A GUIDE TO MOSAICOS ICONS

Readiness Check
This icon, located at the beginning of the first *Funciones y formas* section, reminds students to take the Readiness Check in MySpanishLab to test their understanding of the English grammar related to the Spanish grammar concepts in the chapter. A Study Plan with English Grammar Tutorials is generated for those topics students might need to review.

eText Activities
This icon indicates that a version of the activity is available in MySpanishLab. eText activities are automatically graded and provide detailed feedback on incorrect answers.

Video
This icon indicates that a video segment is available for the *¡Cineastas en acción!* video that accompanies the *Mosaicos* program. The video is available on DVD and in MySpanishLab.

Text Audio Program
This icon indicates that recorded material to accompany *Mosaicos* is available online. In addition, audio for all in-class listening activities and *En directo* dialogues is available on CD.

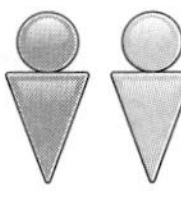

Pair Activity
This icon indicates that the activity is designed to be done by students working in pairs.

Group Activity
This icon indicates that the activity is designed to be done by students working in small groups or as a whole class.

Interactive Globe
This icon indicates that additional cultural resources in the form of videos, web links, interactive maps, and more, relating to a particular country, are organized on an interactive globe online.

Art Tour
This icon accompanies the works of art highlighted in each chapter opener. It links to a virtual art tour and interactive activity in MySpanishLab about the work of art.

MediaShare
This icon, presented with all *Situación* activities, refers to the video-posting feature available online.

Mosaicos:

Spanish as a World Language

It's time to talk! ...and have a cultured conversation. Providing the truly communicative, deeply culture-focused approach professors believe in along with the guidance and tools students need to be successful using a program with highly communicative goals—with ***Mosaicos***, there is no need to compromise. Recognizing the primacy of the relationship between culture and language, the new Sixth Edition of ***Mosaicos*** places culture up front and center, and everywhere in-between!

- Over 1,000 language instructors have partnered with Pearson to create solutions that address the needs of today's students and instructors.
- 100 Faculty Advisors have reviewed, tested, and collaborated with colleagues across North America to make Pearson's **MyLanguageLabs™** the most effective online learning and assessment college language learning system available today.

Challenge:

8 out of 10 language instructors told us that better tools are needed to help students develop oral proficiency so that they will be confident in speaking Spanish.

Solution:

- Almost 1,000,000 students have used Pearson's **MyLanguageLabs** to help them succeed in learning Spanish, French, Italian, German, Russian, Chinese, Portuguese, and Latin.
- **MyLanguageLabs** helps to **improve student results** by offering a robust set of tools that allow students to hear native speakers, and practice their speaking. We include pronunciation guides, Blackboard™ Voice, videos, and audio recordings and are the only online learning and assessment system that includes Versant™ Test of Spanish and MediaShare.

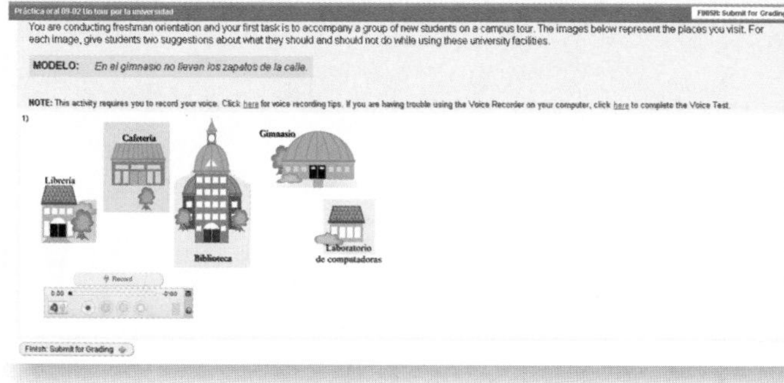

Students love the recording aspect of MyLanguageLabs, which allows them to listen to their own pronunciations, compare, and adjust to match the native speakers. Students' communicative skills have improved significantly with MyLanguageLabs.

—Charles Hernando Molano Álvarez

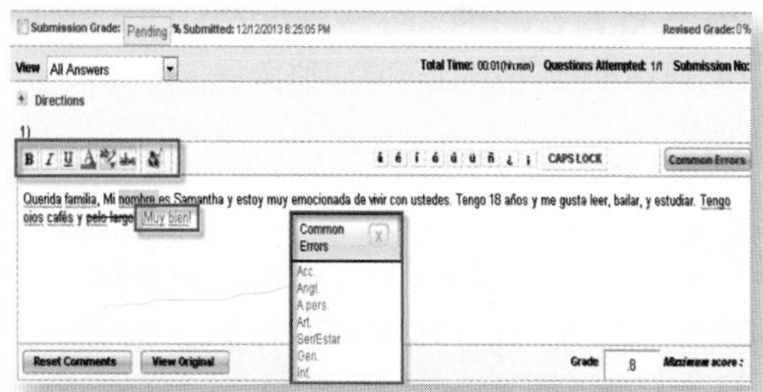

MyLanguageLabs automates teaching chores that are non-meaningful. Let MyLanguageLabs grade homework and quizzes. This gives you time to spend on meaningful pedagogical activities like engaging and interacting with your students.

—Anne Prucha, University of Central Florida

Challenge:

8 out of 10 language instructors voiced that they are teaching more students than ever before, and consequently feel that they no longer have time to provide students with careful guidance to foster speaking and writing skills.

Solution:

- **MyLanguageLabs** allows instructors to easily create the course syllabus, and assign and grade homework, providing you with the time to work with individual students, helping them **achieve higher proficiency levels** in speaking and writing, in particular.

Did you know that...?

- **100% of College Students are internet users**
- **50% are online more than 6 hours every week**
- **Community College Students are even more likely than those at 4 year institutions to use mobile devices**
- **71% of students would prefer to use digital learning materials over print**

Zou, J.J. (2011, July 19). Gadgets, study finds. *Chronicle of Higher Education*

Challenge:

6 of 10 college language programs either have completed or are planning to complete an Introductory Spanish Course Redesign, which will likely result in less face-to-face class time and greater numbers of hybrid or fully online classes.

Solution:

- Pearson Education is the undisputed leader in Higher Education Course Redesign.
- Pearson is an **experienced partner** with over 1150 faculty selecting Pearson to implement a Course Redesign.
- **Evidence-based ongoing Case Studies and Success Stories** demonstrate improved student performance in Course Redesigns that implemented **MyLanguageLabs**.
- **MyLanguageLabs** offers the most extensive opportunities for course personalization that enables instructors to modify instruction according to individual needs, teaching style, grading philosophies, and more, which results in a more **engaging experience** for students.

Redesigning courses around MyLanguageLabs has been a success. The curriculum and course requirements are uniform across all sections so students receive a consistent learning experience. Because MyLanguageLabs automates the grading process, instructors report that they have more time to offer students one-on-one assistance. When I examine the data from before and after MyLanguageLabs, it is clear to me what a great success MyLanguageLabs is and how useful it is for our students.

—Jason Fetters, Purdue University

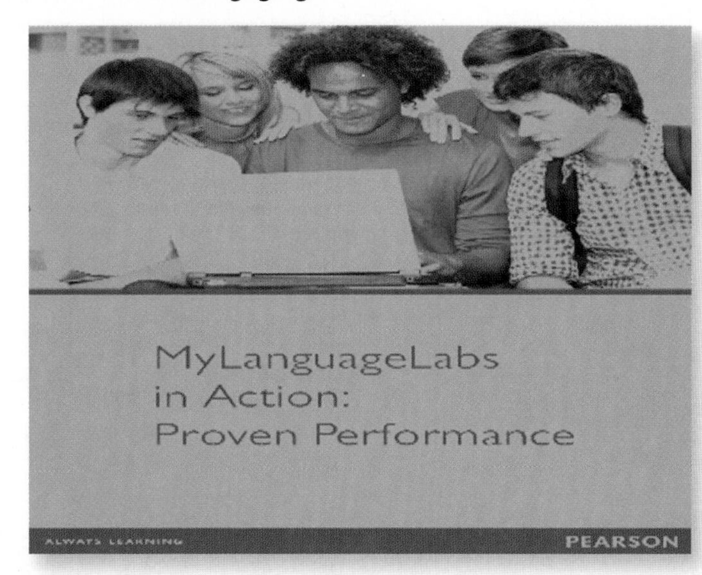

LEARN SMARTER

Boost performance with powerful, personalized learning!

Powered by amplifier and accessible in MySpanishLab, new Dynamic Study Modules combine leading brain science with big-data adaptivity to engage students, drive proficiency, and improve outcomes like never before.

As the language learning and teaching community moves to digital learning tools, Pearson is supercharging its Spanish content and optimizing its learning offerings with personalized Dynamic Study Modules, powered by **amplifier** and MySpanishLab. And, we're already seeing significant gains. Developed exclusively for *Mosaicos*, each study module offers a differentiated digital solution that consistently improves learning results and increases levels of user confidence and engagement with the course materials.

Language instructors observe that they are able to maximize their effectiveness, both in and out of the classroom, because with they are freed from the onerous task of basic knowledge transfer and empowered to:

- reclaim up to 65% more class time for peer to peer communication in the target language;
- tailor presentation and focused practice to address only the most prevalent student knowledge gaps;
- enable livelier, more engaged classrooms.

How does *amplifire* improve learning?

Dynamic Study Modules consist of a comprehensive online learning process that starts with modules of 25 vocabulary and grammar questions that drive deep, contextual knowledge acquisition and understanding.

Based on a Test–Learn–Retest adaptive module, as students respond to each question the tool assesses both knowledge and confidence to identify what students do and don't know. Asking students to indicate their level of confidence engages a different part of the brain than just asking them to answer the question.

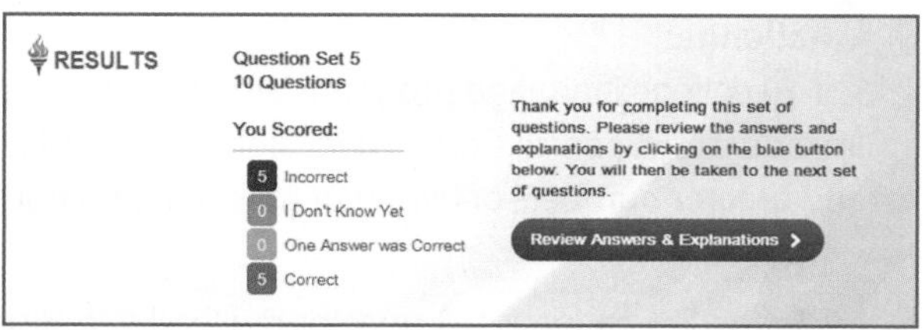

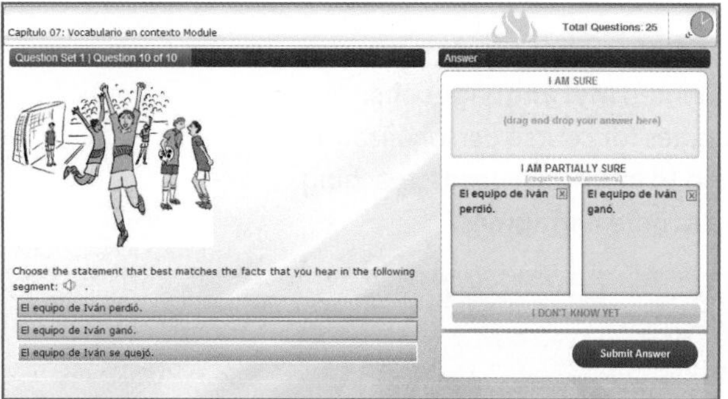

***amplifire* results, embedded explanations, and review opportunities are extremely comprehensive and ideal for fast learning and long-lasting retention.**

After completing the first question set, students are given embedded and detailed explanations for their correct answers, as well as why other answer choices were incorrect. This approach, taken directly from research in cognitive psychology, promotes more accurate knowledge recall. Embedding the learning into the application also saves students valuable study time because they have the learning content at their fingertips!

Dynamic Study Modules cycle students through learning content until they demonstrate mastery of the information by answering all questions confidently and correctly two times in a row.

Once students have reviewed the first set answers and explanations, modules ***amplifire*** presents them with a new set of questions. The ***amplifire*** methodology cycles students through an adaptive, repetitive process of test-learn-retest, until they achieve mastery of the material.

RESULTS!

Based on GAMING and LEARNER ENGAGEMENT techniques, AMPLIFIRE DYNAMIC STUDY MODULES take basic knowledge transfer out of the classroom and improve performance.

Improved student performance and long-term retention of the material ensures students are not only better prepared for their exams, but also for their future classes and careers.

Sixth Edition

mosaicos

SPANISH AS A WORLD LANGUAGE

Volume 3

MATILDE OLIVELLA DE CASTELLS (LATE)
Emerita, California State University, Los Angeles

ELIZABETH E. GUZMÁN
University of Iowa

PALOMA LAPUERTA
Central Connecticut State University

JUDITH E. LISKIN–GASPARRO
University of Iowa

Boston Columbus Indianapolis New York San Francisco Upper Saddle River
Amsterdam Cape Town Dubai London Madrid Milan Munich Paris Montréal Toronto
Delhi Mexico City São Paulo Sydney Hong Kong Seoul Singapore Taipei Tokyo

Senior Acquisitions Editor: Tiziana Aime
Senior Digital Product Manager: Samantha Alducin
Development Editor: Scott Gravina, Celia Meana
MyLanguageLabs Development Editor: Bill Bliss
Director of Program Management: Lisa Iarkowski
Team Lead Program Management: Amber Mackey
Program Manager: Nancy Stevenson
Team Lead Project Managers: Melissa Feimer
Media Coordinator: Regina Rivera
Project Manager: Lynne Breitfeller
Project Manager: Jenna Gray, PreMediaGlobal
Front Cover Design: Black Sun
Cover Image: Maxim Tupikov / Shutterstock
Senior Art Director: Kathryn Foot
Operations Manager: Mary Fischer
Operations Specialist: Roy Roickering
Editorial and Marketing Assistant: Millie Chapman
Editor in Chief: Bob Hemmer
Director of Market Development: Kristine Suárez
World Languages Consultants: Yesha Brill, Mellissa Yokell, Denise Miller

This book was set in 10/13 Serifa Std.

Credits and acknowledgments borrowed from other sources and reproduced, with permission, in this textbook appear on appropriate page within text (or on pages CR-1 to CR-3).

Library of Congress Cataloging-in-Publication Data

Mosaicos : Spanish as a world language / Matilde Olivella de Castells (Late), Emerita, California State University, Los Angeles, Elizabeth E. Guzmán, University of Iowa, Paloma Lapuerta, Central Connecticut State University, Judith E. Liskin-Gasparro, University of Iowa. — sixth Edition.
pages cm
Text is in English and Spanish.
Includes index.
ISBN-13: 978-0-205-25540-5 (alk. paper)
ISBN-10: 0-205-25540-X (alk. paper)
1. Spanish language—Textbooks for foreign speakers—English. I. Castells, Matilde Olivella de. II. Guzmán, Elizabeth E. III. Lapuerta, Paloma. IV. Liskin-Gasparro, Judith E.
PC4129.E5M69 2013
468.2'421—dc23

2013042619

10 9 8 7 6 5 4 3 2 1

Volume 3 ISBN - 10: 0-205-99427-X
Volume 3 ISBN - 13: 978-0-205-99427-4

BRIEF CONTENTS

SCOPE & SEQUENCE

Capítulo	Learning Outcomes	Culture
Preliminar Bienvenidos 2	• Introduce yourself, greet others, and say good-bye • Identify people and classroom objects and tell where they are in the classroom • Listen to and respond to classroom expressions and requests • Spell names and addresses and share phone numbers • Express dates, and tell time, and comment on the weather • Share information about the Spanish language and where it is spoken	**Enfoque cultural:** *El mundo hispano 3*
1 ¿Qué estudias? 30	• Talk about studies, campus, and academic life • Describe daily routines and activities • Specify gender and number • Express location and states of being • Ask and answer questions • Talk about Spain in terms of products, practices, and perspectives • Share information about student life in Hispanic countries and compare cultural similarities	**Enfoque cultural:** *España 31* **Mosaico cultural:** *La vida universitaria en el mundo hispano 41*
2 ¿Quiénes son tus amigos? 64	• Describe people, places, and things • Express origin and possession • Talk about where and when events take place • Describe what someone or something is like • Express emotions and conditions • Identify what belongs to you and others • Discuss the people, things, and activities you and others like and dislike • Present information about Hispanic influences in the United States	**Enfoque cultural:** *Estados Unidos 65* **Mosaico cultural:** *Los estereotipos y la cultura hispana 75*

Capítulo	Learning Outcomes	Culture
3 ¿Qué hacen para divertirse? 100	• Describe free-time activities and food • Plan your daily activities and express intentions • Identify prices and dates • State what and whom you know • Talk about places to visit in Peru • Share information about free-time activities in Hispanic countries and identify cultural similarities	**Enfoque cultural:** *Perú 101* **Mosaico cultural:** *Los hispanos y la vida social 110*
4 ¿Cómo es tu familia? 136	• Talk about family members and their daily routines • Express opinions, plans, preferences, and feelings • Express obligation • Express how long something has been going on • Talk about Colombia in terms of its products, practices, and perspectives • Share information about families and family life in Hispanic countries and compare cultural similarities	**Enfoque cultural:** *Colombia 137* **Mosaico cultural:** *Las familias de la televisión 146*
5 ¿Dónde vives? 170	• Talk about housing, the home, and household activities • Express ongoing actions • Describe physical and emotional states • Avoid repetition in speaking and writing • Point out and identify people and things • Compare cultural and geographic information of Nicaragua, El Salvador, and Honduras	**Enfoque cultural:** *Nicaragua, El Salvador y Honduras 171* **Mosaico cultural:** *Las viviendas en centros urbanos 181*

Capítulo	Learning Outcomes	Culture
6 ¿Qué te gusta comprar? 204	• Talk about shopping and clothes • Talk about events in the past • Indicate to whom or for whom an action takes place • Express likes and dislikes • Describe people, objects, and events • Share information about shopping practices in Hispanic countries and compare cultural similarities	**Enfoque cultural:** *Venezuela* 205 **Mosaico cultural:** *Las tiendas de barrio* 215
7 ¿Cuál es tu deporte favorito? 240	• Talk about sports • Emphasize and clarify information • Talk about past events • Talk about practices and perspectives on sports in Argentina and Uruguay • Share information about sporting events in Hispanic countries and compare cultural similarities	**Enfoque cultural:** *Argentina y Uruguay* 241 **Mosaico cultural:** *Los hinchas y el superclásico* 250
8 ¿Cuáles son tus tradiciones? 276	• Discuss situations and celebrations • Describe conditions and express ongoing actions in the past • Tell stories about past events • Compare people and things • Talk about Mexico in terms of practices and perspectives • Share information about celebrations in Hispanic countries and compare cultural similarities	**Enfoque cultural:** *México* 277 **Mosaico cultural:** *Los carnavales y las tradiciones* 285

Capítulo	Learning Outcomes	Culture
12 ¿Te gusta viajar? 414	• Talk about travel arrangements and preferences • Express possession and clarify what belongs to you and to others • Express affirmation and negation • Express doubt and uncertainty • Talk about travel experiences • Share information about the social and economic impact of the Panama Canal	**Enfoque cultural:** *Costa Rica y Panamá* 415 **Mosaico cultural:** *El mochilero* 425
13 ¿Qué es arte para ti? 448	• Talk about art and culture • Express doubt and uncertainty • Hypothesize about the future • Describe states and conditions • Talk about Bolivia and Paraguay in terms of products, practices, and perspectives • Share information about art and culture in Hispanic countries and identify cultural similarities	**Enfoque cultural:** *Bolivia y Paraguay* 449 **Mosaico cultural:** *El grafiti y la identidad urbana* 460
14 ¿Cómo vivimos los cambios sociales? 478	• Discuss demographics and social conditions • Indicate conditions, goals, and purposes • Express conjecture • Talk about the past from a past perspective • Share information about social change, gender roles, and migration in Hispanic countries and identify cultural similarities	**Enfoque cultural:** *Chile* 479 **Mosaico cultural:** *La migración interna en el mundo hispano* 487
15 ¿Qué nos trae el futuro? 510	• Talk about advances in science and technology • Express wishes and recommendations in the past • Hypothesize and share information about the present and the future • Express unexpected occurrences • Talk about Puerto Rico in terms of its advances in science and technology	**Enfoque cultural:** *Puerto Rico* 511 **Mosaico cultural:** *La investigación tecnológica en Latinoamérica* 520

	Vocabulario en contexto	Funciones y formas	Mosaicos
	Los medios de transporte 417 *El alojamiento y las reservaciones 421* *Viajando en coche 423* 	Expressing affirmation and negation: **Affirmative and negative expressions 426** Talking about things that may not exist: **Subjunctive in adjective clauses 430** Expressing possession: **Possessive pronouns 434** Expressing doubt and uncertainty: **Subjunctive with expressions of doubt 437**	**Escucha** • Use background knowledge to support comprehension 442 **Habla** • Make your presentations comprehensible and interesting 443 **Lee** • Focus on logical relationships 444 **Escribe** • Use facts to offer good advice 446
	La literatura y el cine 451 *La pintura y el arte 454* *La música y la cultura popular 457*	Talking about the past: **Review of the preterit and imperfect 461** Hypothesizing: **The conditional 464** Expressing reciprocity: **Reciprocal verbs and pronouns 468**	**Escucha** • Identify the speaker's intentions 472 **Habla** • Make your presentations comprehensible and interesting 473 **Lee** • Focus on multiple meanings when reading poetry 474 **Escribe** • Write to spark interest 476
	Cambios en la sociedad 481 *El papel de la mujer 484* *Temas de hoy: los jóvenes y la emigración 485*	Expressing conjecture: **Adverbial conjunctions that require the subjunctive 488** Expressing conjecture or certainty: **Adverbial conjunctions that take the subjunctive or indicative 491** Talking about the past from a past perspective: **The past perfect 496** Expressing actions: **The infinitive as subject or object 499**	**Escucha** • Identify the speaker's point of view 503 **Habla** • Organize ideas to present solutions to problems 504 **Lee** • Identify the tone of a text 505 **Escribe** • Use language to express emotions 507
	La ciencia y la tecnología en el mundo de hoy 513 *La conservación del medio ambiente 515* *Otros retos del futuro 517*	Expressing wishes and recommendations in the past: **The imperfect subjunctive 521** Hypothesizing about the present and the future: ***If*-clauses 525** Expressing the unexpected: ***Se* for unplanned occurrences 529**	**Escucha** • Identify the speaker's intention through the main idea and specific information 533 **Habla** • Use drama and humor in telling a personal anecdote 534 **Lee** • Identify the narrator's perspective 536 **Escribe** • Use imagination and humor in writing a narrative 538

NEW to *Mosaicos,* Sixth Edition

Students and instructors will benefit from a wealth of new content and features in this edition. Detailed, contextualized descriptions are provided in the features walk-through that follows.

- **amplifire Dynamic Study Modules,** available in MySpanishLab, are designed to improve learning and long-term retention of vocabulary and grammar via a learning tool developed from the latest research in neuroscience and cognitive psychology on how we learn best. Students master critical course concepts online with **amplifire,** resulting in a livelier classroom experience centered on meaningful communication.
- ***¡Cineastas en acción!,*** a new video program created especially for ***Mosaicos,* sixth edition,** brings together five young filmmakers from different Spanish-speaking countries to attend a summer program at the Los Angeles Film Institute. As part of the program, each will produce documentaries on Hispanic culture in the United States or abroad while competing for a prestigious scholarship for best documentary. Who will win? Students using the ***Mosaicos*** program will decide!

  And, of course, our five young filmmakers will not only learn about making documentaries, but will also learn about each other, and create new bonds as they experience the diversity of Hispanic cultures in Los Angeles.
- Each chapter begins with a robust and interesting two-page cultural section—***Enfoque cultural***—which introduces students to the country of focus and starts the cultural integration that continues throughout the chapter.
- Midway through the chapter, ***Mosaico cultural*** provides a journalistic, thematic cultural presentation. The focus is not on a specific country, but rather on the chapter's theme and how it is reflected in different Spanish-speaking countries, including Hispanic communities in the United States.
- Relevant and interesting cultural information is presented as the introduction to many activities through brief ***Cultura*** sections. Rather than just a boxed aside, the cultural information presented through text and photographs forms the precursor to the activity, making clear and direct connections between language and culture. Accompanying *Comparaciones, Conexiones,* or *Comunidades* questions encourage meaningful communication and cross-cultural reflection.
- Teacher notes provide **additional cultural information** relevant to specific activities that the instructor may wish to highlight to further enrich the cultural aspect of the activities.
- **Learning Outcomes** are provided at the beginning of the chapter giving students a clear idea of the expected performance goals.
- Care has been taken to ensure that the **ACTFL Performance Descriptors**—Presentational, Interpretive, and Interpersonal—are put to consistent use throughout the chapter. A boxed Teacher's Note at the beginning of each chapter details precisely which activities fulfill the requirements for each mode. Additionally, the ***Mosaicos*** skills section is organized around the modes.
- **Advance organizers** accompany the ***Situación*** role plays, providing guidance for students to increase their success in communicating. Each grammar module now culminates with one rather than two *Situaciones* activities with careful attention given to the activity's "situation" being realistic and encouraging meaningful communication among students. Additional ***Situación*** activities are available in MySpanishLab and via the *Situaciones* mobile app including rubrics for activities intended to be completed in real time with Pearson's network of native speakers from around the world.
- The **visual aspect** of the vocabulary presentation has been enhanced providing even more contextualization for the new vocabulary.
- Guided **Vocabulary Tutorials** are provided within **MySpanishLab.** Students work through a series of word recognition activities, most of which culminate with a pronunciation activity in which students compare their pronunciation to that of a native speaker.
- **Pronunciation presentation and practice** is provided for each chapter within MySpanishLab with accompanying text and audio followed by activities.
- Each vocabulary section now begins with an input-based comprehension check. The first vocabulary presentation is followed by an audio-based activity, ***Escucha y confirma***. ***Para confirmar*** follows the second two vocabulary presentations, providing students with the first step towards achieving comprehension.
- A new form-focused activity, ***¿Comprendes?***, follows the presentation of each grammatical structure. This quick, form-focused activity provides students with the opportunity to test themselves in order to ensure they have understood the form of the structure before moving on. ***¿Comprendes?*** activities are also available to be completed online in MySpanishLab.
- ***En directo*** boxes, which provide colloquial expressions for specific activities making speech more native-like, now include **audio** so that students can listen to the expressions used in realistic conversational contexts.
- The ***Mosaicos*** skills section has been edited to make it more manageable for students. Some of the readings for the *Lee* section have been updated, ensuring consistently high-interest readings at the appropriate level. Additionally, the texts featured in the *Lee* section of chapters 13–15 are now pieces of **authentic literature** including stories and a poem.
- ***Comprueba lo que sabes,*** found in MySpanishLab is interactive and encourages students to self-check their mastery of chapter content. Additional practice and games that reinforce chapter vocabulary and grammar is available online.
- **Annotated Scope and Sequence** The authors share their thinking through annotations in the Scope and Sequence of the Annotated Instructor's Edition, explaining the rationale of the grammar scope and sequence.

WHY *MOSAICOS*? WHY THEN… AND WHY NOW?

It has been twenty years since ***Mosaicos*** first appeared in 1994, ushering in a new and evolved vision of how the elements that comprise basic language instruction could be combined in a highly communicative, culturally based language program. Its vision was complete and synthetic, both in the integrity of each element as well as the gathering of these elements into an integrated, connected whole. This vision of wholeness was transformed to become a sound and compelling approach, reflecting the nature of language and how it is learned. The ***Mosaicos*** title was carefully chosen to reflect the principles upon which it was founded and the manner in which it was structured.

The most basic elements of this approach were the following:

- A **guided communicative approach** based on solid methodological principles combined with years of empirical classroom experience, creating an informed and sensible pedagogy that works not only in theory, but also in practice.
- Learning **language in context** with a **focus on meaning.**
- The **integration of culture** as an essential part of language and of the experience of learning it.
- A **synthetic and focused approach** to listening, speaking, reading, and writing.
- The interweaving throughout the program of these elements.

The innovative and evolved approach taken in ***Mosaicos*** set a new standard for language programs and changed basic language publishing. Most important, ***Mosaicos*** has continued to evolve in response to current standards of language teaching, the recommendations of our many reviewers and their experiences in the classroom, as well as the new technologies that transform the potential for achieving more and better communication in the classroom. The new sixth edition of ***Mosaicos*** is more solid and more integrated than ever before, creating for students a multifaceted experience of the intricate mosaic of the Spanish language and its cultures.

Over the past twenty years, many new and reimagined Beginning Spanish programs have appeared, but ***Mosaicos,* sixth edition** continues to offer a unique approach for this reason:

Mosaicos *offers instructors the truly communicative, deeply culture-focused approach they seek while providing the guidance and tools students need to be successful using a program with highly communicative goals. With Mosaicos, there is no need to compromise.*

This inclusiveness of ***Mosaicos,* sixth edition** extends to the broad range of students often found in many Spanish-language classrooms. Accommodating the needs and abilities of all students, from struggling learners to gifted ones, without compromising either group, is a perpetual dilemma for instructors. ***Mosaicos,* sixth edition** provides a highly communicative program with an articulated focus on culture, built in such a way that all students receive the guided learning support they need to succeed and become accomplished learners as they benefit from the rich program and opportunities for communication. Even the struggling student's individual possibilities for learning and communication are not shortchanged; the ***Mosaicos,* sixth edition** program offers the opportunity for achieving more than these students may have thought possible, allowing them to fulfill their true potential.

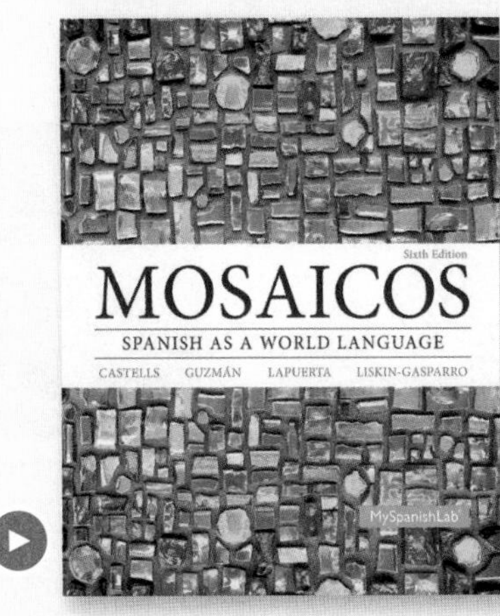

HOW DOES MOSAICOS *DO THIS?*

Integrated Culture | Context | Communication and Guidance | Four-Skills Synthesis

These words have appeared in many programs, but we believe the sixth edition of ***Mosaicos*** meticulously elaborates those simple words into a beautifully conceived, tightly woven, highly articulated program.

CULTURE

Up front and center, and everywhere in between!

All language is enveloped by and imbued with culture—it is the very substance of language. Culture is found both at the forefront and embedded throughout every chapter in ***Mosaicos*, sixth edition.** From its first edition, the authors of ***Mosaicos*** emphasized the link between culture and language and, in response to the broad and emphatic desire from our many users and reviewers, the new sixth edition has taken this coverage to new levels. Let's look at the many ways in which culture is integrated throughout the new ***Mosaicos*, sixth edition** program by looking at examples from Chapter 4.

NEW! *Enfoque cultural:* Each chapter begins with a robust and interesting two-page cultural section that introduces students to the country of focus, giving students a real sense of the vibrancy and uniqueness of the Hispanic cultures. The cultural presentation has been significantly increased at the beginning of the chapter for two reasons. First, many students lack cultural knowledge of the countries in focus, including their geographic location, and thus benefit from this orientation before delving into the chapter. Second, leaving the main cultural presentation for the end of the chapter (as many programs do) makes culture look like an afterthought that is separate from the language itself.

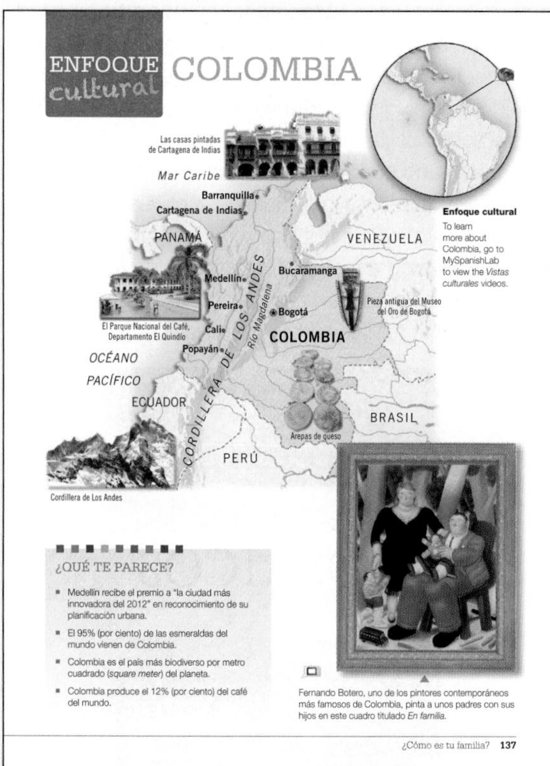

ENFOQUE *cultural* COLOMBIA

Enfoque cultural
To learn more about Colombia, go to MySpanishLab to view the *Vistas culturales* videos.

¿QUÉ TE PARECE?

- Medellín recibe el premio a "la ciudad más innovadora del 2012" en reconocimiento de su planificación urbana.
- El 95% (por ciento) de las esmeraldas del mundo vienen de Colombia.
- Colombia es el país más biodiverso por metro cuadrado (*square meter*) del planeta.
- Colombia produce el 12% (por ciento) del café del mundo.

Fernando Botero, uno de los pintores contemporáneos más famosos de Colombia, pinta a unos padres con sus hijos en este cuadro titulado *En familia.*

¿Cómo es tu familia? **137**

Maps provide geographic location and shared borders with surrounding countries, along with visuals of some cultural and geographic features.

A **work of art** from the country in focus is provided, along with cultural information about the work, and it is enhanced online with a fully **Interactive Art Tour** in MySpanishLab. These tours, developed by experts in language and culture, feature Spanish narrations, offer an in-depth look at the work of art, and enable students to zoom in on details they couldn't otherwise see. At the same time, the tours provide further cultural information.

The **Interactive Globe**, located in the ***Enfoque cultural*** sections and found in MySpanishLab, allows students to further explore the country of focus and the cultural theme of each chapter through ***Vistas culturales*** videos and popular newspapers and magazines.

NEW! *¿Qué te parece?* Far from a dry list of statistics, these interesting and memorable cultural facts, serve to pique students' interest and begin to give shape to the individual countries.

NEW! A full page is devoted to a country-focused, cultural photomontage with captioned readings, giving students a sense of the richness and the accomplishments of the country's culture and facilitates a discussion around culture. Language is carefully controlled, which ensures that students can comfortably comprehend the content. Vocabulary and grammar from previous chapters are recycled, but no new structures are introduced. Any new, non-active vocabulary is either a cognate or is glossed. The photographs also provide context with visual clues.

ENFOQUE cultural

El carnaval de Barranquilla se celebra cada año cuatro días antes de la Cuaresma (*Lent*). Atrae a personas de todas partes que desean disfrutar de las tradiciones, la música y el baile colombianos.

El escritor colombiano y ganador del Premio Nobel de Literatura, Gabriel García Márquez, cuenta con grandes éxitos literarios, entre ellos, su obra maestra, *Cien años de soledad* (*One Hundred Years of Solitude*).

Dieciocho millones de bombillos multicolores iluminan el paseo del río Medellín. Este espectáculo de luces dura (*lasts*) desde el 1 de diciembre hasta el 7 de enero.

Bogotá, la capital de Colombia, está situada en el centro del país, a 2.600 metros sobre el nivel del mar. Es una ciudad moderna, y a la vez tradicional.

¿CUÁNTO SABES?

Completa estas oraciones (*sentences*) con la información correcta.

1. Ecuador, __________ y Brasil están al sur de Colombia.
2. Las casas pintadas de diferentes colores son típicas en la ciudad de __________.
3. __________ es un pintor colombiano.
4. El 95% de las __________ del mundo y el 12% del __________ vienen de Colombia.
5. En Barranquilla se celebra __________ con música y baile en las calles.

138 Capítulo 4

NEW! ***¿Cuánto sabes?*** Brief questions on the two chapter-opening cultural pages serve as a classroom warm-up and help ensure that students are accountable and that they read for meaning.

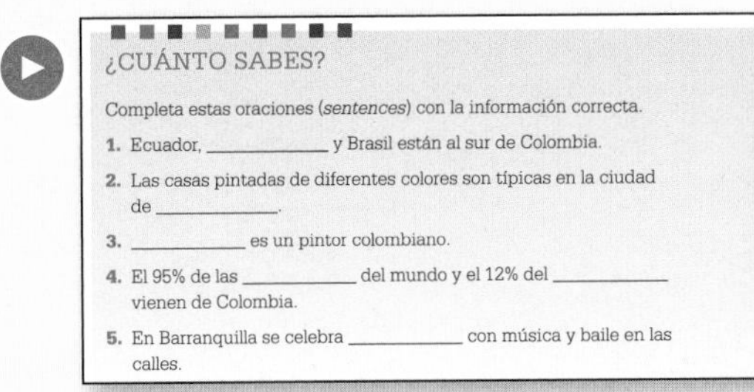

¿CUÁNTO SABES?

Completa estas oraciones (*sentences*) con la información correcta.

1. Ecuador, __________ y Brasil están al sur de Colombia.
2. Las casas pintadas de diferentes colores son típicas en la ciudad de __________.
3. __________ es un pintor colombiano.
4. El 95% de las __________ del mundo y el 12% del __________ vienen de Colombia.
5. En Barranquilla se celebra __________ con música y baile en las calles.

MOSAICO cultural

Las familias de la televisión

Al igual que en Estados Unidos y en muchos países del mundo, la familia ocupa un lugar importante en los programas televisivos. La telenovela *Los Reyes* es una de las más famosas de la televisión colombiana. Esta serie es sobre una familia de clase media que tiene que trabajar mucho para tener una vida tranquila. Los diálogos de esta telenovela son realistas y las situaciones también.

Los Reyes es una crítica social, habla de los conflictos de clase y de los problemas de la sociedad colombiana. Sin embargo, usa a la familia como núcleo de esa discusión. La serie muestra que Colombia es un país moderno y complejo.

Naturalmente, estos conflictos no son exclusivos de Colombia. En México, Argentina y España, este tipo de programa es también muy popular. En España, por ejemplo, la serie *Los Serrano* cuenta la historia de Diego Serrano, un viudo (*widower*) con tres hijos. La historia se complica cuando Diego se casa con Lucía, madre divorciada con dos hijas. Las dos familias tienen que adaptarse para convivir juntas. Al final, como es el caso en muchas familias, la convivencia requiere paciencia y comprensión entre todos los miembros.

La familia ve otro episodio divertido de la serie *Los Reyes*.

El elenco (*cast*) de la serie *Los Serrano*

Compara

1. ¿Qué familias famosas hay en la televisión de tu país? ¿Cuál es tu favorita?
2. Escoge a una familia de una serie televisiva que te gusta. Describe a esta familia.
3. Compara la familia de la serie televisiva con tu propia familia. ¿Qué tienen en común? ¿Qué diferencias hay entre ellas?

146 Capítulo 4

NEW! Chapter theme, learning outcomes, and culture all come together in ***Mosaico cultural***. Midway through the chapter (between the vocabulary and grammar sections), ***Mosaico cultural*** provides a journalistic, thematic, cultural presentation. The focus here is not on a specific country but rather on different cultural aspects of the Hispanic world, including Latinos in the United States, which are relevant to the chapter theme. The communicative *Compara* questions that follow the readings provide the opportunity for cross-cultural reflection.

NEW! *Cultura* Relevant and interesting cultural information is presented when appropriate as the introduction to an activity. The cultural input through text and photographs forms the first step to doing the activity, making the clear and direct connection between language and culture. Accompanying *Comparaciones, Conexiones,* or *Comunidades* questions encourage meaningful communication and cross-cultural reflection.

Cultura

La familia real española

Spain is the only Spanish-speaking country that is a parliamentary system with a constitutional monarchy. The Spanish Royal Family consists of King Juan Carlos, Queen Sofia, and their children Prince Felipe, Infanta Elena and Infanta Cristina. The monarchy is part of the Bourbon Dynasty and has been in Spain since the year 1700.

Conexiones. ¿Sabes qué otros países tienen una monarquía hoy? Busca información en Internet sobre una de ellas y describe a los miembros de su familia para presentar en clase.

4-5

¿Quién es y cómo es?

PREPARACIÓN. Escojan (*Choose*) un miembro de una familia famosa (los Obama, los Jackson, los Kennedy, los Kardashian, etc.) y preparen su árbol familiar.

INTERCAMBIOS. Túrnense (*Take turns*) para describir el árbol familiar de esta persona.

MODELO EL PRÍNCIPE FELIPE

E1: *Es el hijo de los Reyes de España. Su esposa es Leticia. Tienen dos hijas.*

E2: *Sus hijas se llaman Leonor y Sofía. Elena y Cristina son las hermanas mayores del Príncipe Felipe.*

4-6

El arte de preguntar. PREPARACIÓN. Túrnense para preparar las preguntas a estas respuestas.

MODELO Mi madre se llama Dolores.

¿Cómo se llama tu madre?

1. Tengo dos hermanos.
2. Vivo con mi madre y mi padrastro.
3. Tengo dos abuelas y un abuelo.
4. Mis abuelos no viven con nosotros.
5. Tengo muchos primos.
6. Tengo una media hermana, pero no vive con nosotros.

INTERCAMBIOS. Ahora háganse (*ask each other*) preguntas para obtener información sobre la familia de su compañero/a. Después, compartan (*share*) esta información con la clase.

Cultura

Los apellidos

In Hispanic culture, people offically use two surnames, the first is their father's and the second is their mother's. For example, in Pablo's family, his father's name is Jaime Méndez and his mother's name is Elena Sánchez. Pablo's official name, then, is Pablo Méndez Sánchez.

Comparaciones. ¿Cuántos nombres y apellidos tienes? En la cultura hispana, ¿cuál sería (*would be*) tu nombre oficial?

4-7

Mi familia. Busca fotos de tus familiares en tu celular o en Facebook. Luego, muéstrale las fotos a tu compañero/a y describe a tus familiares.

1. nombre y apellido
2. relación familiar
3. personalidad
4. actividades que haces con la persona

142 Capítulo 4

4-27 

Un viaje (*trip*) a Colombia. PREPARACIÓN. Tu familia va a viajar a Colombia. Selecciona la mejor recomendación para cada persona. Después añade (*add*) algo que quieres hacer tú y explica por qué.

1. _____ Mi hermana quiere visitar un lugar religioso muy original.
2. _____ A mis padres les gustaría ver joyas (*jewels*) precolombinas.
3. _____ Mi prima quiere escuchar música colombiana.
4. _____ Mis abuelos prefieren las actividades al aire libre.

a. Tiene que asistir a un concierto de Los Príncipes del Vallenato.
b. Tiene que ir a la Catedral de Sal.
c. Tienen que ir al Museo del Oro.
d. Tienen que conocer el Parque Ecológico El Portal.

INTERCAMBIOS. Busca información en Internet y prepara una breve descripción de uno de los lugares, grupos o eventos siguientes. Incluye la ubicación (*location*) y las actividades asociadas con el lugar, el grupo o los eventos. Luego, comparte la información con la clase.

1. Los Príncipes del Vallenato
2. la Catedral de Sal
3. el Museo del Oro
4. el Parque Arqueológico de San Agustín

Culture Integrated within Activities: Chapter-relevant culture is often integrated within the activities. In this example, the activities for learning to "express obligation with *tener que* + infinitive" are related to the culture of Colombia.

VIDEO

cineasta 1. com. Persona que se dedica al cine, especialmente como director.

***¡Cineastas en acción!**: Where people and cultures come together!*

The Cast

All aspiring documentary filmmakers

Esteban [Costa Rica]

Artistic, free-spirited surfer

Yolanda [Mexico]

Vegan. Green. Hipster.

Esteban's good looks catch her eye, but Federico tries to touch her heart.

Vanesa [Spain]

Madrileña. Trasnochadora. Full of fun and high spirits. Who cannot love fashionista Vanesa?

Federico [Argentina]

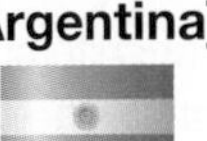

Meat lover. A little macho and full of himself. Can he win over vegan Yolanda who finds him just plain annoying?

Héctor [Peru]

The nice guy and everyone's friend.

THE LOCATION

The Los Angeles Film Institute

Our protagonists' rendezvous point: Blanca's house, their home for the summer

The city of Los Angeles and a myriad of sites throughout the Hispanic world

THE SET-UP

Our five aspiring young filmmakers attend the Los Angeles Film Institute's summer program on documentary filmmaking. Each explores, learns, and then documents the wealth of Hispanic culture in the United States and abroad as part of their course work. Each has also brought previously shot footage from Spanish-speaking countries around the world. Lots of cultural exchange goes on among these new friends as they share aspects of their native cultures and personal experiences through video.

However, our friendly *amigos* are in competition with each other for a prestigious scholarship—spending the next academic year at the Institute—awarded to the student who produces the best work over the course of the summer. Who decides who deserves to win the coveted *beca*? Students using the ***Mosaicos*, sixth edition** program will decide!

Technology also opens up further cultural exchange. The filmmakers are able to virtually share their various projects using tablets and smartphones. In addition, when Vanesa's cousin contacts her on Skype from Guatemala, they hop onto her Facebook page to view her photo album of Guatemala while she narrates her experiences working there. *¡El mundo se convierte en un pañuelo!*

Put five eclectic young filmmakers together and of course some drama will ensue—friendships, rivalries, and maybe even some romance. Watch the dramas unfold!

THE PEDAGOGY

The central theme of each video segment expands on the overarching theme of each ***Mosaicos*, sixth edition** chapter. In the chapter *¿Qué hacen para divertirse?*, we'll visit a Peruvian restaurant in Los Angeles where the chef shares her recipe for *pescado encebollado*. We learn through Federico's eyes what his neighborhood and house in Buenos Aires look like in the chapter *¿Dónde vives?*. In *¿Qué te gusta comprar?,* we'll view a Latino fashion show in Los Angeles and in *¿Cuáles son tus tradiciones?,* we get a close-up look at the exuberance of the La Mercé festival in Barcelona. Tapas culture in Spain, gay marriage in Argentina, surfing in Perú—just a few of the many worlds our friends explore and share!

- Dialogues reinforce each chapter's vocabulary and grammar.
- In-text activities in the ***En acción*** section of the chapter provide pre-, during, and post-viewing activities (continuing the process approach of the ***Mosaicos*** four-skills section).
- Instructors can—at their discretion and reflecting their own methodology—choose whether Spanish captions are available to students. A variety of different types of auto-graded interactive activities are provided within MySpanishLab that assess listening comprehension and cultural knowledge.
- Additional culturally-based video activities are found in MySpanishLab.

CONTEXT

Vocabulary and grammar where they belong—in communicative and cultural context!

In addition to presenting language in the context of culture, one of the hallmarks of ***Mosaicos*** has always been the presentation of vocabulary and grammar in context through a communicatively rich format.

Vocabulario en contexto

New vocabulary is presented in contexts that reflect the chapter theme. Vocabulary is chunked into three modules per chapter so students can learn and practice a manageable amount. Language samples, photos, line drawings, and realia are used to present new material, rather than word lists and translations. Vocabulary is then consistently **recycled in new contexts,** within and across the chapters, blending it with new words and structures.

Boldface type is used within the language samples to highlight key words and phrases that students will need to learn to use actively. Audio icons remind students that recorded versions of the language samples are available online or on CD. A convenient list of these words and phrases with their translation is provided at the end of the chapter with accompanying audio.

NEW! Learning Outcomes clearly listed at the beginning of the chapter give students a clear idea of their goals for this section.

Strategically placed *Lengua* boxes provide students with succinct information right at the point of need to support self-expression.

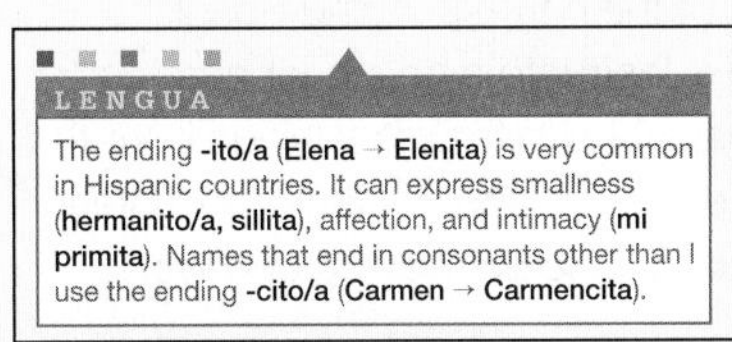

LENGUA

The ending **-ito/a** (**Elena** → **Elenita**) is very common in Hispanic countries. It can express smallness (**hermanito/a, sillita**), affection, and intimacy (**mi primita**). Names that end in consonants other than l use the ending **-cito/a** (**Carmen** → **Carmencita**).

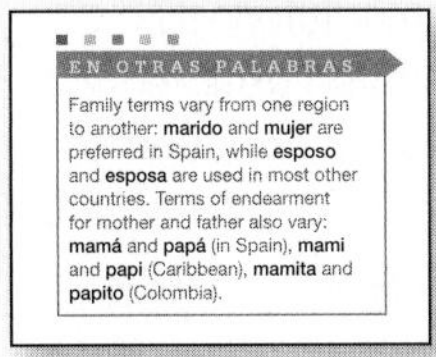

EN OTRAS PALABRAS

Family terms vary from one region to another: **marido** and **mujer** are preferred in Spain, while **esposo** and **esposa** are used in most other countries. Terms of endearment for mother and father also vary: **mamá** and **papá** (in Spain), **mami** and **papi** (Caribbean), **mamita** and **papito** (Colombia).

En otras palabras boxes give examples of regional variations of the language.

Vocabulario en contexto

Talking about family members, what they do, and their daily routines

Los miembros de la familia

NEW! Online Vocabulary Tutorials. Guided online vocabulary tutorials offer students opportunities to work through a series of word recognition activities that help them tie words to images. Most tutorials culminate with a pronunciation activity where students compare their pronunciation to that of a native speaker.

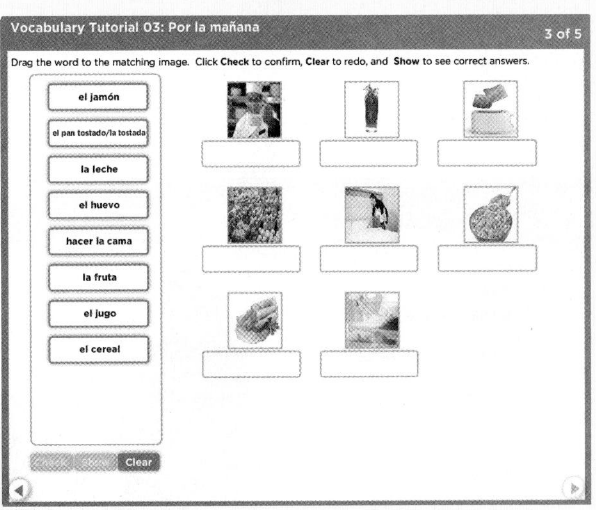

NEW! Pronunciation Presentation and Practice. Within MySpanishLab, a pronunciation topic is presented with accompanying text and audio, followed by three sets of activity types: *Identificación, Las palabras que faltan, Repetición*. In the Annotated Instructor's Edition, notes indicate the specific pronunciation topic covered in that chapter.

Funciones y formas

In ***Mosaicos*, sixth edition,** grammar is presented as a means to effective communication, **moving from meaning to form** and providing an understanding that is both functional and structural. Students are first presented with new structures in meaningful contexts through visuals and brief language samples. The new structures are highlighted in boldface type.

NEW! Audio is provided in MySpanishLab for all of the language samples.

A short, comprehension-based *Piénsalo* activity follows each language sample. These activities form part of the presentation of grammar in context. Students use comprehension and reasoning skills to figure out the answers, by focusing on the connection between meaning (*función*) and the new grammatical structure (*forma*).

Charts and bulleted explanations—clear, concise, and easy to understand—are designed to be studied at home or used for reference in class.

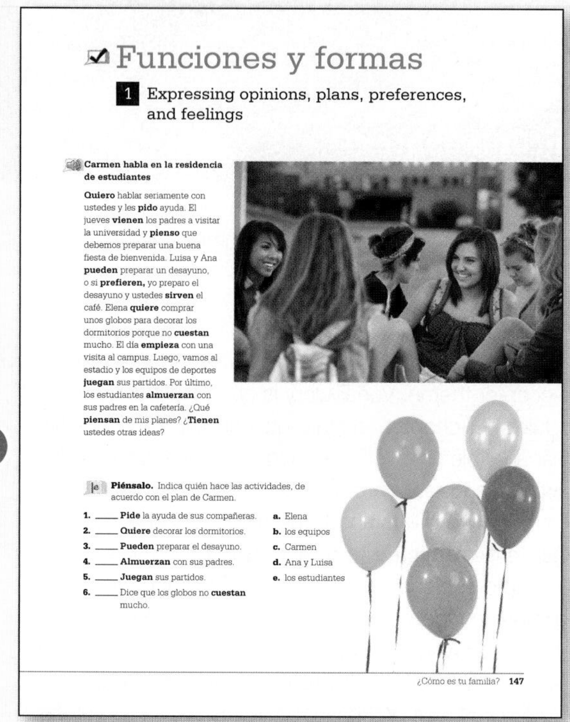

Funciones y formas

1 Expressing opinions, plans, preferences, and feelings

Carmen habla en la residencia de estudiantes

Quiero hablar seriamente con ustedes y les **pido** ayuda. El jueves **vienen** los padres a visitar la universidad y **pienso** que debemos preparar una buena fiesta de bienvenida. Luisa y Ana **pueden** preparar un desayuno, o si **prefieren,** yo preparo el desayuno y ustedes **sirven** el café. Elena **quiere** comprar unos globos para decorar los dormitorios porque no **cuestan** mucho. El día **empieza** con una visita al campus. Luego, vamos al estadio y los equipos de deportes **juegan** sus partidos. Por último, los estudiantes **almuerzan** con sus padres en la cafetería. ¿Qué **piensan** de mis planes? ¿**Tienen** ustedes otras ideas?

Piénsalo. Indica quién hace las actividades, de acuerdo con el plan de Carmen.

1. ____ **Pide** la ayuda de sus compañeras.
2. ____ **Quiere** decorar los dormitorios.
3. ____ **Pueden** preparar el desayuno.
4. ____ **Almuerzan** con sus padres.
5. ____ **Juegan** sus partidos.
6. ____ Dice que los globos no **cuestan** mucho.

a. Elena
b. los equipos
c. Carmen
d. Ana y Luisa
e. los estudiantes

¿Cómo es tu familia? 147

Online English Grammar Readiness Checks and Tutorials: Online English Grammar Readiness Checks assess students' understanding of the English Grammar topics needed to successfully understand the Spanish ones in the chapter and provide personalized remediation via animated English Grammar Tutorials in MySpanishLab. Understanding English grammar terminology greatly facilitates learning of the corresponding Spanish concepts. Instructors no longer need to spend valuable class time talking about the language of language . . . they can instead use the language in meaningful ways.

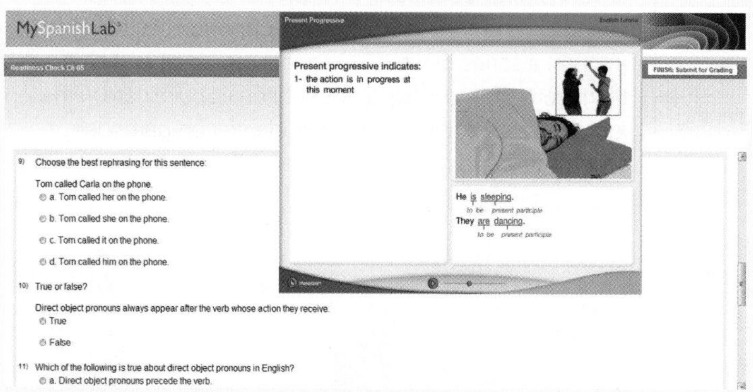

Online Spanish Grammar Tutorials: Online interactive grammar tutorials in MySpanishLab offer narrated explanations and illustrated examples to help students further comprehend the concepts they are learning. The tutorial ends with an auto-scored comprehension check.

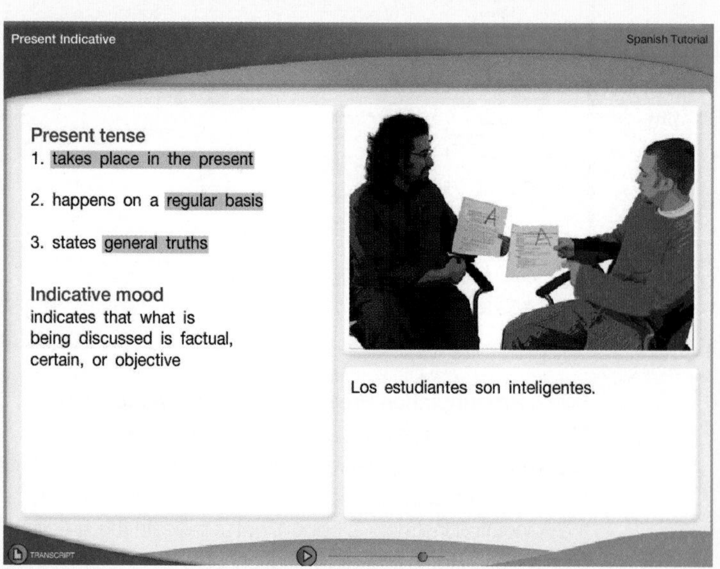

These multiple and complementary means of grammar presentation provide students with different portals for understanding, while serving different learning styles and ensuring that students grasp the concepts.

COMMUNICATION AND GUIDANCE

Providing students the guidance they need to express themselves with confidence!

Just as language and culture are inseparable in ***Mosaicos,* sixth edition,** communication and the guidance provided to foster communication are inseparable as well. Since both the vocabulary and grammar sections contribute unique aspects to the guidance provided, we will look at each one.

With ***Mosaicos,* sixth edition,** almost all of the activities provided in the textbook are communicative in nature. Discrete point practice is primarily provided online through MySpanishLab or in the printed Student Activities Manual. Classroom time is devoted to communicative practice.

The progression within each activity set moves the student along gradually from comprehension to open-ended expression. This carefully stepped progression ensures students are guided through the process and not rushed to produce before they are ready.

COMMUNICATING AND PRACTICING WITH VOCABULARY

NEW! *Escucha y confirma:* A listening activity follows the first of the three vocabulary presentations per chapter. This input-based comprehension check gives students listening practice while allowing them to assess their understanding of the vocabulary and determine if they are ready to move on to additional vocabulary practice in meaningful contexts.

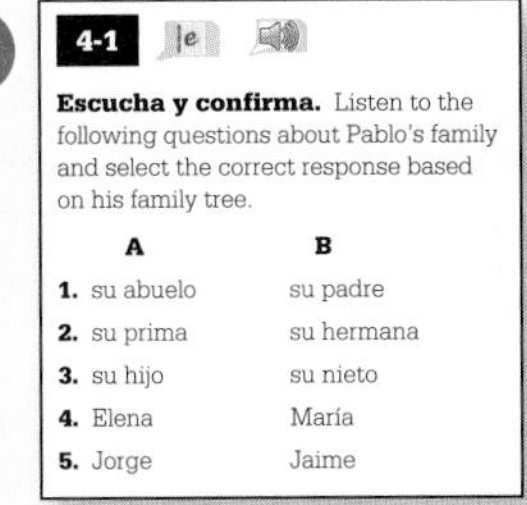

NEW! *Para confirmar:* The first activity of the second two vocabulary presentations is always an input-based comprehension check allowing students to ensure their grasp of the vocabulary before moving on to additional vocabulary practice in meaningful contexts.

NEW! Brief ***Cultura*** presentations introduce selected vocabulary activities to raise awareness of the cultural contexts in which language is used. Accompanying *Comparaciones, Conexiones,* or *Comunidades* questions encourage meaningful communication and cross-cultural reflection.

The activity sequence fosters the use of new and previously learned vocabulary in natural, thematically relevant contexts. Activities foster personalization as students are encouraged to talk about what is known to them, themselves, and the people they know and gradually increase in expectation of output as students become comfortable using the new vocabulary. The vast majority of the activities are done in pairs or groups so that students spend their classroom time in conversation.

COMMUNICATING AND PRACTICING WITH GRAMMAR

NEW! *¿Comprendes?* A new form-focused activity follows the grammar presentation. Students can do the activity in class with the instructor or as graded online homework before coming to class as all *¿Comprendes?* activities are auto-graded and include immediate feedback when completed within MySpanishLab. In these quick, form-focused activities students check that they are able to produce the new grammatical forms before moving to the contextualized and communicative activities.

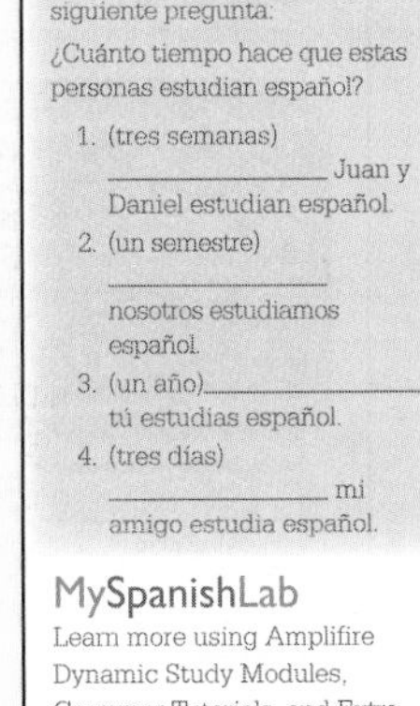

The continuing activity sequence moves students gradually from meaningful, form-focused activities towards production of open-ended, personalized communication. The activities focus attention on the communicative purpose of the linguistic structures while invoking culturally relevant contexts. All activities require students to process meaning as well as form so that they develop skill in using their linguistic knowledge to gather information, answer questions, and resolve problems. For example, even the form-focused activities require students to process meaning, not just fill in the blank with the correct response, making the connection between meaning and form. For good reason, the grammar section is called *Funciones y formas*—a hallmark of the *Mosaicos* approach.

Instructor annotations offer suggestions on how to personalize and expand the activities, guide students through multi-stage activities, and encourage students to engage in metalinguistic processing.

NEW! Brief ***Cultura*** presentations introduce selected grammar activities to raise awareness of the cultural contexts in which language is used. Accompanying *Comparaciones, Conexiones,* or *Comunidades* questions encourage meaningful communication and cross-cultural reflection.

Cultura

La quinceañera

In Hispanic culture, teen girls celebrate their 15th birthday in a special way. The celebration is called a **quinceañera,** and it marks the girl's transition into adulthood. This tradition is celebrated in nearly all Spanish-speaking countries except Spain.

Comparaciones. ¿Cómo se celebra el *sweet sixteen* en tu cultura? ¿Quiénes asisten?

4-22

Una reunión. Ustedes quieren ayudar a su amiga Celeste a organizar una reunión para celebrar el cumpleaños número dieciséis de su prima. Decidan lo siguiente:

1. lugar y hora en que prefieren la reunión
2. número de personas que van a participar
3. comida y bebidas que piensan servir
4. actividades que quieren organizar

Situación

PREPARACIÓN. Lean esta situación. Luego, compartan ejemplos de vocabulario, gramática y otra información que necesitan para desarrollar la conversación.

Role A. You and a family member are planning to visit Colombia. Your friend has heard about your plans and calls with some questions. Answer your friend's questions in detail.

Role B. Your friend is planning to go to Colombia with a relative. Call to find out:

a. when he/she is planning to go;
b. with whom;
c. what places in the country he/she wants to visit and why; and
d. when they are returning.

	ROLE A	ROLE B
Vocabulario	Family member Travel dates	Question words
Funciones y formas	Discussing plans: *Pensar* + infinitive Expressing preferences: *Querer* + infinitive	Discussing plans: *Pensar* + infinitive Expressing preferences: *Querer* + infinitive

INTERCAMBIOS. Practica la conversación con tu compañero/a incorporando el vocabulario y las funciones de *Preparación*. Luego, represéntenla ante la clase.

En directo

These expressions help maintain the flow of conversation:

¡Cuánto me alegro!
I am so happy for you!

Claro, claro...
Of course . . .

¡Qué bien/bueno!
That's great!

Listen to a conversation with these expressions.

152 Capítulo 4

NEW! The *En directo* boxes, which provide colloquial expressions for the activity, now include **audio** so that students can listen to the expressions used in meaningful conversational context.

NEW! *Situación* Advance Organizers. The encompassing goal of these activities has always been embraced by our users. To provide students with guidance to increase their success in communicating through open-ended role plays, the authors have provided advance organizers for the *Situación* activities. Each student prepares by listing specifics for the indicated topics of vocabulary, grammar, and culture (where appropriate) that will facilitate their conversation with their classmate.

Situación. Another of the hallmarks of ***Mosaicos*** has always been the culminating role-play activities for each grammar section. Students have the opportunity to converse in realistic contexts by putting together everything they have learned. These open-ended communicative activities prompt students to integrate relevant grammatical structures, vocabulary, and culture with contexts drawn from the chapter theme. Students also have the opportunity to complete activities and communicate "live" with native speakers around the world.

NEW! Each grammar module now culminates with one rather than two *Situación* activities with careful attention to creating realistic situations for the students to enact.

NEW! *Situaciones* app. Additional *Situación* role-play activities are available in MySpanishLab and via a mobile app that can be easily accessed on tablets and smartphones.

FOUR-SKILLS SYNTHESIS

Bringing it ALL together!

Mosaicos* section:** Not only are listening, speaking, reading, and writing practiced throughout the chapters of ***Mosaicos,* sixth edition** but the final culminating section of each chapter—*Mosaicos*—is devoted to the development and practice of each of these communication skills in a highly focused manner. True to the synthetic nature of this section, the chapter's thematic content and vocabulary are brought together with its linguistic structures and cultural focus. Hence the name, *Mosaicos,* whereby students have the opportunity to bring it ***all together into a coherent whole.

To enhance the development of these skills, **guidance** is provided for each section. First, specific **strategies** are presented for each of the four skills. The strategies build on each other within and across the chapters. Activities are designed so that students systematically practice implementing the strategies presented. Second, a **process approach**, with pre-, during, and post-activities, is applied for all four skills through the *Preparación* and *Un paso más* steps. The cumulative effect of the fifteen *Mosaicos* sections throughout the text will greatly increase students' abilities to effectively listen, speak, read, and write.

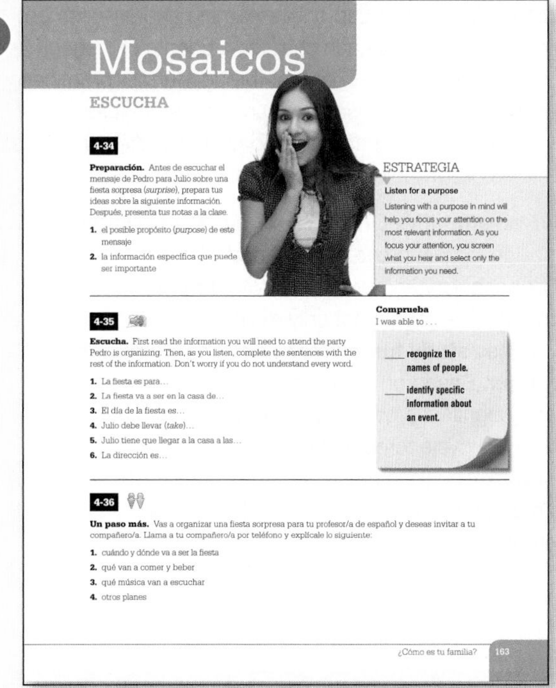

Mosaicos

ESCUCHA

4-34

Preparación. Antes de escuchar el mensaje de Pedro para Julio sobre una fiesta sorpresa (*surprise*), prepara tus ideas sobre la siguiente información. Después, presenta tus notas a la clase.

1. el posible propósito (*purpose*) de este mensaje
2. la información específica que puede ser importante

ESTRATEGIA

Listen for a purpose

Listening with a purpose in mind will help you focus your attention on the most relevant information. As you focus your attention, you screen what you hear and select only the information you need.

4-35

Escucha. First read the information you will need to attend the party Pedro is organizing. Then, as you listen, complete the sentences with the rest of the information. Don't worry if you do not understand every word.

1. La fiesta es para...
2. La fiesta va a ser en la casa de...
3. El día de la fiesta es...
4. Julio debe llevar (*take*)...
5. Julio tiene que llegar a la casa a las...
6. La dirección es...

Comprueba

I was able to . . .

____ **recognize the names of people.**

____ **identify specific information about an event.**

4-36

Un paso más. Vas a organizar una fiesta sorpresa para tu profesor/a de español y deseas invitar a tu compañero/a. Llama a tu compañero/a por teléfono y explícale lo siguiente:

1. cuándo y dónde va a ser la fiesta
2. qué van a comer y beber
3. qué música van a escuchar
4. otros planes

¿Cómo es tu familia? 163

NEW! *Comprueba* boxes provide a self-check guide for students to help them determine if they have covered the main points accurately and sufficiently.

NEW! Each set of activities is now organized around the three ACTFL Performance Descriptors of the three Modes of Communication: Presentational, Interpretive, and Interpersonal. This organization maximizes learning as three parts of a single goal: communication. By consistently using all three interrelated modes, students' opportunity to use the language in relation to the theme is multiplied. Instructor annotations indicate the mode for each activity.

NEW! Based on pre-revision survey feedback from our users, some readings for the Lee section have been updated, ensuring consistently **high-interest readings at the appropriate level.** Additionally, the last three chapters, 13–15, now introduce students to **authentic literature,** enriching the program while giving those students who go on to the intermediate level an introduction to reading and interpreting literature.

If students need more practice with any of the four skills, **additional practice** is provided for each skill within the Student Activities Manual, available in print or in Pearson's award-winning online learning and assessment MySpanishLab platform.

CHAPTER SELF-ASSESSMENT

A check to ensure that all the pieces are firmly in place!

Within the MySpanishLab online learning and assessment system, at the end of each chapter, students can check their mastery of chapter content through further practice in a variety of activities, resources, and games that reinforce chapter vocabulary, grammar, and culture in different ways. Examples of available resources are:

- NEW! **amplifire Online Dynamic Study Modules** are designed to improve learning and long-term retention of vocabulary and grammar. With **amplifire** study modules, students not only master critical concepts, but they **study faster, learn better, and remember longer.** Based on the latest research in neuroscience and cognitive psychology on how we learn best, learners cycle through a process of test/learn/retest until they achieve mastery of the content. The result is a personalized, adaptive approach—tailored to individual students' needs.

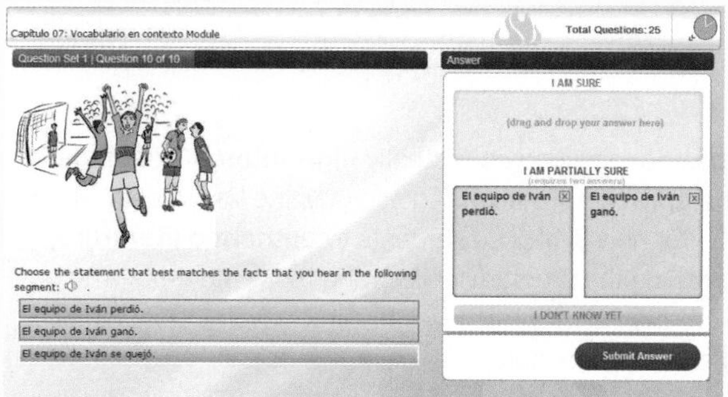

amplifire is the only assessment available that is able to quickly and effectively pinpoint knowledge gaps and areas of misinformation—where learners were confident but incorrect about their answer choices. Instructors can use the results to determine what information the learners retained and where misinformation and gaps still exist, and adjust their curricula accordingly.

- **Vocabulary Flashcards** with audio recordings by a native speaker help students review words and quiz themselves on the active vocabulary. Flashcards can be accessed via mobile devices for practice on the go.
- NEW! **Games** are a painless, enjoyable, and effective way to practice new skills. Games vary from *Concentration* (flip cards to match words to visuals), to *Soccer* (provide the appropriate word in a context), to a *Quiz Show* game in which students choose the appropriate response in a multiple-choice format. Questions are contextualized and move beyond simple form-based exercises to more meaningful, engaging activities.
- **Oral Practice:** Provides two oral activities. Students record their response to the activity and submit it for instructor grading.
- NEW! The **Practice Test with Study Plan** is an auto-scored, full-length test that reviews chapter vocabulary and grammar. Students are given a study plan based on their performance. The study plan refers them to explanations in the eText, extra practice activities, and tutorials to help them review concepts where they need additional practice.

Informed by National Standards

The National Standards for Foreign Language Learning: Preparing for the 21st Century, whose five goal areas (Communication, Cultures, Connections, Comparisons, and Communities) have served as an organizing principle for language instruction for more than a decade, inform the pedagogy of the sixth edition of ***Mosaicos.*** Marginal notes throughout the Annotated Instructor's Edition draw attention to the way specific activities and other elements of the program help students develop proficiency in the five goal areas. A number of strategies have been implemented to achieve success.

Communication. Students are prompted to engage in meaningful conversations throughout the text, providing and obtaining information, expressing their opinions and preferences, and sharing their experiences. Readings and listening activities invite them to interpret language on a variety of topics, while *presentaciones* and writing assignments call on them to present information and ideas in both written and oral modes. The **ACTFL Performance Descriptors of the three Modes of Communication**—Presentational, Interpretive, and Interpersonal—are used consistently throughout the chapters and are the organizing principle for the *Mosaicos* skills' section. By consistently using all three modes, students' opportunity to use the language in relation to the theme is multiplied.

Cultures. Many features of the ***Mosaicos*** program give students an understanding of the relationship between culture and language: The ***Enfoque cultural*** opening spread; the maps, the art, and the accompanying Art Tour; the ***Mosaico cultural*** section; the cultural vignettes in the ***¡Cineastas en acción!*** video; the *Cultura* sections; and the culture integrated within the activities.

Connections. Ample opportunities are provided for students to makes connections with other disciplines through realia, readings, the ***Enfoque cultural*** section, the ***Mosaico cultural*** section, the *Conexiones* questions which accompany the *Cultura* sections, the diverse cultural vignettes of the ***¡Cineastas en acción!*** video, and the conversation activities throughout the text. Students gain information and insight into the distinctive viewpoints of Spanish speakers and their culture.

Comparisons. *Lengua* and *En otras palabras* boxes, the *Compara* questions in each ***Mosaico cultural*** section, and the *Comparaciones* questions in the *Cultura* sections—all provide students with points of comparison between English and Spanish (and among the varieties of Spanish spoken in different parts of the world). Readings and activities frequently juxtapose U.S. and Hispanic cultural products, practices, and perspectives.

Communities. Students are encouraged to extend their learning through guided research on the Internet and/or other sources, and many of the topics explored in ***Mosaicos*** can stimulate exploration, personal enjoyment, and enrichment beyond the confines of formal language instruction. *Comunidades* questions which accompany many of the *Cultura* sections encourage reaching out to the community and cross-cultural reflection.

The Complete *Mosaicos* Program

Mosaicos is a complete teaching and learning program that includes a variety of resources for students and instructors, including an innovative offering of online resources.

FOR THE STUDENT

Student Text (ISBN 10: 0-205-25540-X)

The ***Mosaicos*, sixth edition** Student Text is available in a complete, hardbound version, consisting of a preliminary chapter followed by Chapters 1 through 15. The program is also available as three paperback volumes rather than the single hardcover version. Volume 1 of the paperback series contains the preliminary chapter plus Chapters 1 to 5; Volume 2, Chapters 5 to 10; and Volume 3, Chapters 10 to 15. All three volumes include the complete front and back matter.

Student Activities Manual (ISBN 10: 0-205-24796-2)

The Student Activities Manual (SAM), thoroughly revised for this edition, includes workbook activities together with audio- and video-based activities, all designed to provide extensive practice of the vocabulary, grammar, culture, and skills introduced in each chapter. The organization of these materials parallels that of the student text and include a *Repaso* section at the end that provides additional activities designed to help students review the material of the chapter as well as to prepare for tests.

The online Student Activities Manual found in MySpanishLab now features premium content which includes a variety of interactive activities not available in print.

Answer Key to Accompany Student Activities Manual (ISBN 10: 0-205-25544-2)

An Answer Key to the Student Activities Manual is available separately, giving instructors the option of allowing students to check their homework. The Answer Key now includes answers to all SAM activities.

Audio CDs to Accompany Student Text (ISBN 10: 0-205-25542-6)

A set of audio CDs contains recordings of the *Vocabulario en contexto* and *Funciones y formas* language samples, the ***Mosaico cultural*** reading passages, and the audio material for the *Escucha y confirma* listening activities included in the student text. These recordings are also available online.

Audio CDs to Accompany Student Activities Manual (ISBN 10: 0-205-25541-8)

A second set of audio CDs contains audio material for the listening activities in the Student Activities Manual. These recordings are also available online.

Video on DVD (ISBN 10: 0-205-25545-0)

¡Cineastas en acción! is a newly shot video filmed to accompany the sixth edition of ***Mosaicos.*** Vocabulary and grammar structures of each chapter are used in realistic situations while gaining a deeper understanding of Hispanic cultures.

Pre-viewing, viewing, and post-viewing activities are found in the ***¡Cineastas en acción!*** sections of the textbook and the Student Activities Manual. The video is available for student purchase on DVD, and it is also available within MySpanishLab.

MySpanishLab with Pearson eText, Access Card, for *Mosaicos*: Spanish as a World Language (multi-semester access) (ISBN 10: 0-205-99724-4)

MySpanishLab, part of our MyLanguageLabs suite of products, is an online homework, tutorial, and assessment product designed to improve results by helping students quickly master concepts, and by providing educators with a robust set of tools for easily gauging and addressing the performance of individuals and classrooms. **MyLanguageLabs** has helped almost one million students successfully learn a language by providing them everything they need: full eText, online activities, instant feedback, **amplifire** dynamic study modules, and an engaging collection of language-specific learning tools, all in one online program. For more information, including case studies that illustrate how MyLanguageLabs improves results, visit www.mylanguagelabs.com.

FOR THE INSTRUCTOR

Annotated Instructor's Edition (ISBN 10: 0-205-25543-4)

The Annotated Instructor's Edition contains an abundance of marginal annotations designed especially for novice instructors, instructors who are new to the ***Mosaicos*** program, or instructors who have limited time for class preparation. The format allows ample space for annotations alongside full-size pages of the student text. Marginal annotations suggest warm-up and expansion exercises and activities and provide teaching tips, additional cultural information, and audioscripts for the in-text listening activities. Answers to discrete-point activities are printed in blue type for the instructor's convenience.

Instructor's Resource Manual (available online)

The Instructor's Resource Manual (IRM) contains complete lesson plans for all chapters, integrated syllabi for regular and hybrid courses, as well as helpful suggestions for new and experienced instructors alike. It also provides videoscripts for all episodes of the ***¡Cineastas en acción!*** video, audioscripts for listening activities in the Student Activities Manual, and a complete guide to all ***Mosaicos*** supplements. The Instructor's Resource Manual is available to instructors online at the ***Mosaicos*** Instructor Resource Center and in MySpanishLab.

Supplementary Activities (available online)

Available in MySpanishLab, the Supplementary Activities ancillary consists of a range of engaging activities that complement the vocabulary and grammar themes of each chapter. It offers instructors additional materials that can serve to energize and enrich their students' classroom experience.

Testing Program (available online)

The Testing Program has been thoroughly revised and expanded for this edition. The testing content correlates with the vocabulary, grammar, culture, and skills material presented in the student text. For each chapter of the text, a bank of testing activities is provided in modular form; instructors can select and combine modules to create customized tests tailored to the needs of their classes. Two complete, ready-to-use tests are also provided for each chapter. The testing modules are available to instructors online in MySpanishLab for those who wish to create computerized tests (MyTest) or in the ***Mosaicos*** Instructor Resource Center as downloadable Word documents.

Testing Audio CD (ISBN 10: 0-205-25549-3)

A special set of audio CDs, available to instructors only, contains recordings corresponding to the listening comprehension portions of the Testing Program.

PowerPoint™ Presentations (ISBN 10: 0-205-99712-0)

A PowerPoint™ Presentation is available for each chapter of the text. These dynamic, visually engaging presentations allow instructors to enliven class sessions and reinforce key concepts. The presentations are available to instructors online in MySpanishLab or in the ***Mosaicos*** Instructor Resource Center.

Situaciones adicionales (available online)

The downloadable *Situaciones adicionales* provide instructors with additional opportunities for reinforcing and assessing students' speaking skills. The activities are also available via the *Situaciones* mobile app.

Instructor Resource Center

Several of the instructor supplements listed above—the Instructor's Resource Manual, the Testing Program, the PowerPoint™ Presentations,—are available for download at the access-protected ***Mosaicos*** Instructor Resource Center (www.pearsonhighered.com/mosaicos). An access code will be provided at no charge to instructors once their faculty status has been verified.

ONLINE RESOURCES

MySpanishLab with Pearson eText—Access Card—for *Mosaicos*: Spanish as a World Language

MySpanishLab, part of our MyLanguageLabs suite of products, is an online homework, tutorial, and assessment product designed to improve results by helping students quickly master concepts, and by providing educators with a robust set of tools for easily gauging and addressing the performance of individuals and classrooms. **MyLanguageLabs** has helped almost one million students successfully learn a language by providing them everything they need: full eText, online activities, instant feedback, **amplifire** dynamic study modules, and an engaging collection of language-specific learning tools, all in one online program. For more information, including case studies that illustrate how MyLanguageLabs improves results, visit www.mylanguagelabs.com.

COMPANION WEBSITE

The open-access Companion Website (www.pearsonhighered.com/mosaicos) includes audio to accompany listening activities and sample language from the textbook and audio to accompany the listening activities in the Student Activities Manual.

Acknowledgments

Mosaicos is the result of a collaborative effort among the authors, our publisher, and our colleagues. In particular, the cultural content of the sixth edition has been enhanced by the work of the contributors who created content and activities for the program: María Lourdes Casas, Óscar Martín, Frances Matos-Shultz, Sergio Salazar, Kristine Suárez, Lilián Uribe, and U. Theresa Zmurkewycz. We also extend our thanks to Alicia Muñoz Sánchez and Raúl J. Vázquez-López, who wrote ancillary materials. We are also indebted to the members of the Spanish teaching community for their time, candor, and insightful suggestions as they reviewed drafts of the sixth edition of ***Mosaicos.*** Their critiques and recommendations helped us to sharpen our pedagogical focus and improve the overall quality of the program. We gratefully acknowledge the contributions of the following reviewers:

Sissy Alloway,
Morehead State University

Debra Ames,
Valparaiso University

Ashlee S. Balena,
University of North Carolina at Wilmington

Fleming L. Bell,
Valdosta State University

Talia Bugel,
Indiana University-Purdue University, Fort Wayne

Stephen Buttes,
Indiana University-Purdue University, Fort Wayne

Sara Casler,
Sierra College

Jens Clegg,
Indiana University-Purdue University Fort Wayne

Hilda Coronado,
Glendale Community College

Lisa DeWaard,
Clemson University

Neva Duffy,
Chicago State University

Ari Gutman,
Auburn University

Crista Johnson,
University of Delaware

Keith Johnson,
California State University, Fresno

Maribel Manzari,
Washington & Jefferson College

Bryan Miley,
Glendale Community College

John Andrew Morrow,
Ivy Tech Community College

Margarita Orro,
Miami Dade College, North Campus

Claudia Ospina,
Wake Forest University

Leon Palombo,
Miami Dade College, North Campus

Yelgy Parada,
Los Angeles City College

Kristina Primorac,
University of Michigan

Terri Rice,
University of South Alabama

Lee J. Rincón,
Moraine Valley Community College

Pamela Rink,
Tulsa Community College

Angelo J. Rodriguez,
Kutztown University of Pennsylvania

Felipe E. Rojas,
Chicago State University

Anita Saalfeld,
University of Nebraska at Omaha

Michael Sawyer,
University of Central Missouri

Rachel Showstack,
Wichita State University

Gayle Vierma,
University of Southern California

Maida Watson,
Florida International University

Amanda Wilcox,
Auburn University

Kelley L. Young,
University of Missouri-Kansas City

Hilma-Nelly Zamora-Breckenridge,
Valparaiso University

U. Theresa Zmurkewycz,
Saint Joseph's University

Mosaicos Advisory Board

Silvia Arroyo,
Mississippi State University

Donna Binkowski,
Southern Methodist University

Joelle Bonamy,
Columbus State University

Robert Cameron,
College of Charleston

Susana Castillo-Rodríguez,
University of New Hampshire

Juliet Falce-Robinson,
University of California, Los Angeles

Ronna Feit,
Nassau Community College, SUNY

Chris Foley,
Liberty University

Leah Fonder-Solano,
University of Southern Mississippi

Muriel Gallego,
Ohio University

Kathryn Grovergrys,
Madison Area Technical College

Marie Guiribitey,
Florida International University

Todd Hernández,
Marquette University

Yun Sil Jeon,
Coastal Carolina University

Lauri Kahn,
Suffolk County Community College

Rob Martinsen,
Brigham Young University

Teresa McCann,
Prairie State College

Eugenia Muñoz,
Viriginia Commonwealth University

Michelle Orecchio,
University of Michigan

Susana García Prudencio,
Pennsylvania State University

Bethany Sanio,
University of Nebraska, Lincoln

Virginia Shen,
Chicago State University

Julie Sykes,
University of Oregon

Kelley L. Young,
University of Missouri - Kansas City

Gabriela C. Zapata,
University of Southern California

Nancy Zimmerman,
Kutztown University

We are also grateful for the guidance of Celia Meana and Scott Gravina, the Developmental Editors, for all of their work, suggestions, attention to detail, and dedication to the text. Their support and efficiency helped us achieve the final product. We are very grateful to the many other members of the Pearson World Languages team who provided guidance, support, and fine attention to detail at all stages of the production process: Samantha Alducin, Senior Digital Product Manager, and Regina Rivera, Media Editor, for helping us produce the new MySpanishLab program, the new video, audio programs, and Companion Website. Thanks to Jonathan Ortiz and Millie Chapman, Editorial Assistants, for their hard work and efficiency in managing the reviews and attending to many editorial details.

We are very grateful to our World Languages Consultants, Denise Miller, Yesha Brill, and Mellissa Yokell, for their creativity and efforts in coordinating marketing campaigns and promotion for this edition. Thanks, too, to our program and project management team, Nancy Stevenson and Lynne Breitfeller, who guided *Mosaicos, sixth edition,* through the many stages of production; to our partners at PreMediaGlobal, especially Jenna Gray, for her careful and professional production services and to the PreMediaGlobal design team for the gorgeous interior. A special thank you to Kathryn Foot, Senior Art Director and designer Michael Black of Black Sun for their creative work on the cover. Finally, we would like to express our sincere thanks to Steve Debow, Senior Vice President for World Languages, Bob Hemmer, Editor in Chief, Tiziana Aime, Senior Acquisitions Editor, and Kristine Suárez, Director of Market Development, for their guidance and support through every aspect of this new edition.

About the Authors

Elizabeth with her husband in Petra, Jordan

PALOMA LAPUERTA

My Ph.D. is from... Université de Genève, Switzerland, but I did my "licenciatura" in Universidad de Salamanca, Spain.

My research area is... Spanish Language and Peninsular Literature.

One of my proudest teaching moments was... when I noticed that everybody was having a good time... and learning!

My favorite vacation spot in the Hispanic world is... I have two: Castellón, Spain, which is by the sea, and Pereira, Colombia, which is near the Andes.

I can't live without my... Moleskine®.

My favorite feature in Mosaicos is... that it takes you to places beyond the textbook.

The movie I have seen most often is... *Volver*, by Pedro Almodóvar.

My favorite activity is... to travel.

The site that I found most beautiful was... Machu Picchu.

The landscape I found most impressive was... Namibia.

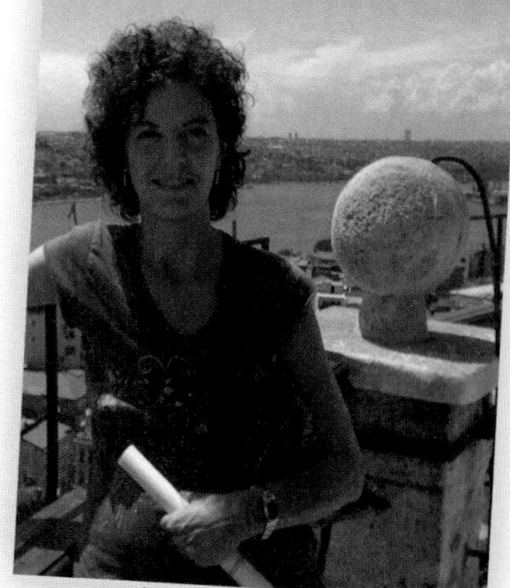
Paloma in Istanbul, Turkey

ELIZABETH E. GUZMÁN

I did my graduate studies in Spanish Applied Linguistics at the University of Pittsburgh.

One of my proudest teaching moments was... when my former students have shown me what a difference I can make in my students through my love of teaching.

My favorite vacation spots in the Hispanic world are... the lake regions of my native Chile and Peru.

I can't live without... my laptop and Pandora radio.

My favorite feature in Mosaicos is... that it opens the doors to the fascinating Spanish-speaking world, its people, and its diverse cultures.

My favorite activities are... traveling, gardening, and listening to music.

The people closest to my heart are... my family, my friends, and the people who value freedom and justice as much as I do.

What makes me happy is... knowing that my work transcends me.

The people I admire are... those from whom I can learn something.

My favorite classroom is... one in which students and I become part of one community working toward common goals.

Judy with student Jia and her first apple pie

JUDITH E. LISKIN-GASPARRO

My Ph.D. is from... the University of Texas–Austin

My research area is... classroom-based second language acquisition.

One of my proudest teaching moments was... when my doctoral student won the ACTFL-MLJ Birkmaier Award for Doctoral Dissertation Research. There have been four proudest moments, because four of my SLA students have won this award since 2007.

My favorite vacation spot in the Hispanic world is... For its mystery and sheer beauty, Machu Picchu. For the lifestyle and amazing *tortillas de patatas*, San Sebastián.

I can't live without my... laptop.

My favorite feature in Mosaicos is... its clickability (my made-up word). It invites students and instructors to challenge linear patterns of learning.

My public talent is... baking cookies—all kinds, and for all occasions. I also give pie workshops.

My secret talent is... making up cool games to play with toddlers.

I am thrilled when... people think I am a native speaker of Spanish.

mosaicos

SPANISH AS A WORLD LANGUAGE

10 ¿Cuál es tu comida preferida?

ENFOQUE CULTURAL
Ecuador

VOCABULARIO EN CONTEXTO
Los productos y las recetas
En el supermercado
La mesa

MOSAICO CULTURAL
Comida callejera

FUNCIONES Y FORMAS
Se + verb constructions
Present perfect and participles used as adjectives
Informal commands
The future tense

EN ACCIÓN
¡Hay que celebrar!

MOSAICOS
ESCUCHA Make notes of relevant details
HABLA Give and defend reasons for a decision
LEE Learn new words by analyzing their connections with known words
ESCRIBE Summarize information

EN ESTE CAPÍTULO...
Comprueba lo que sabes
Vocabulario

LEARNING OUTCOMES

You will be able to:

- talk about ingredients, recipes, and meals
- state impersonal information
- talk about the recent past
- give instructions in informal settings
- talk about the future
- present information, concepts, and ideas about food and public health in Ecuador and other Latin American countries

ENFOQUE cultural ECUADOR

Enfoque cultural

To learn more about Ecuador, go to MySpanishLab to view the *Vistas culturales* videos.

¿QUÉ TE PARECE?

- Charles Darwin visitó las islas Galápagos en 1835. Este viaje influyó en su idea de la evolución mediante la selección natural.
- Ecuador declaró en la Nueva Constitución Ecuatoriana de 2008 que la naturaleza tiene derechos constitucionales. Fue el primer país en reconocer a la naturaleza como sujeto de derecho.
- En Quito, la capital de Ecuador, el punto de ebullición del agua es 90 grados centígrados (194 ºF) debido a la altura de la ciudad.
- Ecuador es el mayor exportador de bananas; produce el 32% de las bananas en el mercado mundial.
- Rafael Correa fue elegido presidente de Ecuador por tercera vez en 2013. Aprendió a hablar quechua durante su año de servicio militar en las montañas.

▲ Este cuadro del siglo XVIII presenta a un indígena yumbo cerca de Quito, Ecuador. Junto a él hay árboles y frutas típicas de su país.

Cuy con papas

Unos típicos platos ecuatorianos son ceviche de camarones, cuy (*guinea pig*), llapingachos (papas con queso), pan de yuca y choclo (maíz) con queso. Se sirve mucha comida con ají criollo (una salsa picante).

Las tortugas de las islas Galápagos son unos animales vertebrados muy antiguos, y pueden vivir hasta 150 años.

Las islas Galápagos tienen plantas y animales que no se encuentran en ningún otro lugar del mundo. El ecoturismo está muy desarrollado en las islas.

Quito fue construida en las ruinas de una ciudad inca. Tiene una rica historia precolombina. Fue designada Patrimonio de la Humanidad por la UNESCO.

¿CUÁNTO SABES?

Asocia la información de las dos columnas.

1. _____ la capital de Ecuador	**a.** islas Galápagos
2. _____ territorio ecuatoriano en el Pacífico	**b.** los Andes
3. _____ llapingachos, cuy y choclo con queso	**c.** Nueva Constitución Ecuatoriana
4. _____ animal protegido	**d.** tortuga
5. _____ cadena de montañas	**e.** Quito
6. _____ protección de la naturaleza	**f.** platos tradicionales

Vocabulario en contexto

Talking about ingredients, recipes, and meals

Los productos y las recetas

MySpanishLab
Learn more using Amplifire Dynamic Study Modules, Pronunciation, and Vocabulary Tutorials.

(a) En Ecuador se cultiva mucha fruta, sobre todo **piña, limón, melón, papaya, maracuyá** y **plátano.** Mucha de esta fruta se exporta a Estados Unidos y a otros países. Aquí vemos a unas personas trabajando en una compañía de exportación de plátanos cerca de Guayaquil.

(b) En los mercados ecuatorianos, como en los de otros países hispanoamericanos, hay buenos puestos de **pasteles** donde se venden los **dulces** típicos de la región.

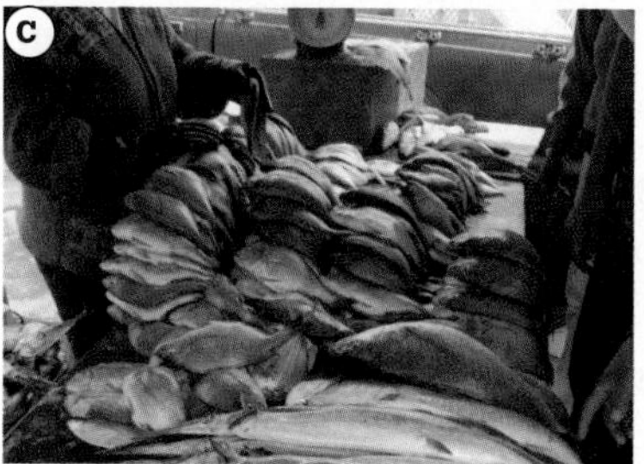

(c) El pescado y los **mariscos** son muy importantes en la dieta de algunos países hispanoamericanos como Chile, Perú y Ecuador. En la provincia de Esmeraldas, en Ecuador, uno de los platos típicos es el encocado, pescado que se cocina con **leche de coco.**

(d) Este joven ecuatoriano cuida sus **ovejas** cerca del Parque Nacional Chimborazo. De las ovejas se aprovechan la carne en comida y la lana en suéteres, mantas, etc. Además, los **campesinos** usan la leche para hacer queso y yogur. Junto a la carne de **cordero,** la de **res** y la de **cerdo** son las que más se usan en la comida de Ecuador y se venden en los mercados y en las carnicerías.

(e) En el mercado de Zumbahua se encuentran los productos que se usan en las muchas **recetas** de la comida de Ecuador. La forma de combinar estos productos con el cilantro y otras **hierbas** y **especias** dan fama a la gastronomía ecuatoriana.

PRÁCTICA

10-1  

Escucha y confirma. Match the letter of the photo to the description you hear.

1. _____
2. _____
3. _____
4. _____
5. _____

10-2 

Definiciones. Asocia las definiciones a continuación con las palabras que aparecen en los textos y fotos anteriores.

1. una lista de ingredientes y de instrucciones para elaborar una comida
2. un animal del que se aprovecha la lana, la leche y la carne
3. una fruta alargada que se pela y que les gusta mucho a los monos
4. un plato ecuatoriano que se cocina con pescado y leche de coco
5. una tienda donde se vende pescado
6. las personas que cultivan productos del campo
7. dulces que se venden en las pastelerías y en los mercados
8. la carne de una oveja pequeña

10-3 

Una receta ecuatoriana. Lean la siguiente receta y clasifiquen sus ingredientes según las categorías. Después, díganse cuál es su comida favorita y por qué les gusta.

1. carnes o pescados:
2. vegetales:
3. condimentos:
4. frutas:

Pescado encocado

Ingredientes:
1 coco
1 libra de camarones
2 libras de pescado crudo

Refrito:
1 cebolla paiteña finamente picada
¼ taza de cebolla blanca finamente picada
1 pimiento picado
4 cucharadas de cilantro picado
4 cucharadas de perejil picado
2 dientes de ajo machacados
4 cucharadas de aceite
1 un tomate grande rojo, pelado y picado
un poquito de achiote
sal, pimienta, comino al gusto

Elaboración:
Haga un refrito con los ingredientes. Agréguele una libra de camarones crudos, pelados y limpios y dos libras de pescado crudo, cortado en trozos. Refríalos durante un rato y luego agregue la mitad de la leche del coco. Tape la olla y deje cocinar durante 20 o 30 minutos. Después, añada la otra mitad de la leche de coco. Sirva inmediatamente, acompañado de arroz blanco y plátano verde asado.

10-4 

Cómo hacer una pizza. Ordenen cronológicamente los pasos para preparar una pizza. ¿Falta algún ingrediente para preparar su pizza favorita? Inclúyanlo y preséntenlo a la clase.

__1__ Se compran los ingredientes para la pizza.

_____ Se calienta el horno a 350 °F.

_____ Se echa un poco de aceite (*oil*) antes de poner la masa en la bandeja de horno.

_____ Se agregan el queso (*cheese*), algún tipo de carne, vegetales y especias.

_____ Se pone la salsa de tomate.

_____ Se trabaja bien la masa y se extiende para formar un círculo.

_____ Se hornea por unos 20 a 25 minutos.

LENGUA

These are some useful words that appear in the recipe: **almejas** (*clams*), **perejil** (*parsley*), **paiteña** (*a type of onion*), **diente de ajo** (*clove of garlic*), **picado** (*chopped*), and **comino** (*cumin*). Other cooking expressions include **picar** (*chop*), **pelar** (*peel*), **machacar** (*crush*), **tapar** (*cover*), **agregar/añadir** (*add*), **taza** (*cup*), and **cucharada** (*spoonful*).

En el supermercado

Las frutas y las verduras

Los productos lácteos y los huevos

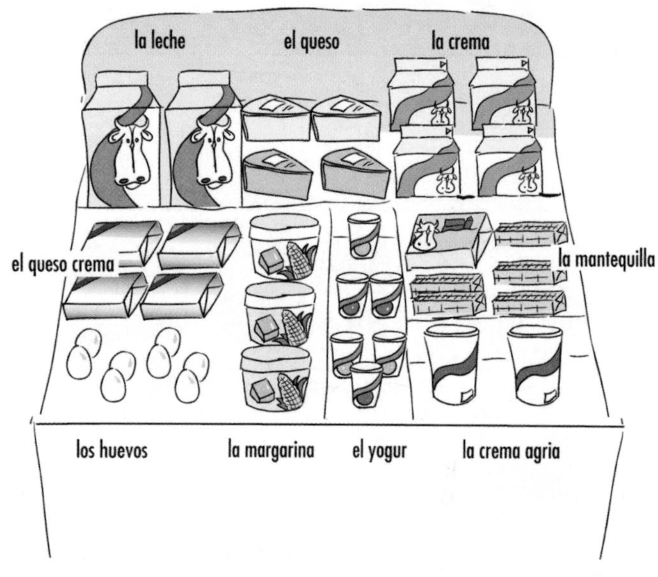

El pescado y la carne

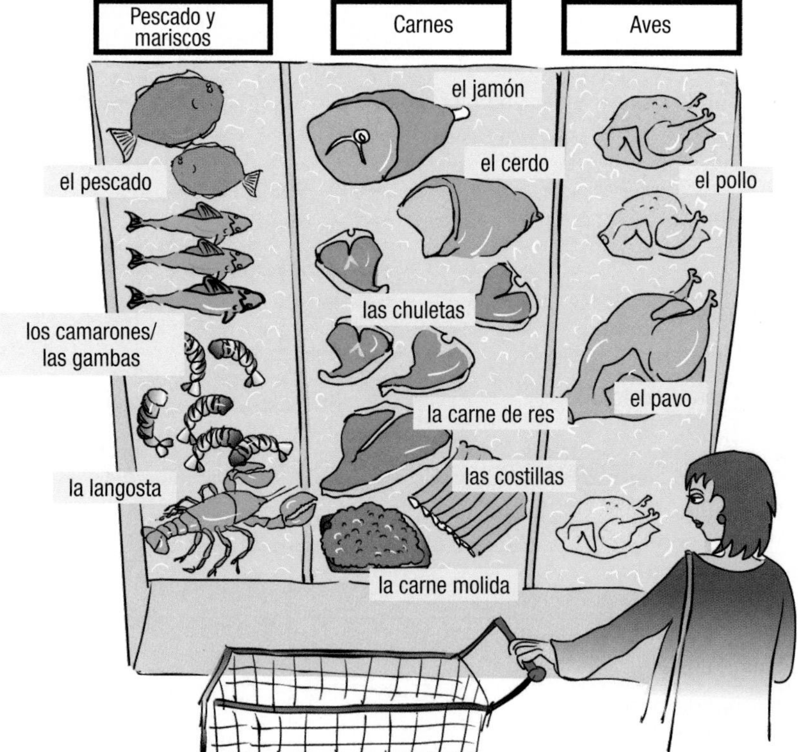

EN OTRAS PALABRAS

The words for some vegetables and spices vary from region to region. **Aguacate** is known as **palta** in some South American countries; **maíz** is known as **elote** in Mexico and in some Central American countries and as **choclo** in parts of South America.

Names of fruits also vary: **plátano** in Spain becomes **cambur** in Venezuela; in other places, **banano** (Colombia) or **banana** (Uruguay) is used. Other examples include **melocotón** (Spain)/**durazno** (Latin America); **fruta de la pasión** (Spain)/**maracuyá** (Colombia)/**parchita** (Venezuela, Mexico).

EN OTRAS PALABRAS

Other names of foods that vary by country are **pavo,** which is **guajolote** in Mexico, and **camarones,** which are **gambas** in Spain. **Puerco** is also commonly used in place of **cerdo.**

Los condimentos y las legumbres

El pan y las bebidas

PRÁCTICA

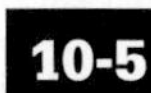  

10-5

Para confirmar. Asocien cada explicación con la palabra adecuada y comenten si les gustan o no estos alimentos.

1. _____ Se toma mucho en el verano, cuando hace calor.	**a.** el jamón
2. _____ Se pone en la ensalada.	**b.** las uvas
3. _____ Se usan para hacer vino.	**c.** la mayonesa
4. _____ Se come en el desayuno con huevos fritos.	**d.** el helado
5. _____ Se prepara para el Día de Acción de Gracias.	**e.** el aderezo
6. _____ Se usa para preparar un sándwich de atún o de pollo.	**f.** el pavo

10-6 

Dietas diferentes.

PREPARACIÓN. Completen la tabla con las comidas o productos adecuados para estas dietas.

DIETA	SE DEBE COMER	NO SE DEBE COMER
vegetariana		
para diabéticos		
para fortalecer (*strengthen*) los músculos		
para bajar de peso (*lose weight*)		

INTERCAMBIOS. Completen las siguientes oraciones con sus recomendaciones para cada una de estas personas. Digan por qué recomiendan eso.

1. Laura, que es vegetariana,...
2. Mi padre, que es diabético,...
3. Luis, que levanta pesas (*weights*),...
4. Joaquín y Amalia quieren bajar de peso. Por lo tanto,...

Cultura

Muchos hispanohablantes que viven en Estados Unidos mantienen las tradiciones y costumbres alimentarias de su país natal (*native*). Estas tradiciones y costumbres, que varían mucho de un país a otro, se reflejan en las recetas, maneras de cocinar y aun en las horas diferentes de comer. Hay productos, como los frijoles, el arroz, los chiles, los plátanos y el maíz, que constituyen la base de la dieta de muchos países de Hispanoamérica y que se encuentran en casi todos los supermercados de Estados Unidos.

Comparaciones. ¿Qué productos son populares en la comida de tu país o región? ¿Qué platos se preparan con estos productos? ¿Cuáles son los postres especiales? ¿Se comen en una época determinada?

10-7

¿Qué necesitamos?

PREPARACIÓN. Ustedes son estudiantes de intercambio en Ecuador y quieren preparar una cena para su familia ecuatoriana. Describan el menú y hagan una lista de los ingredientes que necesitan.

INTERCAMBIOS. Compartan su menú con otra pareja.

10-8

Los estudiantes y la comida. **PREPARACIÓN.** Respondan a las siguientes preguntas.

1. ¿Qué comieron hoy?
2. ¿Cuándo y dónde comieron?
3. ¿Cuánto gastaron en comida?

INTERCAMBIOS. Hagan una lista de recomendaciones para una dieta estudiantil más saludable (*healthier*) y compártanla con el resto de la clase.

En directo

To give some general advice:

Deben + *infinitive* (comer/beber/etc.)...

Para bajar de peso/comer saludable, recomendamos + *noun* (las verduras, el agua, etc.)

Para obtener calcio/proteínas/fibra es bueno + *infinitive* (comer/beber/etc.)

Listen to a conversation with these expressions.

La mesa

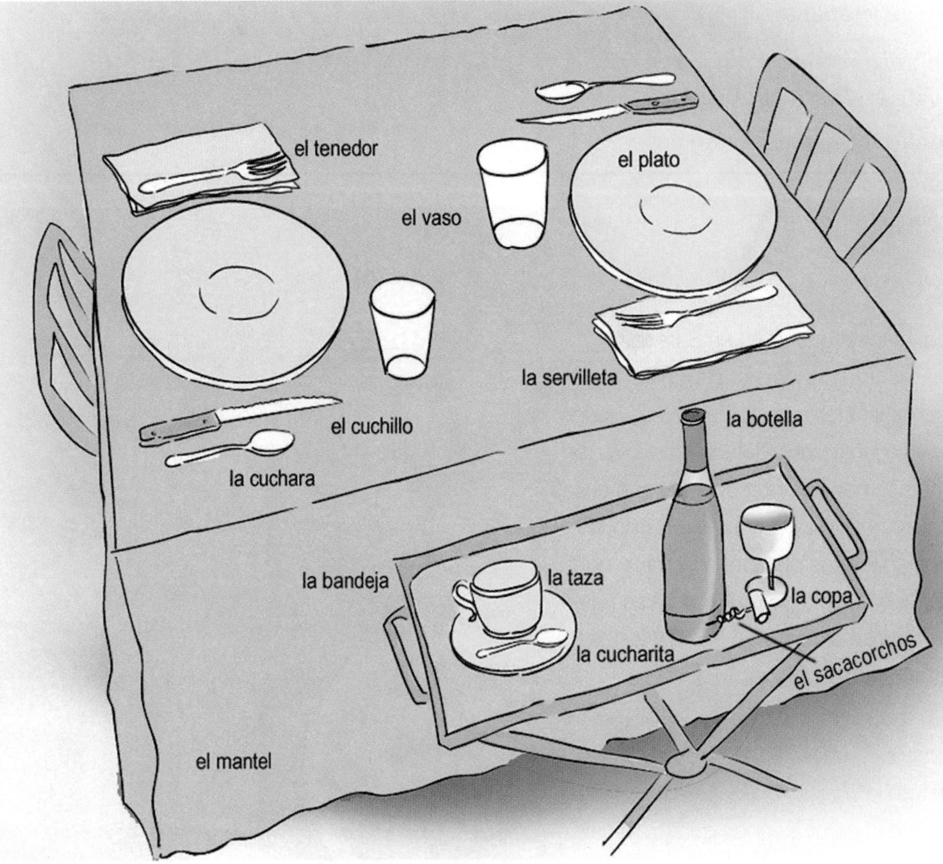

PRÁCTICA

10-9 

Para confirmar. Indica qué tipo de utensilios se necesitan en las siguientes situaciones. Compara tus respuestas con las de tu compañero/a.

1. para cortar un bistec
2. para tomar sopa
3. para beber vino
4. para poner azúcar en el café
5. para llevar comida a la mesa
6. para cubrir la mesa
7. para limpiarse la boca (*mouth*)
8. para destapar una botella de vino

10-10 

El camarero nuevo. Ustedes son camareros/as en un restaurante pero uno/a de ustedes es nuevo/a. El/La experto/a debe decirle a la persona nueva dónde debe poner cada cosa de acuerdo con la foto. Después, cambien de papel.

E1: *Pon el cuchillo a la derecha del plato.*

E2: *Muy bien. ¿Y dónde pongo la copa?*

10-11 

Los preparativos. Ustedes deben organizar una fiesta formal para sus mejores amigos que se gradúan de la universidad este año. Primero, preparen un presupuesto (*budget*), una lista de invitados, un menú y una lista de compras. Luego, divídanse el trabajo y dense instrucciones entre ustedes sobre lo siguiente:

1. la decoración del salón
2. la preparación de la mesa
3. la comida y las bebidas
4. los invitados
5. el lugar, la hora, el día
6. ...

10-12 

Una cena. Estuviste muy ocupado/a ayer porque tuviste invitados a cenar. Dile a tu compañero/a todas las cosas que hiciste. Él/Ella te va a preguntar dónde hiciste las compras, a quién invitaste, qué serviste y si lo pasaste bien. Después, cambien de papel.

En directo

To express that you had a good time:

Lo pasé muy bien./Lo pasamos muy bien. *I/We had a great time.*

Fue estupendo. *It was wonderful.*

Estuvo muy divertido. *It was very fun.*

 Listen to a conversation with these expressions.

Cultura

Platos típicos

En Ecuador, al igual que en Perú, el ceviche de pescado o de camarón es muy popular. Otro plato ecuatoriano muy popular es la fritada, una combinación de diversas carnes con plátano (*plantain*) maduro, plátano tostado y maíz. Y entre los postres, además de los pasteles, es muy sabroso el dulce de higos (*candied figs*).

Comunidades. Piensa en los supermercados que hay en tu ciudad. ¿Qué productos típicos de la cultura hispana puedes encontrar en ellos? ¿Cuáles de estos productos se usan en tu casa?

▲ Dulce de higos

10-13 

Una cena perfecta. PREPARACIÓN. You will listen to a couple talk about their plans for their dinner party tonight. Before you listen, make a list of four ingredients that you will need for a salad and an entrée. Share your list with a classmate.

 ESCUCHA. Now listen to the conversation. As you listen, mark (✓) the appropriate ending to each statement.

1. Rodolfo es...

_____ un buen cocinero.

_____ muy perezoso.

_____ vegetariano.

2. Manuela va a...

_____ preparar ceviche.

_____ poner la mesa.

_____ llamar a los invitados.

3. Rodolfo va a comprar...

_____ pescado y maíz.

_____ limón y camarones.

_____ espinacas y aguacates.

4. Manuela tiene...

_____ todos los ingredientes.

_____ muchos vegetales y frutas.

_____ casi todos los ingredientes.

MOSAICO cultural

Comida callejera

Para Claudia Acosta, encontrar comida en la Ciudad de México no es nada difícil. "La variedad de restaurantes en la ciudad es increíble", comentó Acosta; pero estas opciones no siempre son económicas para una estudiante, especialmente para una que viene

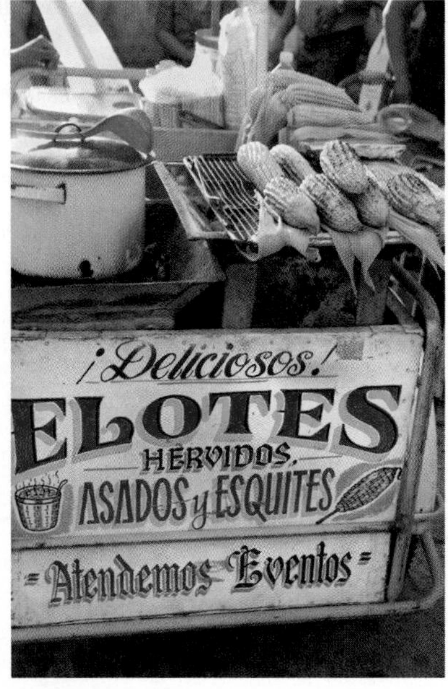

de fuera. Por esta razón ha preferido comer en los puestos de la calle durante los cuatro años que lleva viviendo en México y estudiando en la UNAM. "En mis primeros años cuando vine de Ecuador a estudiar aquí, siempre encontraba un puesto de tacos y tortillas cada tres o cuatro calles", dijo Acosta.

En una ciudad de casi nueve millones de personas, la cantidad de puestos de comida callejera crece constantemente. La mayoría se encuentra en estaciones de metro, áreas de negocios, estadios y parques. Los puestos ofrecen una variedad de carnes, verduras y tortillas para hacer una comida. ¡Y es más barata que en los restaurantes!

Los puestos callejeros han existido en Latinoamérica desde la época de la colonia. Cada país ha mantenido sus costumbres de alimentación y en los puestos se venden productos típicos. En Argentina están los choripanes (pan con chorizo) y las empanadas. En Venezuela se venden arepas rellenas (*filled*) con carnes y vegetales. En todo el mundo hispano se puede conseguir gran variedad de platos típicos. Claudia ha disfrutado de la comida mexicana, pero también ha extrañado (*missed*) la comida de su país: "He tenido días en que cambiaría todo por un buen plato de arroz con menestra y carne asada como el que comía en casa".

Compara

1. ¿Es común encontrar puestos de comida callejera en tu comunidad? ¿Qué tipo de comida venden? Explica detalladamente.
2. En general, ¿cuáles son las comidas que más has consumido en tu vida como estudiante?
3. ¿Se venden comidas extranjeras en tu comunidad?
4. ¿Probaste alguna vez las arepas, los choripanes, los tacos, las empanadas u otras comidas hispanas callejeras? ¿Cómo son en comparación con las comidas callejeras típicas de tu región?

▼ Empanadas argentinas

Funciones y formas

1 Stating impersonal information

PROFESOR: En Estados Unidos **se consumen** muchos carbohidratos y mucha grasa. ¿Sabían ustedes que en este país **se comen** 23 libras de pizza por persona al año?

RICARDO: [*piensa*] ¿Cuánta cerveza **se bebe** con 23 pizzas?

PROFESOR: **Se comen** solo 16 libras de manzanas, bla bla bla...

RICARDO: [*piensa*] En esta clase **se duerme** mucho.

Piénsalo. ¿Cuánto más sabes sobre la dieta estadounidense? Indica si las siguientes afirmaciones son ciertas (**C**) o falsas (**F**), según la información del profesor y lo que sabes.

1. _____ **Se consumen** muchas grasas (*fats*).
2. _____ **Se compra** más fruta en el supermercado ahora que en el pasado.
3. _____ **Se dice** que los niños comen más y hacen menos actividad física.
4. _____ **Se bebe** mucho café, especialmente en las universidades.
5. _____ **Se consume** más pizza que manzanas.
6. _____ **Se recomienda** desayunar todos los días.

Se + verb constructions

- Spanish uses the ***se*** + *verb* construction to emphasize the occurrence of an action rather than the person(s) responsible for that action. The noun (what is bought, sold, offered, etc.) usually follows the verb. The person who buys, sells, offers, and so on, is not mentioned. This is normally expressed in English with the passive voice (is/are + *past participle*).

Se habla español en este restaurante.	*Spanish is spoken in this restaurant.*

- Use a singular verb with singular nouns and a plural verb with plural nouns.

Se necesita un horno para hacer galletas.	*An oven is needed to make cookies.*
Se venden vegetales allí.	*Vegetables are sold there.*

- Use a singular verb when the ***se*** + *verb* construction is followed by an adverb, an infinitive, or a clause. This is expressed in English with indefinite subjects such as *they, you, one,* and *people.*

Se trabaja mucho en ese manzanal.	*They work a lot in that apple orchard.*
Se puede comprar una variedad de manzanas allí.	*You can buy a variety of apples there.*
Se dice que venden sidra excelente también.	*People say they sell excellent cider too.*

¿COMPRENDES?

Completa las oraciones con la forma correcta de **se** + el verbo entre paréntesis.

1. ____ ________ pasteles en la pastelería. (vender)
2. El ceviche ____ ________ con pescado. (preparar)
3. ____ ________ freír o asar la carne de res. (poder)
4. ____ ________ que la comida de ese restaurante es excelente. (decir)
5. Los llapingachos, tortillas de papas con queso, ____ ________ en muchos restaurantes ecuatorianos. (servir)

MySpanishLab

Learn more using Amplifire Dynamic Study Modules, Grammar Tutorials, and Extra Practice activities.

PRÁCTICA

Asociaciones. **PREPARACIÓN.** Asocia las actividades con los lugares donde ocurren. Compara tus respuestas con las de tu compañero/a.

1. _____ Se cambian cheques en...
2. _____ Se vende ropa en...
3. _____ Se toma el sol y se nada en...
4. _____ Se sirven comidas en...

a. un almacén o tienda.
b. un restaurante.
c. un banco.
d. una playa.

INTERCAMBIOS. Piensa en un edificio o lugar público que te gusta mucho y dile a tu compañero/a qué se hace allí.

Me gusta mucho la zona peatonal (pedestrian area) *de mi ciudad. Allí se camina mucho y en el verano se escucha la música de grupos locales.*

10-15 

El supermercado y las tiendas del barrio. Indica (✓) los productos y/o servicios que se encuentran solo en los supermercados y los que se encuentran en las tiendas de tu barrio. Compara tus respuestas con las de tu compañero/a. Después, dile a tu compañero/a qué productos compras con más frecuencia.

PRODUCTOS/SERVICIOS	SUPERMERCADO SOLAMENTE	SUPERMERCADO Y TIENDA DEL BARRIO
productos lácteos	________	________
carnes orgánicas	________	________
frutas de América del Sur	________	________
detergente para lavadoras	________	________
alimentos enlatados (*canned*)	________	________
pescado fresco	________	________
DVD para alquilar	________	________

EN OTRAS PALABRAS

The concept of *convenience stores* is expressed differently depending on the country. In Mexico they are **tiendas de conveniencia,** translated directly from English. In Costa Rica the term **tiendas de gasolinera** is used. **La tienda de la esquina** o **del barrio** is frequently used in several Spanish-speaking countries to refer to the small or medium-sized stores located in residential neighborhoods. Convenience stores in Spain that are open 24/7 are called **tiendas de 24 horas.**

10-16 

Recetas creativas.

PREPARACIÓN. Lean estas recetas originales. Luego, intercambien opiniones sobre cuáles les gustaría probar y cuáles no. Digan por qué.

Ponche a la romana: Se muelen (*grind*) unas rodajas de piña. Se mezcla con una botella de champaña y helado de piña; se agrega azúcar; se enfría en el refrigerador antes de servir.

E1: *Me gustaría probar el ponche, pero no bebo alcohol. ¿Se puede preparar sin champaña?*

E2: *Por supuesto, se puede hacer con jugo de piña.*

1. Plátano derretido (*melted*): Se corta un plátano en rebanadas (*slices*) no muy finas. Se echa azúcar. Se calienta en el microondas por uno o dos minutos.
2. Batido de tarta de manzana (*Apple pie smoothie*): Se ponen en la licuadora (*blender*): media taza de jugo de manzana, tres cucharadas de helado de vainilla y media cucharadita de canela (*cinnamon*). Se bate por un minuto.
3. Hamburguesa y salsa con queso (*nacho cheese sauce*): Se calienta la parrilla. Se pone la hamburguesa en la parrilla. Se pone la salsa con queso en el panecillo y se calienta. Se pone la hamburguesa en el panecillo.
4. Ensalada de pollo: Se abre una bolsa de lechuga prelavada. Se cortan en rebanadas dos pechugas de pollo (*chicken breasts*) cocidas, y se corta media libra de queso en cubos pequeños. Se combinan los ingredientes en una fuente (*bowl*). Se agrega un aderezo de vinagre balsámico.

INTERCAMBIOS. Escriban juntos una receta para compartir con la clase. Si es posible, prepárenla para la clase.

10-17 

¿Cómo se prepara este plato? **PREPARACIÓN.** Tu compañero/a y tú quieren darle una sorpresa a otra persona y deciden prepararle su plato favorito. Primero, seleccionen uno de estos platos.

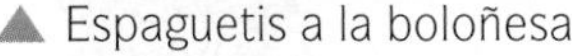
▲ Espaguetis a la boloñesa

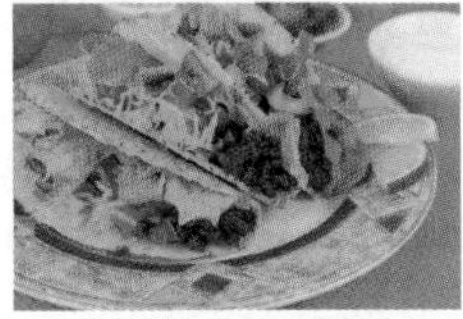
▲ Tacos al carbón

Luego, escriban en cada columna una lista de los ingredientes que se necesitan para hacer este plato.

CARNES	VERDURAS/ VEGETALES	ESPECIAS	OTROS

INTERCAMBIOS. Tú sabes cocinar, pero tu amigo/a no. Responde a sus preguntas mientras preparan el plato. Los siguientes verbos pueden ser útiles.

asar	dorar (*brown*)	rallar (*grate*)
cocinar	hervir	(so)freír
cortar	hornear	tostar

MODELO E1: *Vamos a preparar pollo asado. ¿Cómo se hace?*

E2: *Primero se lava bien el pollo. Luego se ponen la sal y pimienta.*

E1: *¿Y después?*

E2: *Se asa en el horno por dos horas.*

En directo

To propose an idea:

Tengo una idea. *I have an idea.*

¿Qué te parece esto? *What do you think of this?*

Se me ocurrió una idea. *I just thought of an idea.*

To agree with someone's idea:

Me parece perfecto. *That seems perfect.*

Suena muy bien. *Sounds great.*

¡Qué buena idea! *What a great idea!*

Listen to a conversation with these expressions.

Situación

PREPARACIÓN. Lean la situación. Luego, compartan ejemplos de vocabulario, gramática y otra información que necesitan para desarrollar la conversación.

Role A. You are an international student who has just arrived in town. A student has offered to help with your orientation. You are not familiar with shopping in the United States, so you ask:

a. where one buys personal items like vitamins and toothpaste (**pasta de dientes**);
b. where on campus one can find a decent meal;
c. where one goes to buy fresh fruit; and
d. where one can get good American pizza.

Ask follow-up questions to be sure you understand the answers.

Role B. You have offered to show a new international student around campus. Answer his/her questions about where one goes to buy different things. Offer several options, and be prepared to answer your new friend's questions.

	ROLE A	ROLE B
Vocabulario	Vocabulary related to food Question words	Vocabulary related to food Question words
Funciones y formas	Asking and answering questions Verifying information Thanking someone	Answering questions Giving instructions on how things are done Making comparisons between options

INTERCAMBIOS. Practica la conversación con tu compañero/a incorporando el vocabulario y las funciones de *Preparación.* Luego, represéntenla ante la clase.

2 Talking about the recent past

ALICIA: Hola, César, ¿qué tal?

CÉSAR: Hola, Alicia. ¿**Has visto** a Javier? ¡Estoy muy molesto!

ALICIA: ¿Por qué? ¿Qué te pasa?

CÉSAR: Como sabes, el examen de literatura es pasado mañana y yo no **he leído** el libro todavía. ¿Lo **has leído** tú? ¿Lo **ha leído** Javier? ¿Javier te **ha dado** sus notas? No sé qué voy a hacer sin sus notas. ¡Las necesito para estudiar!

ALICIA: Cálmate, César. Yo **he leído** el libro y **he escrito** unas notas. **He hablado** con Javi. No **ha terminado** el libro todavía, pero va a llamarte esta tarde.

Piénsalo. Lee las afirmaciones e indica a quién(es) se refiere cada una: a Alicia (**A**), a César (**C**) y/o a Javier (**J**).

1. _____ **Ha hablado** con Javier.
2. _____ **Ha escrito** unas notas.
3. _____ **Ha leído** una parte del libro.
4. _____ No **ha hecho** mucho en su curso de literatura.
5. _____ No **han visto** a Javier.
6. _____ No **ha abierto** el libro.

Present perfect and participles used as adjectives

- **Present perfect.** Use the present perfect to refer to a past event, action, or condition that has some relation to the present.

  He lavado **los platos.** — *I have washed the dishes.*

  Cecilia nunca ha vivido **en otro país.** — *Cecilia has never lived in another country.*

- Form the present perfect by using the present tense of **haber** as an auxiliary verb with the past participle of the main verb. In English, past participles are often formed with the endings *-ed* and *-en,* as in *finished* or *eaten.*

PRESENT TENSE OF HABER		+	PAST PARTICIPLE
yo	**he**		
tú	**has**		
Ud., él, ella	**ha**		**hablado**
nosotros/as	**hemos**		**comido**
vosotros/as	**habéis**		**vivido**
Uds., ellos/as	**han**		

Los cocineros **han trabajado** mucho en el banquete. — *The cooks have worked a lot at the banquet.*

Unos miembros de la organización ya **han traído** los manteles. — *Some members of the organization have already brought the tablecloths.*

- All past participles of **-ar** verbs end in **-ado,** whereas past participles of **-er** and **-ir** verbs generally end in **-ido.** If the stem of an **-er** verb ends in a vowel, use a written accent on the **i** of **-ido** (leer → le**ído**).

Lucho, ¿ya **has leído** la receta de la paella? — *Lucho, have you read the recipe for paella yet?*

No, no **he leído** la receta todavía. — *No, I have not read the recipe yet.*

- Some **-er** and **-ir** verbs have irregular past participles. Here are some of the more common ones:

IRREGULAR PAST PARTICIPLES			
hacer	**hecho**	abrir	**abierto**
poner	**puesto**	escribir	**escrito**
romper	**roto**	cubrir	**cubierto**
ver	**visto**	decir	**dicho**
volver	**vuelto**	morir	**muerto**

- Place object and reflexive pronouns before the auxiliary **haber.** Do not place any word between **haber** and the past participle.

¿**Le** has dado las servilletas a César? — *Have you given César the napkins?*

No, todavía no **se las** he dado. — *No, I have not given them to him yet.*

LENGUA

To state that something has just happened use the present tense of **acabar** + **de** + *infinitive,* not the present perfect.

Acabamos de volver del supermercado.

We have just returned from the supermarket.

Acabo de probar la sopa y está deliciosa.

I have just tasted the soup, and it is delicious.

Participles used as adjectives. Spanish uses **estar** + *past participle* to express a state or condition resulting from a previous action.

ACTION	RESULT
Ella preparó la sopa.	La sopa **está preparada.**
Luego cerró las ventanas.	Las ventanas **están cerradas.**

- When a past participle is used as an adjective, it agrees with the noun it modifies.

una puerta **cerrada** — *a closed door*

los restaurantes **abiertos** — *the open restaurants*

unas botellas **lavadas** — *some washed bottles*

e ¿COMPRENDES?

Escribe la forma correcta del presente perfecto para indicar la acción y la forma del participio pasado para indicar el resultado de esa acción.

Acción	Resultado
1. Yo ___________ la comida. (preparar)	1. La comida está _________. (preparar)
2. Nosotros ___________ los ingredientes. (comprar)	2. Los ingredientes están _________. (comprar)
3. Tú no ___________ la mesa todavía. (poner)	3. La mesa aún no está _________. (poner)
4. El niño ___________ dos ventanas. (romper)	4. Las ventanas están _________. (romper)
5. Los estudiantes ya ___________ su tarea. (hacer)	5. Las tareas ya están _________. (hacer)

MySpanishLab

Learn more using Amplifire Dynamic Study Modules, Grammar Tutorials, and Extra Practice activities.

10-18 

Lo que no he hecho. Tu compañero/a y tú deben decir las cosas de cada lista que no han hecho. Después, comparen sus respuestas con las de otros estudiantes.

1. Yo nunca he estado en...
   - **a.** Paraguay.
   - **b.** Guatemala.
   - **c.** Ecuador.
2. Yo nunca he visto...
   - **a.** las islas Galápagos.
   - **b.** un volcán activo.
   - **c.** un huracán.
3. Yo nunca he comido...
   - **a.** aguacate.
   - **b.** un postre con leche de coco.
   - **c.** langosta.
4. Yo nunca he roto...
   - **a.** una taza.
   - **b.** un vaso.
   - **c.** un plato.

10-19 

Robo (*Robbery*) en un restaurante. El siguiente incidente ocurrió en el restaurante del chef Marco Tovares. Llena los espacios con la forma correcta del participio pasado de los verbos entre paréntesis.

El chef Marco Tovares salió de la cocina para asegurarse de que todo iba bien. Vio que el locutor de televisión Jorge Ramos estaba (1) _________ (sentar) en una mesa con otras personas. Marco vio que la bolsa de una de las mujeres estaba (2) _________ (abrir) y que un hombre en otra mesa la miraba. Como la mujer estaba (3) _________ (distraer), el hombre aprovechó el momento (4) _________ (esperar). Sacó la billetera de la bolsa de ella. Marco lo vio todo. Se acercó a la mesa y le dijo al hombre: "¿Cómo está la comida esta noche?". El hombre parecía muy nervioso, y curiosamente tenía las manos (5) _________ (cerrar). Marco le dijo: "¿Podría acompañarme, por favor?". El hombre fue con Marco, le dio la billetera (6) _________ (robar) y salió. Marco se acercó a la mesa de Jorge Ramos y les explicó lo ocurrido. Todos estaban muy (7) _________ (sorprender). La mujer dijo: "Hace diez años que vivo en Nueva York, y ¡nunca he (8) _________ (ser) víctima de un robo hasta esta noche!".

10-20 

Hispanos famosos.

PREPARACIÓN. Piensen en un hispano famoso/una hispana famosa y preparen una lista de cinco cosas que creen que ha hecho para tener éxito (*to be successful*). Después, compartan su lista con la de otra pareja.

E1: *Cameron Díaz es una actriz famosa.*
E2: *Ha protagonizado más de treinta películas...*

INTERCAMBIOS. Digan tres cosas que ustedes han hecho que los/las han ayudado a tener éxito en su vida personal, académica o profesional.

10-21 

Una cena importante. Ustedes van a preparar una cena para su profesor/a de español. Háganse preguntas para ver qué preparativos ha hecho cada uno/a para la cena.

comprar la carne

E1: *¿Has comprado la carne?*
E2: *No, no la he comprado todavía.*

1. leer las recetas
2. cortar los vegetales
3. hacer el postre
4. decidir qué música tocar
5. poner la mesa
6. decorar el lugar de la cena
7. ...

10-22 

Justo ahora. Digan qué han hecho estas personas. Den la mayor información posible.

Maricarmen y sus amigos ya no tienen hambre.

E1: *Han comido toda la comida.*
E2: *Han dejado la nevera vacía.*

1. Juan y Ramiro salen del estadio.
2. Pedro y Alina salen de una tienda donde se alquilan películas.
3. Mercedes y Paula traen palomitas de maíz (*popcorn*) para todo el grupo.
4. Un hombre sale corriendo de un banco.
5. Jorge y Rubén salen de un supermercado.
6. Frente a todos sus amigos, Rubén le da una sorpresa a su novia.

10-23 

¿Qué ha pasado? Después de unas horas de haber limpiado y ordenado su apartamento, ustedes encuentran todo muy desordenado. Túrnense para describirle al/a la policía lo que han hecho hoy para ordenar el apartamento y lo que ven ahora.

las ventanas (cerrar, abrir)

E1: *¿Qué ha pasado con las ventanas?*

E2: *Las he cerrado esta mañana... pero ahora están abiertas.*

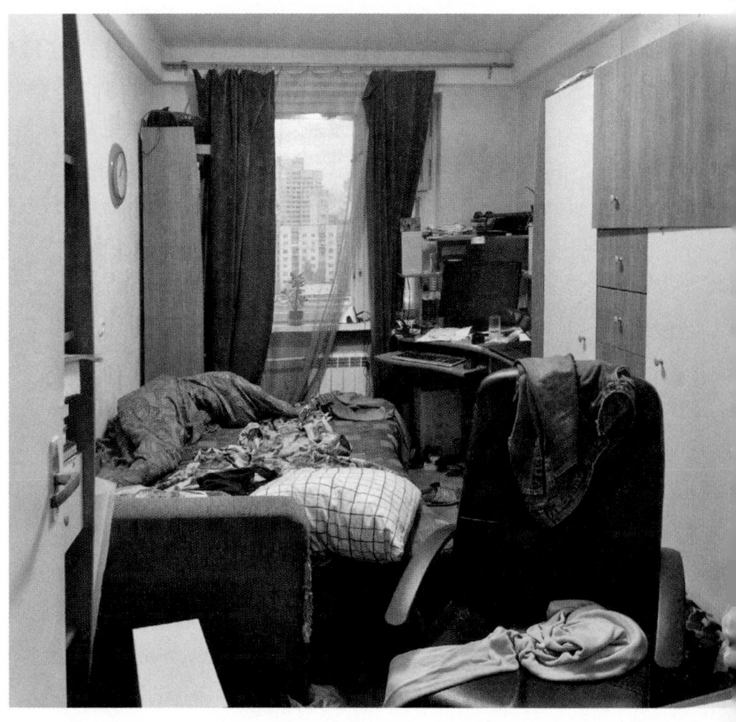

1. el espejo (usar, romper)
2. la cama (tender, desordenar)
3. el televisor (apagar, encender)
4. las camisas (colgar, tirar al piso)
5. la puerta del apartamento (cerrar, abrir)
6. la comida en el refrigerador (tapar [*cover*], destapar [*to uncover*])

Situación

PREPARACIÓN. Lean esta situación. Luego, compartan ejemplos de vocabulario, gramática y otra información que necesitan para desarrollar la conversación.

Role A. You are a student residence hall assistant at your university. Today you are meeting with a student who lives in the dorm. Explain that other students have complained that:

a. he/she has had parties in the dorm;
b. his/her friends have broken furniture in the public areas; and
c. his/her loud music has bothered everyone on the floor.

Say that you are worried about him/her and ask questions to find out what is prompting this behavior.

Role B. You live in a dorm at your school. The residence hall assistant tells you about complaints that he/she has received regarding your behavior. Respond to his/her comments and questions in detail.

	ROLE A	ROLE B
Vocabulario	University life Music Furniture	University life
Funciones y formas	Talking about the recent past Asking questions Giving advice	Talking about the recent past Stating your case Giving details

INTERCAMBIOS. Practica la conversación con tu compañero/a incorporando el vocabulario y las funciones de *Preparación.*. Luego, represéntenla ante la clase.

3 Giving instructions in informal settings

Marcos, la buena alimentación es fundamental para la buena salud. **Desayuna** siempre. Es la comida más importante del día. Para tener energía, **consume** carbohidratos y proteínas en las tres comidas. **Come** carbohidratos complejos, como pasta y pan, pero siempre integrales (*made from whole grains*). **No olvides** las frutas, las verduras y la leche; son muy buenas para la salud. **Evita** comer grasas y azúcares en grandes cantidades.

Piénsalo. Según las sugerencias del enfermero, escoge los alimentos o bebidas que Marcos debe consumir o evitar para alimentarse bien.

1. _____ Come...
2. _____ Evita...
3. _____ Bebe...

a. helado todos los días.
b. pan blanco.
c. manzanas, peras, plátanos, uvas.
d. suficiente leche.
e. pollo y pescado.
f. refrescos.

Informal commands

- To ask a friend to do or not to do something, use an informal command. Use that form with anyone else you address as **tú,** such as someone your own age or someone with whom you have a close relationship.

Pásame la sal.	*Pass me the salt.*
Mira esta foto.	*Look at this photo.*
Lee las instrucciones.	*Read the instructions.*
Préstame tu lápiz.	*Lend me your pencil.*

- To form the affirmative **tú** command, use the present indicative **tú** form without the final -s.

	PRESENT INDICATIVE	AFFIRMATIVE *TÚ* COMMAND
cocinar	cocinas	**cocina**
beber	bebes	**bebe**
consumir	consumes	**consume**

- For the negative **tú** command, use the negative **usted** command form and add the final **-s.**

	NEGATIVE *USTED* COMMAND	NEGATIVE *TÚ* COMMAND
preparar	no prepar**e**	no prepar**es**
comer	no com**a**	no com**as**
subir	no sub**a**	no sub**as**

- Placement of object and reflexive pronouns with **tú** commands is the same as with **usted** commands.

AFFIRMATIVE COMMAND	NEGATIVE COMMAND
Prepárelo (usted).	No **lo** prepare (usted).
Bébela (tú).	No **la** bebas (tú).

- The plural of **tú** commands in Spanish-speaking America is the **ustedes** command.

Cocina (tú).	**Cocinen (ustedes).**
Bebe (tú).	**Beban (ustedes).**
Sube (tú).	**Suban (ustedes).**

- Some **-er** and **-ir** verbs have shortened affirmative **tú** commands, but their negative command is regular.

	AFFIRMATIVE	NEGATIVE
poner	**pon**	**no pongas**
salir	**sal**	**no salgas**
tener	**ten**	**no tengas**
venir	**ven**	**no vengas**
hacer	**haz**	**no hagas**
decir	**di**	**no digas**
ir	**ve**	**no vayas**
ser	**sé**	**no seas**

Sal a las tres si quieres llegar a las cuatro.	*Leave at 3:00 if you want to arrive at 4:00.*
No salgas sin paraguas; va a llover.	*Don't leave without an umbrella; it is going to rain.*
Sé generoso con tus amigos.	*Be generous with your friends.*
No seas impaciente.	*Don't be impatient.*
Dime la verdad.	*Tell me the truth.*
No nos digas mentiras.	*Don't tell us any lies.*

e ¿COMPRENDES?

Completa la siguiente conversación con la forma correcta del verbo entre paréntesis.

MARIO: ¿Cómo preparo un buen asado?

XIMENA: (1) _______ (Comprar) carne blanda.
No (2) _______ (comprar) carne barata.

MARIO: ¿Y luego?

XIMENA: (3) _______ (Poner) sal y pimienta a la carne.
No (4) _______ (poner) demasiada sal.

MySpanishLab

Learn more using Amplifire Dynamic Study Modules, Grammar Tutorials, and Extra Practice activities.

PRÁCTICA

10-24 

Consejos. Escoge los consejos más adecuados, según cada situación. Compara tus respuestas con las de tu compañero/a y después añade otra situación. Tu compañero/a te va a dar un consejo.

1. _______ Tu compañero/a comió demasiado en una fiesta de cumpleaños y ahora le duele mucho el estómago.

a. Come más para recuperarte.
b. Llama al médico.
c. Ve a la farmacia y compra medicamentos.
d. Camina una hora esta tarde.
e. Practica deportes para olvidarte del dolor de estómago.
f. No te acuestes.

2. _______ Tu hermana está enferma. Está congestionada y tiene fiebre.

a. Toma sopa de pollo.
b. Come una hamburguesa.
c. No duermas mucho.
d. Bebe jugos y agua.
e. No bebas vino ni cerveza.
f. No consumas mucha cafeína.

3. _______ A tu amiga le fascina la comida basura (*junk food*), por eso, subió diez libras en un mes.

a. Ve a los restaurantes de comida rápida.
b. Bebe muchas gaseosas.
c. Come en casa, no en restaurantes.
d. No tomes alcohol.
e. Evita los batidos de McDonald's.
f. No pidas ensaladas.

4. _______ Tu mamá quiere alimentarse mejor para tener más energía y bajar de peso.

a. Evita la grasa.
b. Toma muchos helados.
c. Come huevos moderadamente.
d. Compra papas fritas.
e. Acuéstate y descansa.
f. Si no tienes energía, consume mucha cafeína.

5. _______ Tu mejor amigo quiere preparar una cena espectacular para su novia.

a. Compra pizza.
b. Haz un plato sofisticado.
c. No te olvides de comprar un buen vino.
d. Prepara la mesa el día anterior.
e. No le pongas chile picante al plato. Ella detesta la comida picante.
f. Ponle mucha sal a la comida.

Cultura

Las termas de Papallacta

En la cordillera de los Andes, a una hora de la capital de Quito, se encuentran las termas de Papallacta. Son famosas por sus características curativas. Además, es un gran centro turístico por su ubicación en un área medioambiental muy diversa e interesante, cercana a reservas ecológicas y a la región amazónica.

Comparaciones. ¿Dónde se pueden encontrar baños medicinales en Estados Unidos? ¿Has visitado tú o alguien de tu familia uno de estos lugares? Busca información sobre uno de ellos y descríbeselo a la clase.

10-25 

Una cura de reposo. Tu amigo/a estuvo muy enfermo/a y su médico le recomendó pasar dos semanas de descanso en las termas de Papallacta en Ecuador. Como tú has visitado este lugar, dile a tu amigo/a qué puede hacer allí. Después, cambien de papel.

disfrutar de la tranquilidad

E1: *Disfruta de la tranquilidad y no escuches música en tu iPod.*
E2: *Y, ¿qué más puedo hacer?*

1. disfrutar del sol
2. respirar aire puro y descansar
3. no hacer la tarea
4. tomar fotos y hacer videos
5. probar un plato típico ecuatoriano
6. salir por las noches y conversar con las personas del lugar
7. tomar baños termales a diario
8. asistir a un concierto de música andina

10-26 

Buenos hábitos alimenticios. PREPARACIÓN. Ustedes están preocupados por los hábitos de comida de su amigo/a. Lean lo que esta persona come y bebe en un día típico e identifiquen los problemas que tiene.

> Todos los días se levanta al mediodía. Tan pronto se levanta, toma varias tazas de café. Una hora más tarde, come tres huevos fritos con tocino y tostadas. Toma dos tazas de café cubano con bastante azúcar. Luego, lee el periódico en su dormitorio, mira televisión y come chocolate mientras habla por teléfono con sus amigos. Por la tarde, llama por teléfono al restaurante de la esquina, pide una hamburguesa con papas fritas y toma unas cervezas. Después, duerme una siesta larga. Por la noche, tiene problemas para dormir, por eso, toma un batido.

INTERCAMBIOS. Hagan una lista con cinco recomendaciones o instrucciones que su amigo/a debe seguir. Comparen su lista con las de otros grupos.

10-27 

Cocina paso a paso (*step by step*). PREPARACIÓN. Escojan una receta para un plato que se consume en su país y escriban una lista de los ingredientes.

INTERCAMBIOS. Presenten su receta a la clase. Sigan los siguientes pasos: a) describan el plato; b) presenten sus ingredientes; y c) expliquen cómo se prepara.

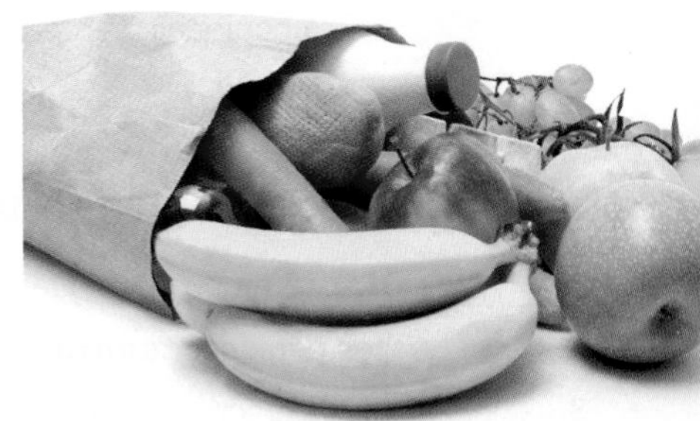

Situación

PREPARACIÓN. Lean esta situación. Luego, compartan ejemplos de vocabulario, gramática y otra información que necesitan para desarrollar la conversación.

Role A. To improve your health, you call your friend who is studying to become a nutritionist. Explain what you generally eat for breakfast, lunch, and dinner. Ask questions and answer the nutritionist's questions.

Role B. You are studying to become a nutritionist and a friend calls you for help with eating habits. Ask what he/she eats for breakfast, lunch, and dinner. Advise him/her:

a. to eat fruits, vegetables, fish, and chicken;
b. not to drink soft drinks or alcohol;
c. to consume foods with lots of fiber; and
d. to do physical activity daily.

Answer your friend's questions.

	ROLE A	ROLE B
Vocabulario	Food-related vocabulary	Food-related vocabulary
Funciones y formas	Explaining food habits Asking and answering questions Thanking someone for the advice	Asking and answering questions Giving advice Giving instructions

INTERCAMBIOS. Practica la conversación con tu compañero/a incorporando el vocabulario y las funciones de *Preparación*. Luego, represéntenla ante la clase.

4 Talking about the future

CIENTÍFICA: Según los expertos, para el año 2030 la población geriátrica **se duplicará** en comparación con la del presente. La gente **comerá** mejor, **vivirá** más años y **tendrá** buena salud.

JULIA: ¿Y nuestra dieta **será** semejante a la de hoy? ¿Qué **comeremos?**

CIENTÍFICA: Se piensa que **consumiremos** más alimentos naturales, porque más gente **comprenderá** sus beneficios. Al mismo tiempo, muchos alimentos **serán** modificados genéticamente. Los individuos **tratarán** de protegerse de ciertas afecciones y enfermedades, como la diabetes y el cáncer.

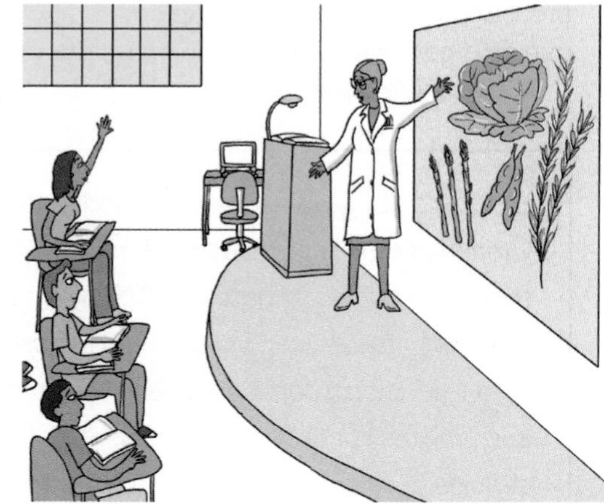

Piénsalo. Indica si las siguientes afirmaciones son ciertas (**C**) o falsas (**F**) o no se sabe (**NS**).

1. ________ **Habrá** menos personas mayores en el futuro.
2. ________ Las personas **tendrán** una vida más larga.
3. ________ Más personas **comprenderán** los beneficios de los alimentos naturales.
4. ________ La gente **será** más alta.
5. ________ La gente **podrá** comer grasas y dulces porque la ciencia los protegerá contra las enfermedades.

The future tense

- You have been using the present tense and **ir a** + *infinitive* to express future plans. Spanish also has a future tense. Although you have other ways to express a future action, event, or state, it is important to be able to recognize the future tense in reading and in listening.
- The future tense is formed by adding the endings **-é, -ás, -á, -emos, -éis,** and **-án** to the infinitive. All verbs, **-ar, -er, -ir,** regular or irregular, use these endings.

FUTURE TENSE			
	HABLAR	**COMER**	**VIVIR**
yo	hablar**é**	comer**é**	vivir**é**
tú	hablar**ás**	comer**ás**	vivir**ás**
Ud., él, ella	hablar**á**	comer**á**	vivir**á**
nosotros/as	hablar**emos**	comer**emos**	vivir**emos**
vosotros/as	hablar**éis**	comer**éis**	vivir**éis**
Uds., ellos/as	hablar**án**	comer**án**	vivir**án**

Rafael **visitará** Ecuador el mes próximo.	*Rafael will visit Ecuador next month.*
Él y sus colegas **volverán** después de dos semanas.	*He and his colleagues will return after two weeks.*
Se reunirán con los dueños de unas haciendas de café.	*They will meet with the owners of some coffee plantations.*

- Some verbs have irregular stems in the future tense and can be grouped into three categories according to the irregularity. The first group drops the **-e** from the infinitive ending.

IRREGULAR FUTURE—GROUP 1		
Infinitive	**New Stem**	**Future Forms**
poder	**podr-**	podré, podrás, podrá, podremos, podréis, podrán
querer	**querr-**	querré, querrás, querrá, querremos, querréis, querrán
saber	**sabr-**	sabré, sabrás, sabrá, sabremos, sabréis, sabrán

- The second group replaces the **e** or **i** of the infinitive ending with a **-d.**

IRREGULAR FUTURE—GROUP 2		
poner	**pondr-**	pondré, pondrás, pondrá, pondremos, pondréis, pondrán
salir	**saldr-**	saldré, saldrás, saldrá, saldremos, saldréis, saldrán
tener	**tendr-**	tendré, tendrás, tendrá, tendremos, tendréis, tendrán
venir	**vendr-**	vendré, vendrás, vendrá, vendremos, vendréis, vendrán

- The third group consists of two verbs whose stems in the future tense are quite different from their respective infinitives.

IRREGULAR FUTURE—GROUP 3		
decir	**dir-**	diré, dirás, dirá, diremos, diréis, dirán
hacer	**har-**	haré, harás, hará, haremos, haréis, harán

Los estudiantes **sabrán** más sobre la nutrición después de tomar el curso.	*The students will know more about nutrition after taking the course.*
Tendrán que leer mucho.	*They will have to read a lot.*
También **harán** un proyecto de investigación.	*They will also do a research project.*
¿A qué hora **vendrán** a cenar?	*What time will they be coming for dinner?*
Querrán probar un poco de todo.	*They will want to try a little of everything.*

e ¿COMPRENDES?

Completa las siguientes ideas sobre el futuro, usando el verbo entre paréntesis.

1. En 20 años, _______ más productos orgánicos. (haber)
2. La gente _______ más cuidado con su alimentación para vivir más años. (tener)
3. La comida _______ más sana. (ser)
4. Los seres humanos _______ de menos enfermedades crónicas. (sufrir)
5. Además de comer bien, nosotros _______ ejercicio. (hacer)

MySpanishLab

Learn more using Amplifire Dynamic Study Modules, Grammar Tutorials, and Extra Practice activities.

PRÁCTICA

Cultura

Quito y Guayaquil

Tanto Quito como Guayaquil son dos ciudades grandes y dinámicas de Ecuador. Quito, la capital, está situada en lo alto de los Andes mientras que Guayaquil está cerca de la costa del Pacífico. Las dos son importantes centros de turismo y de poder económico. El centro histórico de Quito es el mejor preservado de Latinoamérica mientras que en Guayaquil los proyectos de regeneración urbana, como el del Malecón 2000, reflejan su tradición comercial. Aunque muy diferentes entre sí, cada ciudad tiene su verdadero encanto.

Comparaciones. En tu opinión, ¿cuál es la ciudad más importante y dinámica en tu país? ¿Por qué? Explica.

▲ El Malecón 2000, Guayaquil

▲ Basílica del Voto Nacional, Quito

10-28 

¿Qué lugares de Ecuador visitarán estas personas? Completa las oraciones de la izquierda con la acción en la columna de la derecha. Añade un lugar que te interesa y dile a tu compañero/a lo que harás o adónde irás.

1. A Carlos y Eugenia les gusta comer bien. ________ al restaurante especializado en la cocina de Guayaquil.
2. A doña Lourdes y a su hija les fascinan la zoología y la botánica. ________ un viaje juntas a las islas Galápagos para ver la gran variedad de especies animales.
3. Don Jorge y yo ________ el mercado indígena de Cuenca para comprar artesanía ecuatoriana.
4. A ti te gusta disfrutar del aire libre, ver la arquitectura colonial y las montañas. ________ por la Plaza San Blas en Quito.
5. A mí... ____________.

a. caminarás
b. irán
c. visitaremos
d. harán

Cultura

Reservas ecológicas

Ecuador tiene muchos parques nacionales y reservas ecológicas cuyo propósito es conservar la riqueza natural de las cuatro regiones del país: las islas Galápagos, la costa, la sierra y la selva amazónica. En las reservas se encuentran muchas especies de flora y fauna. Para los visitantes, hay muchas maneras de explorar las reservas y gozar de la naturaleza.

Comparaciones. ¿Hay reservas naturales en tu país? ¿Dónde están? ¿Qué se protege? ¿Alguna vez has visitado alguno de estos lugares? ¿Qué se puede hacer allí?

Un viaje a Guayaquil. **PREPARACIÓN.** Ramiro va a Guayaquil a visitar a su familia y a conocer lugares nuevos. Háganse preguntas y contesten según la agenda que preparó Ramiro.

E1: *¿Qué hará Ramiro el jueves por la mañana?*

E2: *Viajará al Parque Nacional Cajas.*

E1: *¿Cuándo irá al cine con los primos?*

E2: *Irán al cine el martes.*

LUNES	MARTES	MIÉRCOLES	JUEVES	VIERNES
salir para Guayaquil	visitar el Parque de las Iguanas	salir de compras al Mercado Artesanal	viajar al Parque Nacional Cajas	empacar las maletas
cenar con los tíos	visitar a otros familiares	ir a un museo	caminar en la reserva, sacar fotos	almorzar con toda la familia
acostarse temprano	ir al cine con los primos	cenar con unos amigos	dormir en el parque	regresar a Estados Unidos

INTERCAMBIOS. Hagan una lista de cinco actividades que Ramiro probablemente hará al regresar a Estados Unidos. Expliquen por qué.

10-30 

Planes de fiesta. **PREPARACIÓN.** Planifiquen una fiesta de matrimonio para sus amigos ecuatorianos José y Silvia. Consideren lo siguiente:

- número de invitados
- lugar de la fiesta
- menú que ofrecerán (comida y bebida)
- actividades para los invitados (música, baile, etc.)

INTERCAMBIOS. Compartan sus planes con otra pareja. Hagan una lista de tres semejanzas y tres diferencias entre las dos fiestas.

10-31 

¿Qué recomendaciones seguirá? Maricela sufre de estrés, insomnio y anemia. Después de leer las recomendaciones que le hacen su mejor amiga y su nutricionista, decidan qué hará ella probablemente.

RECOMENDACIONES DE LA NUTRICIONISTA	RECOMENDACIONES DE SU MEJOR AMIGA
1. Coma en pequeñas cantidades por lo menos cuatro veces al día.	**1.** Come cuando quieras. Si subes de peso puedes seguir una dieta.
2. No consuma cafeína para tener energía. Consuma proteínas.	**2.** Para tener energía, come mucho chocolate y, luego, haz ejercicio.
3. Consuma calcio. Beba leche y coma espinacas.	**3.** Toma helado todos los días porque la leche tiene mucho calcio.
4. Para eliminar la tensión y relajarse, haga yoga.	**4.** Escucha música suave y no contestes el teléfono de la oficina.
5. Compre verduras y carnes orgánicas en supermercados especializados en productos naturales.	**5.** Pide ensalada con pollo en los restaurantes de comida rápida y un refresco de dieta.

Situación

PREPARACIÓN. Lean esta situación. Luego, compartan ejemplos de vocabulario, gramática y otra información que necesitan para desarrollar la conversación.

Role A. You are organizing a picnic and some of the guests are vegetarians. Call your nutritionist friend (your classmate) to discuss what food to serve. Say that:

a. you will prepare vegetarian and non-vegetarian food;
b. for the vegetarians, you will make salads and a Spanish tortilla;
c. for the meat eaters, you will serve a chicken salad and hamburgers; and
d. you will serve beer, soft drinks, and juice.

Ask your friend for advice.

Role B. A friend is calling to ask for advice regarding the menu for a picnic that will include both vegetarian and non-vegetarian guests. Give your friend feedback on the proposed menu and offer additional advice.

	ROLE A	ROLE B
Vocabulario	Food-related vocabulary Drinks	Food-related vocabulary Drinks
Funciones y formas	Asking for advice Thanking someone Using proper phone etiquette	Asking and answering questions Giving advice Using proper phone etiquette

INTERCAMBIOS. Practica la conversación con tu compañero/a incorporando el vocabulario y las funciones de *Preparación*. Luego, represéntenla ante la clase.

EN ACCIÓN

¡Hay que celebrar!

10-32 Antes de ver

El restaurante ideal. En este segmento, Esteban invitará a Yolanda a comer en un restaurante para celebrar su cumpleaños. Marca (✓) las cinco sugerencias que tú le harías (*you would make*) a Esteban para elegir el restaurante ideal.

1. _____ Visita el restaurante antes de hacer la reservación.
2. _____ Busca un restaurante en el centro.
3. _____ Acuérdate que Yolanda es vegana.
4. _____ Pregunta si tienen descuento para estudiantes.
5. _____ Mira si el menú es variado.
6. _____ Habla con los camareros.
7. _____ Prueba la especialidad de la casa.
8. _____ Haz investigación en Internet sobre el restaurante.
9. _____ Consulta el libro de quejas (*complaints*).
10. _____ Averigua quién es el chef.

10-33 Mientras ves 

A comer. Esteban, Yolanda, Fernando y Vanesa hablan sobre sus comidas favoritas y sobre las comidas típicas de sus países. Indica si las siguientes oraciones son ciertas (**C**) o falsas (**F**) según la información de este segmento de video. Corrige las oraciones falsas.

En el restaurante:

1. _____ Yolanda pedirá dos pupusas.
2. _____ Federico pedirá bistec con ensalada.
3. _____ Esteban probará la yuca con chicharrones y plátanos.

Comidas típicas de Costa Rica:

4. _____ Lo más típico de la comida costarricense es el arroz con frijoles.
5. _____ La *soda* es un tipo de restaurante caro y elegante.
6. _____ El *gallo pinto* es un plato que se come en la cena.
7. _____ En los restaurantes de barrio se sirve comida fresca.

Las tapas españolas:

8. _____ Se preparan solamente en casa.
9. _____ El origen de las tapas es muy antiguo.
10. _____ Se sirven en porciones pequeñas.

10-34 Después de ver 

La comida. **PREPARACIÓN.** Marca (✓) los temas que aparecen en este episodio, implícita o explícitamente.

1. _____ las comidas tradicionales de algunos países hispanos
2. _____ algunas costumbres asociadas con comidas típicas
3. _____ los peligros del consumo excesivo de carne
4. _____ la importancia de hacer ejercicio
5. _____ el origen de algunas comidas

INTERCAMBIOS. Comparen sus respuestas de *Preparación* y háganse las siguientes preguntas relacionadas.

1. ¿En qué ocasiones se ve la importancia de la comida como conexión social?
2. ¿Cómo cambiarán nuestras costumbres alimentarias en el futuro? Expliquen o den ejemplos.

Mosaicos

ESCUCHA

10-35

Preparación. Antes de escuchar, prepara una lista de productos que compras regularmente y otra de aquellos que solo compras en ocasiones especiales. Compártela con la clase.

ESTRATEGIA

Make notes of relevant details

In previous chapters, you have practiced the strategy of focusing on information that is relevant to your purpose for listening. Note-taking is a useful strategy for remembering important information. Listening more than once also helps you to remember relevant details.

10-36

Escucha. Andrea, Carolina, Roberto, and Darío have each offered to contribute a dish for their friend Óscar's birthday party. Each has bought some kind of vegetable, meat, or seafood to prepare his/her dish. As you listen, mark (✓) the foods that each of them bought. Note that not all the items purchased are listed below.

Comprueba

I was able to …

_____ **distinguish between key and secondary information.**

_____ **listen for and make note of relevant details.**

ANDREA	CAROLINA	ROBERTO	DARÍO
_____ sal	_____ ajos	_____ mermelada	_____ huevos
_____ pollo	_____ cerdo	_____ pepinos	_____ ajos
_____ carne molida	_____ espinacas	_____ pimienta	_____ fruta
_____ azúcar	_____ jamón	_____ aceite	_____ jamón
_____ zanahorias	_____ langosta	_____ pavo	_____ aderezo
_____ aguacates	_____ maíz	_____ aguacates	_____ pimientos verdes
_____ camarones	_____ pollo	_____ zanahorias	_____ pasta

10-37

Un paso más. Túrnense para hacerse las siguientes preguntas.

1. ¿Cuál es tu plato favorito?
2. ¿Qué productos o ingredientes necesitas para prepararlo?
3. ¿Con quién compartes generalmente tu plato favorito? ¿Por qué?
4. ¿Qué dice esta persona cuando preparas este plato?

LENGUA

Pimienta refers to the spice (*ground pepper*) and **pimiento** refers to the vegetable. Therefore, **pimienta roja** is the red (*cayenne*) pepper that one sprinkles on pizza, and **pimiento rojo** is a red bell pepper. The word for hot, spicy peppers is **chile** or **ají**, as in **chile habanero, chile jalapeño,** and so forth.

HABLA

10-38

Preparación. Marca cuáles de los siguientes alimentos son más saludables (+) o menos saludables (−).

____ los camarones	____ las espinacas	____ el jamón	____ el pollo
____ la carne de res	____ la fruta	____ las legumbres	____ el queso
____ la cerveza	____ las galletas	____ el pan blanco	____ los refrescos
____ los dulces	____ el helado	____ las papas	____ el vino

Intercambios. Escribe en la tabla los productos o alimentos de *Preparación* que en general producen los siguientes efectos. Explica por qué.

ENGORDAN	NO ENGORDAN	DAN ENERGÍA	AUMENTAN EL COLESTEROL

10-39 

Habla. Entrevista a tres compañeros/as para averiguar las preferencias de comida en las siguientes categorías. ¿Qué comida les gusta más y cuál les gusta menos?

los mariscos

E1: *¿Te gustan los mariscos?*
E2: *Me encantan. ¿Y a ti?*
E1: *A mí no me gustan.*

ALIMENTO	ENCANTAR	GUSTAR MUCHO	GUSTAR	NO GUSTAR
la fruta				
las verduras				
la carne				
los mariscos				
los productos lácteos				
los pasteles				

ESTRATEGIA

Give and defend reasons for a decision

When you make a decision that you wish to communicate effectively to others, it is important to a) state your decision clearly; b) present and explain your reasons logically; and c) urge your listeners to consider your point of view.

En directo

To influence someone's decision:

Es mejor/menos dañino (*harmful*) + *infinitive ...*

¿No te/le(s) parece más saludable + *infinitive ...* ?

¿Qué te/le(s) parece si + *indicative ...* ?

Listen to a conversation with these expressions.

Comprueba

In my conversation ...

____ **I expressed my decision clearly.**

____ **I explained my reasons logically.**

____ **I encouraged my listener to consider my point of view.**

10-40 

Un paso más. Preparen un informe comparando los resultados obtenidos en la actividad 10-39 sobre las categorías de alimentos que más consumen los estudiantes. Usen las siguientes preguntas como guía. Después, presenten su informe a la clase.

1. ¿Qué tipos de comida se comen más?
2. En general, ¿sus compañeros se alimentan bien o mal? ¿Por qué?
3. ¿Deben ustedes mejorar su dieta? ¿Qué deben hacer?

LEE

10-41 

Preparación. Lean el título y los subtítulos de la lectura en la página siguiente, miren las fotos y lean sus leyendas. Luego, hablen entre ustedes de lo que esperan encontrar en el artículo guiándose por las preguntas siguientes. Expliquen sus respuestas.

1. ¿Qué información esperan encontrar en el artículo?
   - **a.** ____ una definición del término *fusión culinaria*
   - **b.** ____ recetas para platos de cocina fusión
   - **c.** ____ información sobre la influencia china en la cocina de un país
   - **d.** ____ información sobre la cocina Tex-Mex
2. Marquen (✓) los elementos que los ayudaron a responder a la pregunta 1.
   - **a.** ____ el título y los subtítulos
   - **b.** ____ las fotos junto con sus leyendas
3. ¿Qué es la fusión culinaria? Marquen (✓) la definición más lógica.
   - **a.** ____ la combinación de la cocina con otras artes, como la decoración de interiores
   - **b.** ____ una cocina que combina la influencia de dos tradiciones culinarias
4. Preparen una lista de comidas Tex-Mex que conozcan. ¿Cuáles les gustan más?

ESTRATEGIA

Learn new words by analyzing their connections with known words

As you read in a second language, you encounter words that are unfamiliar to you. In some cases, you can skip over a word and still understand the overall meaning of the sentence or paragraph. In other cases, you should focus on the unfamiliar word and guess its meaning. You can figure out the meanings of unfamiliar words and expand your vocabulary by mentally linking them to words you know that are related in meaning or in grammatical form.

10-42 

Lee. Según el contenido del artículo, ¿son las siguientes afirmaciones ciertas (**C**) o falsas (**F**)? Si la afirmación es falsa, corrige la información.

1. _____ El artículo afirma que la cocina fusión se limita a la combinación de influencias asiáticas en la cocina del Oeste.
2. _____ La cocina peruana incorpora influencias culinarias de muchos países.
3. _____ La inmigración de muchos chinos a Perú empezó al principio del siglo XX.
4. _____ El chifa es un término que se refiere a la cocina chino-peruana.
5. _____ La cocina Tex-Mex es igual a la cocina mexicana.
6. _____ Se usa menos carne y menos queso en la cocina Tex-Mex que en la cocina mexicana tradicional.
7. _____ Los nachos y los tacos fritos son invenciones de la cocina Tex-Mex.
8. _____ El chile con carne que se come en San Antonio, Texas, se prepara con especias similares a las que se usan en Marruecos, en el norte de África.

Comprueba

I was able to ...

____ **use words I know to guess the meaning of new words.**

____ **understand the main points of the reading.**

LA FUSIÓN CULINARIA: UNA TENDENCIA NUEVA CON UNA HISTORIA LARGA

LA FUSIÓN EN LA COCINA CONTEMPORÁNEA

Todos hemos comido platos que combinan la cocina de dos países o culturas. El llamado *California roll* es un ejemplo; la *taco pizza* es otro. La fusión culinaria, o cocina fusión, ejemplifica la mezcla de ingredientes y estilos culinarios de diferentes culturas en el menú de un restaurante o en un mismo plato. Hoy en día es común encontrar restaurantes en Estados Unidos con nombres como *Roy's Hawaiian Fusion Cuisine* o *Fusion Restaurant and Lounge.* Hay muchas posibles combinaciones, limitadas solamente por la creatividad del chef y los gustos de los clientes.

LA FUSIÓN EN LA HISTORIA CULINARIA

A pesar de la creciente popularidad de estas combinaciones gastronómicas, sería un error pensar que la cocina fusión es un fenómeno nuevo. Dos ejemplos de este antiguo fenómeno en las Américas son la cocina chino-peruana y la cocina mexicano-norteamericana, o Tex-Mex.

EL CHIFA: LA COCINA FUSIÓN DE PERÚ

La cocina peruana es una mezcla de muchas influencias: indígena, española, africana, china y japonesa. El chifa, o cocina chino-peruana, es el resultado de la mezcla de la comida criolla de Lima con la cocina traída por los inmigrantes chinos desde mediados del siglo XIX.

▲ Plato chino-peruano o chifa

Los chinos que fueron a Perú se adaptaron a la sociedad y a sus costumbres, pero siempre mantuvieron sus tradiciones culinarias. Con el progreso económico, importaron de China especias y otros productos esenciales para su comida, pero por lo general tenían que cultivar las verduras que necesitaban o sustituirlas por ingredientes locales.

La cultura chino-peruana revolucionó la gastronomía. Algunos platos considerados típicamente peruanos, como el arroz chaufa (preparado con carne picada, cebollitas, pimentón, huevos y salsa de soja) y el tacu-tacu (una tortilla hecha de un puré de frijoles, arroz, ajo, ají y cebolla) reflejan la influencia de la cocina china.

LA COMIDA TEX-MEX: LA COCINA MEXICANA EN ESTADOS UNIDOS

Un ejemplo de la cocina fusión que se conoce en todas partes de Estados Unidos es la cocina Tex-Mex. Se trata de la fusión del estilo de México y del de Texas. La cocina que conocemos hoy en día como Tex-Mex empezó como una mezcla de la comida del pueblo nativo de Texas y la cocina española.

▲ Nachos, un plato popular de la cocina Tex-Mex

Los indígenas contribuyeron con ingredientes como los frijoles pintos, los nopales (las hojas de un cacto), las cebollas silvestres[1] y el mesquite. La influencia española empezó con la llegada del ganado[2] a la región, traído por los colonizadores al final del siglo XVI. Pero también hay influencias del norte de África. Un grupo de colonizadores de las islas Canarias y de Marruecos inmigraron en el siglo XVIII a lo que es ahora San Antonio, Texas. De ellos vinieron nuevas especias, cilantro y chiles. El *chili con carne* de San Antonio todavía retiene los sabores de la cocina marroquí.

En los últimos treinta años se ha intentado separar *la cocina mexicana* de *la cocina mexicana americanizada,* o Tex-Mex. La Tex-Mex utiliza más carne y usa las tortillas para envolver mayor variedad de rellenos. Los nachos, los tacos fritos, las chalupas, el chile con queso y el chile con carne son invenciones Tex-Mex que no se encuentran en la cocina mexicana tradicional. La costumbre universal en los restaurantes Tex-Mex de servir las *tortilla chips* con salsa picante como aperitivo tampoco existe en la cocina mexicana tradicional.

[1]*wild* [2]*cattle*

10-43 

Un paso más. PREPARACIÓN. Hagan una lista de platos que se sirven en restaurantes y que son ejemplos de la cocina fusión. Luego, seleccionen uno de estos platos.

INTERCAMBIOS. Preparen una presentación sobre algún plato de cocina fusión que conocen y sus antecedentes culinarios, y preséntenla a la clase.

ESCRIBE

10-44

Preparación. Lee una vez más el artículo "La fusión culinaria: una tendencia nueva con una historia larga". Identifica las secciones del artículo y pasa tu marcador (*highlighter*) por las ideas centrales de cada sección.

ESTRATEGIA

Summarize information

A good summary maintains the structure of the original text, synthesizes its principal ideas and information, and accurately captures the central meaning of the original. To write a summary:

- Read the text carefully for the main ideas more than once.
- In your own words, write one or two sentences that summarize the main idea of each section you identify in the text.
- Do not inject your own opinion or add anything not in the original text.

10-45

Escribe. Escribe en tus propias palabras un resumen del artículo, usando las ideas principales que marcaste en *Preparación.*

10-46 

Un paso más. Envíale tu resumen a un compañero editor/una compañera editora para que te dé su opinión.

Comprueba

I was able to …

____ identify the main ideas in each section of the reading.

____ relay the main ideas in my own words.

____ focus on factual information rather than my opinion.

En este capítulo...

Comprueba lo que sabes

Go to ***MySpanishLab*** to review what you have learned in this chapter. Practice with the following:

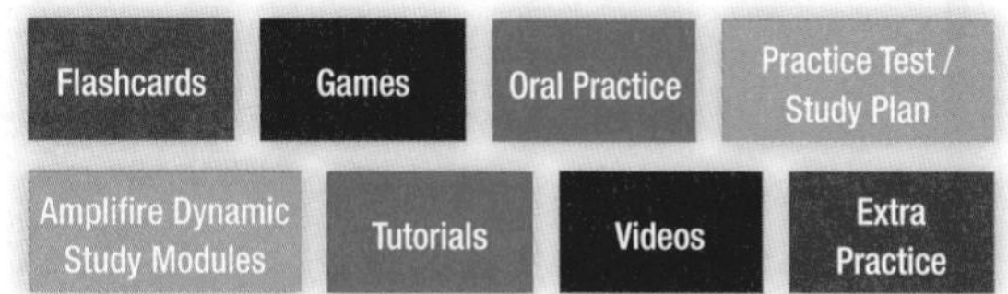

Vocabulario

LAS ESPECIAS Y LOS CONDIMENTOS *Spices and seasonings*

el aceite *oil*
el aderezo *salad dressing*
el azúcar *sugar*
las especias *spices*
las hierbas *herbs*
la mayonesa *mayonnaise*
la mostaza *mustard*
la pimienta *pepper*
la sal *salt*
la salsa de tomate *tomato sauce*
la vainilla *vanilla*
el vinagre *vinegar*

LAS FRUTAS Y LAS VERDURAS *Fruits and vegetables*

el aguacate *avocado*
el ajo *garlic*
la cebolla *onion*
la cereza *cherry*
las espinacas *spinach*
la fresa *strawberry*
el limón *lemon*
el maíz *corn*
la manzana *apple*
el maracuyá *passion fruit*
el melón *melon*
la papaya *papaya*
el pepino *cucumber*
la pera *pear*
el pimiento verde *green pepper*
la piña *pineapple*
el plátano/la banana *banana, plantain*
la toronja/el pomelo *grapefruit*
la uva *grape*
la zanahoria *carrot*

EL PESCADO Y LA CARNE *Fish and meat*

las aves *poultry, fowl*
el camarón/la gamba *shrimp*
la carne *meat*
  molida *ground meat*
  de res *beef/steak*
el cerdo *pork*
la chuleta *chop*
el cordero *lamb*
la costilla *rib*
la langosta *lobster*
los mariscos *shellfish*
la oveja *sheep*
el pavo *turkey*

VERBOS *Verbs*

agregar/añadir *to add*
batir *to beat*
consumir *to consume*
freír (i) *to fry*
hervir (ie, i) *to boil*
probar (ue) *to try, to taste*
recomendar (ie) *to recommend*
tapar *to cover*

LAS DESCRIPCIONES *Descriptions*

agrio/a *sour*
dulce *sweet*
asado/a *roasted*
frito/a *fried*
lácteo/a *dairy (product)*

OTROS PRODUCTOS *Other products*

los churros *fried dough*
la crema *cream*
el dulce *candy/sweets*
la galleta *cookie*
los garbanzos *garbanzo beans*
la harina *flour*
la leche de coco *coconut milk*
las legumbres *legumes*
las lentejas *lentils*
la manteca/la mantequilla *butter*
la margarina *margarine*
el pan dulce *bun, small cake*
el pastel *pastry*
el queso crema *cream cheese*
el yogur *yogurt*

EN LA MESA *On the table*

la bandeja *tray*
la botella *bottle*
la copa *(stemmed) glass*
la cuchara *spoon*
la cucharita *teaspoon*
el cuchillo *knife*
el mantel *tablecloth*
el plato *plate, dish*
el sacacorchos *corkscrew*
la servilleta *napkin*
la taza *cup*
el tenedor *fork*
el vaso *glass*

PALABRAS Y EXPRESIONES ÚTILES *Useful words and expressions*

el/la campesino/a *peasant*
la receta *recipe*
todavía *still, yet*
ya *already*

11 ¿Cómo te sientes?

LEARNING **OUTCOMES**

You will be able to:

- discuss health and medical treatments
- express expectations and hopes
- describe emotions, opinions, and wishes
- express goals, purposes, and means
- share information about public health and medical practices in Cuba and the Dominican Republic, and compare cultural similarities

ENFOQUE *cultural* CUBA Y REPÚBLICA DOMINICANA

El Malecón de la Habana

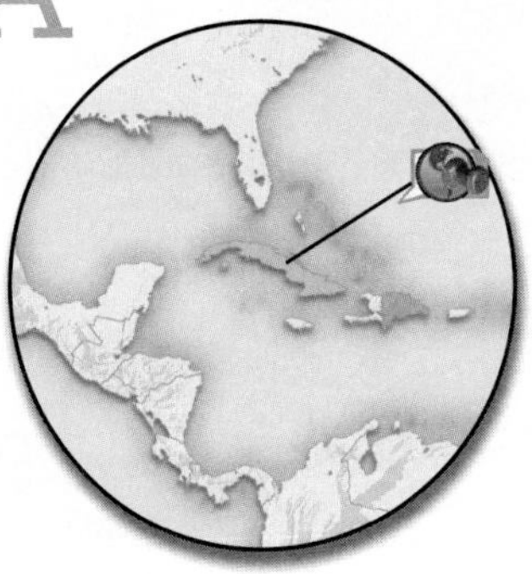

OCÉANO ATLÁNTICO

La Habana
Pinar del Río
Cienfuegos
CUBA
Camagüey
Santiago de Cuba
Guantánamo

Un mojito cubano

REPÚBLICA DOMINICANA
Puerto Plata
Sabana de La Mar
Punta Cana
HAITÍ
Santiago
San Juan
Santo Domingo
Isla Saona
JAMAICA
PUERTO RICO
Mar Caribe

La Catedral de Santo Domingo

Paracaidismo em el Isla Saona

Enfoque cultural

To learn more about Cuba and the Dominican Republic, go to MySpanishLab to view the *Vistas culturales* videos.

Las divinidades Oxum, Xangó y Yemayá del pintor cubano Almeri

¿QUÉ TE PARECE?

- Vista desde el aire, la isla de Cuba se parece a un cocodrilo. Por eso los cubanos la llaman El Cocodrilo o El Caimán.
- El sistema de servicios de salud está muy desarrollado en Cuba tanto para sus ciudadanos como para los extranjeros. Cuba cuenta con un próspero negocio de turismo médico.
- En Cuba, el béisbol y el dominó son actividades de entretenimiento muy populares.
- El merengue, un estilo de música y de baile, se originó en República Dominicana. Algunos de los artistas más famosos son Juan Luis Guerra, Elvis Crespo y Los Hermanos Rosario.
- En Nueva York viven más dominicanos que en Santiago, la segunda ciudad más poblada de República Dominicana.

ENFOQUE cultural

◀ El paseo marítimo de La Habana, Cuba, se llama El Malecón.

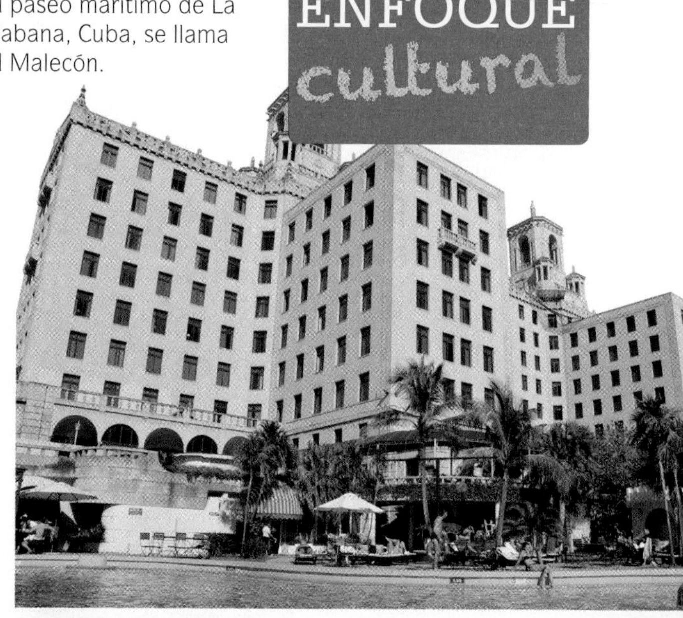

Muchos de los hoteles que se encuentran en Cuba tienen propietarios franceses y españoles. El turismo es una parte importante de la economía cubana. ▶

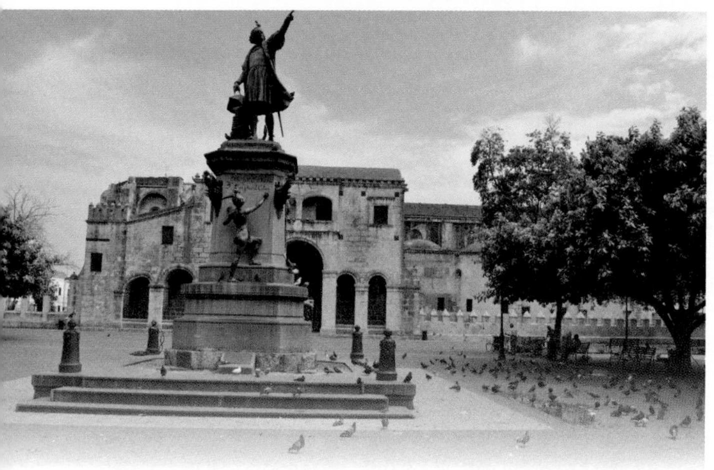

▲ Cristóbal Colón dio el nombre de La Española (*Hispaniola*) a la isla que hoy comprende las naciones de República Dominicana y Haití. Esta isla se escuentra entre Cuba y Puerto Rico.

▲ Punta Cana es una de las playas más conocidas de República Dominicana y uno de los centros turísticos más populares de la isla. Hay muchos hoteles de enclave (*all-inclusive resorts*) allí.

¿CUÁNTO SABES?

Escribe las palabras que corresponden a las descripciones.

1. El turismo médico es importante en este país. ______________
2. Esta capital fue la primera ciudad española construida en las Américas. Cristóbal Colón llegó hasta aquí en uno de sus viajes. ______________
3. Juan Luis Guerra es uno de los artistas de este estilo musical. ______________
4. Los hoteles que incluyen comidas, bebidas y algunas actividades se llaman así. ______________
5. Es una playa turística que se sitúa al extremo oriental de República Dominicana. ______________
6. Es la capital de Cuba. ______________

Vocabulario en contexto

Talking about health, medical care, and the body

MySpanishLab
Learn more using Amplifire Dynamic Study Modules, Pronunciation, and Vocabulary Tutorials.

Médicos, farmacias y hospitales

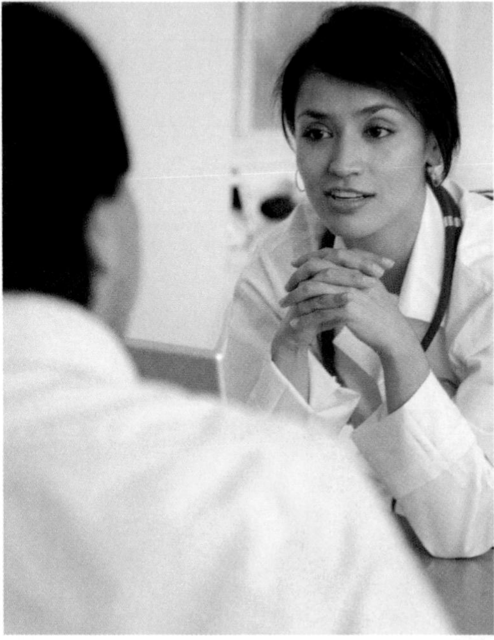

▲ En la mayor parte de los países hispanos existen **hospitales, clínicas** o **sanatorios** y **centros de salud** financiados por el **gobierno** donde los **enfermos** pueden ir sin tener que pagar nada por los servicios o **medicinas** que reciben.

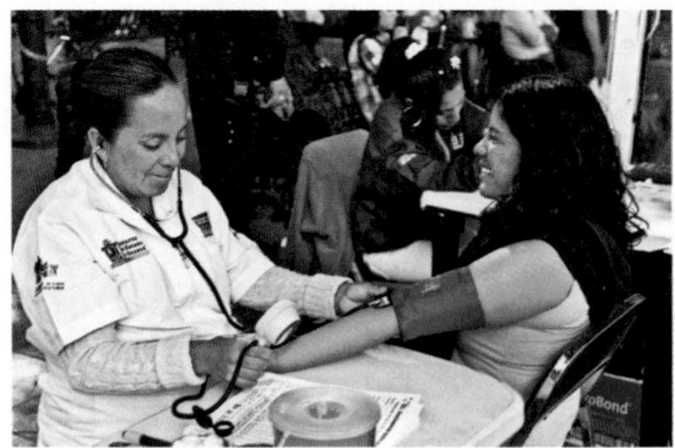

▲ Esta enfermera le toma la **tensión/presión arterial** a una **paciente** en un **sanatorio.**

▲ En las **farmacias** se venden todo tipo de **remedios** y **artículos de belleza.** Al igual que en Estados Unidos, en muchos lugares se necesita tener **receta** médica para comprar **antibióticos.** Muchas veces los clientes de la farmacia le preguntan **al farmacéutico/a la farmacéutica** qué remedio deben comprar para **curar** o **tratar** su **enfermedad.**

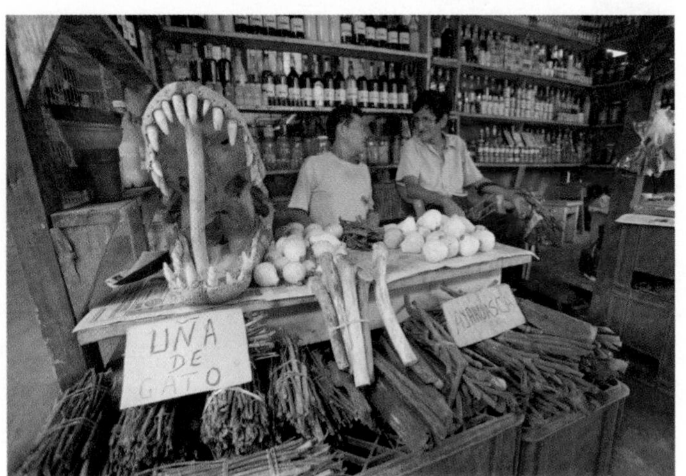

▲ Algunas personas prefieren curarse con hierbas medicinales. Por ejemplo, para el **dolor de estómago** se recomienda tomar un té de manzanilla (*chamomile*). Otra hierba medicinal muy conocida es la uña de gato (*cat's claw*), que se considera buena para el **tratamiento** de **alergias** y **asma.**

PRÁCTICA

Cultura

Los indígenas del continente americano nos han transmitido muchos conocimientos de medicina natural. Conocían los efectos positivos de las infusiones de hierbas y tenían fórmulas para cerrar las heridas (*wounds*) y curar las úlceras. También trataban fracturas de huesos. Acompañaban muchas de estas prácticas con ceremonias en las que invocaban a sus dioses, pidiéndoles protección y ayuda.

Comparaciones. ¿Qué remedios naturales se usan en tu cultura? ¿Para qué se usan? ¿Recuerdas alguno que se usa en tu familia?

11-1  

Escucha y confirma. Classify the words you hear according to the category to which they belong.

UN HOSPITAL	UNA ENFERMEDAD	UNA PERSONA
1. ________	________	________
2. ________	________	________
3. ________	________	________
4. ________	________	________
5. ________	________	________
6. ________	________	________

11-2  

Definiciones. PREPARACIÓN. Completa las siguientes oraciones con las palabras apropiadas. Compara tus respuestas con las de tu compañero/a.

1. En las ________________ se venden medicinas y productos de belleza.
2. El té de manzanilla se recomienda para el ________________ de estómago.
3. Los/Las ________________ ayudan a los médicos en los hospitales y cuidan de los enfermos.
4. Según la creencia popular, las ________________ medicinales pueden curar las enfermedades.
5. Los/Las ________________ les venden a sus clientes los remedios que necesitan.
6. El ________________ financia muchos hospitales y centros de salud en los países hispanos.
7. Los/Las ________________ son las personas que sufren enfermedades.
8. Algunas personas piensan que la uña de gato es buena para el tratamiento contra el ________________.

 INTERCAMBIOS. Háganse las siguientes preguntas.

1. ¿Cuándo y para qué vas generalmente a la farmacia?
2. ¿Qué tomas cuando tienes dolor de estómago?
3. ¿Conoces a alguien que tome hierbas medicinales? ¿Para qué enfermedad?

11-3 

Conversación. Háganse las siguientes preguntas para intercambiar información.

1. Cuando necesitas una operación o tienes un accidente, ¿adónde vas? ¿Tienes que pagar o no?
2. ¿Hay muchos hospitales en tu ciudad? ¿Cómo se llama el más importante?
3. Cuando estás enfermo/a y necesitas medicinas, ¿adónde vas a comprarlas? ¿Qué necesitas del médico/de la médica para poder comprarlas?
4. ¿Qué venden en las farmacias de tu país? ¿Por qué venden muchos otros productos, además de medicinas?
5. ¿Usas hierbas medicinales? ¿Para qué las usas? ¿Las usa alguien de tu familia?
6. ¿Te interesa la medicina alternativa? ¿Alguna vez usaste la acupuntura, la homeopatía o alguna otra? ¿Cómo fue tu experiencia?

EN OTRAS PALABRAS

In some Spanish-speaking countries, the word **sanatorio** is used instead of **hospital;** in others, **sanatorio** connotes a hospital that specializes in pulmonary and respiratory diseases. In some countries **clínica** refers to a private hospital. **Hospital** may refer to a government- or church-run facility that may provide free medical care.

11-4 

Una emergencia. PREPARACIÓN. Ustedes están de viaje en República Dominicana y ambos/as están enfermos/as por algo que comieron. Lean este anuncio y decidan cuál es el número más apropiado para llamar.

INTERCAMBIOS. En preparación para su consulta médica, escriban las respuestas a las preguntas que les van a hacer.

1. ¿Cuáles son sus síntomas?
2. ¿Cuándo comenzaron a sentirse mal? ¿Cómo se sienten ahora?
3. ¿Saben ustedes qué causó el problema? Explíquenlo.

Las partes del cuerpo

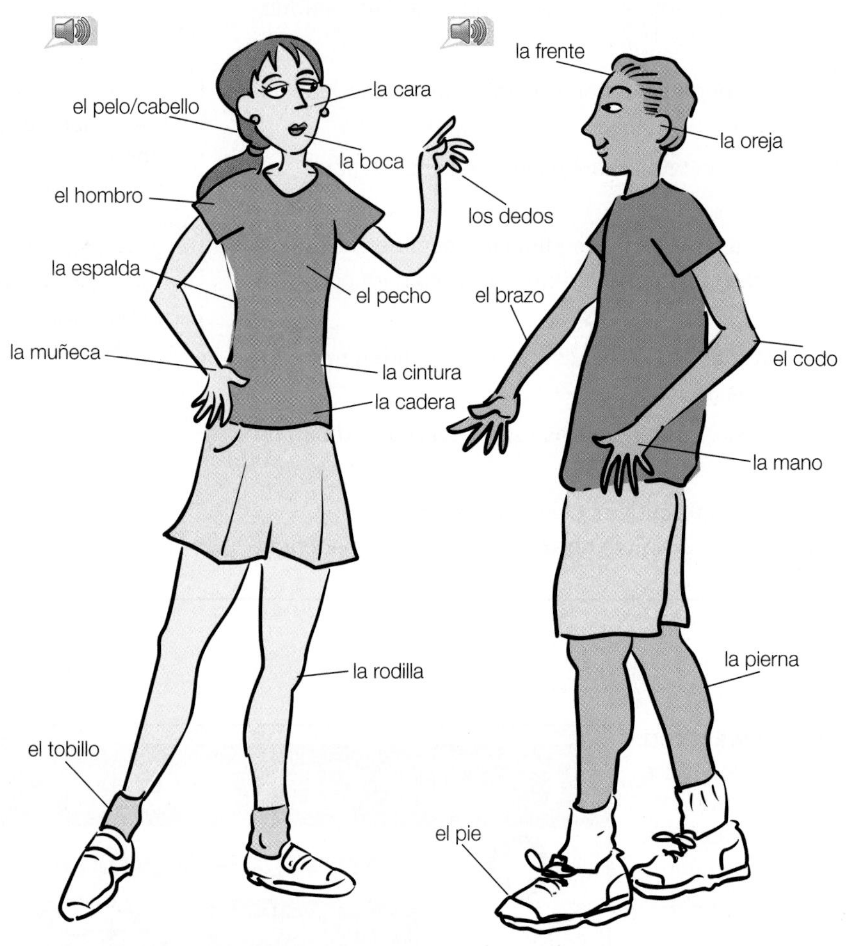

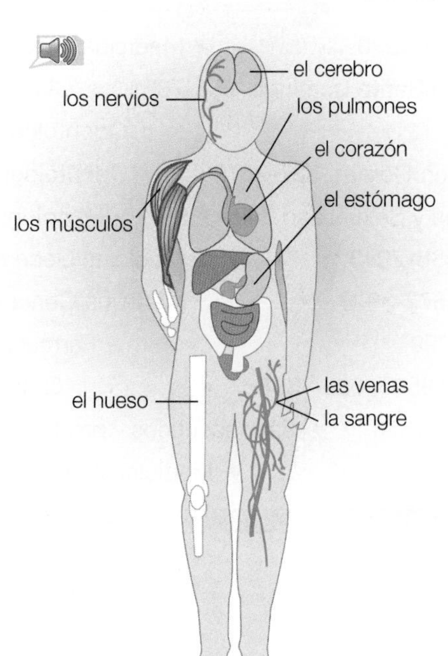

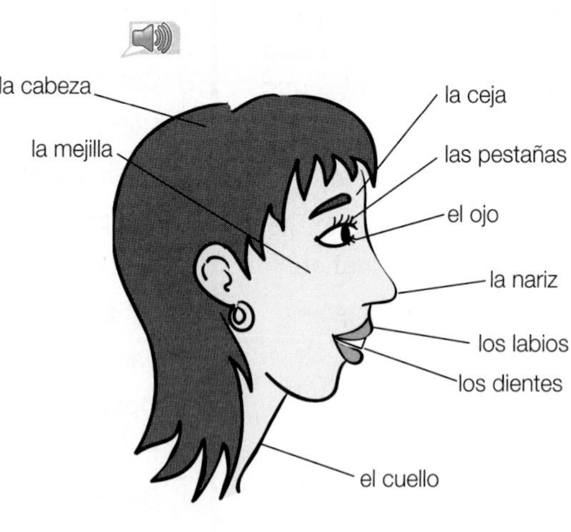

PRÁCTICA

11-5 

Para confirmar. Indica en qué parte del cuerpo se ponen estos accesorios y esta ropa.

1. _____ los calcetines	**a.** la muñeca
2. _____ los guantes	**b.** la cintura
3. _____ el cinturón	**c.** las orejas
4. _____ el collar	**d.** el cuello
5. _____ los aretes	**e.** los pies
6. _____ el reloj	**f.** las manos

11-6  

¿Para qué sirve(n)? Túrnense para completar las siguientes definiciones. Luego, expresen su opinión sobre la importancia de estas partes del cuerpo.

los brazos	la nariz
el cerebro	los ojos
el corazón	las piernas
los dientes	los pulmones
las manos	la sangre

1. __________ unen las manos con el cuerpo.

2. __________ permiten que las personas vean.

3. __________ toman el oxígeno del aire y lo pasan a la sangre.

4. __________ es un líquido rojo que circula por el cuerpo.

5. __________ unen el cuerpo con los pies.

6. __________ se usan para masticar (*chew*) la comida.

7. __________ están al final de los brazos.

8. __________ le da órdenes al cuerpo.

9. __________ impulsa la sangre por las venas del cuerpo.

10. __________ está entre la frente y la boca.

11-7  

Partes del cuerpo. **PREPARACIÓN.** Indiquen qué parte(s) del cuerpo se relaciona(n) con cada una de las siguientes situaciones.

SITUACIÓN	PARTE DEL CUERPO
1. A Felipe le gusta ponerse aretes.	
2. María se maquilla todos los días.	
3. Necesito ponerme gafas porque veo mal.	
4. Un futbolista del Real Madrid le pasa la pelota a un compañero de su equipo.	
5. Se necesitan todos para tocar bien el piano.	
6. Esta mujer ha perdido 30 libras. La falda le queda ancha.	
7. Daniela lleva siempre el mismo collar.	
8. El té de hierbas es muy bueno para la digestión.	

INTERCAMBIOS. Ahora inventen dos adivinanzas para hacer asociaciones con partes del cuerpo.

E1: *Sirven para besar.*

E2: *Los labios.*

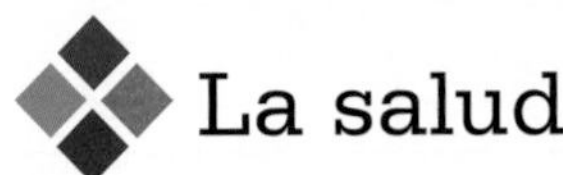

La salud

Jorgito está enfermo

SRA. VILLA: Jorgito, **tienes muy mala cara.** ¿Estás **enfermo?**

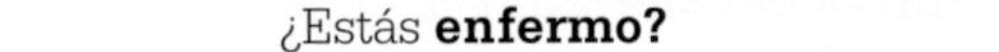

JORGITO: **Me siento** muy mal y **tengo dolor de garganta.** Me duele mucho cuando **toso**.

SRA. VILLA: [Le pone el **termómetro**.] Tienes 39 grados de **fiebre.** Enseguida voy a llamar a la doctora Bosque.

[En la clínica…]

DOCTORA: Vamos a ver, Jorgito. Cuéntame cómo te sientes.

JORGITO: Ahora **me duele** la cabeza y también me duelen los **oídos.** Además **estornudo** y toso mucho.

DOCTORA: Vamos a **examinarte** los oídos y la garganta. Abre bien la boca y di "Ah". Tienes una **infección.** No es **grave,** pero es necesario que **te cuides.**

JORGITO: Doctora, no quiero que me ponga una **inyección.**

DOCTORA: ¡No, qué va! Te voy a **recetar** unas **pastillas.** Debes tomarlas **cada cuatro horas.**

JORGITO: Está bien, doctora.

DOCTORA: Además, tienes **gripe.** Debes descansar y beber mucho líquido. Aquí está la receta, señora.

SRA. VILLA: Gracias, doctora.

¿Qué les pasa a estas personas?

Juan **se torció** el tobillo.

Joaquín **se cayó** y **se fracturó** el brazo.

> **LENGUA**
>
> Most words that refer to medical specialists derive from Latin and thus are similar to English: **pediatra** (*pediatrician*), **psiquiatra** (*psychiatrist*), **cirujano/a** (*surgeon*), **radiólogo/a** (*radiologist*), etc. A construction with **de** may also be used: **especialista** or **médico/a del corazón, del estómago,** etc. The primary care doctor is called **médico/a de familia,** or **médico/a de cabecera.**

PRÁCTICA

11-8 

Para confirmar. Indica si las siguientes afirmaciones se refieren a síntomas (**S**) o recomendaciones (**R**). Compara tus respuestas con las de tu compañero/a. Después, añade otro síntoma para Jorgito. Tu compañero/a va a darle una recomendación.

1. _____ Jorgito tiene que cuidarse.
2. _____ Tiene dolor de garganta.
3. _____ Debe tomar dos pastillas cada cuatro horas.
4. _____ Estornuda y tose mucho.
5. _____ Tiene que beber mucho líquido.
6. …

11-9  

Remedios y consejos. Elige la mejor recomendación para cada uno de los problemas siguientes. Luego, compara tus respuestas con las de tu compañero/a, y piensen en otras dos sugerencias para cada una de estas personas.

1. _____ Esteban tiene una infección en los ojos. Le recomiendo…
a. nadar en la piscina. **b.** tomar antibióticos. **c.** leer mucho.

2. _____ Valeria tiene fiebre y le duele el cuerpo. Le aconsejo…
a. descansar y tomar aspirinas. **b.** comer mucho y caminar. **c.** ir a su trabajo.

3. _____ Carmen se torció un tobillo. Le sugiero…
a. correr todos los días. **b.** tomar clases de baile. **c.** descansar y no caminar.

4. _____ Pablo se fracturó un brazo. Le recomiendo…
a. jugar al tenis. **b.** no usar el ordenador por una semana. **c.** hacer ejercicio.

11-10 

¿A quién debo llamar? Explícale a tu compañero/a tus síntomas o necesidades. Él/Ella te va a decir a quién debes llamar según los anuncios. Después, añadan una situación más.

necesitar un examen médico para el trabajo

E1: *Necesito un examen médico para el trabajo.*

E2: *Debes llamar a la Dra. Corona López.*

1. dolerte la cabeza cuando lees o miras televisión
2. sentirte triste y deprimido/a
3. estar enfermo/a y tener fiebre
4. no poder dormir
5. no poder respirar bien y tener la piel (*skin*) irritada
6. dolerte los dientes cuando comes
7. buscar un/a médico/a para tu sobrino de cinco años
8. ...

Dr. Fco. Javier Amador Cumplido
Cirugía y enfermedades de los ojos
86-43-57
Consultorio 204

Dra. Silvia Corona López
Medicina Interna
86-51-49

Dr. Héctor Molina Oviedo
Psiquiatra
86-51-49
Consultorio 402

Dr. Jaime A. Rodríguez Peláez
Pediatra
Niños y Adolescentes
86-17-15

Clínica de Asma y Alergias
Dr. Rubén Shturman
Amsterdam 219-A
2° piso
294-3866
584-0153

Dra. Gabriela Jacobo de Alcaraz
Cirujano Dentista
86-48-44
Consultorio 314

DR. RAÚL ELGUEZÁBAL R.
Medicina Familiar y Cirugía
86-34-73 EU.
428-4846
Consultorio 309

11-11 

En el consultorio. Tienes un catarro terrible y vas a ver a tu médico/a. Dile cómo te sientes y pregúntale qué debes hacer. Tu médico/a (tu compañero/a) te dará una recomendación y contestará tus preguntas.

E1: *Me siento.../Tengo...*

E2: *Creo que usted...*

E1: *¿Es bueno...?*

E2: *Es excelente.../No es recomendable...*

LENGUA

Traditionally, law and medicine were professions dominated by men. Therefore, only the masculine form was used in Spanish: **el médico, el abogado.** Now that more women practice these professions, the feminine forms have entered the language. The feminine article is sometimes used before a masculine noun (**la médico, la abogado, la juez**), but it is increasingly common to use the feminine forms of the nouns: **la médica, la abogada, la jueza.**

11-12 

Me duele mucho. **PREPARACIÓN.** You will listen to a teenage boy talk to his father about a sports injury. Before you listen, list two symptoms you think he probably has and compare your answers with those of your partner.

ESCUCHA. Pay attention to the general idea of what is said. As you listen, select the letter that indicates the appropriate ending to each statement.

1. _____ Esteban tiene...
   - **a.** una infección en el dedo.
   - **b.** mucho dolor.
   - **c.** fiebre.
2. _____ El padre de Esteban cree que...
   - **a.** su hijo se ha fracturado el dedo del pie.
   - **b.** Esteban debe acostarse.
   - **c.** es necesario que Esteban ponga hielo en el pie.
3. _____ El padre de Esteban quiere...
   - **a.** que Esteban descanse y se cuide.
   - **b.** llevar a Esteban al hospital.
   - **c.** que Esteban tome una aspirina.
4. _____ El padre de Esteban le dice que...
   - **a.** lo ayuda a caminar para llevarlo al hospital.
   - **b.** decida si prefiere descansar o ir al hospital.
   - **c.** el médico puede verlo esa tarde.
5. _____ Esteban decide...
   - **a.** no escuchar a su padre.
   - **b.** jugar al fútbol al día siguiente.
   - **c.** ir al hospital con su padre.

MOSAICO cultural Los remedios caseros

Por poco no se realizó el sueño de Miguel Rojas de conocer la fascinante cultura indígena de Paraguay. Tan pronto como llegó a Asunción desde España, empezó a sentir molestias en la garganta y se sentía cansado. Sin embargo, decidió continuar con sus planes de visitar una comunidad guaraní con sus amigos paraguayos.

Ya en el departamento de Guairá, al este del río Paraná, le dolía la cabeza, tenía fiebre, congestión nasal, escalofríos (*chills*), tosía y estornudaba. Quería ir al médico pero sus amigos le decían que era un simple resfriado y bastante típico entre las personas que visitaban Guairá por primera vez. "Tranquilo", le decía su amiga Zunilda. "Te recomiendo que descanses mucho esta noche y que te tomes un tereré caliente con una infusión de hierbas".

▲ Una mujer guaraní

En Paraguay, como en muchos países latinoamericanos, la medicina occidental y los tratamientos que ofrecen en farmacias y hospitales conviven con la medicina tradicional, cuyo conocimiento ancestral se transmite de generación en generación. El tereré es un tipo de yerba mate que se prepara en Paraguay como una infusión. A Miguel, por ejemplo, le añadieron en la infusión malva[1] blanca para la congestión de la nariz, saúco[2] para la tos y manzanilla, un relajante natural. Miguel siguió las recomendaciones y al día siguiente se sintió mucho mejor. De esta manera pudo realizar su visita y sacar fotos de su encuentro con la comunidad indígena de Paraguay.

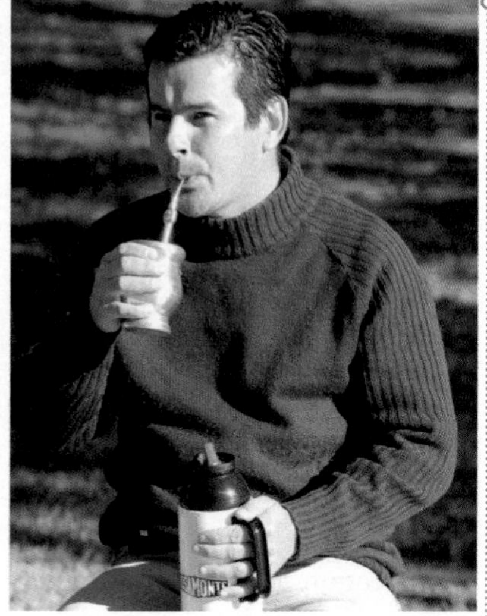

▲ Toma tereré cada cuatro horas para sentirte mejor.

[1]*mallow* [2]*elder*

▼ Los niños posan para una foto.

Compara

1. ¿Te has sentido enfermo/a en algún lugar lejos de casa? ¿Qué tratamientos has seguido en ese caso? Describe tu experiencia con todo detalle.
2. ¿Existe en tu país algún tipo de medicina casera? ¿Es importante en tu cultura? Explica con detalles y ejemplos.
3. ¿Qué le recomiendas a un amigo que tiene gripe?

Funciones y formas

1 Expressing expectations and hopes

ANA: En esta foto estoy con mi madre el día de mi graduación. Ella siempre desea lo mejor para mí: **quiere** que yo **trabaje** mucho, que **tenga** éxito en los estudios, que **piense** en mi futuro.

PEDRO: ¿**Espera** que tú **seas** médica como ella?

ANA: No le importa. **Prefiere** que **tome** buenas decisiones y **siga** mis propios sueños.

Piénsalo. En cada una de estas oraciones, indica cuál es el verbo de deseo (**VD**) y cuál es el verbo de acción (**VA**).

	VD	VA
1. Quiere que yo trabaje mucho.	________	________
2. Quiere que tenga éxito.	________	________
3. Quiere que piense en mi futuro.	________	________
4. ¿Espera que seas médica?	________	________
5. Prefiere que siga mis propios sueños.	________	________

Introduction to the present subjunctive

- To form the present subjunctive, use the **yo** form of the present indicative, drop the final **-o** and add the subjunctive ending. Notice that just like the endings of the **usted/ustedes** commands, **-ar** verbs change the **-a** to **-e,** while **-er** and **-ir** verbs change the **-e** and the **-i** to **-a.**

	HABLAR	COMER	VIVIR
yo	habl**e**	com**a**	viv**a**
tú	habl**es**	com**as**	viv**as**
Ud., él, ella	habl**e**	com**a**	viv**a**
nosotros/as	habl**emos**	com**amos**	viv**amos**
vosotros/as	habl**éis**	com**áis**	viv**áis**
Uds., ellos/as	habl**en**	com**an**	viv**an**

- The present subjunctive of the following verbs with irregular indicative **yo** forms is as follows:

conocer: cono**zca,** cono**zcas...** salir: sal**ga,** sal**gas...** decir: di**ga,** di**gas...**
tener: ten**ga,** ten**gas...** hacer: ha**ga,** ha**gas...** traer: tra**iga,** tra**igas...**
oír: o**iga,** o**igas...** venir: ven**ga,** ven**gas...** poner: pon**ga,** pon**gas...**
ver: v**ea,** v**eas...**

- The present subjunctive of **hay** is **haya.** The following verbs also have irregular subjunctive forms:

dar: **dé, des...** saber: **sepa, sepas...** estar: **esté, estés...**
ser: **sea, seas...** ir: **vaya, vayas...**

- Stem-changing **-ar** and **-er** verbs follow the same pattern as the present indicative.

pensar: p**ie**nse, p**ie**nses, p**ie**nse, pensemos, penséis, p**ie**nsen
volver: v**ue**lva, v**ue**lvas, v**ue**lva, volvamos, volváis, v**ue**lvan

- Stem-changing **-ir** verbs follow the same pattern as the present indicative but have an additional change in the **nosotros/as** and **vosotros/as** forms.

preferir: pref**ie**ra, pref**ie**ras, pref**ie**ra, pref**i**ramos, pref**i**ráis, pref**ie**ran

dormir: d**ue**rma, d**ue**rmas, d**ue**rma, d**u**rmamos, d**u**rmáis, d**ue**rman

- Verbs ending in **-car**, **-gar**, **-ger**, **-zar**, and **-guir** have spelling changes.

sacar: sa**qu**e, sa**qu**es, sa**qu**e, sa**qu**emos, sa**qu**éis, sa**qu**en

jugar: jue**gu**e, jue**gu**es, jue**gu**e, ju**gu**emos, ju**gu**éis, jue**gu**en

recoger: reco**ja,** reco**j**as, reco**j**a, reco**j**amos, reco**j**áis, reco**j**an

almorzar: almuer**c**e, almuer**c**es, almuer**c**e, almor**c**emos, almor**c**éis, almuer**c**en

seguir: si**g**a, si**g**as, si**g**a, si**g**amos, si**g**áis, si**g**an

LENGUA

Remember that you have seen these same orthographic changes in the formal commands:

Siga las instrucciones.
Follow the directions.

Busque la medicina.
Look for the medicine.

- Notice in the examples below that there are two clauses, each with a different subject. When the verb of the main clause expresses a wish or hope, use a subjunctive verb form in the dependent clause (the clause that begins with **que**).

MAIN CLAUSE	DEPENDENT CLAUSE
La doctora **quiere**	que Alfredo **respire** profundamente.
The doctor wants	*Alfredo to breathe deeply.*
Espero	que Alfredo no **tenga** asma.
I hope	*Alfredo doesn't have asthma.*

- When there is only one subject, use the infinitive instead of the subjunctive.

Lola **necesita llamar** a la farmacia para pedir una medicina. — *Lola has to call the pharmacy to order some medicine.*

Ella **quiere recogerla** esta tarde. — *She wants to pick it up this afternoon.*

Desea recogerla antes de las tres. — *She wants to pick it up before 3:00.*

- Some common verbs that express expectations, wants, and hopes are **desear, esperar, necesitar, preferir,** and **querer.**

Los residentes del barrio prefieren que la clínica no **cierre** antes de las siete. — *The residents of the neighborhood prefer that the clinic not close before seven o'clock.*

La niña espera que el enfermero no le **ponga** una inyección. — *The girl hopes that the nurse will not give her a shot.*

- The expression **ojalá (que)** (*I/we hope [that]*), which comes from Arabic, originally meaning *May Allah grant that ...* , is always followed by the subjunctive.

Ojalá (que) ellos **vengan** temprano. — *I hope (that) they will come early.*

Ojalá (que) **puedas** llevarme a la cita con la médica. — *I hope (that) you can take me to the doctor's appointment.*

¿COMPRENDES?

Completa las oraciones con la forma correcta del verbo.

1. ¿Estás enferma? ¿Quieres que yo _______ (ir) a tu casa para ayudarte?
2. ¿Quieres que Amanda y yo te _______ (hacer) una sopa de pollo?
3. Ojalá _______ _______ (sentirse) mejor pronto.
4. Tus amigos esperan que tú _______ (asistir) al concierto mañana con ellos.
5. Todos dicen: "¡Ojalá Sara _______ (poder) ir con nosotros!"

MySpanishLab

Learn more using Amplifire Dynamic Study Modules, Grammar Tutorials, and Extra Practice activities.

PRÁCTICA

11-13 

Comentarios y deseos. Los miembros del Club de Estudiantes de Pre-Medicina están hablando de la fiesta que darán mañana. ¿Cuáles de las afirmaciones siguientes probablemente son comentarios de ellos? Márquenlas (✓) y justifiquen sus selecciones.

1. _____ Queremos que la fiesta empiece puntualmente.
2. _____ Ojalá que no sirvan comida.
3. _____ Preferimos que pongan música caribeña, porque queremos bailar salsa y merengue.
4. _____ Esperamos que también asistan estudiantes de odontología (*dentistry*) y de enfermería.
5. _____ Necesitamos que la fiesta termine temprano.
6. _____ Deseamos que nuestros profesores vayan a la fiesta.
7. _____ Queremos que todos recojan la basura después de la fiesta.
8. _____ Ojalá que nos divirtamos.

11-14 

Trabajo voluntario en el hospital. PREPARACIÓN. Unos estudiantes trabajan de voluntarios en el hospital. ¿Qué espera la directora del programa de voluntarios que ellos hagan? Túrnense para hablar sobre cada escena.

 Elena: llevar flores/conversar con los pacientes

E1: *La directora espera que Elena les lleve flores a los pacientes.*

E2: *También espera que Elena converse con los pacientes. Algunos pacientes se sienten muy solos.*

1. José y Camila: jugar con los niños/hablar con los padres de los niños/leerles libros infantiles a los niños
2. Marisa: trabajar en la tienda de regalos/hacerles recomendaciones a los clientes/poner flores frescas en el mostrador de la tienda
3. Sofía y Eduardo: conversar con los familiares de los pacientes/ofrecerles café/darles almohadas si quieren dormir mientras esperan

 INTERCAMBIOS. ¿Qué más esperan los pacientes que hagan los voluntarios en el hospital? Escriban una lista de cuatro cosas más.

 *Los pacientes esperan que los voluntarios les traigan la comida.*

11-15 

Clínica de familia. En una semana se abre una nueva clínica y ustedes están ayudando con los preparativos. En la tabla siguiente, escriban una lista de lo que ustedes tienen que hacer y otra de lo que esperan que hagan los empleados.

E1: *Tenemos que pintar la sala de espera.*
E2: *Y también tenemos que limpiar los pisos.*

E1: *Espero que los empleados lleguen a tiempo.*
E2: *Y yo espero que los carpinteros terminen su trabajo.*

LO QUE TENEMOS QUE HACER	LO QUE ESPERAMOS QUE OTRAS PERSONAS HAGAN
______________________	la médica especialista: ______________
______________________	los enfermeros: ______________
______________________	la recepcionista: ______________
______________________	la chofer de la ambulancia: ______________
______________________	el anestesista: ______________
______________________	los empleados de limpieza: ______________

Situación

PREPARACIÓN. Lean la situación. Luego, compartan ejemplos de vocabulario, gramática y otra información que necesitan para desarrollar la conversación.

Role A. You are sick today so you will miss the review session for your Spanish midterm. Call a classmate.

a. Say that you need him/her to take notes for you;
b. tell him/her that you hope it is not too much trouble;
c. say when you want your friend to bring you the notes; and
d. thank your friend.

Role B. When a friend from your Spanish class calls to ask a favor, say that you will be happy to take notes for him/her.

a. Ask how your friend is feeling and what he/she has;
b. ask when your friend wants you to bring over the notes; and
c. say that you hope he/she feels better soon.

	ROLE A	ROLE B
Vocabulario	Expressions related to health and parts of the body	Expressions related to health and parts of the body
Funciones y formas	Asking for a favor Expressing hopes and preferences: Subjunctive with verbs of volition Describing symptoms Thanking someone Making polite requests in Spanish	Replying to requests Asking questions Expressing wishes: Subjunctive with verbs of volition

INTERCAMBIOS. Practica la conversación con tu compañero/a incorporando el vocabulario y las funciones de *Preparación.* Luego, represéntenla ante la clase.

2 Expressing requests

PABLO: ¿Qué me recomienda, doctor?

MÉDICO: Le **recomiendo** que **tome** agua y caldo de pollo. **Quiero** que **duerma** mucho y que no **vaya** a clase.

Más tarde...

ALICIA: ¿Qué dice el médico?

PABLO: **Dice** que **me quede** en cama. También **quiere** que tú me **prepares** un caldo de pollo, que **limpies** mi apartamento, que me **traigas** helado...

Piénsalo. Para cada afirmación, indica quién recomienda la acción y quién va a hacer la acción: **el médico**, **Pablo** o **Alicia.**

	Recomienda la acción	Va a hacer la acción
1. Le **recomiendo** que **tome** agua y caldo de pollo.	______	______
2. **Quiere** que tú me **prepares** un caldo de pollo.	______	______
3. **Deseo** que **duerma** mucho.	______	______
4. **Dice** que **me quede** en cama.	______	______
5. **Quiere** que **limpies** mi apartamento.	______	______
6. **Quiere** que me **traigas** helado.	______	______

The subjunctive with expressions of influence

- Verbs that express an intention to influence the actions of others (**aconsejar, pedir, permitir, prohibir, recomendar**) also require the subjunctive in the dependent clause. With these verbs, Spanish speakers often use an indirect object.

El médico **le** recomienda que no **salga** por unos días.	*The doctor recommends that he not go out for a few days.*
La enfermera **me** aconseja que no **coma** por una hora.	*The nurse advises me not to eat for an hour.*

- You may also try to impose your will or express your influence, wishes, and hopes through some impersonal expressions such as **es necesario, es importante, es bueno,** and **es mejor** followed by **que.**

Es necesario que los atletas **duerman** un mínimo de siete horas por noche.	*It is necessary that the athletes sleep a minimum of seven hours a night.*

LENGUA

You have seen that a stressed **i** or **u** requires a written accent when preceded or followed by another vowel (**oír, frío, reúno**). This is because no diphthong results and the vowels are pronounced as two separate syllables. The same rule applies to an **h** between the two vowels (**prohíbo**, **prohíbe**), since the **h** has no sound. When **i** or **u** is not stressed, the vowel combination is pronounced as one syllable, and no accent is required (**prohibir**).

Es mejor que coman pescado porque tiene menos grasa que la carne de res. | *It is better that they eat fish because it has less fat than beef.*

- If you are not addressing or speaking about someone in particular, use the infinitive.

  Es mejor **comer** pescado y pollo. | *It is better to eat fish and chicken.*

- With the verb **decir,** use the subjunctive in the dependent clause when expressing a wish or an order. Use the indicative when reporting information.

  Dice que los atletas **consumen** mucha proteína. (*report information*) | *She says (that) the athletes consume a lot of protein.*

  Dice que los atletas **consuman** mucha proteína. (*express an order*) | *She tells the athletes to eat a lot of protein.*

¿COMPRENDES?

Completa las oraciones con el infinitivo o la forma correcta del subjuntivo.

1. El médico te aconseja que ________ (beber) menos café y más agua.
2. Es necesario que nosotros ________ (cuidarse) si queremos vivir muchos años.
3. La enfermera le dice que ________ (hacer) más ejercicio.
4. Es importante ________ (comer) bien.
5. El especialista le aconseja al paciente que ________ (descansar) mucho.
6. Es bueno que ustedes ________ (pasar) unos días en la playa.

MySpanishLab
Learn more using Amplifire Dynamic Study Modules, Grammar Tutorials, and Extra Practice activities.

PRÁCTICA

Normas de conducta en el trabajo. PREPARACIÓN. Tu amiga Rebeca tiene un trabajo nuevo como recepcionista en un consultorio médico y te pide consejos sobre qué normas de conducta seguir con respecto a los temas de la lista. Escribe cinco recomendaciones para ella y compáralas con las recomendaciones de tu compañero/a.

- llegar unos minutos antes
- llevar chanclas
- almorzar en la oficina
- conversar con los pacientes
- aceptar regalos de los pacientes
- entrar en Facebook

usar el celular
Te recomiendo que no uses tu celular en el trabajo. Es importante que no hagas llamadas personales.

INTERCAMBIOS. Escriban una carta a Rebeca combinando sus recomendaciones. Léanla a la clase.

Juan y yo te aconsejamos que…

11-17

Consejos y sugerencias. Estás organizando un nuevo programa para estudiantes que quieren trabajar en programas de salud en República Dominicana. Explícales a dos compañeros/as los aspectos del programa que aún no están resueltos. Ellos/as te recomendarán qué hacer.

viajar a República Dominicana

E1: *Hay varias opciones: podemos viajar a República Dominicana en grupo, o cada estudiante puede hacer su propia reservación.*

E2: *Es mejor que viajen en grupo, así se consigue mejor precio.*

E3: *Y también es importante que todos los estudiantes lleguen juntos.*

1. empezar clases de español
2. establecer conexiones con las clínicas en la capital
3. buscar alojamiento (*lodging*)
4. escoger actividades de ocio (*free time*)

Cultura

Boca Chica

República Dominicana un país que en los últimos años ha desarrollado una próspera industria turística, gracias en parte a su clima ideal y sus extraordinarias playas. Boca Chica es la playa familiar más famosa de República Dominicana por su arena blanca, agua cristalina y proximidad a la capital. Otras playas conocidas son las de Punta Cana, al este del país, donde predominan los centros turísticos privados (*resorts*). Sin embargo, quedan muchas otras zonas de interés cultural y ambiental relativamente poco exploradas.

Conexiones. ¿Por qué crees que algunas personas prefieren ir de turismo a lugares privados sin conocer realmente el país que visitan?

Excursión a República Dominicana. PREPARACIÓN. Tu clase está planeando una excursión a la playa Boca Chica en República Dominicana. Escribe una lista de todo lo que hay que preparar en cuanto a alojamiento, transporte y equipaje (*luggage*) para la excursión. Después, compártela con tu compañero/a.

E1: *Es importante reservar los pasajes.*

E2: *Sí, y es necesario que compremos unas mochilas.*

INTERCAMBIOS. En grupos de tres o cuatro decidan qué quieren que haga cada persona de su grupo. Compartan la información con la clase.

MODELO

E1: *Queremos que David reserve los pasajes.*

E2: *Sí, y esperamos que Alicia compre las mochilas.*

E1: *Necesitamos que…*

Situación

PREPARACIÓN. Lean la situación. Luego, compartan ejemplos de vocabulario, gramática y otra información que necesitan para desarrollar la conversación.

Role A. You are allergic to (**ser alérgico/a a**) cats, and you have just come back from spending the weekend with your friend who has two cats. Now you have a headache, your eyes itch (**me pican los ojos**), your lungs hurt, and it is hard to breathe. Call the clinic.

a. Explain your situation;
b. describe your symptoms; and
c. ask what the nurse recommends that you do.

Ask questions to be sure you understand the recommendations.

Role B. You work as a nurse at the clinic, and someone calls for advice about an allergic reaction. Ask about the person's symptoms and offer advice about what he/she should do.

	ROLE A	ROLE B
Vocabulario	Health symptoms	Health symptoms and remedies
Funciones y formas	Explaining health conditions Asking clarification questions Asking for recommendations Thanking someone Addressing medical professionals appropriately	Giving medical advice Answering questions Wishing someone a prompt recovery

INTERCAMBIOS. Practica la conversación con tu compañero/a incorporando el vocabulario y las funciones de *Preparación*. Luego, represéntenla ante la clase.

3 Expressing emotions, opinions, and attitudes

Ernesto Sara

 ERNESTO: **Me molesta** que **fumen.** Y no me gusta que **hablen** tan alto.

SARA: **Estoy contenta de** que **se vayan** pronto. Ya han terminado de comer.

 **Piénsalo.** Indica si los verbos de cada oración expresan un sentimiento o una acción y escríbelos en el espacio correcto.

	VERBO/FRASE DE SENTIMIENTO	VERBO DE ACCIÓN
1. **Les molesta** que **fumen.**	____________	____________
2. No **les gusta** que **hablen** tan alto.	____________	____________
3. **Están contentos de** que **se vayan** pronto.	____________	____________
4. **Es triste** que **permitan** fumar en su restaurante.	____________	____________
5. **Es una lástima** que **fumen** en la mesa, tan cerca de otra gente.	____________	____________

Cultura

Fumar perjudica la salud

Tradicionalmente, los países hispanos han sido más permisivos en el consumo del tabaco en lugares públicos, especialmente por la importancia de cafés, bares y restaurantes en la vida cotidiana. Sin embargo, recientemente la mayor parte de los países han adoptado medidas que prohíben o limitan el uso del tabaco en las zonas públicas. Esto ha producido una gran reducción del consumo del tabaco entre los jóvenes y una mayor concienciación sobre sus efectos nocivos.

Comparación: ¿Cuáles son las normas relacionadas con el uso del tabaco en tu país? ¿Te parecen suficientes? ¿Son excesivas? Explica.

The subjunctive with expressions of emotion

- When the verb of the main clause expresses emotion (e.g., fear, happiness, sorrow), use a subjunctive verb form in the dependent clause. Note that the subjects of the two clauses must be different.

Sentimos mucho que el niño **tenga** fiebre.	*We are very sorry (that) the child has a fever.*
Me alegro de que **estés** con él.	*I am glad (that) you are with him.*

- Some common verbs that express emotion are:

alegrarse (de)	*to be glad (about)*	**molestar(le)**	*to bother*
encantar(le)	*to love*	**sentir (ie, i)**	*to feel*
estar contento/a (de)	*to be happy (about)*	**temer**	*to fear*
gustar(le)	*to like*		

- Impersonal expressions and other expressions that show emotion are also followed by **que** + *subjunctive*.

Es triste que el niño **esté** enfermo.	*It is sad that the child is sick.*
¡Qué lástima que no **pueda** ir a la fiesta!	*What a shame that he cannot go to the party!*

¿COMPRENDES?

Completa las oraciones con la forma correcta de los verbos indicados.

1. Juan, me alegro mucho de que tú _______ (venir) a verme las próximas vacaciones.
2. Yo también _______ (estar) contento de que nosotros _______ (poder) pasar tiempo juntos.
3. A mi madre le va a gustar que tú _______ (visitar) a los primos durante las vacaciones.
4. Sí, ya sé, es una lástima que nosotros _______ (vivir) tan lejos.

MySpanishLab

Learn more using Amplifire Dynamic Study Modules, Grammar Tutorials, and Extra Practice activities.

PRÁCTICA

11-19 

Estoy enfermo. Asocien cada comentario con la reacción apropiada. Después, túrnense para añadir nuevos comentarios y reacciones.

1. _____ Estoy muy enfermo/a.
2. _____ Mis padres llegan hoy para estar conmigo.
3. _____ Creo que el doctor Pérez me va a operar.
4. _____ Dicen que es una operación seria.
5. _____ No voy a poder participar en el campeonato.
6. ...

a. Me alegro de que vengan.
b. Siento mucho que estés tan mal.
c. ¡Qué bueno que sea ese el médico!
d. Es una lástima que no puedas jugar.
e. Ojalá que no tengas complicaciones.

11-20 

Una visita. Estás en la clínica para visitar a tu compañero/a, a quien han operado de la rodilla. Tu compañero/a te cuenta sobre su experiencia en la clínica y cómo se siente. Escoge entre las expresiones de *En directo* para responderle e intercambien papeles.

E1: *No me gusta la comida del hospital.*

E2: *Siento que la comida no sea buena. ¿Qué te sirven?*

E1: ...

1. Me duele bastante la rodilla.
2. Tengo fiebre y dolor de cabeza.
3. Estoy mal del estómago porque las medicinas son muy fuertes.
4. Mis amigos me mandan flores y tarjetas.
5. Detesto estar en cama tanto tiempo.
6. Hay tanto ruido que no puedo dormir.
7. Las enfermeras vienen a verme cada media hora.

En directo

To express empathy:

Siento que...
Me alegro de que...
Temo que...
Espero que...
No me gusta que...
¡Qué agradable que...!

Listen to a conversation with these expressions.

11-21

Reacciones. Túrnense para reaccionar a las actividades que Luisa y Rafael piensan hacer la próxima semana.

Luisa/no desayunar

E1: *Luisa no va a desayunar.* E2: *No me gusta que Luisa no desayune.* E1: *Y yo siento/lamento que...*

PERSONAS	LUNES	MIÉRCOLES	VIERNES	DOMINGO
Luisa	empezar una dieta	ir al gimnasio	hacer ejercicio en su casa	caminar 2 kilómetros
Rafael	trabajar en el hospital todo el día	salir del hospital temprano para ir al cine	quedarse en su casa	reunirse con sus amigos

11-22

¿Qué me molesta? PREPARACIÓN. Haz una lista de los hábitos que te molestan de otras personas. Compara tu lista con la de tu compañero/a.

Me molesta que mis amigos lleguen tarde.

INTERCAMBIOS. En pequeños grupos, comparen sus listas y escojan seis hábitos que les molestan más a todos y digan por qué. Compartan sus resultados con el resto de la clase.

Situación

PREPARACIÓN. Lean la situación. Luego, compartan ejemplos de vocabulario, gramática y otra información que necesitan para desarrollar la conversación.

Role A. You and your housemate disagree about health and exercise. You exercise regularly, ride your bike, and hike on the weekends, and want only healthful foods in the refrigerator. Your housemate buys a lot of junk food, leaves a mess in the living room and bathroom, and disturbs you with loud music at all hours. You have a serious conversation to tell him/her what is bothering you.

Role B. Your housemate is uptight and conventional and doesn't know how to enjoy life. When he/she tells you what is bothering him/her about your behavior, you should:

a. react to his/her complaints;
b. respond with your complaints about his/her excessive tidiness; and
c. regret that you do not agree on anything.

	ROLE A	ROLE B
Vocabulario	Activities for a healthy lifestyle Household chores Verbs of emotions, likes, and dislikes	Household chores Verbs of emotions, likes, and dislikes
Funciones y formas	Expressing emotion about someone's actions	Expressing emotion about someone's actions

INTERCAMBIOS. Practica la conversación con tu compañero/a incorporando el vocabulario y las funciones de *Preparación.* Luego, represéntenla ante la clase.

4 Expressing goals, purposes, and means

Vive más

- **Para** vivir más no necesitas más dinero. No pagues miles de pesos **por** aparatos de ejercicio. ¡Muévete!
- Sube a tu clase u oficina **por** las escaleras; no tomes el ascensor.
- Cuando vayas **para** el centro, no conduzcas. Es mejor ir a pie.
- Si caminas 30 minutos **por** día vivirás más. Pasea **por** el parque con tus amigos o tu familia y guarda tu dinero **para** cosas necesarias.
- Relájate mientras caminas al aire libre y vive con menos estrés **por** ti y **para** ti.

Piénsalo. Indica si las afirmaciones son ciertas (**C**) o falsas (**F**). Luego, escoge de la lista el significado de **por** o **para** en cada afirmación.

a causa de algo o alguien	en dirección a un lugar
en beneficio de alguien	medio de transporte
duración	objetivo

	CIERTO/ FALSO	SIGNIFICADO DE POR/PARA
1. **Para** tener una vida larga es importante mantenernos activos.	______	______
2. Caminar **por** 30 minutos al día ayuda a vivir más años.	______	______
3. Es mejor ir en automóvil cuando vamos **para** el supermercado y otras tiendas.	______	______
4. Debemos relajarnos y vivir con menos estrés **por** nosotros mismos.	______	______

Uses of *por* and *para*

- As you learned in *Capítulo 3,* the prepositions **por** and **para** have several meanings and uses. You have used them easily in some contexts in which they are similar to "for" in English:

  Compré estas vitaminas **para** Anita. *I bought these vitamins for Anita.*

- Other uses of **por** and **para** that are not similar to English can be learned by grouping them into functional categories: expressions of movement, time, purpose, and means.

POR	PARA
Movement	
• through or by a place Caminaron **por** el hospital. *They walked through the hospital.*	• toward a destination Caminaron **para** el hospital. *They walked toward the hospital.*
Time	
• duration of an event Estuvo con la médica **por** una hora. *He was with the doctor for an hour.*	• deadline Necesita el antibiótico **para** el martes. *He needs the antibiotic by Tuesday.*
Purpose	
• reason or motive Ana fue al consultorio **por** el dolor de garganta. *Ana went to the doctor's office because of a sore throat.*	• for whom something is intended or done Compró el antibiótico **para** Ana. *He bought the antibiotic for Ana.*

- **Por** is also used to express the following:
  - means of transportation

Mandaron los órganos para el trasplante **por** avión.	*They sent the organs for the transplant by plane.*

  - exchange or substitution

Irma pagó $120 **por** las pastillas.	*Irma paid $120 for the pills.*
Cambió esas pastillas rojas **por** las amarillas.	*She exchanged those red pills for the yellow ones.*

  - unit or rate

Yo camino 5 kilómetros **por** hora.	*I walk 5 kilometers per hour.*
El seguro de salud cubre el sesenta **por** ciento de las cuentas.	*The health insurance covers 60 percent of the bills.*

  - object of an errand

Sara fue a la farmacia **por** jarabe para la tos.	*Sara went to the drugstore for the cough syrup.*
Pasamos **por** ti a las 5:00.	*We'll come by for you at 5:00.*

- **Para** is also used to express the following:
  - judgment or point of view

Para nosotros, esta es la mejor farmacia.	*For us, this is the best drugstore.*
Es un caso difícil **para** un médico joven.	*It is a difficult case for a young doctor.*

  - intention or purpose, when followed by an infinitive

Fueron a la farmacia **para** comprar jarabe para la tos.	*They went to the drugstore to buy cough syrup.*
Come bien **para** vivir más.	*Eat well to live longer.*

e ¿COMPRENDES?

Completa las oraciones con **por** o **para.**

1. Te llamo ________ pedirte un favor.
2. Todos los días caminamos ________ el parque.
3. ¿Puedes pasar ________ mi casa a las cinco?
4. Es muy fuerte ________ un niño de siete años.
5. Ella siempre trabaja ________ mí cuando estoy enferma.

MySpanishLab

Learn more using Amplifire Dynamic Study Modules, Grammar Tutorials, and Extra Practice activities.

PRÁCTICA

11-23 e

Un episodio. PREPARACIÓN. Selecciona la preposición correcta, según el significado entre paréntesis.

1. Salimos **por/para** el consultorio del médico a las nueve de la mañana. (*toward a destination*)
2. Fuimos **por/para** el túnel para llegar más rápido. (*through*)
3. Ana fue a ver al médico **por/para** su dolor de garganta y tos. (*reason or motive*)
4. El médico recetó un antibiótico **por/para** Ana. (*for whom it is intended*)
5. Yo fui a la farmacia **por/para** el antibiótico. (*object of an errand*)
6. ¿Cuánto pagaste **por/para** el antibiótico? (*exchange or substitution*)

INTERCAMBIOS. Túrnense para hablar del siguiente episodio.

1. ¿Cuándo fue la última vez que fuiste al médico?
2. ¿Por qué fuiste?
3. ¿Qué te recomendó el médico y para qué?
4. ¿Cuánto pagaste por la consulta?
5. ¿Cuánto pagaste por los medicamentos?

11-24

La graduación de un nuevo médico. Completa estos párrafos sobre la graduación de Fernando con **por** o **para,** según el contexto. Luego, de la lista de funciones a continuación, escoge la letra que corresponde a cada uso de **por** o **para.**

El 14 de junio es la graduación de Fernando en la Facultad de Medicina de la Universidad Católica Madre y Maestra de Santiago de los Caballeros en República Dominicana. Sus padres, los señores Rovira, viven en Puerto Plata, pero van a Santiago **(1) por/para** (_______) asistir a la graduación y quieren llevarle un regalo. El lunes pasado fueron a una tienda y pagaron cien dólares **(2) por/para** (_______) un regalo muy bonito **(3) por/para** (_______) Fernando. Graciela, su hermana gemela, vive en Miami y no puede ir **(4) por/para** (_______) su trabajo. Ella también le compró un regalo y se lo envió **(5) por/para** (_______) avión porque quiere que llegue **(6) por/para** (_______) el día de la graduación.

El día 14, los padres de Fernando salieron **(7) por/para** (_______) la universidad. Estaba lloviendo, y **(8) por/para** (_______) eso salieron temprano. Normalmente, ellos pueden estar en la universidad en una hora más o menos, pero **(9) por/para** (_______) la lluvia, el viaje duró casi dos horas. **(10) Por/Para** (_______) ellos, que son mayores, el viaje fue un poco largo, pero al final pudieron pasar ese día con su hijo.

To express or indicate...
a. intention or purpose (with infinitive)
b. judgment or point of view
c. means of transportation
d. exchange or substitution
e. toward a destination
f. deadline
g. for whom something is intended or done
h. reason or motive

11-25 

En el laboratorio. Túrnense para averiguar cuándo estarán listos los resultados del análisis (*test*) de unos pacientes. Consulten la tabla para obtener información.

 Alfredo Benítez/2:00 de la tarde

E1: *¿Cuándo va a estar listo el análisis del Sr. Benítez?*

E2: *Va a estar listo para las dos de la tarde.*

PACIENTE	RESULTADOS DEL ANÁLISIS
Hilda Corvalán	11:00 de la mañana
Alfonso González	esta tarde
Jorge Pérez Robles	3:15 de la tarde
Aleida Miranda	mañana por la mañana
César Gómez Villegas	martes
Irene Santa Cruz	...

Cultura

Nuestra Señora de Altagracia

En un país profundamente católico como República Dominicana, la devoción a Nuestra Señora de Altagracia ocupa un lugar preeminente. Los dominicanos consideran a esta virgen como la protectora de la nación. El 21 de enero celebran con devoción y emoción el día de su festividad. Ese día no se trabaja en República Dominicana y muchas personas peregrinan al templo de Higüey para rezar, dar gracias y pedirle protección.

Comparación. ¿Hay lugares espirituales en tu país donde la gente va para reflexionar o dar las gracias?

11-26 

Una cura para el estrés. Aconséjale a tu compañero/a que vaya a República Dominicana para curarse del estrés. Sugiérele algunas actividades y escoge de la lista el propósito para cada actividad. Después cambien de papel.

 ACTIVIDAD: *caminar por el Jardín Botánico de Santo Domingo*

PROPÓSITO: ver la gran variedad de plantas

Camina por el Jardín Botánico para ver la gran variedad de plantas.

ACTIVIDAD	PROPÓSITO
1. participar en la fiesta nacional de Nuestra Señora de Altagracia en Higüey	■ escuchar música y bailar merengue
2. ir a la Bahía de Samaná	■ visitar el santuario de las ballenas jorobadas (*humpback whales*)
3. ir a un club en la Zona Colonia de la capital	■ conocer el significado de esta figura espiritual del pueblo dominicano
4. explorar la Cueva de las Maravillas cerca de La Romana	■ nadar, hacer kayak y tomar el sol
5. salir a cenar en el Mesón de la Cava en Santo Domingo	■ explorar las cavernas y ver unas pinturas antiguas hechas por los aborígenes taínos
6. pasar unos días en las playas de Punta Cana	■ comer comida típica dominicana

Situación

PREPARACIÓN. Lean la situación. Luego, compartan ejemplos de vocabulario, gramática y otra información que necesitan para desarrollar la conversación.

Role A. You hurt your ankle while playing soccer, so you go to the health center at your college or university. Tell the doctor that:

a. you fell during the game;
b. your ankle is swollen (**hinchado**); and
c. you cannot walk.

Ask questions and answer your doctor's questions.

Role B. A patient comes to see you with a sports injury. After you hear how the injury happened, ask:

a. what the coach did for him/her, and;
b. how he/she got to the health center.

After determining that the ankle is not broken, recommend that the patient:

a. rest for three or four days;
b. take medication (**una pastilla**) for the pain; and
c. put ice on his/her ankle to reduce the swelling (**reducir la hinchazón**).

Add that because of the injury, he/she should not play soccer for a month.

	ROLE A	ROLE B
Vocabulario	Health and injuries	Health and injuries
Funciones y formas	Explaining reason for a condition Describing symptoms Asking and answering questions: *Por/para*	Asking and answering questions Giving advice: *Por/para* Subjunctive

INTERCAMBIOS. Practica la conversación con tu compañero/a incorporando el vocabulario y las funciones de *Preparación*. Luego, represéntenla ante la clase.

EN ACCIÓN

No me encuentro bien

11-27 Antes de ver 

¿No te sientes bien? Asocia las definiciones de la columna de la izquierda con las palabras de la columna de la derecha.

1. _____ Vende productos naturales y hierbas medicinales.
2. _____ Vamos a este lugar cuando estamos muy enfermos o en caso de emergencia.
3. _____ Lo tomamos cuando tenemos una infección.
4. _____ Aquí compramos medicamentos con receta médica y también artículos de belleza.
5. _____ Es un sitio para curas físicas y espirituales.
6. _____ Es la parte del cuerpo que nos duele cuando comemos mucho.

a. la botánica
b. el hospital
c. el estómago
d. la farmacia
e. el herbolario
f. el antibiótico

11-28 Mientras ves  

Problemas de la salud. Después de su celebración de cumpleaños, Yolanda no se siente bien. Indica si las siguientes afirmaciones son ciertas (**C**) o falsas (**F**) según la información de este segmento de video. Corrige las afirmaciones falsas.

1. _____ A Yolanda le duele el estómago porque comió mucho.
2. _____ Yolanda quiere consultar a su médico.
3. _____ Cuando era niña, Vanesa tomaba antibióticos frecuentemente.
4. _____ En general, Yolanda goza de buena salud.
5. _____ La familia de Yolanda prefiere tomar productos naturales y caseros.
6. _____ El herbolario Morando es uno de los más modernos de Madrid.
7. _____ El herbolario Morando se especializa en plantas medicinales.
8. _____ En México, las botánicas venden medicinas para enfermedades graves.
9. _____ Las personas van a las botánicas por problemas de salud y también espirituales.
10. _____ En Los Ángeles no hay botánicas.

11-29 Después de ver 

Consejos. PREPARACIÓN. Escoge la mejor recomendación para las siguientes situaciones.

1. Yolanda tiene dolor de estómago. Le recomiendo que...
   a. tome un té de manzanilla (*chamomile*).
   b. coma solamente pasta por unos días.
   c. beba mucha leche.
2. A Vanesa no le gustan los antibióticos y las inyecciones. Le recomiendo que...
   a. vaya a la sala de emergencia.
   b. visite un herbolario.
   c. hable con un farmacéutico.
3. Muchas personas tienen problemas espirituales. Les recomiendo que...
   a. visiten una botánica.
   b. hagan más ejercicio.
   c. aumenten la cantidad de agua que toman diariamente.

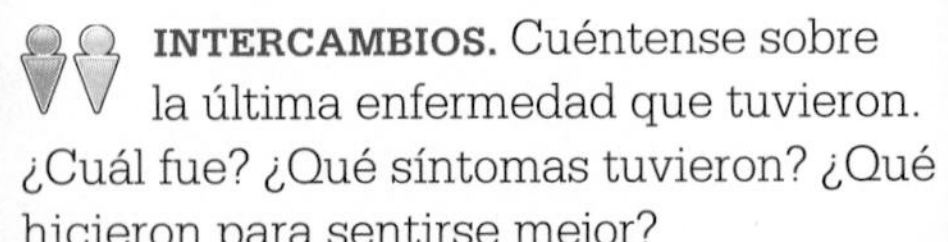

INTERCAMBIOS. Cuéntense sobre la última enfermedad que tuvieron. ¿Cuál fue? ¿Qué síntomas tuvieron? ¿Qué hicieron para sentirse mejor?

Mosaicos

ESCUCHA

Preparación. Van a escuchar una conversación entre un nutricionista y un grupo de estudiantes universitarios. Antes de escuchar, escriban dos preguntas que los alumnos probablemente le harán al nutricionista y dos sugerencias que les dará el nutricionista. Presenten sus preguntas y sugerencias a la clase, y escriban entre todos una lista.

ESTRATEGIA

Listen for the main idea

You can focus your attention on the main ideas when you listen by following these tips:

1. Rely on knowledge of the topic to make connections.
2. Think about the specific words or concepts you may hear.
3. Pay attention to the introduction and the conclusion, where the main ideas are usually stated.
4. Listen for transitional phrases that signal main ideas, such as **Lo importante es..., Recuerde(n)..., Otro punto importante/central...**

11-31  

Escucha. Mark (✓) the statements that best identify the main ideas of what you heard.

1. _____ Consultar al médico una vez por año es importante para evitar enfermedades.
2. _____ El consumo de tomates, lechugas, uvas, naranjas, cerveza y carne de res es recomendable para tener energía.
3. _____ La buena alimentación y el ejercicio tienen un efecto positivo en la salud.
4. _____ Se recomienda comer bastante y hacer muchísimo ejercicio para mantener una vida saludable.
5. _____ Bajar de peso afecta positivamente la salud y la apariencia de las personas.
6. _____ La buena salud requiere disciplina.

Comprueba

I was able to ...

_____ use my knowledge of the topic to anticipate what I would probably hear.

_____ listen for parts of the conversation where main ideas are about to be presented.

_____ identify the main ideas.

11-32 

Un paso más. Háganse las siguientes preguntas. ¿Tienen los mismos hábitos de salud? Comparen sus puntos de vista.

1. ¿Qué hábitos de comida y actividad física tienes? ¿Son tus hábitos buenos o malos?
2. ¿Crees que eres lo que comes?
3. ¿Qué aspecto de tu vida piensas que puedes cambiar para mejorar tu estado físico?

HABLA

11-33

Preparación. Marca (✓) los hábitos o condiciones que ayudan a prolongar la vida de las personas.

1. _____ hacer ejercicio físico regularmente
2. _____ trabajar poco
3. _____ poner el cuerpo bajo mucho estrés
4. _____ ser vegetariano/a
5. _____ beber vino con el almuerzo o la cena
6. _____ llevar una vida sedentaria
7. _____ tomar remedios caseros para curar el catarro
8. _____ evitar fracturarse los huesos

ESTRATEGIA

Select appropriate phrases to offer opinions

When you are talking with someone, it is natural to offer opinions and evaluations of what the other person has said and to express agreement or disagreement. An effective way to do this is to acknowledge the value of what the other person has said and then express your reaction to it.

11-34 

Habla. Entrevista a tu compañero/a sobre los temas siguientes. Reacciona y opina según lo que escuches. Da recomendaciones cuando sea necesario.

1. sus actividades
2. sus hábitos de comida
3. las bebidas que toma cuando sale con sus amigos

En directo

To congratulate or praise someone:

Felicitaciones por mantenerte en forma.

Te felicito. Te cuidas muy bien.

¡Qué bien! Vas a vivir por muchos años.

To express happiness at someone's success:

Me alegro de que + *subjunctive...*

¡Qué fabuloso que + *subjunctive...!*

To introduce a contrasting opinion:

Lo que dices es interesante, pero mi perspectiva es diferente./Yo lo veo diferente.

Entiendo tu punto de vista, pero no estoy de acuerdo contigo.

 Listen to a conversation with these expressions.

Comprueba

In my conversation, I ...

_____ used the correct expressions to praise and encourage.

_____ used the appropriate expressions to acknowledge what the speaker said and then express a different opinion.

_____ used expressions effectively to make recommendations.

11-35

Un paso más. Usa la información de la entrevista a tu compañero/a para escribir un informe que incluya lo siguiente:

1. las actividades y hábitos de tu compañero/a.
2. una comparación con los tuyos.
3. tu opinión y recomendaciones para tener una vida más saludable.

En directo

To make a general recommendation:

Es importante/bueno/conveniente/aconsejable + *infinitive...*

To make a recommendation to someone specific:

Es importante que + *name(s)* + *subjunctive...*

 Listen to a conversation with these expressions.

LEE

11-36

Preparación. De la siguiente lista, indica las enfermedades tropicales que conoces. Después, habla con tu compañero/a sobre las ideas que esperan encontrar en el artículo.

1. _____ la viruela (*smallpox*)

2. _____ la tuberculosis

3. _____ el dengue

4. _____ el virus del Nilo

5. _____ la malaria

6. _____ la enfermedad del sueño

ESTRATEGIA

Focus on relevant information

Identifying the relevant information in a text and disregarding what you think is irrelevant helps you read faster and understand more. Techniques that help you identify what is important include a) reading the titles and subtitles; b) looking at the visuals and reading the captions; c) brainstorming possible content by using your knowledge of the topic; and d) comparing those ideas with what you find as you read.

11-37

Lee. Según el contenido del artículo en la página siguiente, selecciona las expresiones de la derecha que se relacionan con los siguientes temas.

TEMAS	EXPRESIONES RELACIONADAS
enfermedades tropicales	las infecciones la viruela la tuberculosis el virus del Nilo
desafíos de las enfermedades para los expertos	la infección la adaptabilidad el desarrollo la evolución la resistencia
medidas que los gobiernos toman para enfrentar estas enfermedades	campañas inmunización reproducción vacunas prevención

Comprueba

I was able to …

____ **distinguish between main and secondary ideas.**

____ **identify key terms related to the main ideas.**

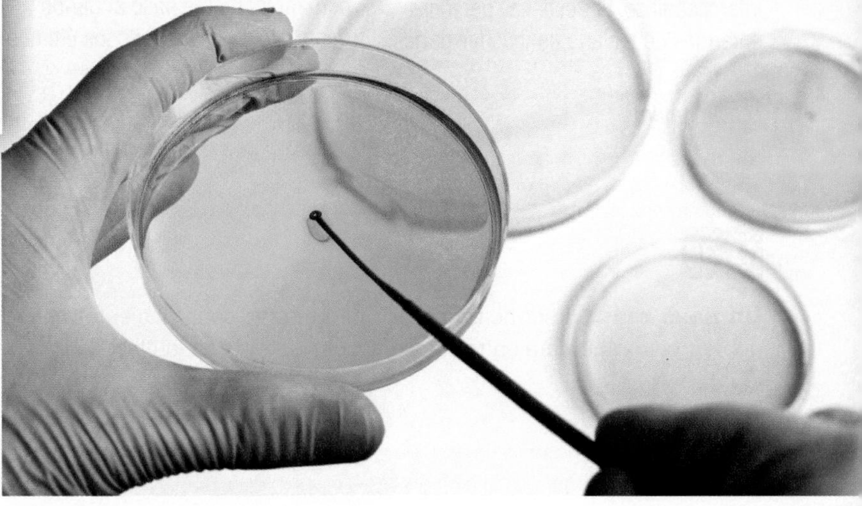

LAS ENFERMEDADES Y LA GLOBALIZACIÓN

Enfermedades tropicales como el dengue, la viruela, la malaria, la tuberculosis y el virus del Nilo que, según muchos expertos, ya no existían, ahora reaparecen y se extienden por todo el mundo. Las causas de su reaparición son evidentes: cambios en el medio ambiente[1] y el constante movimiento de personas entre los continentes. Los turistas, los trabajadores migratorios y los inmigrantes transportan estos virus e infecciones. De la misma manera, los cambios climáticos facilitan la adaptación de los virus a nuevos ambientes y los hacen resistentes.

BACTERIAS, PARÁSITOS Y VIRUS VIAJEROS Y RESISTENTES

Un claro ejemplo de la adaptabilidad de estas enfermedades infecciosas es la tuberculosis. Los científicos pensaban que estaba controlada en los países desarrollados. Sin embargo, los hechos nos muestran que esta enfermedad ha evolucionado y ha retornado.

La Organización Mundial de la Salud (OMS) expresa gran preocupación por la malaria. El mosquito que la provoca puede sobrevivir largos viajes interoceánicos. Por eso, hay personas enfermas de malaria en muchas partes del mundo. La malaria es peligrosa si no se detecta a tiempo. Los médicos sin experiencia en este tipo de enfermedades la pueden confundir con la gripe y tratarla con medicamentos inadecuados.

El virus del Nilo constituye otra enfermedad que afecta a los turistas. Se reportaron 3.500 casos de la enfermedad en Estados Unidos en el 2007, de los que murieron más de cien personas.

LAS ENFERMEDADES MIGRATORIAS

A fines del siglo XX, gracias a una campaña mundial contra la viruela, casi toda la población mundial fue inmunizada contra esta enfermedad. Sin embargo, en Estados Unidos ha sido necesario fabricar vacunas contra la viruela que no se producían desde hacía años.

El dengue es indudablemente la enfermedad más extendida del mundo en los últimos años. Los expertos afirman que es posible que el 40% de la población del mundo contraiga[2] esta mortal fiebre. Geográficamente, el dengue nació en el suroeste de Asia, pero rápidamente pasó al Caribe y Centro y Sudamérica. En los últimos años se han descubierto casos incluso en España.

▲ La malaria aumenta a causa de las inundaciones del río Amazonas.

La lista de enfermedades que surgen de nuevo por la movilidad de la población del mundo actual es larga, pero los fondos mundiales para realizar investigaciones sobre las enfermedades que causan el 90% de las muertes en el mundo son mínimos y limitados. Sin duda, la globalización ha resuelto algunos problemas, pero ha creado otros.

[1] *environment*

[2] *contracts*

Un paso más. Escribe un párrafo informativo sobre las enfermedades tropicales y las medidas que los gobiernos toman para enfrentarlas, y compártelo con la clase.

ESCRIBE

11-39

Preparación. Lee este correo electrónico de uno de tus buenos amigos. Después, escribe tres problemas que tiene Tomás y algunas ideas para ayudarlo a resolver cada problema.

Hola:

Perdón por no escribirte antes, pero últimamente no me siento bien. No puedo trabajar un día completo y no tengo apetito. No tengo energía para cocinar, así que a veces como solo sopa enlatada. Otras veces voy a un restaurante de comida rápida. Tomo café constantemente, porque necesito la cafeína para sobrevivir, pero luego no puedo dormir. Mi vida es una pesadilla. Quisiera ver a un médico, pero no tengo dinero. ¿Qué me aconsejas?

Bueno, escríbeme para saber de ti. Te contestaré tan pronto pueda.

Un fuerte abrazo,

Tomás

PROBLEMAS DE TOMÁS	ALGUNAS POSIBLES SOLUCIONES
1.	1.
2.	2.
3.	3.

ESTRATEGIA

Persuade through suggestions and advice

Well-structured suggestions and advice are important for effective persuasion in writing. Remember to …

- decide whether to address your reader as **tú** or **usted,** based on your relationship (e.g., friend vs. supervisor at work).
- select suggestions that match the nature of your relationship.

En directo

To express concern or sympathy:

Me preocupa (mucho) que…

Siento/Lamento que…

Qué lástima que…

To persuade a friend through suggestions:

Te recomiendo/sugiero/aconsejo que…

Es importante/necesario/urgente/mejor que…

Ojalá (que)…

 Listen to a conversation with these expressions.

11-40

Escribe. Responde al correo electrónico de Tomás. Usa la información de la actividad 11-39 y expresa tus sentimientos o preocupación por los problemas. Indícale algunas sugerencias para que los resuelva.

Comprueba

I was able to ...

____ **use a familiar tone to communicate with a friend.**

____ **use appropriate expressions to express concern and sympathy.**

____ **use appropriate suggestions for effective persuasion.**

____ **use transitions effectively to move from one idea to the next.**

En directo

To put ideas together coherently:

Por un lado...

On one hand ...

Por otro (lado)...

On the other (hand) ...

En primer/segundo lugar...

In the first/second place ...

Además...

Besides/In addition/Furthermore ...

To contrast ideas:

No obstante... *However ...*

Sin embargo... *Nevertheless ...*

 Listen to a conversation with these expressions.

11-41

Un paso más. Lean los correos electrónicos que cada uno/a le escribió a Tomás y comenten lo siguiente:

1. ¿Qué problemas de Tomás les parecen más serios? ¿Por qué?
2. ¿Qué soluciones le proponen ustedes? ¿Por qué?

En este capítulo…

Comprueba lo que sabes

Go to ***MySpanishLab*** to review what you have learned in this chapter. Practice with the following:

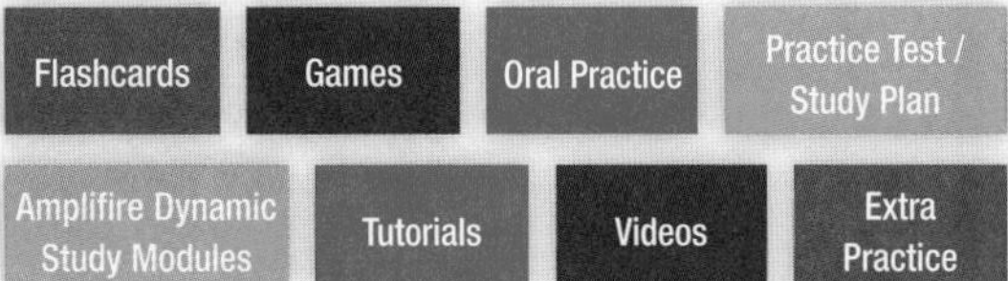

Vocabulario

EL CUERPO HUMANO
The human body

la boca *mouth*
el brazo *arm*
la cabeza *head*
la cadera *hip*
la cara *face*
la ceja *eyebrow*
el cerebro *brain*
la cintura *waist*
el codo *elbow*
el corazón *heart*
el cuello *neck*
el dedo *finger*
el diente *tooth*
la espalda *back*
el estómago *stomach*
la frente *forehead*
la garganta *throat*
el hombro *shoulder*
el hueso *bone*
el labio *lip*
la mano *hand*
la mejilla *cheek*
la muñeca *wrist*
el músculo *muscle*
la nariz *nose*
el nervio *nerve*
el oído *(inner) ear*
la oreja *(outer) ear*
el pecho *chest*
el pelo/cabello *hair*
la pestaña *eyelash*
el pie *foot*
la pierna *leg*
el pulmón *lung*
la rodilla *knee*
la sangre *blood*
el tobillo *ankle*
la vena *vein*

LOS PROVEEDORES DE SALUD
Healthcare providers

la clínica/el centro de salud/el sanatorio *clinic*
el/la farmacéutico/a *pharmacist*
la farmacia *pharmacy*
el gobierno *government*
el hospital *hospital*

LOS TRATAMIENTOS MÉDICOS
Medical treatments

el antibiótico *antibiotic*
la inyección *injection*
la medicina *medicine*
la pastilla *pill*
la receta *prescription*
el remedio *remedy, medicine*
el termómetro *thermometer*

LA SALUD
Health

la alergia *allergy*
el asma *asthma*
el catarro *cold*
el dolor *pain*
la enfermedad *illness*
el/la enfermo/a *ill person*
la fiebre *fever*
la gripe *flu*
la infección *infection*
el/la paciente *patient*
el síntoma *symptom*
la tensión/la presión (arterial) *(blood) pressure*
la tos *cough*

VERBOS
Verbs

alegrarse (de) *to be glad (about)*
caer(se) *to fall*
cuidar(se) (de) *to take care of*
curar *to cure*
doler (ue) *to hurt, ache*
estornudar *to sneeze*
examinar *to examine*
fracturar(se) *to fracture, break*
fumar *to smoke*
molestar(le) *to bother, be bothered by*
recetar *to prescribe*
respirar *to breathe*
sentir (ie, i) *to feel*
temer *to fear*
torcer(se) (ue) *to twist*
toser *to cough*
tratar *to treat*

PALABRAS Y EXPRESIONES ÚTILES
Useful words and expressions

el artículo de belleza *beauty item*
cada… horas *every … hours*
¿Qué te/le(s) pasa? *What's wrong (with you/them)?*
tener dolor de… *to have a(n) … ache*
tener mala cara *to look terrible*

LAS DESCRIPCIONES
Descriptions

enfermo/a *sick*
grave *serious*
serio/a *serious*

12 ¿Te gusta viajar?

ENFOQUE CULTURAL
Costa Rica y Panamá

VOCABULARIO EN CONTEXTO
Los medios de transporte
El alojamiento y las reservaciones
Viajando en coche

MOSAICO CULTURAL
El mochilero

FUNCIONES Y FORMAS
Affirmative and negative expressions
Subjunctive in adjective clauses
Possessive pronouns
Subjunctive with expressions of doubt

EN ACCIÓN
Lugares fantásticos

MOSAICOS
ESCUCHA Use background knowledge to support comprehension
HABLA Make your presentations comprehensible and interesting
LEE Focus on logical relationships
ESCRIBE Use facts to offer advice

EN ESTE CAPÍTULO...
Comprueba lo que sabes
Vocabulario

LEARNING **OUTCOMES**

You will be able to:

- talk about travel arrangements and preferences
- express possession and clarify what belongs to you and to others
- express affirmation and negation
- express doubt and uncertainty
- talk about travel experiences
- share information about the social and economic impact of the Panama Canal

ENFOQUE cultural COSTA RICA Y PANAMÁ

Enfoque cultural

To learn more about Costa Rica and Panama, go to MySpanishLab to view the *Vistas culturales* videos.

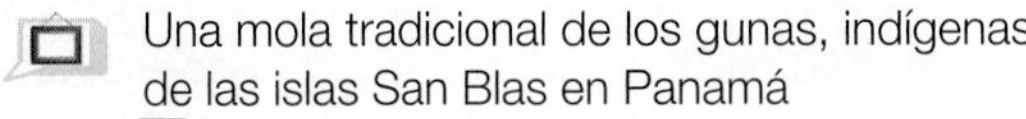

Una mola tradicional de los gunas, indígenas de las islas San Blas en Panamá

¿QUÉ TE PARECE?

- Para muchos estadounidenses, Costa Rica y Panamá son países predilectos para retirarse.
- Panamá, también llamada la nueva Suiza, es uno de los centros bancarios del mundo.
- Panamá es el país natal de varios cantantes de reguetón, como Flex (Félix Danilo Gómez), Eddy Lover (Eduardo Mosquera), El General (Edgardo Franco), La Factoría, Makano (Ernán Enrique Jiménez) y Nando Boom.
- Costa Rica es el único país latinoamericano sin ejército.

ENFOQUE cultural

◀ La mola es una prenda hecha de varias piezas de tela. Algunas molas son de colores brillantes, otras tienen dibujos geométricos. Los gunas las usan para hacer blusas y fundas de almohada. Algunas molas son verdaderas obras de arte.

▲ El Canal de Panamá tiene 48 millas. El viaje dura unas quince horas y los barcos pasan por tres esclusas (*locks*). El Canal de Panamá une el océano Atlántico y el océano Pacífico.

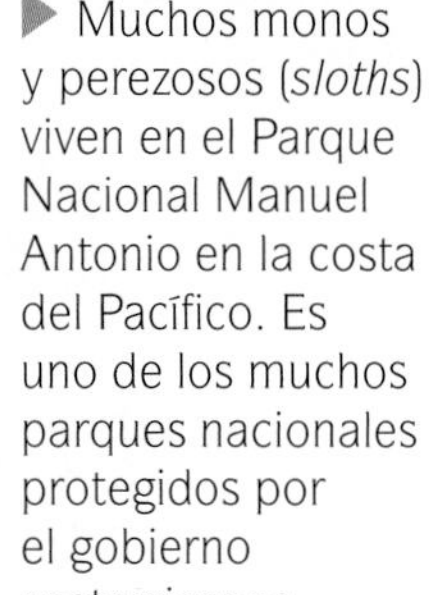

▶ Muchos monos y perezosos (*sloths*) viven en el Parque Nacional Manuel Antonio en la costa del Pacífico. Es uno de los muchos parques nacionales protegidos por el gobierno costarricense.

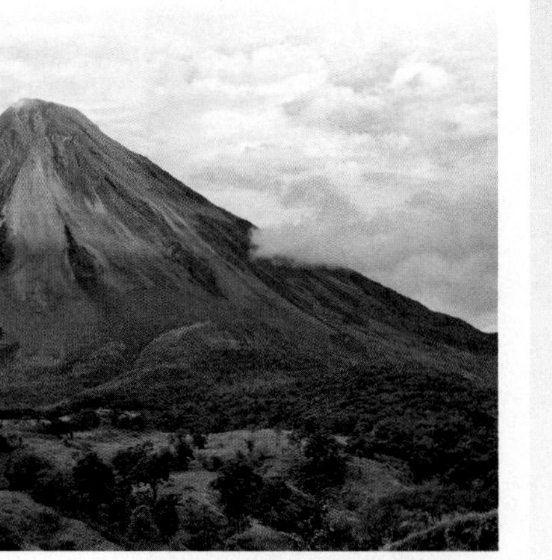

▲ Costa Rica tiene montañas, volcanes activos, playas bonitas, lagos y mucha diversidad de flora y fauna.

¿CUÁNTO SABES?

Completa las siguientes oraciones con la información correcta.

1. Una de las atracciones turísticas de Costa Rica es ____________.
2. Un animal que vive en los parques nacionales es ____________.
3. Los miembros de una tribu indígena que vive en Panamá se llaman ____________.
4. La mola se usa para hacer ____________ y ____________.
5. El Canal de Panamá conecta ____________ y ____________.
6. Un tipo de música popular en Panamá es ____________.
7. El único país latinoamericano sin ejército es ____________.

Vocabulario en contexto

Talking about travel arrangements and modes of travel

Los medios de transporte

MySpanishLab
Learn more using Amplifire Dynamic Study Modules, Pronunciation, and Vocabulary Tutorials.

▲ Mucha gente usa el transporte público. Los **autobuses** son populares en las ciudades y también para **viajar** largas distancias. Son la solución para las personas que no tienen carro, o a quienes simplemente no les gusta **manejar** en las **carreteras** y **autopistas.** El **metro** es otra forma de transporte eficiente en los centros urbanos, como Madrid, Barcelona, Santiago, Buenos Aires, Caracas y la Ciudad de México.

▲ El AVE, el **tren** español de alta **velocidad** entre Madrid y otras grandes ciudades españolas, viaja a unos 300 kilómetros por hora. La RENFE (Red Nacional de Ferrocarriles Españoles) es tan importante en España como las **líneas aéreas** en Estados Unidos. Gracias al turismo se ha recuperado en Costa Rica la antigua tradición de **recorrer** el país en tren. Algunas agencias organizan **excursiones** desde San José a la costa este.

◀ El **crucero** es otra forma de viajar. En **barcos** modernos con una capacidad de 400 hasta más de 2.000 **pasajeros,** se puede hacer de todo. En las **escalas** en los diferentes puertos hay excursiones organizadas y oportunidades para ir de compras. De noche, la diversión continúa en la discoteca, el casino y el teatro. El barco es un medio de transporte y también puede servir para pasar las vacaciones.

En el avión

El avión es la manera, aunque más cara, de viajar rápidamente de un lugar a otro, especialmente en zonas como las selvas y en las montañas, donde es difícil construir carreteras por la geografía o el clima. Hoy en día, los viajes en avión son más comunes; se ofrecen **vuelos** domésticos entre muchas ciudades de los países hispanos.

EN OTRAS PALABRAS

Other words for **auxiliar de vuelo** are **azafato/a,** used especially in Spain, and **aeromozo/a,** used mostly in Latin America. To buy a ticket in Latin America you will most likely hear people use the terms **pasaje** or **boleto,** while in Spain the word **billete** is more common.

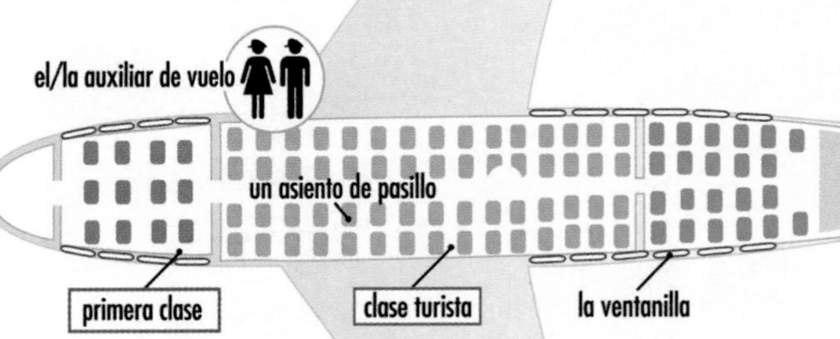

En el aeropuerto

Los pasajeros **hacen cola** frente al **mostrador** de la **aerolínea** para **facturar** el **equipaje,** pedir un **asiento** y conseguir la **tarjeta de embarque** para su **vuelo.** Algunos prefieren hacer esto por Internet.

 **En el mostrador de la línea aérea**

EMPLEADA: Buenos días. Su **pasaporte** y su **boleto,** por favor.

VIAJERO: Aquí están. Y si es posible, prefiero un asiento cerca de una **salida de emergencia.**

EMPLEADA: Muy bien. ¿**Ventanilla** o **pasillo**?

VIAJERO: Pasillo, por favor. Señorita, ¿me puede decir dónde hay un **cajero automático** aquí en el aeropuerto?

EMPLEADA: Sí, hay una oficina del Banco Popular enfrente a la derecha.

VIAJERO: Gracias. ¿Me acreditó los kilómetros a mi programa de viajero frecuente?

EMPLEADA: Sí, y su **pasaje** es **de ida y vuelta,** así que va a tener bastantes kilómetros. Su asiento a San José es el 10F. Aquí tiene su tarjeta de embarque. La puerta de salida es la C20. ¡Que tenga un buen viaje!

PRÁCTICA

12-1

Escucha y confirma. Listen to the following questions about transportation and select the correct response.

1. **a.** el metro **b.** el autobús
2. **a.** el AVE **b.** la RENFE
3. **a.** el crucero **b.** el avión
4. **a.** facturar el equipaje **b.** hacer escalas
5. **a.** en el mostrador **b.** en el cajero automático
6. **a.** el boleto de ida y vuelta **b.** el pasaporte

EN OTRAS PALABRAS

Depending on the region, different words for **autobús** are used: **camión** (Mexico), **ómnibus** (Peru), **bus, guagua** (Puerto Rico, Cuba), **colectivo** (Argentina), **micro** (Chile), or **chiva** (Colombia).

12-2

Asociaciones. Asocia cada palabra con su descripción. Luego, compara tus respuestas con las de tu compañero/a y dile qué medio de transporte prefieres y por qué.

1. _____ transporte público para viajar por las calles de la ciudad
2. _____ viaje en un barco grande de pasajeros
3. _____ persona que atiende a los pasajeros en un vuelo
4. _____ transporte subterráneo
5. _____ lugar de inspección al llegar a otro país
6. _____ identificación necesaria para viajar al extranjero
7. _____ pasaje para ir y volver
8. _____ se viaja en un asiento cómodo y se come bien

a. el/la auxiliar de vuelo
b. pasaporte
c. primera clase
d. autobús
e. metro
f. aduana
g. boleto de ida y vuelta
h. crucero

12-3 **Salidas y llegadas.** Miren los horarios y la puerta de salida de los siguientes vuelos y háganse preguntas.

MODELO E1: *¿A qué hora sale el vuelo para San José?*

E2: *El avión para San José sale a las tres y media por la puerta 1A.*

SALIDA DEPARTURE	ABORDAR BOARDING	PUERTA GATE	DESTINO DESTINATION
3:30	3:00	1A	SAN JOSÉ
3:50	3:20	4	MANAGUA
4:10	3:40	6	GUATEMALA
4:25	3:55	10	PANAMÁ
4:45	4:15	8	LIMÓN
5:10	4:40	5	MÉXICO D.F.
6:00	5:30	5	KINGSTON

12-4 **Problemas en los viajes.** Túrnense para completar las conversaciones y resolver los problemas.

MODELO E1: *Estoy en Madrid y tengo que ir a Barcelona inmediatamente.*

E2: *Te recomiendo que tomes el AVE. El tren va muy rápido.*

	ESTUDIANTE 1	ESTUDIANTE 2
1.	No me gusta manejar en las ciudades grandes. ¿Qué hago?	No hay problema. En las ciudades grandes, hay... Te recomiendo que tomes...
2.	No pude imprimir mi tarjeta de embarque en casa porque no tengo Internet. ¿Qué hago?	No es difícil. Al llegar al aeropuerto, tienes que...
3.	Tengo miedo de viajar por avión pero quiero ir de Chicago a Seattle.	Si te gustan los paisajes espectaculares pero no quieres manejar, te sugiero que...
4.	Dejé mi pasaporte en casa y mi vuelo para San José sale en cuatro horas.	¡Ay, qué problema! Te aconsejo que...

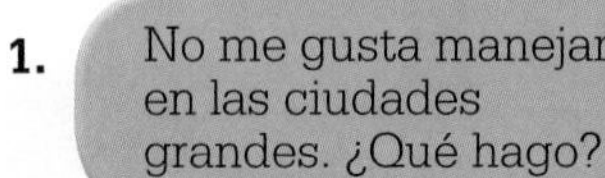

Cultura

Parque Nacional de Isla del Coco

El Parque Nacional Isla del Coco se encuentra en el océano Pacífico a unos 550 kilómetros de la costa costarricense. Es un espacio protegido y una reserva natural con numerosas especies animales y vegetales autóctonas. Los visitantes llegan atraídos por la naturaleza salvaje y limpia con el deseo de encontrarse en una isla deshabitada llena de bosques y cascadas donde se puede pescar y caminar. Solo se puede llegar a la isla por barco en un viaje que dura unas 36 horas. Por su interés natural viven allí numerosos biólogos e investigadores del medio ambiente. Debido a la riqueza del ecosistema, el turismo está muy regulado para proteger el equilibrio medioambiental.

Comparaciones. ¿Existe en tu país un parque nacional de características semejantes a las del Parque Nacional Isla del Coco? ¿Qué parque nacional de tu país te gusta más? ¿Por qué?

12-5 **Haciendo turismo en Costa Rica o Panamá.** Tu compañero/a y tú quieren viajar a Costa Rica o Panamá. Seleccionen su destino y usen la información cultural del capítulo para planear su itinerario. Incluyan en el itinerario la información de la lista. Después, presenten su itinerario a la clase y digan por qué eligieron ese destino.

DESTINOS:	
COSTA RICA	**PANAMÁ**
• Parque Nacional Isla del Coco	• Canal de Panamá

Itinerario:

1. destino y por qué lo seleccionaron
2. fechas de viaje (número de días)
3. tipo de boleto aéreo (primera clase o clase turista) y asiento (ventanilla, etc.) y por qué lo seleccionaron
4. medio de transporte que prefieren utilizar en el lugar
5. sus actividades

El alojamiento y las reservaciones

Buscando alojamiento

EMPLEADO: Buenas tardes. ¿En qué les puedo servir?

SRA. CANO: Buenas tardes. Tenemos dos **habitaciones** reservadas a nuestro nombre, señores Cano.

EMPLEADO: Sí, señora. Tengo una **doble** y una **sencilla.**

SRA. CANO: Muy bien. Una es para nosotros y otra para nuestro hijo. Quisiera dejar los pasaportes en un lugar seguro. ¿Podría usted…?

EMPLEADO: ¿Por qué no los deja en la **caja fuerte** de su habitación?

SRA. CANO: Muy bien.

EMPLEADO: Bueno, aquí tiene dos **tarjetas magnéticas.** Ya no usamos **llaves.** Sus habitaciones están en el segundo piso.

SR. CANO: Y…, ¿nos puede indicar cómo llegar a la Plaza Cinco de Mayo?

EMPLEADO: Sí, cómo no. Mire, **salgan** del edificio y **doblen** a la derecha. **Sigan derecho** por esta calle hasta la próxima **esquina.** Allí, **doblen** a la izquierda y caminen una **cuadra** hasta la plaza que está a la derecha. No pueden **perderse.**

SR. CANO: Muchísimas gracias.

PRÁCTICA

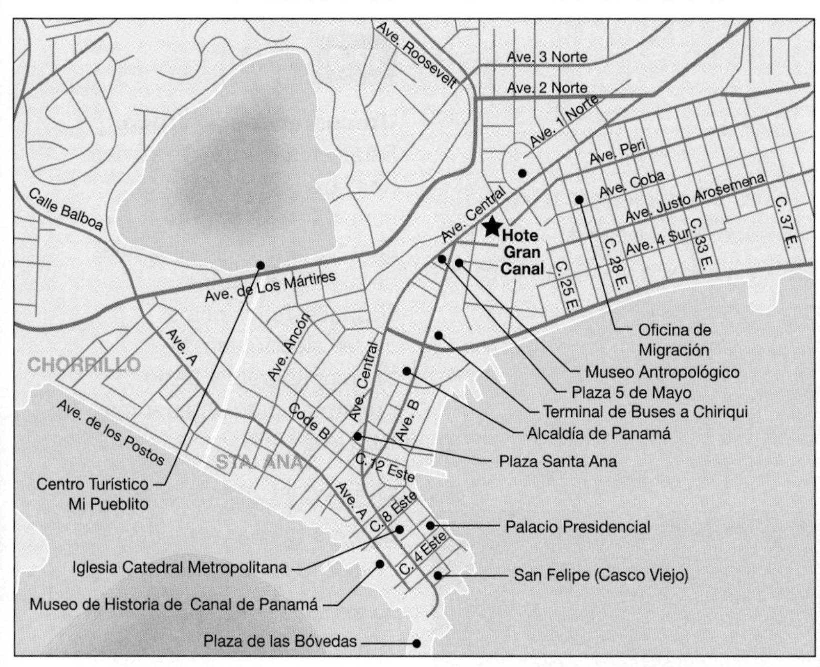

 **12-6** 

Para confirmar. Estás perdido/a en la Ciudad de Panamá. Usando el plano, pregúntale a una persona en la calle (tu compañero/a) cómo ir a ciertos lugares. Tu compañero/a debe explicarte cómo llegar.

ESTÁS EN…	DESEAS IR…
la Plaza 5 de Mayo	al Palacio Presidencial
la Avenida Ancón y la Avenida A	a San Felipe
el Museo de Historia del Canal de Panamá	al Centro Turístico Mi Pueblito

 Estás en el Hotel Gran Canal. Quieres ir a la Oficina de Migración.

E1: *¿Me puede decir cómo llegar a la Oficina de Migración, por favor?*

E2: *Sí, cómo no. La Oficina de Migración está cerca del hotel. Siga derecho por la Avenida Peri. Doble a la derecha en la Calle 27 E. Camine una cuadra y doble a la izquierda en la Avenida Coba. La Oficina de Migración está en la Avenida Coba entre la Calle 27 Este y la Calle 28 Este.*

12-7 

En el hotel. Túrnense para hacer el papel de recepcionista de hotel y cliente en las siguientes situaciones. Usen el vocabulario y las expresiones de la lista. Después, escojan una situación y preséntenla a la clase.

una habitación doble/sencilla	la tarjeta magnética	Quisiera...
la llave	el equipaje	¿Dónde...?
una reservación	la caja fuerte	¿Podría...?

	CLIENTE	RECEPCIONISTA
SITUACIÓN 1	Llega al hotel y necesita una habitación.	Hace muchas preguntas.
SITUACIÓN 2	Necesita una habitación con dos camas para él/ella y su amigo/a pero no tiene reservación.	Solo tiene una habitación sencilla.
SITUACIÓN 3	Quiere reservar una habitación por teléfono, pero no quiere dar su número de tarjeta de crédito.	Para garantizar la reservación debe dar el número de tarjeta de crédito.

Cultura

Bocas del Toro

Isla Colón es la isla principal del archipiélago de Bocas del Toro en el noroeste de Panamá. La ciudad principal lleva el nombre del archipiélago. Esta ciudad es uno de los centros turísticos más importantes de Panamá. Se puede acceder a ella mediante barco o avión, pues cuenta con un aeropuerto internacional. Los turistas viajan a Isla Colón durante todo el año atraídos por las playas y el clima templado. Una atracción turística importante es el surf y la práctica de deportes acuáticos.

Comparaciones. ¿Por qué crees que mucha gente prefiere pasar sus vacaciones cerca del mar? En tu opinión, ¿hay otro lugar mejor para pasar las vacaciones? Explica.

12-8 

Un correo electrónico. Estás en Panamá y le envías un correo electrónico a tu compañero/a. Cuéntale algunos aspectos especiales de tus experiencias. Después, reacciona al correo electrónico de tu compañero/a y hazle preguntas para obtener más detalles.

1. lugar(es) que visitaste
2. lugar donde te quedaste y el tipo de alojamiento
3. personas que conociste
4. experiencias divertidas o especiales que viviste
5. comida nueva que probaste
6. regalos que compraste

Viajando en coche

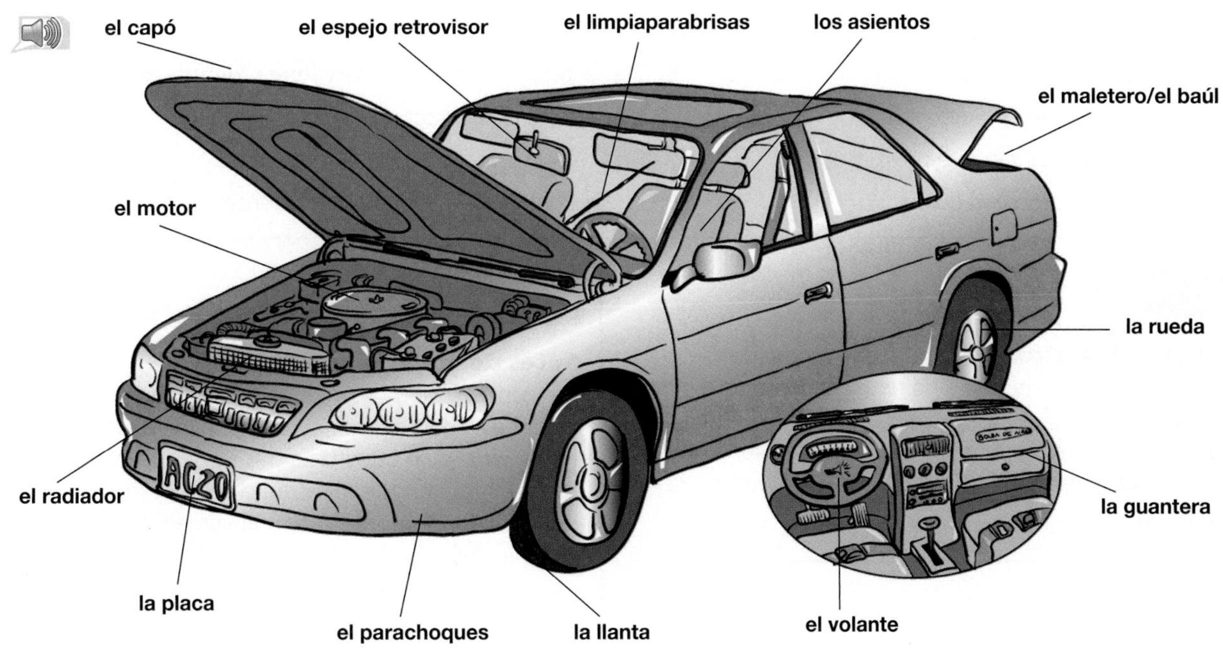

Un episodio desafortunado

Estaba en la **autopista** 95. Mi carro **se descompuso.** Por las **luces** de la consola pensé que era el **radiador** o el **motor.** Saqué el manual de la **guantera.** Traté de bajarme del carro, pero por el **espejo retrovisor** vi que venía una larga fila de vehículos. Mientras esperaba, puse las **luces intermitentes.** Me quedé con las manos al **volante** y quise limpiar el **parabrisas,** pero el **limpiaparabrisas** no funcionaba y el motor se apagó. Me bajé para abrir el **capó** cuando vi un carro patrulla de la policía. Sin decirme una palabra, el policía tomó nota de la **placa** de mi carro, se acercó a mí y me pidió la **licencia de conducir.** Intenté explicarle que tenía problemas eléctricos con el carro, pero me puso una **multa** por estar **mal aparcado.**

PRÁCTICA

12-9 

Para confirmar. Digan la palabra que corresponde a las siguientes descripciones. Después, describan otras partes del coche para ver si otra pareja sabe cómo se llama cada una.

1. Es para poner el equipaje.
2. Permite ver bien cuando llueve.
3. Son negras y llevan aire por dentro.
4. Controla la dirección del coche.
5. Tiene letras y números, y sirve para identificar el coche.
6. Le permite al conductor ver los carros que vienen detrás.
7. Se abre para ver el motor, el radiador, etc.
8. Protege al coche en caso de accidentes.

12-10 

Mi auto favorito. Averigüen qué medio de transporte usa cada uno/a de ustedes con más frecuencia. Después, pregúntense cuál es el auto favorito de cada uno/a y por qué. Cada persona debe decir cuatro características del auto para explicar su preferencia.

Cultura

Los autos y el transporte público

Aunque en los países hispanoamericanos se usa mucho el transporte público, el tráfico y la contaminación son problemas serios en las ciudades grandes. Además, cada vez es más difícil encontrar estacionamiento. Por eso se usan mucho las motos y los carros pequeños.

Comparaciones. ¿Qué medios de transporte hay en tu comunidad? ¿Cuáles son más populares entre los jóvenes? ¿Cuáles son más populares entre los mayores? ¿Qué problemas se asocian con el transporte en tu comunidad y tu región?

12-11 

Para evitar accidentes. Escriban un anuncio con recomendaciones para evitar accidentes de tráfico. El anuncio debe tener la siguiente información:

1. un título o eslogan
2. el nombre de la compañía o grupo que patrocina (*sponsors*) el anuncio
3. tres recomendaciones para evitar accidentes

12-12 

Antes de viajar. **PREPARACIÓN.** You will listen to a conversation between a man who is checking in at the airport and an airline employee. Before you listen, write two questions you think the employee will ask him and the answers you think the man will provide. Compare your answers with those of your partner.

ESCUCHA. Now listen to the exchange, and choose the appropriate ending to each statement.

1. El empleado le pide al viajero...
   - **a.** su boleto de ida y vuelta.
   - **b.** su tarjeta de embarque.
   - **c.** su pasaporte y su pasaje.
2. El viajero va a facturar...
   - **a.** tres maletas.
   - **b.** un maletín de mano.
   - **c.** dos maletas.
3. El viajero prefiere un asiento...
   - **a.** al lado de la ventanilla.
   - **b.** en el pasillo.
   - **c.** en la parte posterior del avión.
4. El empleado le puede conseguir un asiento...
   - **a.** de pasillo, el 28C.
   - **b.** en el centro, entre la ventanilla y el pasillo.
   - **c.** en la ventanilla en primera clase.
5. El empleado le dice al pasajero que...
   - **a.** tiene tiempo para llamar por teléfono.
   - **b.** puede llamar desde el avión.
   - **c.** no tiene que pasar por seguridad.

MOSAICO cultural

El mochilero

Cuando Edmundo celebró su cumpleaños número 22 —al mismo tiempo que terminó la universidad— decidió hacer un viaje por los lugares más atractivos del mundo hispano. En junio, Edmundo tomó su mochila, que estaba cargada con poca ropa y sus utensilios de *camping,* y se fue de viaje con poco dinero.

▲ **De excursión por el bosque en Panamá**

Edmundo decidió hacer algo común entre los jóvenes hispanos: ser *mochilero.* El plan de *mochilero* significaba viajar sin muchas complicaciones, adaptándose a las circunstancias inmediatas. Edmundo tomaba el transporte que tenía a la mano y dormía en los lugares donde le permitían usar su tienda (*tent*). "Fue un periodo muy bonito, conocí a mucha gente linda y aprendí mucho de la cultura de varios lugares que no conocía", dijo Edmundo.

▲ **Subiendo a la cima de Machu Picchu**

Para empezar, Edmundo tomó un autobús que lo llevó desde su casa en La Paz, Bolivia, hasta Oruro, a mitad del camino entre La Paz y Sucre. Allá acampó por dos días y conoció a un par de mochileros norteamericanos que estaban de visita. Luego de dos días y muchas experiencias, Edmundo salió para Perú. Este viaje le tomó cuatro días, porque lo hizo *echando dedo* (haciendo autostop). Edmundo se ubicaba al lado de las autopistas y esperaba que alguien lo llevara hasta Machu Picchu. Es una forma arriesgada de viajar porque no es muy eficiente y puede ser peligrosa, pero es mucho más económica que comprar boletos de avión. Cuando llegó a Machu Picchu, Edmundo le envió una postal a su mamá: "Mami, pasé por el lago Titicaca, ¡me encantó! Monté en bus, canoa, bicitaxi y ¡en un burro!".

Ir de Bolivia a Perú fue el primer tramo (*stretch*) de un camino mochilero extenso que se conoce como la ruta del gringo. Recibe este nombre por la gran cantidad de norteamericanos que lo visitan. Después de Machu Picchu, otros destinos comunes son Bocas del Toro en Panamá, Antigua y Tikal en Guatemala, Moctezuma en Costa Rica, y por supuesto, Chichén Itzá y Tulum en México. Edmundo viajó por dos meses antes de volver a La Paz.

▲ **La playa Cocles, Costa Rica**

Compara

1. ¿En tu cultura hay una palabra equivalente a mochilero? ¿En qué contextos se usa?
2. ¿Has oído la expresión *echar dedo?* ¿Es algo común en tu país? ¿Has practicado el autostop? Explica con detalles.
3. En tu cultura, ¿existe un viaje simbólico que hacen los jóvenes para ser adultos? Explícalo con ejemplos.
4. ¿Te gustaría tener la experiencia de viajar como mochilero? ¿Qué lugares te gustaría visitar y qué precauciones tomarías?

Funciones y formas

1 Expressing affirmation and negation

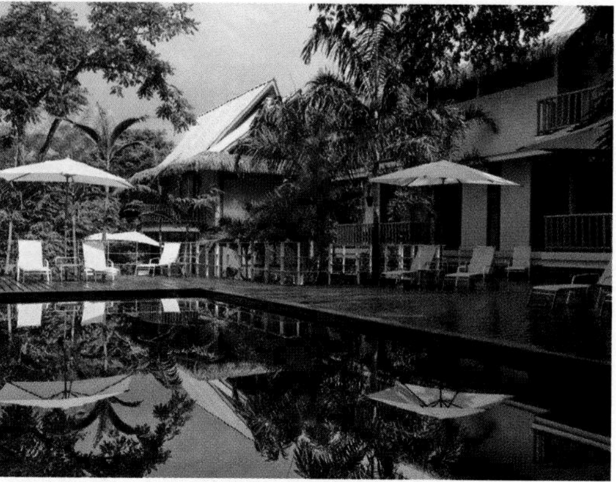

JOSEFINA: Alberto, tenemos que hablar de nuestro viaje a Costa Rica. **Siempre** trato de buscar alojamiento económico, pero no me gusta **ningún** hotel de hotelesbaratos.com. **Todos** parecen viejos y malos. Ese sitio web casi **nunca** nos da buenas recomendaciones; no lo voy a usar más.

ALBERTO: A mí **tampoco** me gusta ese sitio. **Nunca** encuentro **nada** que me guste. ¿Por qué no le pedimos una recomendación a tu amiga Maricelle? Es de San José, ¿no?

JOSEFINA: Buena idea. Seguramente tendrá **algunas** recomendaciones.

Piénsalo. Indica quién hace cada una de las afirmaciones a continuación: Josefina (**J**) o Alberto (**A**).

1. _____ **Siempre** trato de buscar alojamiento económico.
2. _____ No me gusta **ningún** hotel de hotelesbaratos.com.
3. _____ Casi **nunca** nos da buenas recomendaciones.
4. _____ A mí **tampoco** me gusta ese sitio.
5. _____ **Nunca** encuentro **nada** que me guste.
6. _____ Seguramente tendrá **algunas** recomendaciones.

Affirmative and negative expressions

- You have already seen and used some affirmative and negative expressions in previous chapters. In this section you will study the most frequently used expressions.

AFFIRMATIVE		NEGATIVE	
algo	*something, anything*	**nada**	*nothing*
todo	*everything*		
alguien	*someone, anyone*	**nadie**	*no one, nobody*
todos/as	*everybody, all*		
algún, alguno/a (-os, -as)	*some, any, several*	**ningún, ninguno/a**	*no, not any, none*
o... o	*either ... or*	**ni... ni**	*neither ... nor*
siempre	*always*	**nunca**	*never, (not) ever*

AFFIRMATIVE		NEGATIVE	
una vez	*once*		
alguna vez	*sometime, ever*	**jamás**	*never, (not) ever*
algunas veces	*sometimes*		
a veces	*at times*		
también	*also, too*	**tampoco**	*neither, not*

- Negative words may precede or follow the verb. If they follow the verb, use the word **no** before the verb.

Nadie va a ese museo.
No va **nadie** a ese museo.
No one/Nobody goes to that museum.

- **Alguno** and **ninguno** shorten to **algún** and **ningún** before masculine singular nouns.

¿Ves **algún** monumento interesante? — *Do you see any interesting monuments?*

No veo **ningún** monumento interesante. — *I do not see any interesting monuments.*

- Use the personal **a** when **alguno/a/os/as** and **ninguno/a** refer to persons and are the direct object of the verb. Use it also with **alguien** and **nadie** since they always refer to people. Note that negative statements are expressed in the singular.

¿Conoces a **alguno** de los guías? — *Do you know any of the guides?*

No, no conozco **a ninguno.** — *No, I do not know any (of them).*

¿Conoces **alguna** de las agencias de turismo? — *Do you know any tourism agencies?*

No, no conozco **ninguna.** — *No, I do not know any (of them).*

¿COMPRENDES?

Completa las afirmaciones para expresar lo contrario.

1. **Siempre** trato de buscar alojamiento económico.
   ________ trato de buscar alojamiento ecónomico. Prefiero los hoteles de lujo.
2. No me gusta ________ hotel de este sitio web porque son baratos y malos. Pero a Marcos le gustan ________ porque no tiene mucho dinero.
3. **Nunca** encuentro **nada** que me guste. Maricelle tiene mejor suerte. Ella ________ encuentra ________ hoteles que le gustan.
4. **Algunos** de mis amigos se alojan en albergues cuando viajan.
   Pero ________ amigo de mis padres se aloja allí. Las personas mayores prefieren los hoteles.

MySpanishLab
Learn more using Amplifire Dynamic Study Modules, Grammar Tutorials, and Extra Practice activities.

PRÁCTICA

Nada de nada. Asocia cada pregunta con su probable respuesta. Luego, comparen sus respuestas y añadan una pregunta más para hacerle a su compañero/a.

1. _____ ¿Visitaste Panamá alguna vez?
2. _____ ¿Conoces a alguien en Costa Rica?
3. _____ ¿Bailas alguno de los bailes típicos de la región?
4. _____ ¿Sabe alguien quién escribió la novela *Pasiones griegas?*
5. _____ ¿Conoces alguna canción de Maribel Guardia?
6. …

a. No, ninguna.
b. No, ninguno.
c. No, nadie.
d. No, a nadie.
e. No, nunca.

12-14 

¿Con qué frecuencia? Indica con qué frecuencia haces cada una de las actividades de la tabla siguiente y explica por qué las haces. Después pregúntale a tu compañero/a.

 ver una película en español

E1: *Veo una película en español todas las semanas porque me gusta escuchar la lengua. ¿Y tú?*

E2: *Yo nunca veo películas en español porque no me gustan los subtítulos.*

ACTIVIDAD	YO	RAZÓN	COMPAÑERO/A	RAZÓN
viajar a otro países				
salir de vacaciones con amigos				
hacer reservaciones en Internet				
comprar pasajes de avión en Internet				
usar transporte público				
ir a restaurantes mexicanos				
ver películas extranjeras				

Ecoturismo

Costa Rica y Panamá, en general, han decidido apostar por un ecoturismo de calidad en vez de un turismo de masas. En este sentido, Costa Rica fue el país pionero. Apoyado en una estabilidad política y económica singular dentro de la zona, Costa Rica fue uno de los primeros países en crear una extensa red de parques naturales y áreas protegidas donde se respetan la biodiversidad y el equilibrio medioambiental. Hoy en día esta red ocupa casi el 25% de la superficie total del país gracias a las decisiones del gobierno costarricense en los años 80.

Comparaciones. ¿Cuáles son las ventajas del ecoturismo? ¿Prefieres hacer ecoturismo o turismo más convencional? Explica.

12-15 

Una excursión de ecoturismo. Estás en Costa Rica y vas a hacer una excursión de ecoturismo. Tu compañero/a ya hizo la excursión y piensa que fue un desastre. Él/Ella va a contestar tus preguntas negativamente. Añade una pregunta más.

 ofrecer excursiones

E1: *¿Ofrecieron excursiones para ver la fauna y la flora?*

E2: *No, no ofrecieron ninguna excursión.*

1. ver tortugas en la playa
2. ver las vistas panorámicas
3. comer un almuerzo típico costarricense
4. dejar entrar a muchas áreas protegidas
5. …

12-16 

¡La negatividad es contagiosa! Después de pasar tus vacaciones con tu amigo/a negativo/a, te sientes influenciado/a y contestas a todo negativamente. Túrnense para preguntarse y añadan alguna actividad más.

 llamar a un amigo

E1: *¿Vas a llamar a un amigo?*

E2: *No, no voy a llamar a nadie. ¿Y tú vas a… ?*

1. visitar Panamá alguna vez en el futuro
2. ver alguna película latinoamericana este fin de semana
3. leer un artículo sobre los siete pueblos indígenas de Panamá
4. invitar a alguien a ver un documental sobre los parques nacionales de Costa Rica
5. …

Comarca Guna Yala

Guna Yala, conocida como San Blas hasta 1998, es una región de Panamá que incluye parte de la costa caribeña de Panamá y numerosas islas pequeñas a las que se accede en barco. Es la tierra de los gunas, un pueblo indígena que ha luchado por sus derechos sobre la tierra. En la tierra de los gunas se mantienen activas tradiciones locales en torno a la agricultura y pesca, aunque últimamente se ha desarrollado una industria turística basada en el ecoturismo.

Comparaciones. ¿Existen en tu país comunidades como las de Guna Yala? ¿Qué tradiciones tienen? ¿Qué actividades se asocian con esta comunidad?

Planeando un viaje. PREPARACIÓN. Quieren hacer un viaje a Panamá para conocer su cultura. Comenten qué van a hacer allí.

 pasar unos días en la capital

E1: *Quiero pasar unos días en la capital.*

E2: *Yo también. Es una ciudad interesante.*

1. conocer la Comarca Guna Yala
2. comprar unos textiles de mola, hechos por artesanos indígenas gunas
3. hacer una excursión al Canal de Panamá
4. tomar una clase de cumbia, un baile folclórico
5. asistir a un partido de fútbol

 INTERCAMBIOS. Conversen sobre dos o tres actividades que quieren hacer en Panamá. Después, reúnanse con otra pareja, explíquenle sus planes y escuchen los planes de sus compañeros/as. Respondan negativamente a los planes de la otra pareja.

Situación

PREPARACIÓN. Lean esta situación. Luego, compartan ejemplos de vocabulario, gramática y demás información que necesitan para desarrollar la conversación.

Role A. You call a travel agency to purchase tickets for an all-day excursion. When the clerk answers, ask:

a. if sometimes they offer free tickets for students;
b. if they have any tickets for Friday or Saturday; and
c. whether lunch at a restaurant is included in the price.

You may express your annoyance at all the negative answers you receive when you thank the clerk for his/her help.

Role B. You work in a travel agency. A customer calls to ask about tickets for an excursion. Reply that:

a. they never give free tickets to anyone (not students, not young children);
b. there aren't any tickets for the days the customer inquires about; and
c. there will be two breaks for snacks (**merienda**), but not a restaurant meal.

You are in a bad mood and you let it show during the conversation.

	ROLE A	ROLE B
Vocabulario	Question words Travel vocabulary	Travel vocabulary
Funciones y formas	Asking questions Expressing annoyance in a formal setting	Giving information Expressions of negation Expressing annoyance in a formal setting

INTERCAMBIOS. Practica la conversación con tu compañero/a incorporando el vocabulario, las funciones y demás información. Luego, represéntenla ante la clase.

2 Talking about things that may not exist

MUJER: Por favor, ¿dónde está el tren que **sale** a las 9:00?

AGENTE: No hay trenes que **salgan** por la noche, señorita. El último tren salió a las 6:00 de la tarde.

MUJER: ¡Ay, Dios mío! ¿Hay un tren que **salga** temprano por la mañana?

AGENTE: Sí, señorita. El primer tren sale a las 7:00.

MUJER: Bueno, tendré que esperar hasta mañana, entonces. ¿Me puede recomendar un hotel que **esté** cerca? Necesito uno que no **sea** caro.

AGENTE: Sí, cómo no. Le recomiendo el Hotel Colonial. Es un buen hotel que **tiene** precios baratos.

Piénsalo. Para cada oración, indica si la persona habla de algo que existe (**E**), de algo que no existe (**NE**) o de algo que posiblemente exista (**PE**).

1. _____ ¿Dónde está el tren que **sale** a las 9:00?
2. _____ No hay trenes que **salgan** por la noche.
3. _____ ¿Hay un tren que **salga** temprano por la mañana?
4. _____ ¿Me puede recomendar un hotel que **esté** cerca?
5. _____ Necesito un hotel que no **sea** caro.
6. _____ Es un buen hotel que **tiene** precios baratos (*moderate*).

Subjunctive in adjective clauses

- As you have learned, the subjunctive in Spanish is used primarily in sentences that have two clauses. In this section, you will learn about using the subjunctive in adjective clauses.

LENGUA

Que introduces a dependent clause, and it may refer to persons or things.

El cuarto **que** reservé es muy caro.	*The room I reserved is very expensive.*
Ese es el agente **que** me alquiló el coche.	*That is the agent who rented the car for me.*

Use **quien(es)** after a preposition when referring to people.

Allí está el recepcionista **con quien** hablé esta mañana.	*There is the receptionist with whom I spoke this morning.*

- Both adjectives and adjective clauses provide descriptive information about a noun in the independent clause.

Vamos a ir a un hotel muy **moderno.** (ADJECTIVE)

Vamos a ir a un hotel **que es muy moderno.** (ADJECTIVE CLAUSE)

- Use the indicative in an adjective clause that refers to a person, place, or thing (antecedent) that exists or is known. Use the subjunctive in an adjective clause that refers to a person, place, or thing that does not exist or whose existence is unknown or in question. Study the examples to see the differences.

INDICATIVE	SUBJUNCTIVE
Hay un buen hotel que **queda** cerca de la playa. *There is a good hotel that is near the beach.* (You are familiar with the hotel.)	Busco un buen hotel que **quede** cerca de la playa. *I am looking for a good hotel that is near the beach.* (The existence of such a hotel is uncertain or unknown to you.)
Visité el museo que **tiene** una exposición de molas. *I visited the museum that has a molas exhibit.* (You went there, so there is such a museum.)	Aquí no hay ningún museo que **tenga** una exposición de molas. *There is no museums here that has a molas exhibit.* (There is no such museum.)

¿COMPRENDES?

Completa las oraciones con el indicativo o el subjuntivo de los verbos.

1. Buscamos un guía que (ofrece/ofrezca) excursiones a las pirámides.
2. Buscamos a alguien que (trabaja/trabaje) los sábados.
3. No conozco a nadie que (visita/visite) Costa Rica este año.
4. Encontramos un hotel que (está/esté) en el centro.
5. Hay tres itinerarios que me (gustan/gusten).
6. Necesito un restaurante que (sirve/sirva) comida vegetariana.

MySpanishLab

Learn more using Amplifire Dynamic Study Modules, Grammar Tutorials, and Extra Practice activities..

LENGUA

Use the personal **a** before specific persons or animals that function as direct objects. If the person or animal is unknown or specific, use the subjunctive and do not use the personal **a.** Always use the personal **a** before **alguien** and **nadie.**

Busco **a** la auxiliar que trabaja en ese vuelo.
I am looking for the (specific) flight attendant who is working on that flight.

Busco **una** auxiliar que **trabaje** en ese vuelo.
I am looking for a (any) flight attendant who is (happens to be) working on that flight.

Busco **a** alguien que me **acompañe** al museo.
I am looking for someone who will go with me to the museum.

LENGUA

In questions, use the indicative or the subjunctive according to the degree of certainty you have about the matter. For example, if you want to ask: *Are there any travelers here who are leaving on flight 420?*

If you don't know for sure but think there are, then use the indicative:
¿Hay viajeros aquí que **salen** en el vuelo 420?

If you don't know, but doubt there are, then use the subjunctive:
¿Hay viajeros aquí que **salgan** en el vuelo 420?

PRÁCTICA

12-18 

¿Cuál es la respuesta correcta? Selecciona el indicativo o el subjuntivo de los verbos indicados, según el contexto.

1. No hay ningún vuelo que _____ por la noche.	**a.** sale	**b.** salga
2. Pero hay un vuelo que _____ a las 7:00 de la mañana.	**a.** queda	**b.** quede
3. Me interesa encontrar un hotel (*any hotel*) que _____ cerca del centro.	**a.** habla	**b.** hable
4. Hay un hotel que no es muy caro y que _____ en el centro.		
5. Busco al empleado que _____ inglés.		
6. ¿Hay algún empleado (*any employee*) en este departamento que _____ inglés?		

12-19 

Por curiosidad. Túrnense para hacerse preguntas sobre la familia de cada uno/a. Respondan con detalles adicionales.

 tu familia/dormir mucho durante los viajes largos en auto.

E1: *¿Hay alguien en tu familia que duerma mucho durante los viajes largos en auto?*

E2: *Sí, mi hermano siempre duerme mucho en el auto. El año pasado fuimos a la casa de mis abuelos y él durmió durante todo el viaje.*

1. tu familia/viajar mucho
2. tus amigos/trabajar en vez de viajar durante las vacaciones de la primavera
3. tus amigos/conocer los lugares más interesantes de Costa Rica
4. tu familia/saber pilotear un avión
5. tus amigos/ir a esquiar en sus vacaciones
6. tu familia/viajar a Panamá este año

12-20 

Emergencia en el aeropuerto. Túrnense para hacer los papeles de dos jefes de personal de una aerolínea que buscan empleados que puedan hacer ciertos trabajos. Sigan el modelo.

 programar la computadora (alguien)

E1: *Necesito a alguien que programe la computadora para los itinerarios.*

E2: *No hay nadie en el aeropuerto que pueda programarla.*

E1: *Bueno, es necesario buscar a alguien que lo haga.*

1. hablar inglés, japonés y español para el vuelo a Tamarindo (auxiliar)
2. recibir el vuelo que viene de Puerto Jiménez (agente)
3. darles esta información a los pasajeros del vuelo 562 (empleado/a)
4. llevar a los pasajeros a inmigración (empleado/a)
5. poder trabajar este fin de semana (dos auxiliares)
6. ...

En directo

To express annoyance at something in a formal or business setting:

Perdón, pero ¿está seguro/a de que…?

Excuse me, but are you sure that … ?

¡Esto es increíble!

This is incredible.

Perdón, pero ¿no hay ninguna posibilidad de + *infinitive*?

Sorry, but isn't there any chance to …?

 Listen to a conversation with these expressions.

12-21 

Un lugar para ir de vacaciones. PREPARACIÓN. Túrnense para hacerse preguntas sobre un lugar adonde ir de vacaciones. Contesten según la información de la tabla.

 hotel/tener piscina

E1: *¿Hay un hotel que tenga piscina?*

E2: *Sí, hay un hotel que tiene piscina./No, no hay ningún hotel que tenga piscina.*

HAY	NO HAY
tiendas/vender ropa para esquiar	autobús/llegar por la mañana
cines/dar películas en español	cafetería/servir comida vegetariana
restaurantes/tener cajero automático	restaurantes/aceptar cheques personales

INTERCAMBIOS. Ahora ustedes deben describir cómo es su lugar ideal de vacaciones, explicando su ubicación, ambiente y atracciones. Después, intercambien ideas con otra pareja.

 E1: *Quiero ir de vacaciones a una isla que tenga playas blancas y un ambiente tranquilo. ¿Y tú?*

E2: *Mi lugar de vacaciones ideal es diferente. Quiero ir a una ciudad que tenga muchos conciertos y obras de teatro.*

Situación  

PREPARACIÓN. Lean esta situación. Luego, compartan ejemplos de vocabulario, gramática y otra información que necesitan para desarrollar la conversación.

Role A. Your family owns a small inn near the college that houses international faculty who visit the campus. You need to hire two people for your staff, so you call an employment agency. Explain that you are looking for:

a. a receptionist who speaks French, German, or Spanish (preferably two of those languages) and who has experience as a secretary; and
b. a chef who is familiar with European cuisines and who is able to work nights and weekends.

Role B. You work at an employment agency, and you receive a call from an innkeeper who is looking for a receptionist and a chef. Listen to the innkeeper's requirements and ask about any other qualifications that may be desired. Tell the innkeeper you will start looking right away.

	ROLE A	ROLE B
Vocabulario	Question words Employment qualifications Words and expressions related to cooking Time and schedules	Question words Employment qualifications Words and expressions related to cooking Time and schedules
Funciones y formas	Asking questions Giving information Subjunctive with adjectival clauses to express uncertainty	Asking questions Giving information Subjunctive with adjectival clauses to express uncertainty Expressing reassurance and guarantee of assistance

INTERCAMBIOS. Practica la conversación con tu compañero/a incorporando el vocabulario, las funciones y demás información. Luego, represéntenla ante la clase.

3 Expressing possession

MADRE: Ramiro, mi maleta casi está lista. ¿Y **la tuya?**

RAMIRO: ¡**La mía** no! Después del programa la empaco. ¿Ya empacaste tus libros, mamá?

MADRE: **Los míos** ya están en mi maletín. ¿Y las muñecas (*dolls*) de Susana?

RAMIRO: **Las suyas** están en su mochila, pero **las de** Laurita no sé dónde están.

Piénsalo. Lee las siguientes afirmaciones de la conversación anterior. Indica a qué se refieren las palabras en negrita.

1. ***¡La mía** no!*

   La mía se refiere ____.

   a. al programa de Ramiro

   b. a la maleta de Ramiro

2. ***Los míos** ya están en mi maletín.*

   Los míos se refiere a ____.

   a. los libros de la madre

   b. las muñecas de Susana

3. ***Las suyas** están en su mochila.*

   Las suyas se refiere a ____.

   a. los maletines de mano

   b. las muñecas de Susana

4. ***Las de Laurita** están en su cuarto.*

   Las de Laurita se refiere a ____.

   a. sus libros

   b. sus muñecas

Possessive pronouns

- Possessive pronouns express ownership or possession. They are used to avoid repetition of the noun to which they refer.

SINGULAR				PLURAL			
	Masculine		**Feminine**		**Masculine**		**Feminine**
el	mío	la	mía	los	míos	las	mías
	tuyo		tuya		tuyos		tuyas
	suyo		suya		suyos		suyas
	nuestro		nuestra		nuestros		nuestras
	vuestro		vuestra		vuestros		vuestras

- The definite article precedes the possessive pronoun, and both article and pronoun agree in gender and number with the noun to which they refer.

  ¿Tienes la mochila de Mario? — *Do you have Mario's backpack?*

  Sí, tengo **la suya** y **la mía** también. — *Yes, I have his and mine too.*

- After the verb **ser,** the article is usually omitted.

  Esa maleta es **mía.** — *That suitcase is mine.*

- To be clearer and more specific, the following structures may be used to replace any corresponding form of **el suyo/la suya.**

la de usted	*yours* (singular)
la de él	*his*
la de ella	*hers*
la mochila suya → **la suya** or	
la de ustedes	*yours* (plural)
la de ellos	*theirs* (masculine, plural)
la de ellas	*theirs* (feminine, plural)

LENGUA

Stressed possessive adjectives, which have the same forms as possessive pronouns, emphasize to whom a particular object belongs. Because they are adjectives, they always immediately follow the noun to which they refer. They are often used to emphasize a contrast.

El cuarto mío es grandísimo.	*My room is very big.*
La maleta tuya está en la recepción.	*Your suitcase is at the front desk.*
Las llaves nuestras están encima del escritorio.	*Our keys are on the desk.*
Esos primos míos llegan hoy.	*Those cousins of mine arrive today.*

¿COMPRENDES?

Usa una expresión con el pronombre correcto para indicar posesión.

1. mi maleta: ________ ________
2. los pasajes de ustedes: ________ ________
3. nuestras llaves: ________ ________
4. el viaje de ellos: ________ ________
5. tus planes: ________ ________
6. el equipaje de Marta y Sara: ________ ________

MySpanishLab

Learn more using Amplifire Dynamic Study Modules, Grammar Tutorials, and Extra Practice activities..

PRÁCTICA

12-22  

¿De quién(es) son estas cosas? PREPARACIÓN. En la clase de español decidieron hacer un viaje de estudios a Costa Rica. En este momento van a tomar el bus para ir al aeropuerto. Escoge la respuesta correcta para cada una de las preguntas. Compara tus respuestas con las de tu compañero/a.

1. Miguel, ¿es tuya esta mochila?	**a.** Sí, es mía.	**b.** Sí, es tuya.
2. ¿Son estas maletas de Pedro?	**a.** Sí, son suyas.	**b.** Sí, son mías.
3. ¿El maletín de color café es de Alicia?	**a.** No, es tuya.	**b.** No, no es suyo.
4. Este mapa de San José, ¿es tuyo?	**a.** Sí, es mía.	**b.** Sí, es mío.
5. ¿Son nuestros estos boletos?	**a.** Sí, son suyos.	**b.** Sí, son suyas.

INTERCAMBIOS. Ve por la clase y pregunta a varios compañeros/as de quién son algunos de los objetos que ves o encuentras.

12-23 

¿Quién tiene carro? PREPARACIÓN. Entrevístense para saber quién(es) tiene(n) carro. Hablen de sus carros: marca, modelo, año y color. Tomen apuntes sobre la información.

E1: *Mi carro es un Toyota Corolla rojo del 2009. ¿Y el tuyo?*

E2: *El mío es un Ford Focus azul del 2012.*

E3: *Yo no tengo carro, pero mi hermana me presta el suyo de vez en cuando. Es una camioneta negra del 2002.*

INTERCAMBIOS. Combinen la información de todos los grupos y preparen un informe sobre las características más comunes de los carros de los miembros de la clase.

12-24 

Preparándose para un viaje. Van a hacer un viaje en auto y deben tomar varias decisiones antes de salir. Háganse preguntas para decidir lo que van a hacer y den una razón.

usar mi coche o tu coche

E1: *¿Vamos a usar mi coche o el tuyo?*

E2: *Prefiero usar el tuyo porque es más nuevo.*

1. llevar tus maletas o las de mi hermano
2. usar mis mapas o tus mapas
3. llevar tu cámara o mi cámara
4. llevar tu portátil o mi portátil
5. usar tu GPS o el de mis padres

Situación

PREPARACIÓN. Lean esta situación. Luego, compartan ejemplos de vocabulario, gramática y otra información que necesitan para desarrollar la conversación.

Role A. On the plane home from an ecotourism trip to Costa Rica, you sit next to a student returning from a similar trip. Ask your seatmate:

a. why he/she went on an ecotourism trip;
b. what national park he/she liked best, and why;
c. one thing he/she learned from the trip; and
d. whether he/she has plans to return to Costa Rica.

Answer your seatmate's questions about your trip.

Role B. On the plane home from an ecotourism trip to Costa Rica, you sit next to a student returning from a similar trip. After answering your seatmate's questions, ask him/her similar questions about his/her trip. Comment on how your experience was similar to that of your seatmate.

	ROLE A	ROLE B
Vocabulario	Greetings Question words Vacation activities Ecoturism activities Future plans	Greetings Question words Vacation activities Ecoturism activities Future plans
Funciones y formas	Talking about a past experience: Possessive pronouns Preterite Discussing plans: Future tense Making small talk	Asking and answering questions about the past and future: Possessive pronouns Preterite Future Comparisons of equality and inequality Making small talk

INTERCAMBIOS. Practica la conversación con tu compañero/a incorporando el vocabulario, las funciones y demás información. Luego, represéntenla ante la clase.

4 Expressing doubt and uncertainty

ANA MARÍA: ¡Qué buenos son! Es seguro que **ganan** el premio.

JULIO: No creo que **sean** tan buenos, y dudo que **salgan** bien en el concurso.

ANA MARÍA: Es posible que **tengan** éxito, ¿no?

JULIO: Creo que no. No tienen ni melodía ni ritmo. Es dudoso que **ganen.**

Piénsalo. Indica (✓) si las siguientes afirmaciones expresan certeza (*certainty*) o duda (*doubt*).

	CERTEZA	DUDA
1. Es seguro que **ganan** el premio.	_____	_____
2. No creo que **sean** tan buenos.	_____	_____
3. Dudo que **salgan** bien en el concurso.	_____	_____
4. Es posible que **tengan** éxito.	_____	_____
5. Es dudoso que **ganen.**	_____	_____

Subjunctive with expressions of doubt

You learned in *Capítulo 11* to use the subjunctive to express emotions, opinions, expectations, and wishes. In this chapter you will learn to use the subjunctive for a related communicative function: to express doubt and uncertainty.

- When the verb in the main clause expresses doubt or uncertainty, use a subjunctive verb form in the dependent clause (the clause that begins with **que**).

Dudo que **vendan** libros en español.	*I doubt (that) they sell books in Spanish.*
Es dudoso que el guía **llegue** tarde a la excursión.	*It's unlikely (that) the guide will arrive late to the tour.*

¿COMPRENDES?

Completa las oraciones con la forma correcta de los verbos.

1. Es seguro que el avión _______ (llegar) tarde.
2. Es posible que _______ (llover) el día de la excursión.
3. Dudo que la compañía nos _______ (dar) boletos para otro día.
4. Creo que los autobuses _______ (tener) un horario diferente los domingos.
5. Quizás _______ (ser) mejor tomar un taxi.
6. Es verdad que los turistas _______ (divertirse) mucho en Costa Rica.

MySpanishLab

Learn more using Amplifire Dynamic Study Modules, Grammar Tutorials, and Extra Practice activities.

- Use the subjunctive with impersonal expressions that denote doubt or uncertainty, such as **es dudoso que, es difícil que, es probable que,** and **es posible que.**

Es dudoso que **encontremos** artesanía panameña en ese mercado.	*It is doubtful that we will find Panamanian handicrafts in that market.*
Es posible que **tengan** textiles.	*It is possible that they have textiles.*

- Use the indicative with impersonal expressions that denote certainty: **es cierto/verdad que, es seguro que,** and **es obvio que.** When these expressions are negative, the following verb is in the subjunctive.

Es verdad que el tamborito y la cumbia **son** bailes populares en Panamá.	*It is true that the tamborito and the cumbia are popular dances in Panama.*
No es cierto que los bailes panameños se **conozcan** mucho en Estados Unidos.	*It is not true that Panamanian dances are well known in the United States.*

- When the verbs **creer** and **pensar** are used in the negative, the subjunctive is used in the dependent clause. In questions with these verbs, the subjunctive may be used to express uncertainty or to anticipate a negative response. If the question simply seeks information, use the indicative.

SUBJUNCTIVE	
Hace sol. No creo que **llueva.**	*It is sunny out. I don't think it will rain.*
¿Crees que **haga** calor en San José?	*Do you think it is/will be hot in San José?* (I am not sure.)

INDICATIVE	
¿Crees que **llueve** mucho en la costa?	*Do you think it rains a lot on the coast?* (I think so, and I am seeking confirmation.)

- Since the expressions **tal vez** and **quizá(s)** convey uncertainty, the subjunctive is normally used.

Tal vez el conjunto **toque** un tamborito panameño.	*Perhaps the group will play a tamborito panameño.*
Quizá(s) todos **empiecen** a bailar.	*Perhaps everyone will start to dance.*

PRÁCTICA

12-25 

¿Están de acuerdo? Lee las siguientes opiniones y marca (✓) si estás de acuerdo o no. Luego, compara tus respuestas con las de tu compañero/a. Explíquense las razones de sus respuestas.

	SÍ	NO
1. Yo creo que los bailes folclóricos son fáciles de aprender.	_____	_____
2. Yo dudo que el transporte público sea más popular en Estados Unidos que en América Latina.	_____	_____
3. Creo que los parques nacionales de Costa Rica son muy importantes para la ecología del planeta.	_____	_____
4. Es posible que viajar en tren sea más costoso que viajar en avión.	_____	_____
5. Es obvio que el precio de la gasolina en Estados Unidos afecta el turismo.	_____	_____
6. No creo que los estudiantes hoy viajen a otros países tanto como viajaban los estudiantes hace veinte años.	_____	_____

En directo

To report agreement:

Todos creemos/pensamos que…
We all believe/think that...

Nosotros estamos de acuerdo con que…
We all agree that...

To report different opinions:

No hay consenso entre nosotros/ellos. Unos piensan que…, otros creen que…
We/They do not agree. Some think that..., while others believe that...

 Listen to a conversation with these expressions.

12-26 

Opiniones. Intercambia opiniones sobre los siguientes temas con tu compañero/a. Después, comparen sus opiniones con las de otras parejas y compartan sus conclusiones con la clase.

1. los cruceros
2. ir de vacaciones con la familia
3. los bailes folclóricos
4. ver exposiciones de arte

 MODELO el ecoturismo

E1: *Creo que el ecoturismo es aburrido. Prefiero disfrutar de la vida de noche en las ciudades grandes. Y tú, ¿qué opinas?*

E2: *Dudo que las grandes ciudades del mundo sean diferentes de las cuidades grandes de Estados Unidos. Yo prefiero conocer la naturaleza.*

12-27 

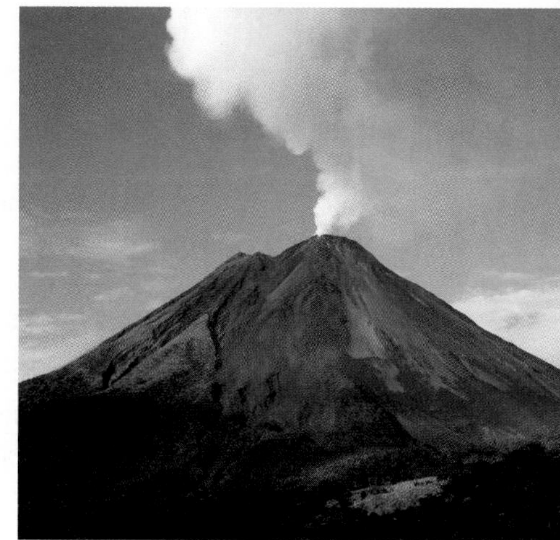

Un viaje. PREPARACIÓN. En un concurso, ustedes ganaron un viaje de una semana a cualquier ciudad del mundo hispano. Escojan una ciudad y hagan una lista de tres cosas que posiblemente ocurran durante la semana y tres cosas que dudan que pasen. Expliquen por qué.

 Puntarenas, Costa Rica

E1: *Esperamos que alguien nos invite a un club porque nos gusta mucho bailar. También es posible que vayamos de excursión al volcán Arenal porque dicen que es muy impresionante.*

E2: *Dudamos que llueva, porque hace buen tiempo casi todo el año. Es poco probable que volvamos otra vez; por eso queremos hacer muchas actividades.*

INTERCAMBIOS. Reúnanse con otra pareja y explíquenle qué ciudad escogieron y por qué. Infórmenle sobre sus expectativas y dudas con respecto a su viaje. Comenten si están de acuerdo con lo que dicen sus compañeros/as.

Situación

PREPARACIÓN. Lean esta situación. Luego, compartan ejemplos de vocabulario, gramática y otra información que necesitan para desarrollar la conversación.

Role A. A friend borrowed your car and brought it back a whole day later than the two of you had agreed, which caused you a lot of inconvenience. Ask your friend for an explanation. Express doubt about at least three reasons your friend gives you. To avoid ongoing conflict with your friend, make sure the situation is resolved.

Role B. You borrowed your friend's car, and you brought it back a whole day later than the two of you had agreed, which caused your friend a lot of inconvenience. Now you have to explain yourself. You don't want to tell the real reason, so you make up a detailed story of what happened. Your friend is skeptical, so you have to try hard to be convincing. To avoid ongoing conflict with your friend, make sure the situation is resolved.

	ROLE A	ROLE B
Vocabulario	Words and expressions related to travel	Words and expressions related to travel
Funciones y formas	Expressing doubts or disbelief Subjunctive with expressions of doubt and disbelief Resolving a problem with a friend	Telling a story Preterit and imperfect Making excuses Apologizing Resolving a problem with a friend

INTERCAMBIOS. Practica la conversación con tu compañero/a incorporando el vocabulario, las funciones y demás información. Luego, represéntenla ante la clase.

EN ACCIÓN

Lugares fantásticos

12-28 Antes de ver

De viaje. Imagínate que vas de vacaciones a un lugar que nunca has visitado. Indica cuáles son las tres actividades más importantes que debes hacer antes de llegar allí.

1. ___ Hacer una reservación de hotel.
2. ___ Comprar un mapa del lugar.
3. ___ Buscar información en Internet sobre los sitios más representativos.
4. ___ Hablar con alguien que viva allí.
5. ___ Hacer las maletas.
6. ___ Despedirte de tus amigos.
7. ___ Comprar ropa para el viaje.

12-29 Mientras ves 

Lugares inolvidables. En este segmento de video se describen tres lugares de interés turístico. Indica si las siguientes oraciones se refieren a las Cataratas del Iguazú (**I**), Costa Rica (**CR**) o San Francisco (**SF**).

1. _____ Vanesa siempre ha querido visitar este lugar.
2. _____ Hay un río que pasa por tres países distintos.
3. _____ Es muy popular por su ecoturismo.
4. _____ Las corrientes (*currents*) son muy poderosas.
5. _____ Una de sus atracciones más conocidas es un enorme puente que cruza la bahía.
6. _____ Muchas personas van a este lugar para hacer *surf*.
7. _____ Su nombre viene de una palabra guaraní que significa *agua grande*.

12-30 Después de ver 

Lugares y preferencias. PREPARACIÓN. Indica si las siguientes afirmaciones se refieren a Esteban (**E**), a Vanesa (**V**) o a Federico (**F**).

1. _____ Prefiere los sitios que tengan vida nocturna.
2. _____ Le encantan los sitios donde se pueda hacer *surf*.
3. _____ Muestra mucho orgullo al hablar de la industria turística en su país.

Intercambios. Imagínense que Uds. tienen la oportunidad de hacer un video para promocionar un lugar especial. ¿Qué lugar eligen? Describan ese lugar y digan qué actividades pueden hacer las personas allí. Indiquen por qué es especial ese lugar y cuáles son sus principales atractivos. Escriban un eslogan para promocionarlo.

Mosaicos

ESCUCHA

ESTRATEGIA

Use background knowledge to support comprehension

When you listen to a conversation or a lecture in Spanish, your experience may lead you to expect certain content. To support your comprehension, do the following:

Before you listen...

- brainstorm a list of ideas you expect to hear about the topic.
- read about the topic on the Internet if you are not familiar with it.

As you listen ...

- use your prior knowledge to help you understand. For example, when you hear numbers announced at an airport, they probably refer to flight or gate numbers.

12-31 

Preparación. Vas a escuchar una conversación telefónica entre una agente de viajes y el Sr. Hernández, quien busca un hotel para él y su familia en San José. Antes de escuchar, escribe tres características que el Sr. Hernández probablemente desea que tenga el hotel y tres preguntas que probablemente le hará la agente. Compártelas con la clase.

12-32  

Escucha. As you listen to the conversation between Sr. Hernández and the travel agent, check (✓) the statements that best report what was said.

1. _____ El Sr. Hernández dice que quiere un hotel económico que esté cerca del centro de la ciudad.
2. _____ La agente tiene varias posibilidades y le describe tres hoteles para que escoja.
3. _____ El Sr. Hernández afirma que prefiere que sus hijos y esposa estén cómodos aunque (*even though*) él tenga que tomar un taxi o manejar mucho.
4. _____ La agente le dice al cliente que su elección no es buena porque el hotel es muy caro y está muy lejos del centro de la ciudad.

Comprueba

I was able to ...

_____ **understand the main points of the conversation.**

_____ **use experience and logic to confirm what I understood.**

Un paso más. Háganse las siguientes preguntas.

1. Cuando buscas un hotel, ¿es más importante que sea económico o que sea de lujo (*luxurious*)?
2. ¿Qué servicios o comodidades prefieres que ofrezca un hotel?
3. ¿Cuál es el hotel más cómodo en el que has estado? Explica.

HABLA

12-34 

Preparación. Escojan a una de las personas de la lista. Busquen información sobre esa persona para completar la tabla. También busquen otra información que les interese a ustedes.

Francisco Amighetti	Félix Danilo Gómez
Óscar Arias Sánchez	Manuel Noriega
Rubén Blades	Carlos Ruiz
Franklin Chang Díaz	Juan Santamaría

NOMBRE	DATOS PERSONALES	PROFESIÓN	LOGROS
________	Fecha de nacimiento: ____________ Lugar de nacimiento/ muerte: ____________	____________ Contribución a su profesión: ____________	

12-35 

Habla. Hagan una breve presentación sobre la persona que escogieron, usando imágenes y algún tipo de audio para mantener el interés de sus compañeros de clase.

Comprueba

In my presentation...

____ **I spoke slowly and clearly to make my presentation understandable.**

____ **I used visuals to make my presentation lively and interesting.**

____ **I engaged the audience and successfully answered their questions.**

En directo

To support a decision:

Hemos elegido a... porque...
We have chosen ... because ...

Lo que más influyó en nuestra decisión fue/fueron...
What most influenced our decision was/were ...

Nuestra decisión está basada en lo siguiente...
Our decision is based on the following ...

 Listen to a conversation with these expressions.

ESTRATEGIA

Make your presentations comprehensible and interesting

When you give a presentation, your two challenges are to a) keep it simple so your classmates understand it; and b) make it interesting so they will listen.

- Keep it simple. Use words and expressions you know. Don't copy whole sentences from other sources, because your audience may not understand you.
- Practice your presentation. If you have notes, don't read them; instead, use them for reference. If you read, your audience will not understand you.
- Make it interesting. Use PowerPoint, photos, and artifacts to make your presentation more lively and interesting. Do not read from your slides. You may have notes, but only for reference.
- Involve your audience. Make eye contact, ask questions, check that they understand you, and invite them to ask questions.

12-36 

Un paso más. Decidan cuál de las figuras famosas de la actividad 12-34 es la persona más admirable o interesante. Expliquen por qué, usando las expresiones de *En directo*.

LEE

Preparación. Hablen de lo siguiente.

1. ¿Prefieren los viajes en avión o por tierra? ¿Por qué?
2. ¿Les gusta organizar sus propios viajes o prefieren una agencia? ¿Por qué?
3. ¿Qué problema serio ha tenido cada uno/a de ustedes en un viaje?
4. ¿Han tenido problemas semejantes o diferentes?

ESTRATEGIA

Focus on logical relationships

Magazine articles often address current issues, such as identity theft, sedentary lifestyles, or travel tips. When you read an article of this type, you can take advantage of its structure to maximize your comprehension. As you read, look for the issues or problems that the author introduces, and then focus on the logical relationships, such as between problems and their causes, or between problems and their solutions. An individual case often appears at the beginning of the article as an example of the problem, and then returns at the end to illustrate a possible solution.

12-38

Lee. Marca (✓) los problemas que enfrentan los viajeros, según el artículo "Vacaciones o pesadilla". Después, busca en el artículo ejemplos de lo que se indica.

Problemas	Ejemplos
1. _____ agencias de viajes deshonestas	**1.** tres problemas que tuvieron Isabel y Mario en sus vacaciones
2. _____ maletas perdidas	**2.** la causa principal de la situación desagradable de Isabel y Mario
3. _____ vuelos cancelados	**3.** recomendaciones para evitar o minimizar problemas
4. _____ choques de avión	
5. _____ robo de las tarjetas de crédito	
6. _____ autos alquilados que no funcionan	
7. _____ problemas para entrar en otro país	
8. _____ enfermedades causadas por la comida	

Comprueba

I was able to …

_____ **identify the problems described by the author.**

_____ **focus on the relationship between different parts of the content to discover key problems, their causes, and their possible solutions.**

VACACIONES O PESADILLA[1]
CÓMO REDUCIR LOS PROBLEMAS EN LOS VIAJES

Isabel y Mario, una pareja estadounidense de origen uruguayo, decidieron celebrar su aniversario de boda en Costa Rica. Para preparar el viaje se pusieron en contacto por Internet con la agencia Viajes Reales. La agencia ofrecía paquetes de excursiones que incluían billete de avión, hotel y coche de alquiler por precios bastante módicos. Las fotos prometían una estancia relajada en un hotel de ambiente exótico al noroeste del país. La variedad de piscinas, la cercanía del mar, la apetecible gastronomía local y los cócteles refrescantes que se veían en lujosas mesitas junto a las hamacas de los afortunados clientes confirmaban que se trataba de un verdadero paraíso.

Isabel y Mario pagaron la cantidad requerida y no dudaron ni un momento de su decisión. Pero al llegar a su destino comprobaron que las fotos no correspondían a la realidad. El hotel no tenía ni vista al mar ni jardines exóticos. Las habitaciones eran pequeñísimas e incómodas y la comida dejaba mucho que desear.

Lamentablemente, esta no es una anécdota aislada entre los viajeros. ¿Quién no ha sufrido alguna vez la pérdida de su equipaje, las incomodidades de un vuelo cancelado, el robo de su pasaporte o sus tarjetas de crédito, los problemas en la aduana por comprar un producto comestible que no se permite pasar?

La experiencia de los viajes nos enseña a ser prudentes y prever los riesgos. La facilidad que proporciona Internet es conveniente, pero cuando se viaja por primera vez es preferible dirigirse a una agencia local para que los especialistas de viajes nos ayuden a elegir las mejores opciones. Frecuentemente es más caro hacerlo así, pero se puede ahorrar tiempo y evitar sorpresas desagradables. Por otra parte, a veces resulta más barato comprar un seguro de cancelación que arriesgarse a perder, por una razón u otra, el costo de un billete de avión.

Algunos incidentes son naturalmente inevitables, pero otros se pueden prevenir. Por ejemplo, es posible minimizar el riesgo de un robo llevando los pasaportes y papeles importantes en una bolsita colgada del cuello que se oculta debajo de la ropa, o en un bolsillo doble del pantalón. En cuanto a los impedimentos en la aduana, hay que tener en cuenta que las medidas de seguridad son cada vez más estrictas. Ya no se puede subir al avión con líquidos de más de tres onzas y solo se permite viajar con las bebidas y comestibles comprados en las tiendas del aeropuerto.

Por suerte, las vacaciones de Mario e Isabel no fueron un desastre total. La pareja pudo disfrutar del maravilloso país en sus excursiones a Puntarenas, Puerto Limón y los parques naturales cercanos a Orosí. También pudieron celebrar su aniversario en un magnífico restaurante. ¡Qué lástima que la experiencia completa no fuera tan agradable! Como dice un conocido refrán[2]: Más vale prevenir… que lamentar.

[1] *nightmare* [2] *proverb*

12-39

Un paso más. La agencia Viajes Reales recibe una carta de Isabel y Mario quejándose de los problemas que tuvieron durante su viaje a Costa Rica. Contesta esa carta de parte de la agencia incluyendo lo siguiente.

1. las excusas de la agencia por la mala experiencia de los clientes
2. una explicación por la falsa publicidad
3. la promesa de devolver el dinero o de ofrecer otro viaje

ESCRIBE

12-40 

Preparación. En un concurso, tu amigo/a ganó diez mil dólares para viajar a San José, Costa Rica. Nunca ha hecho un viaje largo, siente mucha ansiedad (*anxiety*) y te pidió ayuda con la planificación de su viaje. Para ayudarlo, haz lo siguiente:

1. En Internet, lee uno o dos artículos sobre este lugar.
2. Subraya y toma nota de las ideas y los datos concretos más relevantes y útiles.
3. Decide cuáles son tus consejos principales sobre la planificación del viaje, y selecciona la información que lo sustente (*support*).
4. Organiza la información y las ideas en orden de importancia.
5. Selecciona las palabras adecuadas para lograr (*achieve*) el tono adecuado.

ESTRATEGIA

Use facts to offer advice

In your academic work, you are often expected to provide reliable facts, such as statistics and expert opinions. Facts also serve as the basis to support a point of view on an issue. For example, a person may be against texting while driving (personal point of view) because statistics show accidents are caused by drivers who text while behind the wheel (fact). When talking to a friend, facts about different options provide objective support for the advice you give. However, not all sources of information are helpful. Always be sure to ...

- consult reliable sources
- acknowledge your sources
- make it clear how your facts are connected to other sources of information, such as knowledge about your friend.

12-41

Escribe. Escríbele un correo electrónico a tu amigo/a y compártelo con la clase. Incluye la información que preparaste. Además, dale buenos consejos para disminuir su ansiedad.

▲ San José, Costa Rica

Comprueba

I was able to ...

____ **locate and organize key factual information.**

____ **give advice based on factual information.**

____ **use the *En directo* expressions to present and support my perspective.**

12-42

Un paso más. Comparen sus respectivos mensajes. ¿Dieron consejos similares o diferentes? ¿Cuáles son los consejos más importantes? Preparen un informe breve para compartir con la clase.

En este capítulo...

Comprueba lo que sabes

Go to the ***MySpanishLab*** to review what you have learned in this chapter. Practice with the following:

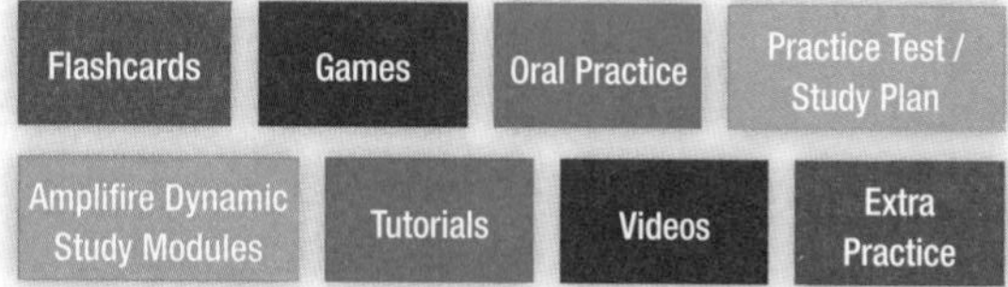

Vocabulario

LOS MEDIOS DE TRANSPORTE
Means of transportation

el autobús/bus *bus*
el avión *plane*
el barco *ship/boat*
el metro *subway*
el tren *train*

EN EL AEROPUERTO
At the airport

la aduana *customs*
la aerolínea/línea aérea *airline*
el asiento *seat*
de pasillo/ventanilla *aisle/window seat*
la clase turista *tourist class*
la llegada *arrival*
el mostrador *counter*
la primera clase *first class*
la puerta (de salida) *gate*
la salida *departure*
la sala de espera *waiting room*
la salida de emergencia *emergency exit*
el vuelo *flight*

LAS PERSONAS
People

el/la agente de viajes *travel agent*
el/la auxiliar de vuelo *flight attendant*
el/la inspector/a de aduana *customs agent*
el/la pasajero/a *passenger*

LOS VIAJES
Trips

la agencia de viajes *travel agency*
la autopista *freeway*
el boleto/el pasaje *ticket*
la carretera *highway*
el crucero *cruise*
el equipaje *luggage*
la escala *stopover*
la excursión *outing, trip*
la maleta *suitcase*
el maletín *briefcase*
el pasaporte *passport*
la tarjeta de embarque *boarding pass*
la velocidad *speed*

EN EL HOTEL
In the hotel

el alojamiento *lodging*
la caja fuerte *safe*
la habitación doble/sencilla *double/single room*
la llave *key*
la recepción *front desk*
la tarjeta magnética *key card*

LOS LUGARES
Places

la cuadra *city block*
la esquina *corner*

LAS DESCRIPCIONES
Descriptions

bien/mal aparcado *well/badly parked*
lleno/a *full*
vacío/a *empty*

VERBOS
Verbs

descomponerse *to break down*
doblar *to turn*
facturar *to check in (luggage)*
manejar *to drive*
perderse (ie) *to get lost*
recorrer *to cover, travel*
reservar *to make a reservation*
salir *to leave*
viajar *to travel*

PALABRAS Y EXPRESIONES ÚTILES
Useful words and expressions

el cajero automático *ATM*
de ida y vuelta *round trip*
hacer cola *to stand in line*
la licencia de conducir *driver's license*
la multa *fine*
nunca *never*
seguir (i) derecho *to go straight*
una vez *once*

LAS PARTES DE UN COCHE
Parts of a car

el capó *hood*
el espejo retrovisor *rearview mirror*
la guantera *glove compartment*
el limpiaparabrisas *windshield wiper*
la llanta *tire*
la luz (las luces) *light(s)*
las luces intermitentes *flashers/hazard lights*
el maletero/el baúl *trunk*
el motor *motor*
el parabrisas *windshield*
la placa *license plate*
el radiador *radiator*
la rueda *wheel*
el volante *steering wheel*

See pages 434 and 435 for a list of stressed possessive adjectives and pronouns.

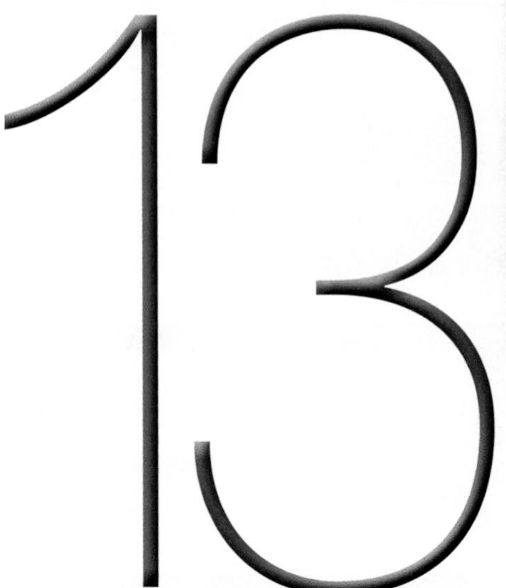

13 ¿Qué es arte para ti?

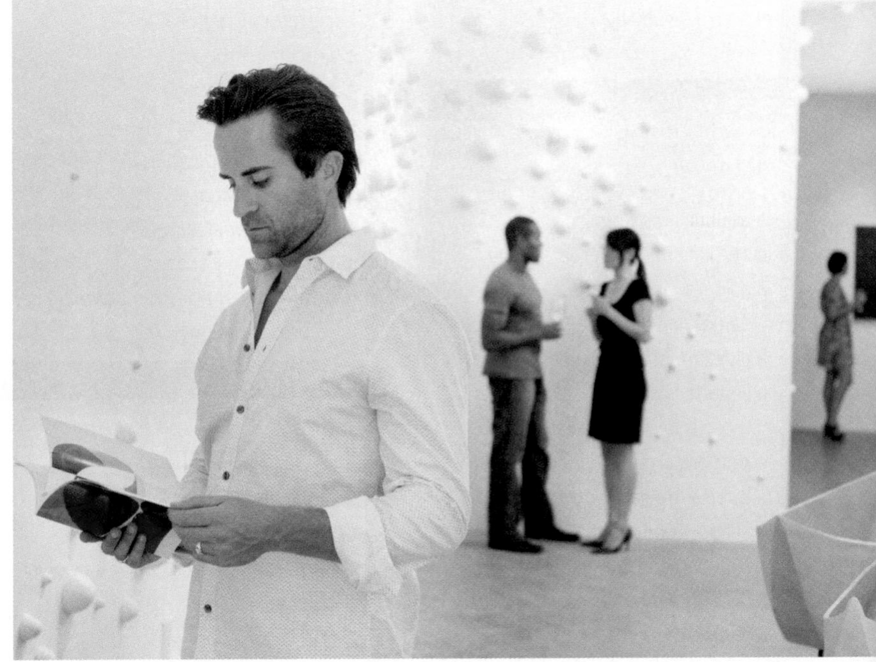

LEARNING **OUTCOMES**

You will be able to:

- talk about art and culture
- express doubt and uncertainty
- hypothesize about the future
- describe states and conditions
- talk about Bolivia and Paraguay in terms of products, practices, and perspectives
- share information about art and culture in Hispanic countries and identify cultural similarities

ENFOQUE cultural BOLIVIA Y PARAGUAY

Enfoque cultural

To learn more about Bolivia and Paraguay, go to MySpanishLab to view the *Vistas culturales* videos.

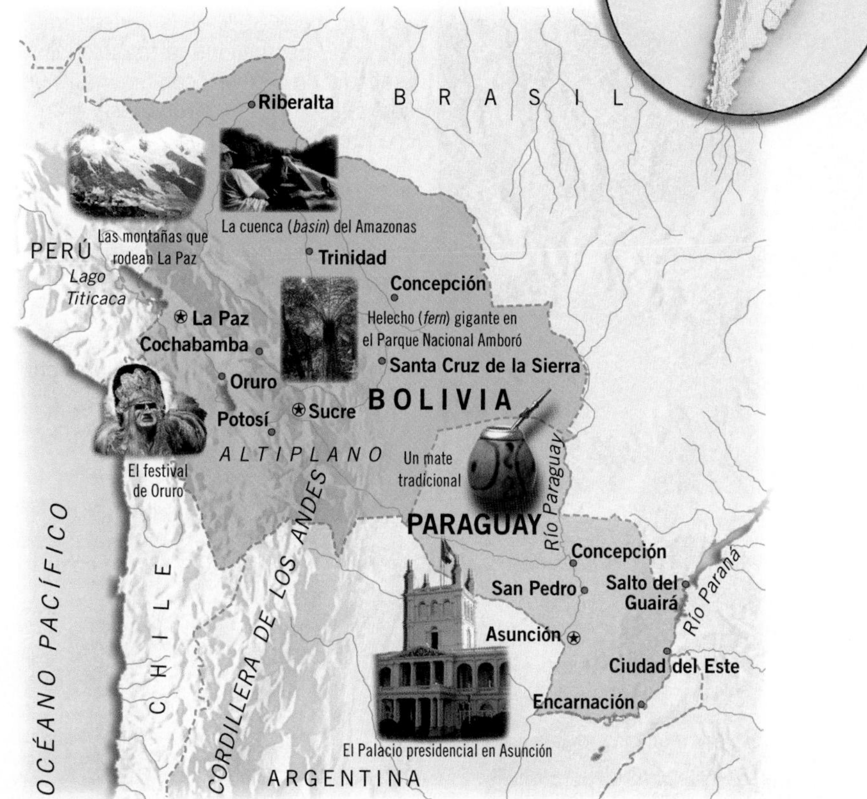

Detalle de tabla de madera pintada, siglo XVI, Museo Casa de Murillo, La Paz, Bolivia

¿QUÉ TE PARECE?

- El Salar de Uyuni en Bolivia es el desierto de sal más grande del mundo y una fuente importante de litio (*lithium*). Tiene hoteles de lujo construidos de sal.
- El Lago Titicaca en Bolivia es el lago comercial y navegable más alto del mundo con una altura de 3.812 metros y es el lago más grande de Sudamérica.
- El presidente boliviano, Evo Morales, salió en el *Daily Show* de Jon Stewart el 25 de septiembre de 2007.
- Paraguay y Bolivia son los únicos países de Sudamérica sin salida directa al mar.
- El español y el guaraní son los dos idiomas oficiales de Paraguay. El guaraní es también el nombre de su moneda.
- El 95% de la población de Paraguay es mestiza, es decir, de ascendencia europea e indígena.

◀ La ciudad de Santa Cruz de la Sierra en Bolivia, ubicada en el corazón del continente, era un puesto fronterizo insignificante de menos de 30.000 habitantes hasta mediados del siglo XX. Hoy en día es la ciudad más grande de Bolivia, con 2,5 millones de habitantes, y produce el 80% de la agricultura del país. Es una ciudad tradicional y sofisticada a la vez, con una multitud de cafés, museos, boutiques y grandes centros de cine.

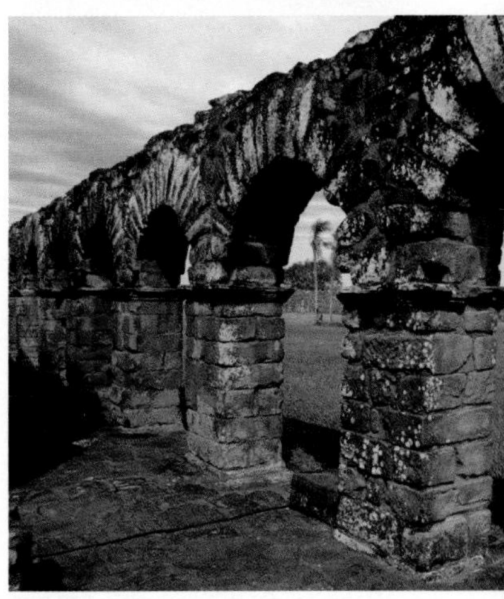

La Santísima Trinidad de Paraná ▶ forma parte de una serie de misiones fundadas por los jesuitas en el siglo XVII. Siete de estas misiones se establecieron en Paraguay. Hoy en día, solo quedan las ruinas de estos centros urbanos y espirituales creados para los indígenas de la zona.

▲ En 2005, Evo Morales fue el primer indígena elegido presidente en Bolivia. Bajo la constitución de 2009, la República de Bolivia cambió su nombre a Estado Plurinacional de Bolivia, en reconocimiento a los diversos grupos indígenas. El mismo año, Morales fue nombrado *World Hero of Mother Earth* por la Asamblea General de las Naciones Unidas. Morales recibió atención global cuando decretó la *Ley de los Derechos de la Madre Tierra* en 2010. Esta ley, única en el mundo, atribuye a la naturaleza los mismos derechos que a los seres humanos. Refleja la antigua y aún vital creencia de los aimaras y los quechuas en la Pachamama (*Mother Earth*), que el ser humano fue creado de la tierra y así tiene un parentesco fraternal con toda la naturaleza.

◀ La Represa Hidroeléctrica de Itaipú en el río Paraná, entre Paraguay y Brasil, suministra el 90% de la energía de Paraguay y el 25% de la de Brasil. En 1994 fue nombrada una de las Siete Maravillas del Mundo Moderno por la *American Society of Civil Engineers*.

¿CUÁNTO SABES?

Indica si las siguientes afirmaciones son ciertas (**C**) o falsas (**F**), según lo que tú sabes sobre Bolivia y Paraguay.

1. _____ El río Paraná está en la frontera entre Paraguay y Argentina.

2. _____ El guaraní es una de las lenguas oficiales de Paraguay.

3. _____ La capital de Bolivia es Santa Cruz.

4. _____ Paraguay no produce suficiente energía hidroeléctrica para exportarla a sus países vecinos.

5. _____ Bolivia tiene grandes depósitos de sal y litio.

6. _____ La República de Bolivia cambió su nombre a Estado Plurinacional de Bolivia en reconocimiento a la diversidad ecológica del país.

Vocabulario en contexto

Discussing the arts: literature, film, art, music, and popular culture

La literatura y el cine

MySpanishLab
Learn more using Amplifire Dynamic Study Modules, Pronunciation, and Vocabulary Tutorials.

Augusto Roa Bastos ▶

Uno de los **novelistas** más importantes de Hispanoamérica es el paraguayo Augusto Roa Bastos (1917–2005). Su novela *Yo, el supremo* (1974) **trata** sobre el **tema** de las dictaduras. Su **personaje principal** se basa en la figura de José Rodríguez de Francia, dictador de Paraguay en las primeras décadas del siglo XIX. Este **escritor** fue uno de los iniciadores del movimiento literario conocido como realismo mágico, que combina elementos mágicos o irracionales con situaciones de aparente normalidad.

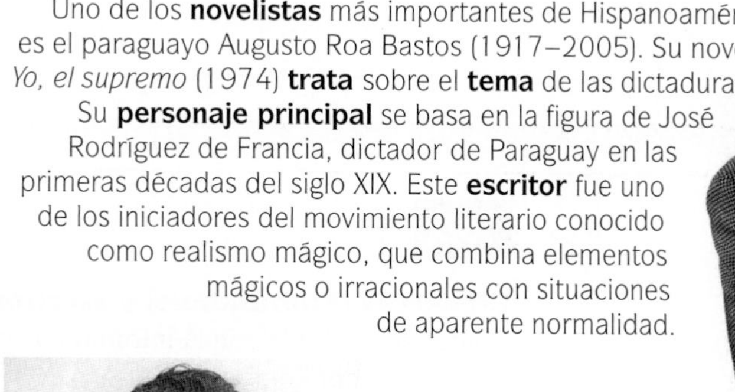

▲ Gabriel García Márquez

Gabriel García Márquez (1928), colombiano, es otro escritor que se asocia con el realismo mágico. **A través de** sus **novelas** y **cuentos** ha sabido recrear un mundo mítico de gran riqueza humana. En su novela *Cien años de soledad* (1967) narra en tono épico la historia de una familia y la **fundación** y **desarrollo** de Macondo, un pueblo imaginario. En 1982 este autor recibió el **Premio** Nobel de Literatura. Algunas de sus obras han sido llevadas al cine; por ejemplo, *El amor en los tiempos del cólera* (2007), con el actor español Javier Bardem.

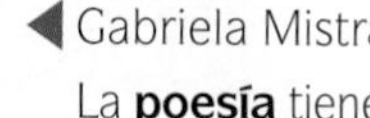

◀ Gabriela Mistral

La **poesía** tiene nombres **destacados** en las letras hispanas. Gabriela Mistral (1889–1957), chilena, fue la primera persona de Hispanoamérica en recibir el Premio Nobel de Literatura, en 1945. Algunos de los temas de su **obra** son **el amor, la amistad** y el mestizaje como característica de la identidad latinoamericana. Otros **poetas** universalmente conocidos son el chileno Pablo Neruda y el peruano César Vallejo.

Iciar Bollaín ▶

El cine hispano ha dado numerosos ejemplos de **calidad** en películas de todos los países. Entre las que han sido **nominadas** o han ganado algún Óscar se encuentran las españolas *Mar adentro* (2004), de Alejandro Amenábar, y *Volver* (2006), de Pedro Almodóvar. La cubana *Fresa y chocolate* (1994), de Tomás Gutiérrez Alea, ganó el Oso de Plata en el festival de Berlín, y la colombiana *La estrategia del caracol* (1993), de Sergio Cabrera, fue premiada en el festival de Valladolid. El cine mexicano ha tenido grandes éxitos en los últimos tiempos con películas de Alfonso Cuarón (*Y tu mamá también*, 2001), de Alejandro González Iñárritu (*Babel*, 2006) y de Guillermo del Toro (*El laberinto del fauno*, 2006). Entre los directores jóvenes más **prometedores** está la española Iciar Bollaín, autora de *Mataharis* (2007) y de *Te doy mis ojos* (2003), que **denuncia** el tema de la violencia doméstica.

PRÁCTICA

13-1  

Escucha y confirma. Listen to the descriptions and select the writer or artist it refers to.

	AUGUSTO ROA BASTOS	GABRIEL GARCÍA MÁRQUEZ	GABRIELA MISTRAL	ICIAR BOLLAÍN
1.				
2.				
3.				
4.				
5.				
6.				

Cultura

Las nominaciones y los premios son muy codiciados (*sought after*) en el mundo del cine. Las películas que compiten en los festivales de cine suelen adquirir más publicidad y tener más éxito económico. Ganar un Óscar a la mejor película extranjera es una de las aspiraciones de muchos directores de todo el mundo, pero hay otros festivales de cine internacionales que tienen gran tradición y repercusión en el mundo hispano, como los de Valladolid (Seminci) y de San Sebastián en España.

Conexiones. Busca información sobre la Semana Internacional de Cine de Valladolid (Seminci) y el Festival de Cine de San Sebastián. ¿Qué películas fueron premiadas en los últimos festivales? ¿Te parecen interesantes estas películas? ¿Conoces algún director o actor entre los ganadores?

13-2 

Cineastas (*Filmmakers*) y escritores. PREPARACIÓN. Completen la tabla con la información que leyeron sobre ciertos hispanos prominentes.

NOMBRE	PROFESIÓN	LUGAR DE ORIGEN	DATOS INTERESANTES	OTRO DATO
	director de cine	Colombia	Ganó un premio en el festival de Valladolid.	
	poetisa	Chile		
Pedro Almodóvar			Es el director de la película *Volver*.	
			Una película suya denuncia el tema de la violencia doméstica.	
	escritor		Ganó el Premio Nobel.	

 **INTERCAMBIOS.** Comparen su tabla con la de otra pareja, y entre todos hagan una lista de otros artistas o escritores hispanos famosos. Pueden incluir a gente del cine, la música, la pintura, el periodismo, la arquitectura, el diseño de ropa, etc. Incluyan el nombre y la siguiente infomación:

1. profesión
2. lugar de origen
3. algunos datos interesantes de su carrera

13-3 

¿De qué trata? **PREPARACIÓN.** Intercambien información sobre un libro que han leído o una película que han visto últimamente. Utilicen las siguientes preguntas como guía.

1. ¿Quién escribió el libro o dirigió la película?
2. ¿Cuál es el tema?
3. ¿Quién es su personaje principal? ¿Cómo es?
4. ¿Te gustó la película/el libro? ¿Por qué?

INTERCAMBIOS. Comparte con la clase la información que has obtenido de tu compañero/a.

13-4 

Un poema. **PREPARACIÓN.** Lean el siguiente poema de Gabriela Mistral y digan si las siguientes afirmaciones son ciertas (**C**) o falsas (**F**). Si son falsas, den la respuesta correcta.

Dame la mano

Dame la mano y danzaremos;
dame la mano y me amarás.
Como una sola flor seremos,
como una flor, y nada más...

El mismo verso cantaremos,
al mismo paso bailarás.
Como una espiga ondularemos,
como una espiga, y nada más.

Te llamas Rosa y yo Esperanza;
pero tu nombre olvidarás,
porque seremos una danza
en la colina y nada más...

1. _____ "Dame la mano" es un poema de amor.
2. _____ El poema habla de tres personas.
3. _____ El tiempo del poema se relaciona con el pasado.
4. _____ Es un poema alegre.

INTERCAMBIOS. Marquen (✓) los temas que trata el poema. Luego, escriban el verso o los versos que ejemplifican cada tema.

1. _____ el baile
2. _____ el amor
3. _____ la familia
4. _____ la naturaleza
5. _____ la música

13-5 

Escritores famosos. Busquen información en Internet sobre uno de estos poetas hispanos y preparen una breve presentación incluyendo la siguiente información.

César Vallejo	Pablo Neruda	Blanca Andreu
Alejandra Pizarnik	Federico García Lorca	Adela Zamudio

1. datos biográficos
2. explicación de uno de sus poemas (tema y características de estilo)

La pintura y el arte

▲ *Las Meninas* de Diego Velázquez

El Museo del Prado tiene una excelente colección de cuadros de **pintores** españoles, como Diego Velázquez, del siglo XVII, y Francisco de Goya, del siglo XVIII. Uno de los cuadros más importantes de Velázquez es *Las Meninas,* donde **retrata** una **escena** en el palacio real. En esta escena vemos a una hija del rey Felipe IV **rodeada** de sus sirvientas. En el cuadro hay un espejo donde **se reflejan** los reyes. También hay un **autorretrato** del pintor.

La persistencia de la memoria de Salvador Dalí ▶

Algunos de los mejores pintores del siglo XX, como Pablo Picasso y Salvador Dalí, también son españoles. En este cuadro vemos el estilo **surrealista** de Dalí, con sus relojes **blandos** y su obsesión por los insectos. Este **paisaje,** con el mar **al fondo,** es un **recuerdo** del pueblo del Mediterráneo donde él vivió, y se repite en muchos de sus cuadros. Picasso desarrolló el estilo **cubista** y fue muy original en el uso de los colores y las **formas.**

◀ *Danza en Tehuantepec* de Diego Rivera

Los mexicanos Frida Kahlo y Diego Rivera muestran en sus **obras** las costumbres y las condiciones sociales de su país. Este cuadro **se titula** *Danza en Tehuantepec* y en él se ve a una pareja bailando una danza tradicional. Rivera es muy famoso por sus grandes **murales.** Algunos de ellos se pueden ver en México, Detroit y San Francisco.

Fernando Botero ▶

El **escultor** y pintor colombiano Fernando Botero es conocido por las voluminosas figuras humanas de sus cuadros y esculturas que **se exponen** en todos los museos del mundo. Botero reconoce la influencia artística de los grandes pintores españoles Velázquez y Goya, así como la de los **muralistas** mexicanos. En su obra, Botero critica con humor una sociedad infantilizada o inmadura en la que **abundan** los **símbolos** de la autoridad y del poder, como clérigos, presidentes y burgueses (*members of the middle class*).

PRÁCTICA

13-6 

Para confirmar. Relaciona las siguientes afirmaciones con los pintores mencionados anteriormente.

1. _____ Pinta con humor retratos de figuras poderosas.
2. _____ Sus cuadros son de estilo surrealista.
3. _____ Es famoso por sus murales.
4. _____ Fue un pintor español del siglo XVIII.
5. _____ Es el pintor de *Las Meninas*.
6. _____ Es una pintora mexicana que retrata las costumbres de su país.
7. _____ Su estilo cubista muestra formas muy originales.

a. Diego Velázquez
b. Francisco de Goya
c. Pablo Picasso
d. Salvador Dalí
e. Frida Kahlo
f. Diego Rivera
g. Fernando Botero

◀ *Saturno devorando a un hijo* de Francisco de Goya

Cultura

Los aparapitas

Enrique Arnal (1932) es uno de los artistas bolivianos más importantes a nivel internacional. Es muy conocido por una serie de pinturas que se enfoca en la figura del aparapita, cargador indígena contratado para llevar objetos y productos en los concurridos mercados de La Paz. La palabra proviene de la lengua aimara y significa *el que carga*. De procedencia rural, los aparapitas se encuentran en una sociedad moderna, desubicados y aislados socialmente. Arnal capta esta alienación en sus cuadros colocándolos entre portales donde parece que pasan de una dimensión a otra. Para expresar su presunta anonimidad ante el público, Arnal borra las facciones de las caras. Al mismo tiempo que los aparapitas están presentes, pasan sin ser percibidos (*noticed*).

▲ *Doble recinto* de Enrique Arnal

13-7 

Otros artistas. Busquen información en Internet sobre algún pintor, escultor o muralista de Bolivia o de Paraguay. Luego, preparen una presentación visual para la clase que incluya lo siguiente.

1. lugar y fecha de nacimiento
2. título y descripción de una de sus obras más famosas
3. algún acontecimiento (*event*) notable de su vida

13-8 

Comparación. Comparen *Las Meninas* de Picasso con *Las Meninas* de Velázquez. Analicen los siguientes aspectos y expliquen cuál de los dos cuadros les gusta más y por qué.

1. el color
2. la ubicación de los personajes
3. las formas
4. el estilo

▲ *Las Meninas,* Diego Velázquez, 1656

▲ *Las Meninas,* Pablo Picasso, 1957

La música y la cultura popular

◀ El boliviano Piraí Vaca es uno de los **guitarristas** más famosos de la **actualidad**. Aparte de su repertorio clásico, Vaca interpreta las tradiciones de la música popular como el tango argentino y el chopi paraguayo. Entre sus muchas distinciones, Vaca ha sido honrado con el *Fellowship of the Americas* por el John F. Kennedy Center for the Performing Arts y declarado el *Boliviano más Destacado en el Exterior* por las Naciones Unidas para la Juventud. Sus conciertos son **inolvidables** por su impresionante talento musical y su carismática presencia sobre el escenario.

La variedad ▶ de la música hispanoamericana, que va **desde** la música afrocaribeña **hasta** las melodías de los Andes, es impresionante. Entre todas estas formas musicales, el tango siempre **se ha distinguido** por la riqueza de las **voces** de sus más notables **intérpretes,** como Carlos Gardel. El tango **surgió** entre los europeos que emigraron a Argentina a comienzos del siglo XX en busca de una vida mejor.

La danza latinoamericana ▶ tiene una larga tradición, tanto en su manifestación clásica como contemporánea. Alicia Alonso, de Cuba, Julio Bocca, de Argentina, y la **bailarina** mexicana Laura Rocha, quien **dirige** su propia **compañía,** Barro Rojo, se han presentado en muchos países de América Latina, en Estados Unidos y en Europa.

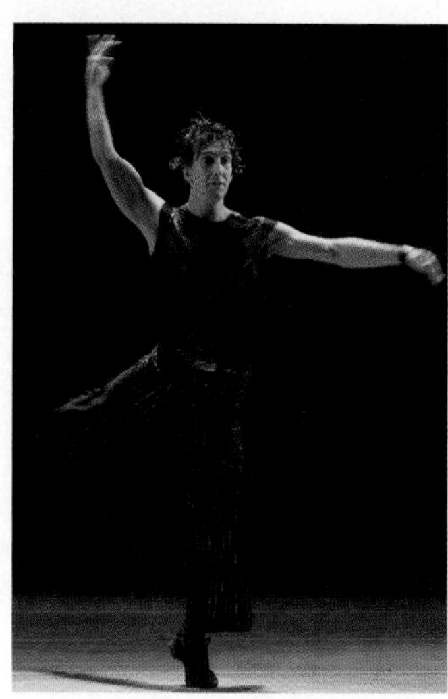

Los actores son a menudo ▶ los protagonistas de las **revistas del corazón.** Los medios de comunicación hablan de sus **éxitos** y de sus **fracasos,** de sus relaciones y de la ropa que llevan. La multifacética actriz Leonor Watling, hija de una británica y un español, ha trabajado en películas tan famosas como *La vida secreta de las palabras,* de Isabel Coixet, y *Hable con ella,* de Pedro Almodóvar. Además, es la cantante principal del grupo Marlango.

Los instrumentos musicales

La música de Hispanoamérica incluye una gran variedad de instrumentos, desde los tambores y trompetas de la música del Caribe hasta las quenas y los charangos característicos de los Andes. La quena es una flauta tradicional, generalmente de bambú, y el charango es parecido a una guitarra pero más pequeño. El instrumento típico del tango argentino es el bandoneón, que es como un acordeón con botones a los lados. La música típica de Paraguay incluye en ocasiones el arpa (*harp*).

Comparaciones. ¿Cuáles son los instrumentos más importantes en la música folclórica norteamericana? Selecciona uno y descríbelo.

PRÁCTICA

13-9  

Para confirmar. Asocia la descripción con la expresión apropiada.

1. _____ lo contrario del éxito
2. _____ un/a artista muy famoso/a
3. _____ una persona cuya (*whose*) profesión es la danza
4. _____ un grupo de artistas que hace un espectáculo
5. _____ un espectáculo de música
6. _____ una publicación sobre la vida de los artistas

a. un bailarín/una bailarina
b. una compañía
c. un concierto
d. una revista del corazón
e. el fracaso
f. una estrella

Cultura

El flamenco

El flamenco es un tipo de música que se originó en Andalucía, en el sur de España, hacia el siglo XV. Inicialmente eran canciones breves, sin acompañamiento instrumental, que los gitanos (*gypsies*) cantaban para lamentarse de sus malas condiciones de vida. A través de los siglos, el flamenco ha continuado su desarrollo y ha añadido instrumentos musicales, principalmente la guitarra. A partir del siglo XVIII adquirió gran popularidad el baile flamenco, que es uno de los más emocionantes y variados del mundo.

Comparaciones. Investiga el origen del *blues* y compáralo con lo que sabes del flamenco. ¿Qué similitudes encuentras?

13-10

Personajes célebres. PREPARACIÓN. Vas a escribir un breve artículo sobre uno de los artistas mencionados en la página 457. Escribe al menos ocho preguntas relacionadas con los siguientes aspectos de su vida que después investigarás para tu artículo.

1. su lugar de origen
2. su familia
3. algún recuerdo o anécdota de su vida
4. los inicios de su carrera artística
5. sus mayores éxitos y sus fracasos
6. sus planes

 **INTERCAMBIOS.** Busca en Internet información sobre este artista y escribe un breve artículo sobre él/ella incluyendo esta información. Comparte el contenido de este artículo con la clase.

13-11

La cultura en los medios de comunicación. **PREPARACIÓN.** En una revista o un periódico en línea, busca un artículo sobre algún concierto o película que te interese, léelo y resúmelo.

INTERCAMBIOS. Comparte con tu grupo el resumen del artículo que leíste. Incluye la siguiente información.

1. ¿Cómo se llama la revista o el periódico de donde obtuviste el artículo?

2. ¿Quién lo escribió?

3. ¿Cuál es el tema del artículo?

4. ¿Cuáles son las ideas centrales que se presentan?

5. ¿Por qué escogiste este artículo?

13-12

¿Adónde vamos? **PREPARACIÓN.** You will listen to a young couple trying to decide where to go on a Friday evening. With your partner, list three places where you think they might want to go.

ESCUCHA. As you listen, focus on the general idea of what is said. Then select the appropriate ending for each statement.

1. Uno de los eventos culturales a los que Alberto y Josefina consideran ir es…

a. una exposición de arte precolombino.

b. una lectura de poemas.

c. un concierto de música popular.

2. Josefina prefiere ir al…

a. concierto de la orquesta sinfónica.

b. museo de arte latinoamericano.

c. lugar que sea más barato.

3. Para averiguar si hay entradas, Josefina va a…

a. usar Internet.

b. llamar por teléfono a todos los lugares.

c. ir personalmente al centro.

4. Según esta conversación podemos ver que…

a. Alberto siempre decide a qué lugar van a ir y no escucha a nadie.

b. Josefina no acepta ninguna sugerencia e impone su voluntad.

c. Alberto y Josefina discuten las posibilidades y deciden juntos.

MOSAICO cultural

El grafiti y la identidad urbana

El grafiti es una manifestación cultural que ha adquirido mucha fuerza en el mundo hispano. Para Oz Montania, un reconocido artista urbano paraguayo, el grafiti es libertad de expresión y es espacio público. Desde los doce años, Oz ha llevado esta forma de arte hasta la gente de una manera absolutamente democrática, como dice él. Históricamente, el grafiti —que es una parte del arte urbano— ha tenido principios políticos: en los periodos de dictadura (*dictatorship*) militar el grafiti fue una de las formas de expresión ideológica más fuerte, especialmente en Argentina, Chile y México. Desde entonces, el grafiti ha ganado importancia entre las otras artes populares, como la música y la danza.

▲ Una calle en la región de Tarapacá, Chile

▲ ¿Arte o vandalismo?

Sin embargo, este arte popular es aún relativamente joven y no es comprendido por algunos sectores de la población. Charqui, un grafitero chileno, ha tenido problemas con la policía porque a veces lo han considerado un criminal y no un artista. "Es probable que las personas no entiendan el humor, la ironía y la inconformidad política de mis grafitis. Quizá por eso piensan que soy un vándalo", comentó Charqui.

Es obvio que esta manifestación artística ha comenzado a definir la identidad de las ciudades. Desde hace años se celebra en Valparaíso el Festival Mundial del Grafiti. En este encuentro se reúnen artistas urbanos de todo el mundo y pintan gran parte de la ciudad de forma colaborativa. Dice Charqui sobre el festival: "El código del grafiti es la solidaridad; la obra de un artista fusionada con el trabajo de otro. Al final, la cultura de la ciudad gana con este proceso artístico".

▲ Valparaíso, Chile

Compara

1. ¿Conoces a algún artista urbano en tu ciudad? ¿Qué tipo de grafiti hace?
2. ¿Piensas que el grafiti es una manifestación artística y que tiene valor cultural? Justifica tu respuesta.
3. ¿Piensas que los grafitis hispanos son diferentes de los estadounidenses? Explica tu opinión con ejemplos.

Funciones y formas

1 Talking about the past

JOSEFINA: Alberto, ¿qué piensas de esta obra?

ALBERTO: Es una expresión magnífica del arte abstracto.

JOSEFINA: ¿Ah, sí? ¿Quién la **pintó?**

ALBERTO: **Fue** un artista que en todas sus obras **pintaba** un ojo abstracto. **Tenía** mucho talento pero **murió** joven. **Empezó** a pintar a los 15 años y **vendió** su primer cuadro a los 17 años. Poca gente lo **conocía.** Sin embargo, **era** uno de los favoritos de los críticos.

JOSEFINA: ¿Qué le **pasó?**

ALBERTO: **Tuvo** un accidente de moto cuando **viajaba** por los Andes. ¡Muy trágico!

Piénsalo. Indica si cada una de las oraciones se refiere a un evento que ocurrió en el pasado (**E**), o si es una descripción (**D**).

1. _____ En todas sus obras **pintaba** un ojo abstracto.
2. _____ **Murió** joven.
3. _____ ¿Quién lo **pintó**?
4. _____ **Era** uno de los favoritos de los críticos.
5. _____ **Tuvo** un accidente de moto.
6. _____ **Tenía** mucho talento.

Review of the preterit and imperfect

- In previous chapters you learned two tenses that Spanish uses to express the past: the preterit (**el pretérito**) and the imperfect (**el imperfecto**). You used the preterit to talk about past events, actions, and conditions that are viewed as completed or ended. You used the imperfect to describe characteristics and conditions in the past; to express habitual or repeated actions, or states in progress at a particular time in the past; and to tell the time and someone's age in the past. In this section you will gain further experience using both tenses to narrate in the past.

REGULAR PRETERIT ENDINGS			
	-ar	**-er**	**-ir**
yo	-é	-í	-í
tú	-aste	-iste	-iste
Ud, él, ella	-ó	-ió	-ió
nosotros/as	-amos	-imos	-imos
vosotros/as	-asteis	-isteis	-isteis
Uds., ellos/as	-aron	-ieron	-ieron

REGULAR IMPERFECT ENDINGS			
	-ar	**-er**	**-ir**
yo	-aba	-ía	-ía
tú	-abas	-ías	-ías
Ud, él, ella	-aba	-ía	-ía
nosotros/as	-ábamos	-íamos	-íamos
vosotros/as	-abais	-íais	-íais
Uds., ellos/as	-aban	-ían	-ían

Refer to *Capítulos 6* through *8* for more information about the past tense.

¿COMPRENDES?

Escoge entre el pretérito y el imperfecto en cada oración.

1. Durante nuestra visita a La Paz, Marcos y yo (fuimos/íbamos) al Museo Nacional de Arte Contemporáneo.
2. (Fue/Era) temprano cuando el museo (abrió/abría) sus puertas.
3. (Hubo/Había) un guardia en cada sala del museo.
4. Toda la gente (caminó/caminaba) en silencio y (admiró/admiraba) las hermosas obras de arte.
5. Marcos y su familia siempre (fueron/iban) al museo cuando él y sus hermanos (fueron/eran) pequeños.

MySpanishLab

Learn more using Amplifire Dynamic Study Modules, Grammar Tutorials, and Extra Practice activities.

PRÁCTICA

13-13  

El arpa de Paraguay. Lee la siguiente historia sobre el arpa en la música paraguaya. Completa las oraciones con la forma correcta del pretérito o el imperfecto de los verbos. Luego, compara tus respuestas con las de tu compañero/a.

Los historiadores afirman que los españoles (**1**) _____________ (traer) el arpa a América. Cuando este instrumento (**2**) _____________ (llegar) a Paraguay, a los habitantes indígenas de lugar les (**3**) _____________ (encantar) la música que (**4**) _____________ (tocar) el español, don Martín Niño. El contacto de la cultura europea y la indígena (**5**) _____________ (resultar) en la fusión de dos culturas. De esa unión (**6**) _____________ (nacer) el arpa paraguaya. Los guaraníes (**7**) _____________ (adoptar) el arpa y la (**8**) _____________ (remodelar), usando materiales americanos, como la madera. También (**9**) _____________ (crear) su propio repertorio musical. (**10**) _____________ (Ser) obvio para los jesuitas y los franciscanos españoles que los mestizos (**11**) _____________ (tener) gran talento musical. Con cada perfeccionamiento del instrumento musical, los clérigos (**12**) _____________ (observar) una mejor sonoridad y claridad en la ejecución del arpa paraguaya. Los mestizos (**13**) _____________ (pasar) sus conocimientos de generación en generación y de esta manera cada una (**14**) _____________ (crear) sus propias técnicas. Por ejemplo, (**15**) _____________ (usar) las uñas de la mano derecha para crear la melodía. El acompañamiento lo (**16**) _____________ (hacer) con la mano izquierda. Con los años el arpa (**17**) _____________ (pasar) a ser parte de diversos tipos de música de México, Venezuela, Perú, Chile y Argentina.

13-14 

Nuestro viaje a Bolivia. Visiten virtualmente las salas del Museo Nacional de Etnografía y Folklore de Bolivia y seleccionen un objeto que les interese. Presenten un informe breve a la clase con la siguiente información.

1. qué tipo de objeto era
2. cuándo y dónde se encontró
3. quiénes lo usaban y para qué lo usaban
4. qué importancia tenía
5. otros detalles interesantes que ustedes descubrieron en su investigación

13-15 

Un espectáculo inolvidable. PREPARACIÓN. Piensa en un espectáculo emocionante al que asististe en el pasado. Habla con tu compañero/a sobre el espectáculo e incluye la siguiente información.

1. lo que sabías acerca del espectáculo y los artistas antes de ir
2. lo que esperabas ver allí
3. algo nuevo que descubriste después de ver el espectáculo y los artistas
4. dos actividades que hiciste y dos actividades que no hiciste
5. lo que más recuerdas del espectáculo

 INTERCAMBIOS. Determinen cuál de los dos espectáculos fue el más interesante y por qué. Compartan con la clase sus experiencias en el espectáculo.

Situación

PREPARACIÓN. Lean la situación. Luego, compartan ejemplos de vocabulario, gramática y otra información que necesitan para desarrollar la conversación.

Role A. Last week you travelled to La Paz, Bolivia and, on the plane, you happened to be seated next to a movie star. Call your best friend and tell him/her:

a. who the famous person was;
b. what he/she looked like;
c. what he/she was wearing;
d. if you spoke to him/her and what you talked about.

Role B. Your best friend calls you to tell you that he/she met a movie star. Listen to his/her descriptions and information about the encounter. Ask him/her additional information:

a. what he/she did on the plane;
b. what he/she ate;
c. why he/she was sitting in economy class; etc.

	ROLE A	ROLE B
Vocabulario	Physical descriptions Clothes	Airplane and travel expressions Food
Funciones y formas	Using the imperfect to describe Using the preterit for actions Topics of conversation	Using the imperfect to describe Using the preterit for actions

INTERCAMBIOS. Practica la conversación con tu compañero/a incorporando el vocabulario y las funciones de *Preparación.* Luego, represéntenla ante la clase.

2 Hypothesizing

GLORIA: Aquí veo solo dos de los instrumentos para el concierto de esta noche. ¿Dónde están los otros?

AMARU: Siempre grabamos digitalmente la música de los otros instrumentos. Yo los **traería** todos, pero **sería** carísimo. **Gastaríamos** demasiado para traer los tambores, las guitarras y las quijadas (*jawbone*), por ejemplo.

GLORIA: ¿Cuánto **costaría** traer los otros instrumentos?

AMARU: Bueno, yo **tendría** que pagar 200 dólares solo para traer mi guitarra. Para traer todos los instrumentos, **pagaríamos** una fortuna.

e **Piénsalo.** Indica (✓) en la columna correspondiente si cada una de las siguientes afirmaciones se refiere a la **realidad** o a una **hipótesis.**

	REALIDAD	HIPÓTESIS
1. Aquí **veo** solo dos de los instrumentos para el concierto.	_____	_____
2. Siempre **grabamos** digitalmente la música de los otros instrumentos.	_____	_____
3. ¿Cuánto **costaría** traer los otros instrumentos?	_____	_____
4. **Sería** carísimo.	_____	_____
5. **Tendría** que pagar $200 solo para traer mi guitarra.	_____	_____
6. **Pagaríamos** una fortuna.	_____	_____

The conditional

- You have used the expression **me gustaría...** to express what you would like. **Gustaría** is a form of the conditional.
- The conditional in Spanish is similar to the English construction *would* + *verb.* It is used to hypothesize about a situation that is not part of the speaker's present reality.

  Yo **saldría** temprano para el concierto, pero trabajo hasta tarde. — *I would leave early for the concert, but I work late.*

- When English *would* implies *used to,* the imperfect is used in Spanish.

  Cuando era chica, mi papá me **llevaba** a los conciertos al aire libre en el parque. — *When I was little, my father would (used to) take me to open-air concerts in the park.*

- The conditional is easy to recognize. It is formed by adding the endings **-ía, -ías, -ía, -íamos, -íais, -ían** to the infinitive.

CONDITIONAL			
	HABLAR	**COMER**	**VIVIR**
yo	hablar**ía**	comer**ía**	vivir**ía**
tú	hablar**ías**	comer**ías**	vivir**ías**
Ud., él, ella	hablar**ía**	comer**ía**	vivir**ía**
nosotros/as	hablar**íamos**	comer**íamos**	vivir**íamos**
vosotros/as	hablar**íais**	comer**íais**	vivir**íais**
Uds., ellos/as	hablar**ían**	comer**ían**	vivir**ían**

¿COMPRENDES?

Completa las oraciones con la forma del condicional de los verbos.

1. De ser el líder del grupo, yo ________ (pagar) dinero para llevar todos los instrumentos a mis conciertos.
2. El público ________ (preferir) escuchar la música en vivo que escucharla digitalizada.
3. Nosotros ________ (ganar) más dinero porque ________ (asistir) más público.
4. Los conciertos ________ (ser) un éxito rotundo.

MySpanishLab

Learn more using Amplifire Dynamic Study Modules, Grammar Tutorials, and Extra Practice activities.

- Verbs that have an irregular stem in the future have that same stem in the conditional.

IRREGULAR CONDITIONAL VERBS		
INFINITIVE	**NEW STEM**	**CONDITIONAL FORMS**
haber	**habr-**	habría, habrías, habría...
poder	**podr-**	podría, podrías, podría...
querer	**querr-**	querría, querrías, querría...
saber	**sabr-**	sabría, sabrías, sabría...
poner	**pondr-**	pondría, pondrías, pondría...
salir	**saldr-**	saldría, saldrías, saldría...
tener	**tendr-**	tendría, tendrías, tendría...
venir	**vendr-**	vendría, vendrías, vendría...
decir	**dir-**	diría, dirías, diría...
hacer	**har-**	haría, harías, haría...

Yo **pondría** el cuadro sobre la chimenea. — *I would put the painting over the fireplace.*

¿**Podrías** escribir un poema de amor en español? — *Would you be able to write a love poem in Spanish?*

PRÁCTICA

13-16

¿Qué harías? **PREPARACIÓN.** Lee las siguientes situaciones y escoge lo que probablemente harías.

1. Es el cumpleaños de tu mejor amigo, quien sigue cursos avanzados de español, y le quieres regalar algo útil.

a. Le compraría una novela de Roa Bastos traducida al inglés.
b. Le regalaría *El Quijote* de Cervantes.
c. Le daría un buen diccionario.

2. El dúo boliviano Tupay va a dar un concierto en tu ciudad este fin de semana.

a. Invitaría a mi novio/a al concierto.
b. Llamaría a mis amigos para ir al concierto.
c. Compraría un charango para tocar con ellos durante el concierto.

3. Van a estrenar (pasar por primera vez) una nueva película de Leonor Watling.

a. La iría a ver la noche del estreno.
b. No vería la película porque no me interesa la actriz.
c. Leería las reseñas (*reviews*) antes de ir a verla.

4. Vas a pasar unos días en Madrid pero tienes poco tiempo para visitar el Museo del Prado. ¿Qué harías?

a. Pasaría algunos minutos en el museo para conocerlo.
b. Me informaría sobre lo que se puede ver en el museo.
c. Solo visitaría las salas donde están las pinturas de mi pintor favorito.

INTERCAMBIOS. Comparen sus respuestas y después digan qué harían ustedes realmente en esas situaciones.

13-17

Desafíos (*Challenges*). PREPARACIÓN. Ganaste una beca de tu universidad. Con los fondos (un millón de dólares), debes despertar el interés de los alumnos universitarios por las artes y las letras. Escribe algunas ideas de qué harías con el dinero y por qué. Considera los siguientes propósitos.

1. promocionar la pintura
2. despertar el interés por las artes populares
3. organizar un foro de expresión artística para los estudiantes con talento artístico

 INTERCAMBIOS. Comenten y comparen sus planes hipotéticos. Luego, seleccionen el mejor plan y explíquenle a la clase por qué lo escogieron.

13-18 

Buscar soluciones. Primero di qué harías en las siguientes situaciones. Después, compara tus respuestas con las de otros estudiantes.

1. Mientras caminas por una calle de tu ciudad, inesperadamente, te encuentras (*run into*) con tu artista favorito/a.
2. Un amigo tuyo es pintor y necesita dinero para montar su primera exposición.
3. Acabas de descubrir que alguien en el campus está vendiendo entradas falsas y muy baratas para un concierto de tu grupo favorito.
4. Alguien confiable (*trustworthy*) te informó que la persona que pintó grafiti en las paredes de la residencia donde vives es uno de tus mejores amigos.

13-19 

Músicos aficionados. PREPARACIÓN. Tienen un grupo de amigos que han creado una banda de música muy buena pero no saben promocionarse. Denles ideas de lo que ustedes harían en su lugar.

INTERCAMBIOS. Compartan sus ideas con otra pareja y escojan las mejores para compartir con la clase.

Cultura

Museo Nacional de Bellas Artes

El Museo Nacional de Bellas Artes de Asunción es el más importante del país. En este museo se puede apreciar la historia del país, caracterizada por la importancia de la cultura indígena y por su aislamiento de corrientes artísticas y emigraciones de influencia europea hasta el siglo XX. Hoy en día, cuenta con una importante colección de arte indígena y con obras de los principales artistas paraguayos del siglo XX que siguieron tendencias cosmopolitas. También cuenta con una colección de artistas internacionales.

Comparaciones. ¿Con qué frecuencia visitas los museos de arte? ¿Qué tipo de obras se pueden ver en el museo de bellas artes de tu ciudad o estado?

Situación

PREPARACIÓN. Lean la situación. Luego, compartan ejemplos de vocabulario, gramática y otra información que necesitan para desarrollar la conversación.

Role A. You are considering visiting Paraguay next summer so you call a friend who has been there. Include the following in your conversation:

a. ask how much money you would need for food and lodging for a month in Paraguay;
b. tell your friend that you are really interested in seeing and studying the indigenous art of Paraguay;
c. ask your friend to recommend some Paraguayan folk music; and
d. find out how long it would take to learn Guaraní, the indigenous language of Paraguay.

Role B. Your friend is thinking of visiting Paraguay, a country you love and know a lot about. Tell your friend the following:

a. he/she would probably need around U.S. $1,500 for food and lodging for a month if he/she stays at youth hostels (**albergues juveniles**);
b. you would recommend the Museo Nacional de Bellas Artes in Asunción for indigenous art; and
c. the Teatro Nacional for concerts of Paraguayan folk music;
d. he/she would probably be able to learn some basic expressions in Guaraní during the trip, but it's totally different from Spanish.

	ROLE A	ROLE B
Vocabulario	Expressions related to traveling and popular art, such as handicrafts Question words	Expressions related to traveling and popular art, such as handicrafts
Funciones y formas	Asking questions	Answering questions Giving suggestions on hypothetical situations

INTERCAMBIOS. Practica la conversación con tu compañero/a incorporando el vocabulario y las funciones de *Preparación*. Luego, represéntenla ante la clase.

3 Expressing reciprocity

En general, los artesanos hispanos forman comunidades donde abundan las relaciones de solidaridad. **Se conocen** entre ellos y, puesto que generalmente viven modestamente, **se ayudan** mutuamente. Así lo indican las afirmaciones de Camilo, uno de los artesanos de este taller. "Mario y yo somos amigos y compartimos casi todo. Cuando uno de los dos no tiene dinero, **nos prestamos** dinero. Pero aún más importante, **nos respetamos** el uno al otro porque **nos necesitamos".**

Piénsalo. Asocia las afirmaciones con su significado.

1. _____ **Se conocen** entre ellos.
2. _____ **Se ayudan** mutuamente.
3. _____ **Nos prestamos** dinero.
4. _____ **Nos respetamos** el uno al otro.
5. _____ **Nos necesitamos**.

a. Yo respeto a Mario y él me respeta a mí.
b. Mario me necesita a mí y yo lo necesito a él.
c. Mario conoce a Camilo y Camilo conoce a Mario.
d. Camilo ayuda a Mario y viceversa.
e. Yo le presto dinero a Mario y él hace lo mismo conmigo.

Reciprocal verbs and pronouns

- Use plural reflexive pronouns (**nos**, **os**, **se**) to express reciprocal actions. In English, reciprocal actions are usually expressed with *each other* or *one another.*

Muchos hispanos **se abrazan** cuando **se saludan.**	*Many Hispanics embrace when they greet each other.*
Los artesanos de este taller **se ven** todos los días.	*The artisans in this workshop see each other every day.*
En este centro de arte **nos ayudamos** mucho.	*In this art center, we help each other a lot.*
Nos llamamos cuando hay una nueva exposición de arte para ir juntos.	*We call each other when there is a new art exhibit so that we can go together.*

¿COMPRENDES?

Completa las oraciones para indicar reciprocidad.

1. Mónica y Pablo ________ (ayudar) a preparar la exposición de la artesanía que ambos han creado.
2. ¿Por qué tú y yo no ________ (ver) después del concierto?
3. Los guardias que cuidan a los artistas famosos ________ (mandar) mensajes de texto cuando ven algo extraño.

MySpanishLab

Learn more using Amplifire Dynamic Study Modules, Grammar Tutorials, and Extra Practice activities.

PRÁCTICA

13-20 

Indicaciones de reciprocidad. Escoge las ideas que completen las oraciones.

1. _____ Cuando Mario y Camilo no se ven durante el día, ellos...
2. _____ El perro y el gato de Mario se pelean todo el tiempo. Ellos...
3. _____ Alberto y yo somos muy buenos amigos, pero vivimos en ciudades diferentes. No hablamos mucho por teléfono, pero...
4. _____ Mario y Alicia son novios y se quieren mucho. Cuando se despiden por la noche, ellos...
5. _____ Mario y Camilo dicen que el secreto de su larga amistad es que ellos...

a. nos mandamos correos electrónicos.
b. se llaman por teléfono.
c. se aprecian y se respetan.
d. se detestan.
e. se abrazan y se besan.

13-21 

¿Qué hacen los buenos colegas? PREPARACIÓN. Determinen si los buenos colegas deben hacer lo siguiente, y bajo qué circunstancias.

respetarse

E1: *Yo creo que los buenos colegas se respetan, a pesar de sus diferencias.*

E2: *Estoy de acuerdo. En las reuniones se escuchan con atención y se tratan con respeto siempre.*

1. ____ llamarse todos los días
2. ____ comprenderse
3. ____ ayudarse cuando tienen problemas
4. ____ insultarse y pelearse
5. ____ regalarse cosas
6. ____ darse consejos cuando los necesitan
7. ____ comunicarse constantemente
8. ____ criticarse continuamente
9. ____ pedirse disculpas (*apologize*) después de una fuerte discusión
10. ____ demostrarse empatía

INTERCAMBIOS. Compartan sus ideas con otra pareja. Luego, hagan lo siguiente:

1. Escojan las cuatro actitudes más importantes para mantener una buena relación con la gente. Justifiquen su selección.
2. Escojan las dos actitudes que consideran más problemáticas en las relaciones con otras personas. Den ejemplos de los problemas que podrían causar entre las personas.
3. Compartan sus conclusiones con la clase.

13-22 

Mis relaciones con... Piensa en la gente con quien te relacionas normalmente y explícale a tu compañero/a cómo son las relaciones entre ustedes. Usa los verbos de la lista.

comunicarse	pelearse
detestarse	quererse
odiarse	respetarse

MODELO *Mi hermano y yo... mucho, pero a veces...*

En directo

To complain about something or someone:

Tengo una queja. *I have a complaint.*

Quisiera quejarme de... *I would like to complain about ...*

Quisiera hablar con usted sobre un problema que tengo con... *I would like to discuss with you a problem that I have with ...*

Listen to a conversation with these expressions.

13-23

Consejos. **PREPARACIÓN.** Identifica los problemas de las siguientes personas. Luego, recomienda una solución en cada situación.

1. Rafael y Magdalena son novios, pero no se ven con mucha frecuencia. Él es un pintor que vive en Monterrey, México, y ella trabaja en Los Ángeles. Mantienen una relación a distancia.
2. Catalina y Raquel trabajan en un taller de arte. Cuando Catalina quiere pintar un cuadro, necesita silencio absoluto para inspirarse. Pero cuando ella llega al taller, siempre encuentra a Raquel hablando por teléfono con su novio.
3. Los empleados de Pablo tienen miedo de expresar sus opiniones sobre las piezas de cerámica que él crea porque Pablo siempre toma los comentarios de sus empleados como un ataque personal o parece no escucharlos. Sus colegas evitan hablar con él de este tema.

INTERCAMBIOS. Discute con tu compañero/a los problemas que identificaste y tus recomendaciones. Luego, determinen la mejor recomendación para cada caso y compártanla con la clase.

E1: *En el caso de Rafael y Magdalena, el problema es la distancia. Se ven con poca frecuencia.*

E2: *Tienes razón. ¿Qué les recomendarías?*

E1: *Les recomendaría conseguir un trabajo en la misma ciudad.*

E2: *Estoy de acuerdo./No estoy de acuerdo. Deberían terminar su relación.*

Situación

PREPARACIÓN. Lean la situación. Luego, compartan ejemplos de vocabulario, gramática y otra información que necesitan para desarrollar la conversación.

Role A. You are talking with the owner of a popular art studio in your community where you are taking a pottery class (**cerámica**). You are new in town and think this will be a good place to meet people. You trust this person enough to ask the following personal questions:

a. if he/she has many good friends;
b. when he/she met his/her best friend (**conocerse**); and
c. what the key (**la clave**) to a long friendship (**amistad**) is.

Role B. You own an art studio that is very popular in your community. You are talking with a new student who is eager to make friends with people in the class. Share with him/her some of your own experiences. Explain:

a. when you and your best friend met (**conocerse**);
b. how your friendship (**amistad**) started;
c. that you do not see each other every day but you stay in touch (**mantenerse en contacto**); and
d. that you respect each other, although you do not always agree on everything.

	ROLE A	ROLE B
Vocabulario	Vocabulary related to relationships	Vocabulary related to relationships
Funciones y formas	Asking questions Expressing reciprocity	Answering questions Expressing reciprocity

INTERCAMBIOS. Practica la conversación con tu compañero/a incorporando el vocabulario y las funciones de *Preparación.* Luego, represéntenla ante la clase.

EN ACCIÓN

¡No te lo pierdas!

13-24 Antes de ver

Artistas del mundo hispanoamericano. ¿Con qué artistas asocias las siguientes obras?

1. _____ *Autorretrato entre México y Estados Unidos*
2. _____ *Cien años de soledad*
3. _____ *La estrategia del caracol*
4. _____ *Don Quijote de la Mancha*
5. _____ *Las Meninas*

a. Gabriel García Márquez
b. Cervantes
c. Velázquez
d. Frida Kahlo
e. Sergio Cabrera

13-25 Mientras ves  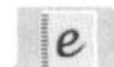

Manifestaciones artísticas. En este segmento de video, cada uno de los chicos se interesa por distintas manifestaciones artísticas del mundo hispanoamericano. Asocia la persona interesada con cada uno de los siguientes temas.

1. _____ obras de pintores latinoamericanos
2. _____ música puertorriqueña
3. _____ teatro infantil
4. _____ muralistas latinoamericanos

a. Vanesa
b. Yolanda y Federico
c. Héctor
d. Esteban

13-26 Después de ver 

Preferencias artísticas. PREPARACIÓN. Indica si las siguientes afirmaciones son ciertas (**C**) o falsas (**F**) de acuerdo con la información en el video.

1. _____ El Museo de Arte Latinoamericano tiene una importante colección de obras de artistas hispanos del siglo XIX.
2. _____ A Héctor le interesan mucho los artistas que hacen un comentario social a través de sus obras.
3. _____ Fede y Yolanda salen a la calle para entrevistar a un novelista hispano.
4. _____ En el festival que grabó Vanesa se celebra la cultura y herencia de todos los latinos en Estados Unidos.
5. _____ Según Choco Orta, la música salsa representa la voz de la gente pobre e invisible.

 **INTERCAMBIOS.** En el video que muestra Héctor se dice que los artistas hispanos enfocan su arte en la realidad política o económica de su país. ¿Están ustedes de acuerdo? Discutan esta idea con sus compañeros e ilustren sus comentarios con la obra de algún artista que conozcan. ¿Ocurre lo mismo en el arte de su propio país? Expliquen con ejemplos.

Mosaicos

ESCUCHA

13-27 

Preparación. Vas a escuchar a cuatro estudiantes universitarios que hablan sobre actividades culturales. Antes de escuchar, haz una lista de tres actividades culturales que te interesarían a ti. Comparte tu lista con la clase.

ESTRATEGIA

Identify the speaker's intentions

When you listen to a speaker, you can frequently infer his or her intentions from the context. Let's imagine that you get this message: "I have a couple of tickets to a recital. Please give me a call." You immediately know the caller wants to invite you to the recital, even though the word *invitation* was never uttered.

To identify correctly a speaker's intention, follow these tips:

- Hypothesize about what the speaker probably means, making logical connections based on what you hear.
- As you listen, see if you can confirm your hypothesis.
- If you get information that does not fit, form a new hypothesis.

13-28  

Escucha. Now read the following statements, and then listen to the students. As you listen, next to each statement write the number of the passage associated with the student who probably uttered it.

_____ Miguel probablemente quiere escuchar o conversar con los artistas latinoamericanos para decidir sus estudios de posgrado.

_____ Joaquín es el pintor a quien le gusta más la pintura mexicana.

_____ Rosa María piensa ir a ver las obras de teatro este año.

_____ Eugenia es pianista y quiere convencer a otra persona de las ventajas de aprender a tocar el piano.

Comprueba

I was able to …

_____ **identify the activities students are interested in.**

_____ **make logical connections between what students say and what they do.**

13-29 

Un paso más. Comparte tu opinión con tu compañero/a.

1. ¿Es importante que los jóvenes aprendan a apreciar las diversas expresiones artísticas (la pintura, la música clásica, el teatro o la escultura)? ¿Por qué?
2. ¿Qué manifestación artística prefieres, la música o la pintura?
3. ¿Cuál es tu pintor o músico favorito? ¿Por qué te gusta?

HABLA

13-30

Preparación. Escoge a una de las personas de la lista y busca la información indicada en la tabla sobre esta persona. También puedes incluir otra información que te interese.

Luis Cañete	Alfonso Gumucio Dagrón
Pablo Casals	Jaime Laredo
Carlos Colombino	Marina Núñez del Prado
Susy Delgado	Maria Luisa Pacheco
Plácido Domingo	Violeta Parra
Carlos Gardel	

NOMBRE	DATOS PERSONALES	PROFESIÓN	LOGROS
	fecha de nacimiento	contribución a su profesión	premios
	lugar de nacimiento/ muerte		reconocimientos

ESTRATEGIA

Make your presentations comprehensible and interesting

When you give a presentation in your Spanish class, your two challenges are a) to make it understandable to your classmates; and b) to make it interesting so they will listen. The following guidelines will help you achieve these goals:

- Keep it simple. If you consulted sources for your presentation, present content in your own words. Look up new words in the dictionary and simplify your speech.
- Practice your presentation, so you can talk, not read, to your audience.
- Use visuals and props to make your presentation more lively and interesting.
- Involve your audience. Make eye contact, ask questions, check that they understand you, and invite them to ask questions.

13-31 

Habla. Haz una breve presentación sobre la persona que escogiste en la actividad 13-30. Incluye la mayor cantidad de información posible.

Comprueba

I was able to ...

____ present the information in my own words.

____ use visuals and props to make my presentation interesting.

____ make eye contact with my classmates.

En directo

To support a decision:

He elegido a... porque... *I have chosen ... because ...*

Lo que más influyó en mi decisión fue/fueron... *What most influenced my decision was/were ...*

Mi decisión está basada en lo siguiente... *My decision is based on the following ...*

 Listen to a conversation with these expressions.

13-32 

Un paso más. Elige a uno de los artistas de la actividad 13-30 como la persona a quién más admiras. Comparte tu elección con tu compañero/a. Dale tres razones para explicar tu elección.

LEE

13-33 

Preparación. Háganse las siguientes preguntas. ¿Piensan igual o diferente?

1. ¿Tienes algunos objetos favoritos? ¿Por qué son especiales?
2. ¿Les hablas a tus objetos a veces? ¿Qué les dices?
3. ¿Es posible tener una relación personal con tus objetos favoritos, aunque sean inanimados Explica tu opinión.
4. ¿Tienes mascota en casa? ¿Cómo es?
5. ¿Qué relación tienes con tu mascota? ¿Tratas a tu mascota como otro miembro de la familia, aunque sea un animal?

ESTRATEGIA

Focus on multiple meanings when reading poetry

When you read a narrative or journalistic text in Spanish, you have learned to increase your comprehension by going for the main ideas and using your prior knowledge to guess what the text is about. When you read poetry in Spanish, you need different strategies. Start by looking up the meanings of unfamiliar words. Then, with a pencil in your hand, read the poem aloud several times. Circle important, unusual, or repeated words. Draw lines to connect related ideas. Try to unfold the language of the poem by paraphrasing it in straightforward sentences: subject, verb, object. This will help you answer the question: "What is this poem about?"

13-34

Lee. Antes de leer el poema, lee primero la siguiente nota biográfica de la autora. Después, relaciona las cosas y objetos con las acciones.

Gloria Fuertes, poeta española (1917–1998), nació en Madrid. Era de una familia pobre: su madre era costurera (*seamstress*) y sirvienta y su padre limpiaba edificios comerciales. Fuertes comenzó a una edad temprana a escribir cuentos y poemas. De adolescente leía sus poemas en Radio España de Madrid. En 1961, recibió la beca Fulbright para dar clases de poesía española en la Universidad de Bucknell en Pensilvania. Los temas principales de su poesía son el amor, la muerte y los derechos humanos. También le interesa mucho el poder de la poesía de revelar el significado profundo de la vida cotidiana (*everyday*). Dada su afinidad por las letras desde muy niña, no es sorprendente que escribiera también cuentos y poemas infantiles.

LAS COSAS

Las cosas, nuestras cosas,
les gustan que las quieran;
a mi mesa le gusta que yo apoye los codos,
a la silla le gusta que me siente en la silla,
a la puerta le gusta que la abra y la cierre
como al vino le gusta que lo compre y lo beba,
mi lápiz se deshace[1] si lo cojo[2] y escribo,
mi armario se estremece[3] si lo abro y me asomo[4],
las sábanas son sábanas cuando me echo sobre ellas
y la cama se queja cuando yo me levanto.
¿Qué será de las cosas cuando el hombre se acabe?
Como perros las cosas no existen sin el amo.

[1] *dissolves* [2] *I hold it* [3] *trembles* [4] *I look inside*

COSAS	ACCIONES
_____ **1.** las cosas	**a.** estremecerse (*tremble*)
_____ **2.** la mesa	**b.** deshacerse (*dissolve*)
_____ **3.** la silla	**c.** quejarse
_____ **4.** la puerta	**d.** quererlas
_____ **5.** el vino	**e.** apoyar los codos
_____ **6.** el lápiz	**f.** cerrarla
_____ **7.** el armario	**g.** beberlo
_____ **8.** la cama	**h.** sentarse

Comprueba

I was able to …

_____ **understand what the poem is about.**

_____ **understand the speaker's relationship to her objects.**

Un paso más. Trabajando en grupos, escriban su interpretación de los dos últimos versos (*lines*) del poema y preséntenla a la clase.

ESCRIBE

13-36

Preparación. Busca información biográfica en Internet sobre una persona hispana que te interese en uno de estos campos: los deportes, las artes, la ciencia o la política. Toma nota sobre los siguientes datos que te ayudarán a expresar información concreta de esta persona.

1. nombre, fecha y lugar de nacimiento: ¿Cuándo y dónde nació?
2. información personal: ¿Es soltero/a, casado/a, divorciado/a? ¿Tiene hijos? ¿Cuántos?
3. estudios y formación profesional: ¿Cuáles son los mayores éxitos personales y/o profesionales de esta persona? ¿Cómo los logró?
4. su comunidad: ¿En qué área se destaca (*stands out*): en la religiosa, étnica, profesional, científica, artística, etc.? Sus éxitos, ¿han beneficiado a la comunidad? ¿Cómo?

ESTRATEGIA

Write to spark interest

To hold the interest of your reader, these tips may prove useful.

1. Be sure you are knowledgeable about the topic before you start to write. Do some research if necessary.
2. Organize the information to keep the text focused on the topic.
3. Vary your vocabulary.
4. When appropriate, add a hint of controversy by including provocative statements or questions.
5. When appropriate, incorporate the element of fun with a personal story or anecdote.
6. Choose a title that will grab the attention of your readers.

13-37

Escribe. Escribe un informe biográfico para una revista electrónica, usando la información obtenida en la actividad 13-36. Tu propósito es despertar la curiosidad de los jóvenes por conocer qué sacrificios han hecho los famosos para tener éxito.

Comprueba

I was able to …

____ **focus on the topic.**

____ **add an interesting element to spark the reader's attention.**

13-38 

Un paso más. Lee la biografía que escribió tu compañero/a y, luego, hazle preguntas sobre otros aspectos de la vida o carrera de este artista de los cuales (*about which*) te gustaría saber más.

En este capítulo...

Comprueba lo que sabes

Go to ***MySpanishLab*** to review what you have learned in this chapter. Practice with the following:

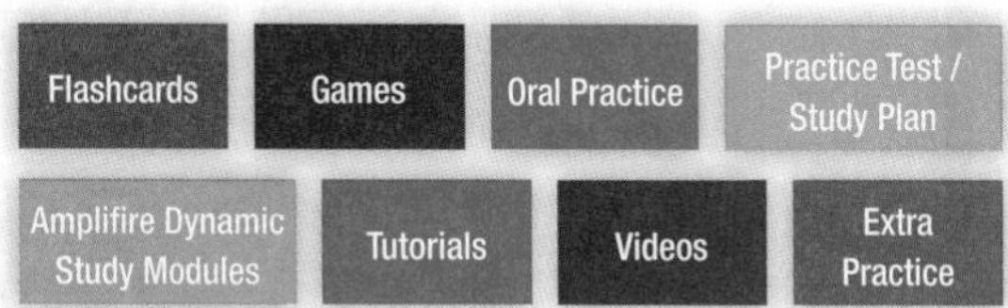

Vocabulario

LAS PERSONAS *People*

el bailarín/la bailarina *dancer*
la compañía (de danza, de teatro) *(dance, theater) company*
el/la escritor/a *writer*
el/la escultor/a *sculptor*
el/la guitarrista *guitar player*
el/la intérprete *performer, artist*
el/la muralista *muralist*
el/la novelista *novelist*
el/la pintor/a *painter*
el/la poeta *poet*

LAS OBRAS DE ARTE *Works of art*

el autorretrato *self-portrait*
el cuento *story*
la escena *scene*
la forma *shape, form*
el mural *mural*
la novela *novel*
la obra *work*
el paisaje *landscape*
el personaje principal *main character*
la pintura *painting*
el poema *poem*
la poesía *poetry*
el símbolo *symbol*
el tema *theme*
el verso *line*
la voz *voice*

PALABRAS Y EXPRESIONES ÚTILES *Useful words and expressions*

a través de *through*
al fondo *at the back, in the rear*
la amistad *friendship*
el amor *love*
la calidad *quality*
cubista *cubist*
el desarrollo *development*
desde *since*
en la actualidad *at the present time*
el éxito *success*
el fracaso *failure*
la fundación *establishment, founding*
hasta *including*
el premio *award, prize*
el recuerdo *memory*
la revista del corazón *gossip magazine*
surrealista *surrealist*
tener éxito *to be successful*

LAS DESCRIPCIONES *Descriptions*

blando/a *soft*
destacado/a *outstanding*
inolvidable *unforgettable*
prometedor/a *promising*

VERBOS *Verbs*

abrazar (c) *to embrace*
abundar *to abound*
besar *to kiss*
denunciar *to denounce*
dirigir (j) *to direct*
distinguir *to distinguish*
exponer (g) *to exhibit*
grabar *to film, to record*
nominar *to nominate*
pintar *to paint*
reflejar *to reflect*
retratar *to portray*
rodear *to surround*
saludar *to greet*
surgir (j) *to emerge*
titular(se) *to be called*
tratar *to treat, be about*

14 ¿Cómo vivimos los cambios sociales?

LEARNING OUTCOMES

You will be able to:

- discuss demographics and social conditions
- indicate conditions, goals, and purposes
- express conjecture
- talk about the past from a past perspective
- share information about social change, gender roles, and migration in Hispanic countries and identify cultural similarities

ENFOQUE cultural CHILE

El desierto de Atacama

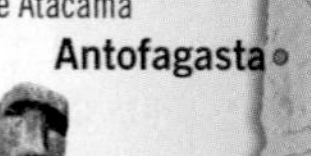

Enfoque cultural

To learn more about Chile, go to MySpanishLab to view the *Vistas culturales* videos.

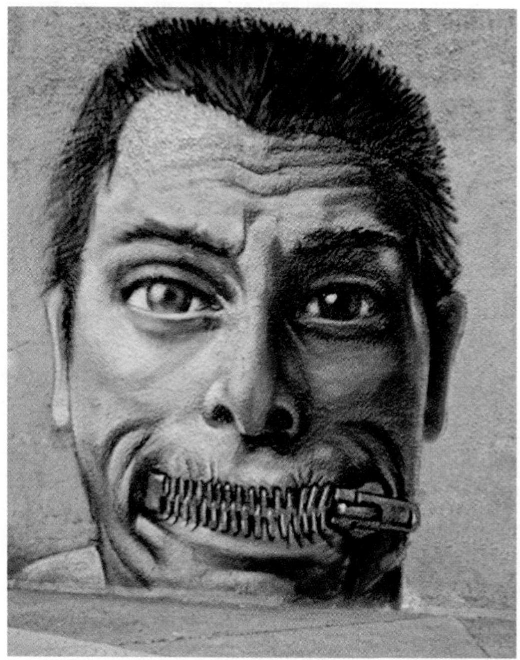

▲ Este mural en las calles de Santiago retrata el sufrimiento y la opresión de los chilenos durante la dictadura militar entre 1973 y 1990.

¿QUÉ TE PARECE?

- Chile es una larga franja de tierra rodeada de montañas: al este, por la Cordillera de los Andes; al oeste, por la cordillera de la costa.
- Sobre su nombre, muchos han especulado que Chile proviene de la palabra quechua *chiri,* que significa frío, helado. Sin embargo, para el cronista Diego Rosales, el nombre probablemente venía de Tili, un cacique picunche, quien gobernó la región de Aconcagua antes de la llegada de los españoles. Hasta hoy no existe consenso del origen del nombre Chile.
- El desierto de Atacama, en el norte de Chile, es el más árido del mundo. Aunque llueve poco, en las últimas décadas, a causa del calentamiento global, el clima está cambiando. En 2013, nevó copiosamente después de 30 años.

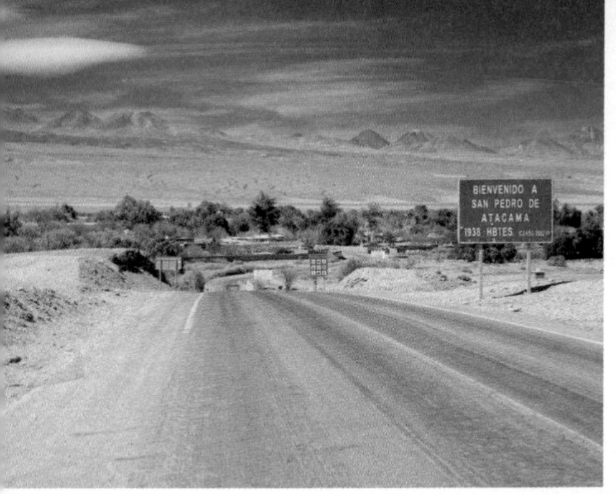

◀ El desierto de Atacama, situado en el norte de Chile, es sin duda el más seco del mundo. En él se encuentran riquezas minerales como el cobre, el hierro, el oro y la plata. Los recursos económicos más importantes de Chile son el cobre, el vino, la fruta y el pescado, los cuales exporta a muchos países en todos los continentes.

▲ Santiago, la capital de Chile, cuenta con una población de más de seis millones y medio de habitantes. En esta antigua ciudad capital, ubicada entre el mar y las montañas, conviven armoniosamente lo antiguo y lo moderno. Es una de las ciudades más importantes de Sudamérica por el comercio y por su alta calidad de vida.

El pastel de choclo y las empanadas son considerados dos platos típicamente chilenos. Preparado con choclo, o maíz, carne y huevos, el pastel de choclo usualmente se come durante el verano. Las empanadas suelen ser de carne o de mariscos. Tanto el pastel de choclo como las empanadas se acompañan con vino tinto o blanco. ▶

▲ Ubicada a aproximadamente 670 kilómetros del puerto de Valparaíso, la isla de Pascua forma parte del territorio chileno. Aparte del español, en la isla se habla el rapanui, una lengua indígena. Por su historia y atractivo natural, la isla de Pascua es un lugar visitado por muchos turistas de todo el mundo. En 1996 UNESCO declaró el Parque Nacional Rapa Nui patrimonio de la humanidad.

Punta Arenas, la ciudad más austral del país, está situada al lado del estrecho de Magallanes. Durante el verano, el sol sale (*rises*) antes de las 6:00 de la mañana y se pone (*sets*) después de las 10:00 de la noche. Así, los habitantes de Punta Arenas gozan de más de dieciocho horas de luz natural. ▼

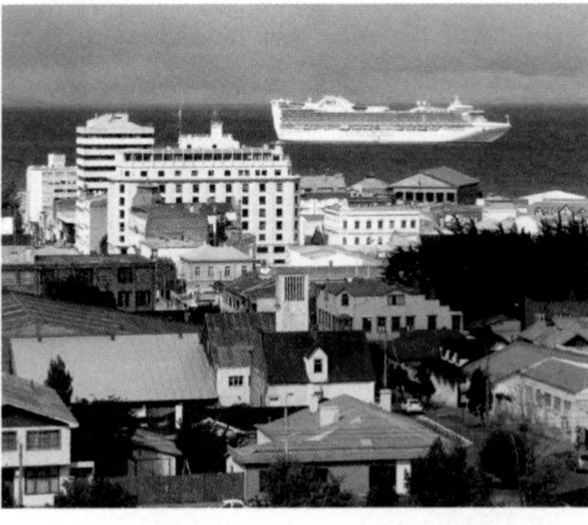

¿CUÁNTO SABES?

Completa las siguientes oraciones con la información correcta.

1. El desierto de ____________, uno de los desiertos más áridos del mundo, está en el norte de Chile.
2. En ____________, la capital de Chile, viven más de seis millones de habitantes.
3. Chile exporta ____________________ a otros países.
4. Punta Arenas es la ciudad más al sur de Chile. Está junto al estrecho de ____________.
5. Santiago está entre el ____________ y las montañas.

Vocabulario en contexto

Talking about social change, gender roles, and migration

Cambios en la sociedad

MySpanishLab
Learn more using Amplifire Dynamic Study Modules, Pronunciation, and Vocabulary Tutorials.

▲ En las últimas décadas ha habido **cambios** muy importantes en el mundo hispano. Varios países, como Chile, Uruguay, Argentina y España, pasaron de tener **regímenes dictatoriales** a ser **democracias** modernas. Michelle Bachelet ganó la presidencia en las **elecciones** democráticas de Chile en 2006 y en 2010 fue nombrada directora ejecutiva de la ONU Mujer. En 2013 anunció su candidatura presidencial por un segundo período. Esta mujer **políglota,** médica de profesión, la primera mujer en llegar a la presidencia de su país, es considerada una de las mujeres más poderosas del mundo.

▲ En Argentina, Cristina Fernández de Kirchner fue **elegida** en 2007 por una **amplia mayoría** y reelegida en 2011. Aunque es la segunda mujer **presidenta** de su país (en los años 70 **gobernó** Isabel Perón), es la primera en ser elegida en un proceso democrático.

Evo Morales, de origen aimara, fue elegido presidente de Bolivia en 2005 y reelegido en 2009. Es el primer presidente indígena de su país desde la conquista española hace 470 años. Desde el comienzo de su carrera política, Morales **se destacó** por su capacidad de organizar a los campesinos en la **lucha** por sus **derechos.** Es un defensor del cultivo de la coca en la región andina. La coca es un producto natural con fines medicinales. Sin embargo, se opone a la comercialización de la coca por las bandas internacionales del **tráfico de drogas.** ▶

Las condiciones de vida aún son difíciles en algunos países de Hispanoamérica donde la **pobreza** y el **analfabetismo** todavía son problemas importantes entre sus **habitantes.** Sin embargo, la economía de algunos países latinoamericanos como Chile, Colombia y México, entre otros, **ha mejorado** considerablemente en las últimas décadas gracias a la **diversificación** de los cultivos, a la intensificación de las **exportaciones** y a mayores índices de educación de sus habitantes. Hoy en día Chile, por ejemplo, exporta cobre, vino, pescado, fruta y otros productos a todo el mundo.

Estos **datos** muestran y comparan algunos de los problemas sociales de Hispanoamérica. Por ejemplo, a pesar de ser un país emergente, el **desempleo** es bastante alto en Colombia. El **porcentaje** de mujeres **analfabetas** es más alto que el de los hombres en casi todos los países. Las mujeres guatemaltecas tienen el **promedio** más alto de hijos. La **esperanza de vida** es en general más alta para las mujeres que para los hombres, y Bolivia tiene la **tasa** más alta de **mortalidad infantil.**

2012-2013	CHILE	BOLIVIA	COLOMBIA	GUATEMALA
Población	17.216.945	10.461.053	45.745.784	14.373.472
Tasa de crecimiento económico (GPD)	5,5%	5,2%	4,0%	3,0%
Esperanza de vida (años)	78,27	68,22	75,02	71,46
Tasa de fertilidad (número de hijos por mujer)	1,9%	2,9%	2,1%	3,8%
Analfabetismo entre los hombres	1,4%	4,2%	6,6%	18,8%
Analfabetismo entre las mujeres	1,5%	13,2%	6,3%	28,9%
Tasa de desempleo	6,4%	7,5%	10,4%	4,1%
Mortalidad infantil (por cada mil nacimientos)	7,19	39,76	15,46	24,32

Fuente: CIA *The World Factbook*

PRÁCTICA

 **14-1**  

Para confirmar. Determinen si las siguientes afirmaciones son ciertas (**C**) o falsas (**F**) de acuerdo con lo que leyeron. En caso de que sean falsas, corrijan la información.

1. _____ Cristina Kirchner fue la primera mujer presidenta de su país.
2. _____ Evo Morales fue elegido presidente de Chile.
3. _____ Michelle Bachelet habla más de dos lenguas.
4. _____ El presidente de Bolivia defiende el cultivo tradicional de la coca.
5. _____ El analfabetismo en algunos países de Latinoamérica ya no es un problema grande.
6. _____ La economía de Chile ha mejorado.
7. _____ En Bolivia hay menos analfabetismo entre las mujeres que entre los hombres.
8. _____ Bolivia tiene menos habitantes que Guatemala.
9. _____ Las chilenas tienen más hijos que las guatemaltecas.
10. _____ En Colombia se mueren más niños que en Bolivia.

Cultura

La natalidad

El índice de natalidad en los países hispanos ha descendido de manera espectacular en los últimos treinta años. Este descenso parece ser la tendencia general, a pesar de las circunstancias particulares de cada país. En Perú y Bolivia, por ejemplo, los gobiernos han apoyado campañas para mostrar las ventajas de los planes familiares y el control de la natalidad. En Venezuela, sin embargo, el promedio de hijos ha bajado en treinta años de 6,7 a 2,7 sin campañas por parte del gobierno. Esto se debe a varios factores, como la crisis económica, la escasez de vivienda y el mayor acceso de las mujeres al trabajo y a la educación. Pero tal vez el caso más extremo de esta tendencia es el de España, que ha pasado de ser el país de Europa con más hijos por pareja en los años sesenta, a ser, junto con Italia, el país europeo con el índice de natalidad más bajo en la actualidad, con un promedio de 1,3 hijos.

Comparaciones. Piensa en el número de hijos en tu familia en las últimas dos o tres generaciones. Después compara tu caso con el de tus compañeros/as. ¿Qué tendencia de natalidad se puede observar? ¿Creen ustedes que hay una crisis de natalidad en Estados Unidos?

14-2 

Los datos demográficos. PREPARACIÓN. Busquen en los textos y en la tabla en la página anterior la información necesaria para contestar las siguientes preguntas. Después comparen sus respuestas con las de otros/as compañeros/as.

1. ¿Cuál de los países en la tabla está más poblado?
2. ¿Cuál tiene menos habitantes?
3. ¿En qué país vive más años la gente?
4. ¿En qué país crece con más rapidez la población?
5. ¿De dónde son las mujeres que tienen más hijos?
6. ¿Dónde hay más analfabetos probablemente, en el campo o en las ciudades?
7. ¿En qué país hay menos desempleo?
8. ¿En qué país se mueren más niños cuando son bebés?
9. ¿En qué país crece más rápido la economía?
10. ¿Qué país probablemente les ofrece más oportunidades educativas a las mujeres?

INTERCAMBIOS. Comparen los datos de los países hispanos en las siguientes áreas con los datos de su propio país.

1. analfabetismo
2. desempleo
3. promedio de hijos
4. mortalidad infantil
5. esperanza de vida

14-3 

Una encuesta sobre las familias.
PREPARACIÓN. Háganse preguntas para obtener los siguientes datos sobre sus respectivas familias.

1. número de personas que forman el núcleo familiar
2. número de hombres y de mujeres
3. edad promedio de los miembros de la familia
4. número de personas que estudian
5. número de personas que trabajan

INTERCAMBIOS. Recopilen (*Compile*) la información obtenida. Con esta información, preparen una tabla que indique el porcentaje de familias que hay en su clase…

1. con menos de tres miembros o más de tres.
2. con mayoría de mujeres o de hombres.
3. con edad promedio de 40 años más o menos.
4. con más o menos de dos personas con títulos (*degrees*) universitarios.
5. donde trabajan más o menos de dos miembros.

El papel de la mujer

■ (FEMPRESS) En un reciente estudio **realizado** en 553 empresas colombianas, Luz Gabriela Arango encontró que solo el 23,7% de las directivas están constituidas por mujeres. Con todo, el estudio muestra que en este terreno, así como en otros, ha habido enormes cambios. En los años cincuenta, por ejemplo, todas las **sucursales** bancarias tenían un varón como gerente. En los años noventa, una alta proporción era dirigida por mujeres.

La encuesta "clase empresarial", realizada a ejecutivos, señala que la **confianza** en el desempeño profesional de la mujer es mayor que en el del hombre. De hecho, el 96,8% de los entrevistados le dio la más alta calificación a su **honestidad;** el 80% a la calidad de su trabajo; el 81,6% en materia de confiabilidad; el 79,2% lo dio a su cumplimiento.

En cuanto al manejo de la autoridad, las ejecutivas entrevistadas por *Dinero* consideran que mientras se valora a un hombre por ser **enérgico,** cuando una mujer asume posiciones fuertes puede causar rechazo. En cuanto al poder, se sienten menos ambiciosas y le dan menor prioridad que los hombres.

Las gerencias administrativas y de recursos industriales en manos de mujeres están aumentando. En algunas entrevistas de *Dinero,* se destaca y se apoya la participación de las mujeres en la empresa pues las consideran más responsables, más comprometidas, más honestas, se ausentan menos del trabajo que los hombres, demuestran mayor **eficiencia** en el manejo del tiempo y son más transparentes en el trabajo.

Es interesante ver, dice CIDER (Centro Interdisciplinario de Estudios Regionales), las áreas en las cuales se ha concentrado la presencia femenina. Estas son, en sectores financieros y de servicios en el caso de la empresa privada, y en instituciones de servicio y manejo de relaciones públicas en el sector público, como son los ministerios de salud, educación, trabajo y relaciones exteriores. La mayor concentración de fuerza laboral femenina en un alto **nivel** se ubica en las labores ejecutivas, mientras que solo el 8,2% de los funcionarios hombres está en ese nivel no directivo.

PRÁCTICA

Para confirmar. Preparen un informe sobre la situación de la mujer en el mundo hispanohablante, utilizando la información que leyeron en las estadísticas (p. 482) y las citas. Comparen su informe con el de otros grupos.

14-5 

Mujeres ejecutivas.

PREPARACIÓN. Cada uno/a de ustedes debe hacer una lista de cinco mujeres que ocupan puestos importantes en países hispanos o en su país. Hablen sobre estas mujeres, basándose en los siguientes puntos.

1. puesto que ocupan y responsabilidades que tienen
2. su personalidad y rasgos (*traits*) de carácter
3. obstáculos que cada una ha tenido que superar en su área de trabajo

INTERCAMBIOS. Ahora, comenten lo siguiente.

1. ¿Qué tipo de personalidad y rasgos de carácter tienen en común estas mujeres?
2. ¿Hacen estas mujeres trabajos tradicionalmente femeninos, o han incursionado en el mundo laboral típicamente masculino?
3. ¿Hay semejanzas entre los obstáculos que estas mujeres han tenido que superar? ¿Cuáles son? ¿Cómo han logrado superarlos?

14-6 

Los tiempos cambian. Conversen sobre los logros de la mujer en este siglo y el pasado. Hagan una lista de los cambios que han afectado a la mujer en las siguientes áreas en los últimos 50 años.

1. la familia
2. el trabajo
3. la casa
4. el gobierno/la política
5. la educación

Temas de hoy: los jóvenes y la emigración

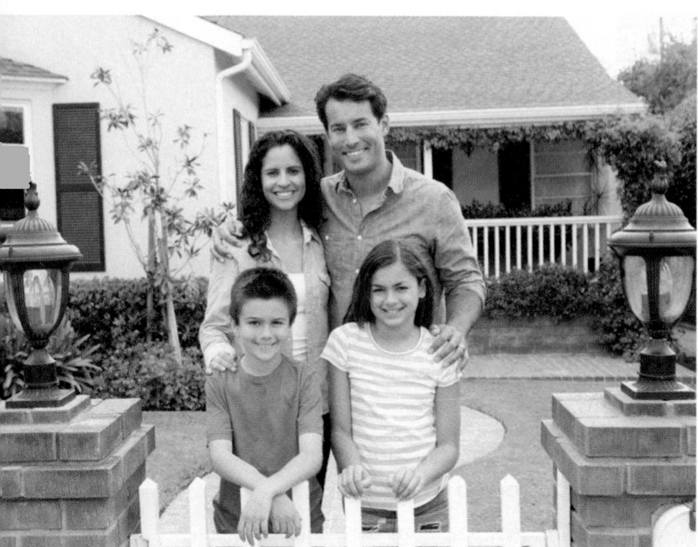

El **desplazamiento** de personas de un país a otro es algo muy común en los últimos tiempos. En general, los jóvenes que emigran de sus países lo hacen por motivos económicos o políticos. Muchos tienen la esperanza de mejorar sus condiciones de vida. Entre los países hispanos, Chile y España son los que más **emigrantes** reciben, aunque debido a la crisis **económica,** la **inmigración** a España ha disminuido en los últimos años.

LENGUA

La emigración refers to the act of *leaving* one's country to settle somewhere else. **La inmigración** refers to *entering* another country for the purpose of setting up permanent residence there.

País de origen de los extranjeros en Chile

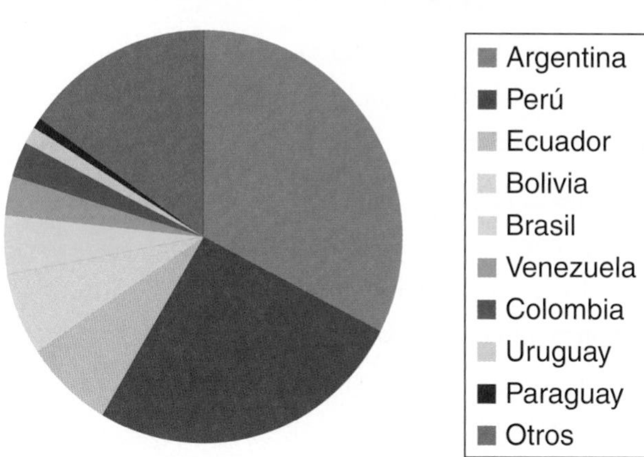

En Chile, los argentinos y los peruanos son los dos grupos de extranjeros más numerosos. En España también las comunidades peruana y argentina son muy numerosas, solo superadas por los **inmigrantes** de origen ecuatoriano. La ventaja de estas **migraciones** interhispanas es que todos hablan la misma lengua y esto hace que las dificultades de **adaptación** sean menores.

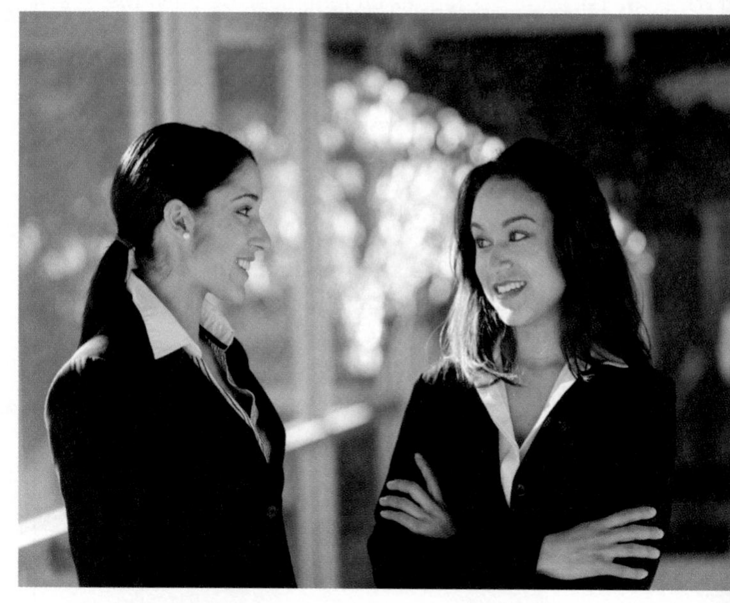

Muchos hispanoamericanos, especialmente mexicanos y caribeños, prefieren **emigrar** a Estados Unidos **en vez de** a Europa en busca de oportunidades económicas y una mayor **proximidad** con sus países. Los jóvenes por lo general se adaptan más fácilmente que sus padres porque aprenden inglés rápidamente. Además, hoy en día las ventajas de ser bilingüe en EE.UU. son evidentes.

PRÁCTICA

14-7 

Para confirmar. Completa las siguientes oraciones con la forma correcta de las palabras de la lista.

bilingüismo	emigración	habitante
condición	emigrante	proximidad

1. En España hay muchos ________________ de nacionalidad ecuatoriana.
2. Una ventaja para los caribeños que emigran a Estados Unidos es la __________ a los países del Caribe.
3. El __________ es útil para los jóvenes hispanos que buscan trabajo.
4. Frecuentemente las personas se desplazan para mejorar sus __________ de vida.
5. La __________ es un fenómeno de nuestros días que está relacionada con la globalización.
6. Chile es uno de los países de Hispanoamérica que más __________ recibe.

14-8 

Los habitantes de su comunidad. Preparen preguntas para entrevistar a un/a compañero/a sobre sus orígenes y las costumbres de su comunidad o grupo étnico. Usen los puntos a continuación como guía para elaborar su cuestionario.

E1: *¿Cuál es el origen de tu familia?*

E2: *Mis abuelos eran italianos.*

E1: *¿Cuándo emigraron a este país?*

E2: *Emigraron cuando mi padre tenía cinco años.*

1. origen de tu apellido
2. grupo(s) étnico(s) que asocias con tu familia
3. área de concentración en Estados Unidos
4. costumbres e idioma
5. fiestas o celebraciones
6. productos que consumen
7. comida típica

14-9  

La mujer en los países hispanos. You will listen to a conversation between a reporter and a professor of sociology at the Universidad de Santiago de Chile about the status of women in the Hispanic world. Before you listen, write two questions the reporter may ask the professor and the answers that you think she may provide.

As you listen, focus on the main ideas of what is said. Indicate the appropriate ending to each statement.

1. La doctora Gómez dice que la situación de la mujer ha mejorado porque...
   - **a.** más mujeres son jefas de empresas.
   - **b.** ahora hay más leyes que las protegen.
   - **c.** hay muchas mujeres que no tienen hijos.
2. Según la doctora Gómez, en comparación con los hombres, las mujeres...
   - **a.** no tienen que trabajar tanto.
   - **b.** tienen que estar mejor preparadas.
   - **c.** no estudian tanto.
3. Las mujeres hispanas ganan...
   - **a.** más dinero que los hombres.
   - **b.** tanto dinero como los hombres.
   - **c.** menos dinero que los hombres.
4. En los hogares hispanos, el trabajo de la casa y la crianza de los hijos...
   - **a.** son la responsabilidad de los empleados domésticos.
   - **b.** son compartidos por todos los miembros de la familia.
   - **c.** están principalmente en manos de las mujeres.

MOSAICO cultural

La migración interna en el mundo hispano

Olga Jaramillo ha vivido en Tegucigalpa, la capital de Honduras, desde hace siete años. Olga nació en una pequeña ciudad llamada Danlí, donde vivía con tres hermanos en una familia campesina (*farming*). "Tan pronto como terminé mis estudios del colegio, supe que quería ir a la universidad", comenta Olga. Las oportunidades de educación superior son limitadas en las ciudades pequeñas, por eso muchas mujeres como Olga prefieren ir a las ciudades principales. "Cuando mi madre tenía mi edad ya había tenido a mis hermanos. Yo sabía que a menos que saliera de Danlí a estudiar, mi futuro sería similar", dice Olga. Olga tuvo que dejar a su familia y pasar momentos difíciles adaptándose a la vida de la ciudad. Como muchos otros jóvenes, Olga trabajaba mientras estudiaba, y después de los cinco años de carrera universitaria, consiguió un trabajo estable como dentista.

Esta decisión de Olga demuestra un cambio de mentalidad en los jóvenes hispanos: tener menos hijos y tomarse más tiempo para educarse. Sin embargo, las oportunidades en educación y seguridad social son estables principalmente en las ciudades grandes. El progreso económico vertiginoso de algunas ciudades capitales no es igual al de las ciudades más pequeñas. Por esta razón, muchas personas deciden buscar suerte en la gran ciudad, en un proceso que se conoce como migración interna. Pero llegar a la ciudad no siempre asegura mejores condiciones; en ocasiones, estas personas enfrentan retos de adaptación demasiado grandes y terminan en situaciones de pobreza. Afortunadamente para Olga, este no fue su caso: "Venir a Tegucigalpa fue muy difícil, pero tenía que salir de Danlí o no habría encontrado la estabilidad que buscaba".

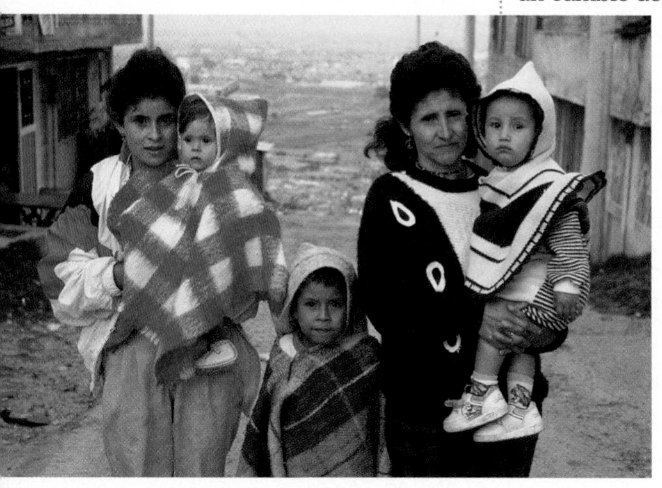

Compara

1. En promedio, ¿cuántos hijos por familia tienen las personas en tu país? ¿Este número ha variado en las últimas décadas? ¿Piensas que esta tendencia varía dependiendo de la región geográfica?
2. ¿Qué importancia social tiene la educación en tu país? Piensa en las regiones que no son predominantemente universitarias. Compara las grandes ciudades con otras zonas más pequeñas.
3. ¿En tu país existe un fenómeno similar a la migración interna? ¿Cuáles son las razones principales de esta migración? Incluye detalles en tu respuesta; piensa en tendencias demográficas que han cambiado en los últimos años.
4. En tu opinión, ¿qué implicaciones sociales tiene la migración interna para las grandes ciudades? ¿Qué ocurre con la economía? ¿Qué ocurre con la seguridad social de los migrantes?

☑ Funciones y formas

1 Expressing conjecture

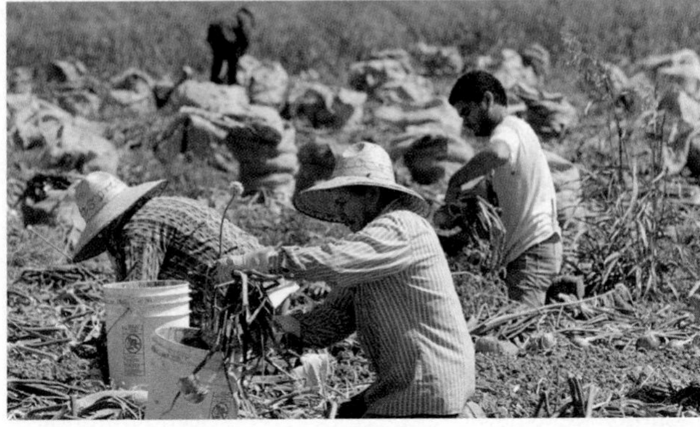

Estos inmigrantes cosechan cebollas en Texas. Según la ley, pueden trabajar en Estados Unidos **con tal de que** tengan estatus legal en el país. Muchos inmigrantes mandan dinero a su familia **para que** sus hijos vivan mejor. Muchos vuelven a su país **a menos que** su familia pueda venir a Estados Unidos también.

Piénsalo. Escoge en la columna de la derecha el significado de las palabras en negrita.

1. _____ Pueden trabajar en Estados Unidos **con tal de que** tengan estatus legal.
2. _____ Mandan dinero a su familia **para que** sus hijos vivan mejor.
3. _____ Volverán a su país **a menos que** su familia pueda venir a Estados Unidos.
4. _____ Para muchos inmigrantes es difícil conseguir trabajo **sin que** sus amigos los ayuden.
5. _____ Los hijos de algunos emigrantes pasan muchos años con solo su madre **antes de que** su padre vuelva a casa.

a. si
b. anterioridad de tiempo
c. si… no
d. con la intención

Adverbial conjunctions that require the subjunctive

- Conjunctions are words or phrases that function as connectors in sentences. Some conjunctions introduce dependent clauses known as adverbial clauses, which communicate how, why, when, and where an action takes place.
- Some conjunctions always require the subjunctive when followed by a dependent clause.

a menos que	*unless*	**para que**	*so that*
antes (de) que	*before*	**sin que**	*without*
con tal (de) que	*provided that*		

Las mujeres tendrán una reunión **antes de que** sus representantes **hablen** con los oficiales.	*The women will have a meeting before their representatives speak with the officials.*
Las mujeres votarán por los oficiales **con tal de que** ellos **implementen** los cambios mencionados en la petición.	*The women will vote for the officials provided that they implement the changes mentioned in the petition.*
Las representantes negocian con los oficiales **para que** todos los niños **tengan** acceso a servicios médicos.	*The representatives negotiate with the officials so that all children have access to medical services.*

- Use an infinitive after the prepositions **antes de, para,** and **sin** when there is no change of subject.

Las comunidades ofrecen clases **para que** los inmigrantes **aprendan** inglés.	*Communities offer classes so that immigrants can learn English.*
Los inmigrantes estudian inglés **para aprender** la lengua rápidamente.	*Immigrants study English to learn the language quickly.*

¿COMPRENDES?

Completa las afirmaciones a continuación con las conjunciones más lógicas en cada contexto.

1. Pagamos impuestos ______________ haya buenas escuelas.
2. Tenemos que limpiar la oficina ______________ lleguen los miembros del comité.
3. Votaremos por ellos ______________ nos guste su plan para la ciudad.
4. No publicamos el panfleto ______________ el presidente lo apruebe.

MySpanishLab

Learn more using Amplifire Dynamic Study Modules, Grammar Tutorials, and Extra Practice activities.

PRÁCTICA

14-10  

En el futuro. PREPARACIÓN. Túrnense para leer la primera parte de cada oración y después busquen el final apropiado a la derecha. Fíjense (*Take note*) en el contexto y también en la forma verbal correcta.

1. _____ Muchos empleados trabajarán en casa sin...
2. _____ Las compañías de limpieza programarán los robots para que...
3. _____ Podremos jubilarnos (*retire*) antes de...
4. _____ Casi todos los cursos universitarios se ofrecerán en Internet sin que...
5. _____ Los jóvenes no tendrán que trabajar a menos que...
6. _____ Habrá computadoras de uso gratis en muchos lugares públicos para...
7. _____ Los empleados de las compañías multinacionales podrán comunicarse fácilmente con tal de que...
8. _____ Después de nacer sus hijos, los padres no volverán a trabajar antes de que los niños...

a. los profesores ni los alumnos tengan que ir a la universidad.
b. tengan aparatos de interpretación simultánea.
c. tener que comunicarse con los clientes o colegas en persona.
d. facilitar la comunicación entre las personas.
e. cumplan 5 años de edad.
f. limpien los edificios sin intervención de los seres humanos.
g. les interese hacer trabajo de voluntariado.
h. los 50 años.

INTERCAMBIOS. Ahora escojan dos de las oraciones de la izquierda y complétenlas de acuerdo con sus propias ideas. Después comparen sus respuestas con las de otra pareja.

14-11 

Una ingeniera se entrevista. La ingeniera industrial María Victoria Martín se entrevista hoy con Sanofi Aventis, una compañía que fabrica medicinas. Para saber qué pasó en la entrevista, completa las oraciones con la forma correcta del verbo apropiado: **decir, hacer, ofrecer, pasar** o **saber.**

María Victoria llega temprano a la cita con la directora, y la secretaria le pide que espere unos minutos antes de (1) ________ a su oficina. María Victoria trata de tranquilizarse para que nadie (2) ________ que está muy nerviosa. Piensa que podrá dar una buena impresión con tal de que la directora le (3) ________ preguntas relevantes a su experiencia. Finalmente la directora se presenta y la invita a entrar en su oficina sin que María Victoria (4) ________ una palabra. Al final de la entrevista la directora le ofrece el puesto. María Victoria dice que no puede aceptar la oferta a menos que la compañía le (5) ________ seguro médico. La directora acepta esta condición.

14-12

¿Estudio en Chile o no? Estás considerando la posibilidad de estudiar en Chile el próximo semestre. Indica lo que piensas sobre esta posibilidad, usando las expresiones adverbiales de la lista. Tu compañero/a va a responder de forma lógica.

a menos que	antes (de) que	con tal (de) que	para que	sin que

el programa sea muy caro

E1: *Voy a estudiar en Chile, a menos que el programa sea muy caro.*

E2: *No participes en el programa a menos que te den una beca.*

1. el semestre termine para el 1 de junio
2. mis compañeros y yo aprendamos mucho español
3. viva con una familia amable
4. mi familia me visite durante el semestre
5. haya oportunidades de viajar a otros países
6. mi amigo/a también participe en el programa
7. conozca la cultura mapuche
8. pasemos las vacaciones esquiando en los Andes

Situación

PREPARACIÓN. Lean la situación. Luego, compartan ejemplos de vocabulario, gramática y otra información que necesitan para desarrollar la conversación.

Role A. You are an exchange student who has recently arrived in the United States. Ask your classmate a) what his/her family does to help him/her attend college; b) if in big lecture classes students can use their cell phones and read e-mail without their professors' knowledge; and c) what he/she hopes to accomplish before graduating.

Role B. You have become acquainted with an international student at your university. Answer his/her questions about university life in the United States and ask about university life in his/her country.

	ROLE A	ROLE B
Vocabulario	Academic subjects Technology	Academic subjects Technology
Funciones y formas	Formulating questions	Adverbial conjunctions with subjunctive

INTERCAMBIOS. Practica la conversación con tu compañero/a incorporando el vocabulario y las funciones de *Preparación*. Luego, represéntenla ante la clase.

2 Expressing conjecture or certainty

SRA. LÓPEZ: ¿Qué te interesa hacer **cuando te gradúes**?

VICENTE: **Después de terminar** mis estudios, me gustaría trabajar en otro país para una organización sin fines de lucro (*non-profit*).

SRA. LÓPEZ: Muy bien. **Tan pronto como terminemos** de hablar, te mandaré una lista de organizaciones. No esperes **hasta que te gradúes** para empezar a buscar trabajo. Familiarízate con las posibilidades ahora, **mientras eres** estudiante.

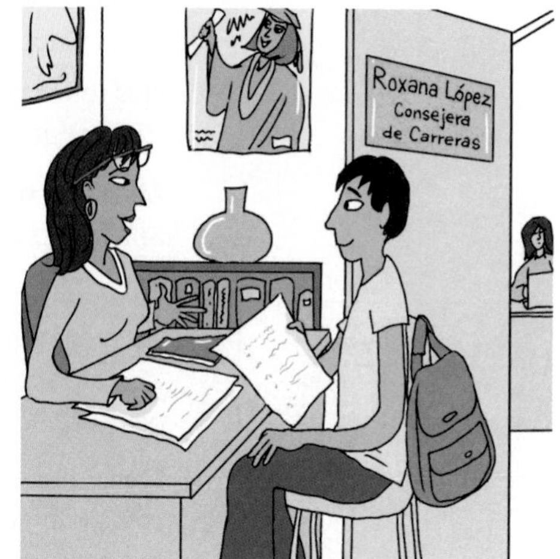

Piénsalo. Indica si la persona que habla se refiere al presente (**P**) o al futuro (**F**).

1. ______ ¿Qué te interesa hacer **cuando te gradúes?**
2. ______ **Tan pronto como terminemos** de hablar, te mandaré una lista de organizaciones.
3. ______ No esperes **hasta que te gradúes** para empezar a buscar trabajo.
4. ______ Familiarízate con las posibilidades ahora, **mientras eres** estudiante.
5. ______ Vicente va a buscar trabajo en una organización sin fines de lucro, **aunque gane** poco dinero.
6. ______ Estas organizaciones siempre apoyan a las comunidades aun (*even*) **después de que** las comunidades **terminan** el proyecto.

Adverbial conjunctions that take the subjunctive or indicative

- Earlier in this chapter you learned about conjunctions that are always followed by the subjunctive. Here you will practice using conjunctions that are followed by a verb in either the subjunctive or indicative, depending on whether the event in the adverbial clause has occurred or not, or whether it is factual or unknown.

aunque	*although, even though, even if*	**en cuanto**	*as soon as*
		hasta que	*until*
cuando	*when*	**mientras**	*while*
después (de) que	*after*	**según**	*according to, as*
donde	*where, wherever*	**tan pronto (como)**	*as soon as*

- These conjunctions require the subjunctive when the event in the adverbial clause has not yet taken place. Note that the main clause expresses future time.

Va a luchar **hasta que** la comunidad **ofrezca** clases gratis para los inmigrantes nuevos.
She is going to fight until the community offers free classes for new immigrants.

Nos reuniremos **después de que comiencen** las clases.
We will meet after classes start.

Me llamará **tan pronto reciba** la aprobación del alcalde.
She will call me as soon as she receives approval from the mayor.

- These conjunctions require the indicative when the event in the adverbial clause has already taken place, is taking place, or usually takes place.

  Nos reunimos **después de que comenzaron** las clases.
  We met after classes started.

  Me llamó **tan pronto recibió** la aprobación del alcalde.
  She called me as soon as she received approval from the mayor.

  La organización apoya a los inmigrantes **hasta que se establecen** en la comunidad.
  The organization supports the immigrants until they become established in the community.

- **Donde** and **según** require the indicative when they refer to something definite or known, and the subjunctive when they refer to something indefinite or unknown.

  Vamos a reunirnos **donde** ella **dice.**
  We are going to meet where she says. (She has already announced the place.)

  Vamos a reunirnos **donde** ella **diga.**
  We are going to meet wherever she says. (She has not yet announced the place.)

  Llena el formulario **según dice** el consejero.
  Fill out the form according to what the adviser says. (Instructions have already been given.)

  Vamos a seguir el procedimiento **según diga** el alcalde.
  We will follow the procedure in accordance with whatever the mayor says. (Instructions have not yet been given.)

- **Aunque** also requires the subjunctive when it introduces a condition not regarded as fact.

Lo compro **aunque es** caro.	*I will buy it, although it is expensive.*
Lo compro **aunque sea** caro.	*I will buy it, although it may (turn out to) be expensive.*

e ¿COMPRENDES?

Completa las oraciones con la forma del subjuntivo o indicativo del verbo entre paréntesis.

1. Por lo general, el jefe lee los informes después de que yo se los ____________ (entregar).
2. Comenzaremos la reunión cuando Sandra ____________ (llegar).
3. Haremos lo que el grupo ____________(decidir).
4. No importa la hora; iré a las protestas aunque ____________ (empezar) a la medianoche.

MySpanishLab
Learn more using Amplifire Dynamic Study Modules, Grammar Tutorials, and Extra Practice activities.

LENGUA

You learned that in Spanish, the subject is normally placed after the verb when asking a question: **¿Les dio instrucciones el alcalde?** (*Did the mayor give them/you instructions?*) You may also place the subject after the verb in statements, especially when you wish to emphasize the subject: **Les habló el alcalde.** (*The mayor talked to them/you.*) To avoid misinterpreting statements with this structure, you should locate the subject first, and not assume that the first noun or pronoun in the sentence is the subject.

PRÁCTICA

Cultura

Regímenes dictatoriales en Latinoamérica

Aunque hoy en día todos los países latinoamericanos tienen sistemas democráticos, a través de la historia ha sido notable la presencia de líderes militares que se han convertido en dictadores de diferentes países. Estas figuras han accedido al poder casi siempre mediante golpes de estado y han consolidado regímenes políticos autoritarios y represivos que han llevado una "guerra sucia" sin respeto por los derechos humanos. Entre otros, se destacan los casos de las juntas militares en Argentina (1976–1983), Chile (1973–1989) y Uruguay (1973–1985) así como las sangrientas dictaduras centroamericanas de Somoza (asesinado en 1979) en Nicaragua, o los escuadrones de la muerte en Guatemala y El Salvador.

Conexiones. ¿Qué tácticas se aplican en una guerra sucia? ¿Qué efecto tienen estas tácticas en la población? ¿Todavía existen regímenes que usen las tácticas de una guerra sucia?

14-13 

¿Cuáles serán los cambios? Escoge la forma verbal correcta para completar las siguientes afirmaciones.

1. A menos que hay/haya elecciones democráticas, un país no puede considerarse democrático.
2. Se suprimió el derecho de libre expresión según lo exige/exigió la Junta Militar.
3. Las familias que tenían miembros desaparecidos reclamaron (*demanded*) justicia cuando se recuperó/se recupere la democracia.
4. Como resultado, la Corte Suprema ha decidido atender los reclamos de las familias de los desaparecidos para que la sociedad pueda/puede recuperar su confianza en las instituciones jurídicas.
5. Muchas personas dicen que no creerán en la justicia hasta que ven/vean a los culpables encarcelados.

14-14 

La educación a distancia. Ustedes toman un curso en Internet sobre la historia de Chile por medio del programa VirtualU de la Universidad de Chile. Todo lo hacen en la computadora y se comunican por mensajes de texto y correo electrónico. Digan lo que van a hacer, completando las oraciones lógicamente con una frase de la siguiente lista.

ser las 12:00	llegar el día del examen final
tener tiempo	escribirme mi compañero/a virtual
ser muy tarde	leer unos mensajes electrónicos de la profesora
tener sus horas de consulta	terminar de leer sobre los regímenes dictatoriales

 Voy a trabajar en la computadora hasta que... empezar las noticias/ser la hora de cenar

E1: *Voy a trabajar en la computadora hasta que empiecen las noticias.*

E2: *Y yo voy a trabajar hasta que sea la hora de cenar.*

1. Voy a hablar con la profesora en cuanto...
2. Comeré después de que...
3. Voy a comprobar los datos tan pronto como...
4. Haré la mayoría del trabajo en nuestro ensayo hasta que...
5. Voy a estudiar el tema de la inmigración chilena esta noche aunque...
6. Le mandaré a la profesora mi informe sobre las lecturas antes de que...

14-15 

Después de que termine el año escolar. PREPARACIÓN. Quieres descansar y divertirte después de que terminen las clases, pero también quieres hacer algo por tu comunidad. Completa dos de las opciones que más te interesen en cada columna y añade una más para expresar tus propias ideas. Después, comparte tus planes con tu compañero/a.

DIVERSIÓN	AYUDA COMUNITARIA
1. Quiero dormir hasta que...	**1.** Trabajaré de voluntario donde...
2. No voy a abrir los libros aunque...	**2.** Ayudaré en la biblioteca después de que...
3. Haré un crucero por... tan pronto como...	**3.** Les serviré comida a los desamparados (*homeless*) cuando...
4. Iré a la playa todos los días a menos que...	**4.** Organizaré juegos infantiles en el parque para que...
5. ...	**5.** ...

INTERCAMBIOS. Preparen un plan para ayudar a su comunidad. En su plan deben indicar lo siguiente:

1. sector de la comunidad
2. tipo de ayuda
3. frecuencia de su participación
4. medios que van a usar
5. resultados que esperan obtener

14-16

El hombre y la mujer en la sociedad. PREPARACIÓN. Indica (✓) si, en tu opinión, las situaciones presentadas en las siguientes afirmaciones existen o no existen hoy en día.

LOS HOMBRES Y LAS MUJERES...	SÍ	NO
1. reciben la misma educación.		
2. son tratados de la misma forma en el trabajo.		
3. ganan el mismo sueldo por el mismo trabajo.		
4. tienen las mismas oportunidades.		
5. hacen las mismas tareas domésticas.		
6. tienen los mismos derechos en un divorcio.		

En directo

To make a polite request or a proposal:

Quiero/Queremos proponer (que)...

Sugiero/Sugerimos (que)...

Listen to a conversation with these expressions.

INTERCAMBIOS. Ahora compara tus respuestas con las de tu compañero/a. Defiende tus opiniones negativas y di cuándo o bajo qué condiciones crees que los cambios necesarios ocurrirán.

E1: *Los hombres y las mujeres ocupan más o menos el mismo número de puestos importantes.*

E2: *No estoy de acuerdo. Los hombres ocupan la mayoría de los puestos importantes en las compañías y en el gobierno. Esto va a cambiar cuando las generaciones jóvenes puedan tomar más decisiones.*

Situación

PREPARACIÓN. Lean la situación. Luego, compartan ejemplos de vocabulario, gramática y otra información que necesitan para desarrollar la conversación.

Role A. You make a presentation to the city council (**concejo municipal**) about starting an adult literacy program. Explain how the lives of participants will improve when they know how to read and write well. In response to questions, say that you will a) organize the program; b) hold classes wherever the council says; and c) decide on class schedules according to the needs of the participants.

Role B. You are the president of the city council (**concejo municipal**). After listening to a presentation by a specialist in adult literacy who wants to start a program in the community, ask a) where and when the classes will be held; and b) who will pay for the program.

	ROLE A	ROLE B
Vocabulario	Social problems Dates and time	Social problems Dates and time
Funciones y formas	Expressing conjecture or certainty Adverbial conjunctions that take the subjunctive or indicative	Expressing conjecture or certainty Adverbial conjunctions that take the subjunctive or indicative

INTERCAMBIOS. Practica la conversación con tu compañero/a incorporando el vocabulario y las funciones de *Preparación*. Luego, represéntenla ante la clase.

3 Talking about the past from a past perspective

VIOLETA: Oye, mamá, mi profesora habló un poco de Gabriela Mistral. ¿Tú sabes algo de ella?

MADRE: ¡Claro que sí! Gabriela Mistral fue una gran poeta chilena que ganó el Premio Nobel de Literatura en 1945. Pero antes de recibir el premio, Gabriela ya **había hecho** muchas cosas importantes.

VIOLETA: ¿Qué **había hecho?** Yo no sé nada de ella.

MADRE: Antes de ser famosa, Gabriela **había tenido** una vida muy difícil. Su padre **había abandonado** a la familia, y eran muy pobres.

VIOLETA: ¡Qué triste la vida de Gabriela, mamá!

MADRE: Sí y no. Ella utilizó su sufrimiento positivamente para lograr mucho. Por ejemplo, a los 15 años, ya **había escrito** sus primeras poesías y **se había graduado** de profesora. Además, antes de ella, ningún escritor latinoamericano **había ganado** el Premio Nobel.

Piénsalo. Indica (✓) las experiencias de Gabriela Mistral y su madre que se refieren a un momento cronológicamente anterior al momento cuando Gabriela se hizo internacionalmente famosa.

1. _____ Gabriela ya **había hecho** muchas cosas importantes.
2. _____ Su madre y ella **habían tenido** una vida muy difícil.
3. _____ **Ganó** el Premio Nobel en 1945.
4. _____ Su padre **había abandonado** a Gabriela y a su madre.
5. _____ **Había escrito** poesías antes de cumplir los 15 años.
6. _____ Ningún escritor latinoamericano **había ganado** el Premio Nobel.

The past perfect

- Use the past perfect to refer to a past event, action, or condition that occurred prior to another past event, action, or state.

Ningún escritor latinoamericano **había ganado** el Premio Nobel de Literatura antes de Mistral.	*No Latin American writer had won the Nobel Prize for Literature before Mistral.*
Otros escritores **habían sido** nominados para el premio, pero ella lo recibió.	*Other writers had been nominated for the award, but she received it.*

- Form the past perfect with the imperfect tense of **haber** and the past participle of the main verb.

IMPERFECT OF *HABER*		PAST PARTICIPLE
yo	**había**	
tú	**habías**	
Ud., él, ella	**había**	**hablado**
nosotros/as	**habíamos**	**comido**
vosotros/as	**habíais**	**vivido**
Uds., ellos/as	**habían**	

¿COMPRENDES?

Completa las afirmaciones con la forma del pluscuamperfecto del verbo entre paréntesis.

1. Cuando Michelle Bachelet ganó la presidencia de Chile, ya ____________ (trabajar) por muchos años en el servicio público.
2. El novelista chileno Roberto Ampuero ya ____________ (escribir) varios libros antes de estudiar para su doctorado.
3. Nosotros sacamos muy malas notas en el examen porque no ____________ (leer) el material.
4. Cuando invité a mis padres al concierto, me dijeron que ya ____________ (hacer) otros planes para esa noche.

MySpanishLab

Learn more using Amplifire Dynamic Study Modules, Grammar Tutorials, and Extra Practice activities.

PRÁCTICA

14-17 

¡Recuerdos! **PREPARACIÓN.** Para cada afirmación, indica la acción que ocurrió primero.

 Cuando yo cumplí diez años, ya había escuchado discusiones políticas.

1. Cuando cumplimos diecisiete años, mis amigos y yo ya nos habíamos inscrito en un partido político.
2. Cuando terminé la escuela secundaria, mis padres ya me habían comprado un carro.
3. Yo ya había trabajado y había ahorrado (*saved*) algún dinero cuando empecé la universidad.
4. Cuando pasó el primer mes de clases en la universidad, yo ya me había acostumbrado a todo el trabajo que tenía que hacer.
5. Mis padres ya sospechaban que yo me había hecho más independiente cuando los visité después de algunos meses.

 **INTERCAMBIOS.** ¿Cuáles de las acciones de *Preparación* concuerdan (*agree*) con tu experiencia personal? Comparte tus respuestas con tu compañero/a.

14-18 

Una investigación. **PREPARACIÓN.** Completa la tabla y dile a tu compañero/a si tú o miembros de tu familia ya habían hecho estas cosas antes del año 2013.

 buscar trabajo en Internet antes del año 2013

E1: *Mi hermano y yo ya habíamos buscado trabajo en Internet. En el año 2012, los dos conseguimos trabajo por Internet.*

E2: *Pues, yo nunca había usado Internet para buscar trabajo. En 2012, yo estaba en la escuela secundaria.*

ANTES DEL AÑO 2013	SÍ	NO	¿QUIÉNES?
1. manejar un carro híbrido			
2. hacer trabajo voluntario			
3. votar en las elecciones presidenciales			
4. leer periódicos digitales muchas veces			
5. comunicarse con los amigos por mensajes de texto			
6. comprar un iPod			
7. diseñar una página web			
8. crear una cuenta de Twitter			

 **INTERCAMBIOS.** Hagan una encuesta para averiguar qué tres actividades de *Preparación* marcaron más personas del grupo. Determinen si más hombres o más mujeres hicieron cada una de las tres actividades.

14-19 

¡Una familia organizada! Los señores Rosales salieron temprano para el trabajo hoy. Cuando volvieron por la noche notaron que sus hijos Carlos, Eduardo y Magdalena habían hecho todo el trabajo doméstico. Túrnense para conjeturar qué había hecho cada uno.

 Al salir, les dijeron a sus hijos que iban a llegar un poco tarde y que no tendrían tiempo para cocinar. *Al volver, vieron que Eduardo había cocinado unos espaguetis para toda la familia.*

1. Después del desayuno dejaron los platos sucios en el lavaplatos.
2. Antes de irse a la oficina, la señora Rosales vio que había un montón de libros de la biblioteca en la mesa del comedor.
3. Cuando salía de casa el señor Rosales notó que el garaje estaba sucio.
4. Los dormitorios de sus hijos estaban desordenados; había ropa y libros en el piso.
5. Como tenía prisa, la señora Rosales olvidó mandar por correo unos cheques importantes.
6. No llevaron a la tintorería (*dry cleaner*) una ropa que querían limpiar en seco (*dry clean*).

Situación  

PREPARACIÓN. Lean la situación. Luego, compartan ejemplos de vocabulario, gramática y otra información que necesitan para desarrollar la conversación.

Role A. You are interviewing a student for your campus newspaper. Ask a) what he/she had planned to study before coming to the university; b) what other schools he/she had considered before choosing this one; and c) how his/her experience has been different from what he/she had expected.

Role B. You are a student who is being interviewed for the campus newspaper. Provide as much information to the reporter as possible, including your expectations (**lo que había pensado**) before you entered college and the reality you found when you started to study here.

	ROLE A	ROLE B
Vocabulario	Studies Extracurricular activities	Studies Extracurricular activities
Funciones y formas	Asking questions Past perfect	Past tense Past perfect

INTERCAMBIOS. Practica la conversación con tu compañero/a incorporando el vocabulario y las funciones de *Preparación*. Luego, represéntenla ante la clase.

4 Expressing actions

LAURA: Mamá, ¿viste la marcha en la tele? Yo también estaba allí con todos mis compañeros de la clase de sociología.

MAMÁ: **Luchar** por la igualdad entre los sexos es tiempo perdido, hija. No hemos avanzado mucho. Mira, yo continúo trabajando en casa, pero no me importa.

LAURA: Pero **quedarse** de brazos cruzados tampoco es una opción para mí, mamá.

MAMÁ: **Trabajar** duro es lo que debemos hacer. Ninguna protesta nos ayudará.

LAURA: Mamá, ¿cómo puedes pensar así? **Guardar** silencio es **hacerse** cómplice de la injusticia. **Exigir** igualdad y respeto por nuestra dignidad es nuestro derecho.

Piénsalo. Indica si crees que las siguientes acciones representan las opiniones de Laura (**L**) o las de su madre (**M**).

1. _____ **Trabajar** en casa no es un problema para la mujer.
2. _____ **Protestar** nos ayudará a cambiar la sociedad.
3. _____ No **resignarse** al trato desigual es fundamental para conseguir el cambio.
4. _____ **Mantenerse** de brazos cruzados significa aceptar la desigualdad y la injusticia.

The infinitive as subject or object

- The infinitive is the only verb form that may be used as the subject of a sentence. As the subject, it corresponds to the English *-ing* form.

Dialogar es necesario para lograr cambios.	*Talking is necessary for changes to occur.*
Hacer comentarios negativos no es bueno para nuestras negociaciones.	*Making negative pronouncements is not good for our negotiations.*

- Use an infinitive after a preposition.

Llama **antes de ir.**	*Call before going.*
No trates de discutir el tema **sin prepararte.**	*Do not try to argue without preparing yourself.*

- **Al +** *infinitive* is the equivalent of **cuando +** *verb.*

Al recibir su carta de despido, llamó al director.	*Upon receiving his pink slip, he called the director.*
Cuando recibió su carta de despido, llamó al director.	*When he received his pink slip, he called the director.*

- When used in signs and instructions, the infinitive functions as a command.

No **comer** en clase.	*No eating in class.* (Lit. *Don't eat in class.*)
Hablar en voz baja.	*Speak softly.*

¿COMPRENDES?

Completa las oraciones con los siguientes verbos.

abrir	hacer
cerrar	nadar
dormir	participar
fumar	

1. ________ está prohibido en los edificios de la universidad.
2. ________ es el mejor ejercicio para el dolor de espalda.
3. La vida es breve: un ________ y ________ de ojos.
4. Al ________ en las protestas, Gonzalo se comprometió aún más con el movimiento.

MySpanishLab

Learn more using Amplifire Dynamic Study Modules, Grammar Tutorials, and Extra Practice activities.

PRÁCTICA

Cultura

Independencia en Latinoamérica

Los países latinoamericanos consiguieron la independencia de España durante el siglo XIX. Las diferentes guerras por la independencia crearon países libres en un tiempo relativamente corto. El primer país en independizarse fue Venezuela, en 1811, y el último Bolivia en 1825. Entre las grandes figuras guerreras independentistas se encuentran Iturbide en México y el "gran libertador de las Américas", Simón Bolívar, que venció a los españoles en la batalla de Ayacucho en 1825. Un caso singular es el de Cuba y Puerto Rico. Tras la guerra entre España y Estados Unidos a finales del siglo XIX, Cuba ganó su independencia en 1898. Puerto Rico, por otra parte, nunca ha sido un país independiente. Primero fue un protectorado de Estados Unidos y posteriormente, un "Estado libre asociado".

Comparaciones. ¿Qué personajes históricos se consideran "grandes libertadores" en la Guerra de Independencia de los Estados Unidos? Prepara una breve presentación.

14-20 

Ciudadanos responsables. Asocia lógicamente las opciones de la columna de la izquierda con las ideas de la columna de la derecha y compara tus respuestas con las de tu compañero/a.

1. _____ Luchar por la libertad...
2. _____ Estudiar idiomas...
3. _____ Expresar una opinión...
4. _____ Aceptar a los inmigrantes...

a. es indispensable para una convivencia sana dentro de una comunidad.
b. es un derecho.
c. es la mejor manera de aprender sobre otras culturas.
d. es una obligación moral de todos.

14-21 

Opiniones. PREPARACIÓN. Indica si las siguientes actividades son necesarias (**N**), opcionales (**O**) o inaceptables (**I**). Después, compara tus respuestas con las de tu compañero/a y explícale las razones de tus respuestas.

ACTIVIDAD	OPINIÓN
1. ofrecer seguro de salud para todos	
2. informarse sobre lo que pasa en el mundo	
3. prohibir la proliferación de armas nucleares	
4. hacer investigación sobre células troncales (*stem cell*)	
5. discriminar a algunas personas por su etnia (*ethnicity*)	

INTERCAMBIOS. Escojan el tema más importante para ustedes de *Preparación*. Expliquen por qué es importante y qué es necesario hacer para lograr la atención de la gente.

14-22 

Interpretar los mensajes. PREPARACIÓN. Observen los siguientes letreros y escriban una nota bajo cada uno de ellos.

1. ____________

2. ____________

3. ____________

4. ____________

INTERCAMBIOS. Preparen su propio letrero. Otra pareja tiene que decir dónde sería bueno ponerlo y por qué.

Situación

PREPARACIÓN. Lean la situación. Luego, compartan ejemplos de vocabulario, gramática y otra información que necesitan para desarrollar la conversación.

Role A. As president of the Student Association, you are designing a campaign to promote cross-cultural understanding in your area. Discuss with a friend: a) what students can do to better understand people from other cultures; and b) how students can reach out to (**comunicarse con**) people from other cultures who live in the community.

Role B. A friend wants to discuss a project to promote cross-cultural understanding in your area. Explain your views about a) what students can do to learn about cultural diversity; and b) how students can reach out to (**comunicarse con**) people from other cultures who live in the community.

	ROLE A	ROLE B
Vocabulario	Social issues Plans and projects	Social issues Plans and projects
Funciones y formas	Expressing opinions Using the infinitive as subject or object *Por/para*	Expressing opinions Using the infinitive as subject or object *Por/para*

INTERCAMBIOS. Practica la conversación con tu compañero/a incorporando el vocabulario y las funciones de *Preparación*. Luego, represéntenla ante la clase.

EN ACCIÓN

Por un mundo mejor

14-23 Antes de ver

Temas de interés social. Asocia las personas o grupos de la columna de la izquierda con los temas de la columna de la derecha.

1. ____ los techos verdes	**a.** la persecución política
2. ____ los refugiados	**b.** la discriminación sexual
3. ____ los indocumentados	**c.** el medio ambiente
4. ____ los indígenas	**d.** la reforma migratoria
5. ____ los homosexuales	**e.** las minorías étnicas
6. ____ los veganos	**f.** la protección de animales

14-24 Mientras ves  

Cambios y más cambios. En este segmento, los chicos hablan sobre sus proyectos. Indica si las siguientes afirmaciones son ciertas (**C**) o falsas (**F**) según la información que aparece en el video. Corrige las afirmaciones falsas.

1. ______ Yolanda ya ha terminado su proyecto de video.
2. ______ El proyecto de Yolanda está relacionado con problemas del medio ambiente.
3. ______ Esteban cree que la pobreza y el analfabetismo ya no existen.
4. ______ El video de Esteban trata de la inmigración.
5. ______ La organización Chirla lucha por los derechos de los homosexuales.
6. ______ Chirla promociona actividades para que haya una sociedad más justa.
7. ______ El proyecto de Federico trata de la legalización de la marihuana en Argentina.
8. ______ Argentina fue el primer país latinoamericano en legalizar el matrimonio entre personas del mismo sexo.

14-25 Después de ver 

Un mundo mejor. **PREPARACIÓN.** Completa las afirmaciones de la izquierda con las ideas de la derecha.

1. ______ Para que haya más conciencia sobre los problemas del medio ambiente...	**a.** para que deje de consumir carne y otros productos derivados.
2. ______ Chirla intentará influir sobre el congresista de Los Ángeles...	**b.** de manera que aumente la conciencia social sobre ellos.
3. ______ Yolanda hablará con Federico sobre los derechos de los animales...	**c.** para que vote a favor de la reforma migratoria.
4. ______ Los chicos van a presentar proyectos sobre problemas sociales...	**d.** la organización techos verdes busca cambiar la actitud de las personas en México.

INTERCAMBIOS. El proyecto de video de Esteban está relacionado con los derechos de los inmigrantes y refugiados. Explíquense las diferencias entre un inmigrante y un refugiado. Hablen de los desafíos (*challenges*) de ser inmigrante o refugiado y sugieran maneras de mejorar la situación de estos grupos.

Mosaicos

ESCUCHA

14-26

Preparación. Dos mujeres mayores conversan sobre los cambios que han ocurrido en la familia hispana. Antes de escuchar su conversación, escribe un cambio que probablemente se mencionará en relación con cada una de estas áreas: los quehaceres de la casa y la crianza de los hijos. Luego, comparte tus ideas con la clase.

ESTRATEGIA

Identify the speaker's point of view

When you listen to someone or see someone talk you may identify the speaker's intention and point of view by paying attention to word choice as well as other cues, such as tone, organization of ideas, and pitch. Identifying the speaker's point of view will help you understand his/her position on the issues.

14-27  

Escucha. Read the statements, then listen to Sonia and Vilma talk about changes in the Hispanic family that have occurred during their lifetime. Pay attention to how each woman organizes her ideas, her choice of words, and the tone she uses to indicate if each statement reflects Sonia's (**S**) point of view or Vilma's (**V**).

1. _____ Los cambios que han ocurrido en la sociedad han sido positivos.
2. _____ Ahora nadie se ocupa de los quehaceres de la casa.
3. _____ No era bueno el papel secundario que tenía la mujer en la casa.
4. _____ Los abuelos han perdido la importancia que tenían en la familia.
5. _____ La mujer debe desarrollarse profesional e intelectualmente.

Comprueba

I was able to ...

_____ **identify words that helped me understand different points of view.**

_____ **identify Sonia and Vilma by the pitch and tone of their voices.**

14-28 

Un paso más. Compartan su punto de vista sobre los siguientes asuntos.

1. ¿Es necesario que uno de los padres se quede en casa mientras los hijos son pequeños? Expliquen su respuesta.
2. Si ambos padres trabajan fuera de casa, ¿cómo se podría resolver la cuestión de la educación de los hijos?

HABLA

14-29

Preparación. Investiga sobre un problema (local, nacional o mundial) en una de las siguientes áreas y anota en qué consiste el problema.

MODELO **Área:** *seguridad*

Problema: *terrorismo*

Explicación del problema: *Hoy existen grupos terroristas que atacan y crean caos en el mundo. Nadie se siente seguro.*

ÁREAS

1. economía

2. igualdad

3. educación

4. salud

ESTRATEGIA

Organize ideas to present solutions to problems

When you present your ideas about how to solve a problem, organize them so that you can communicate clearly to your listeners a) what the problem is, to whom it is important, and why; b) how your proposal is to be implemented and how it addresses the problem; and c) the likely consequences of your solution. Your underlying goal is to convince your listeners of the wisdom of your approach.

14-30 

Habla. Conversen sobre los problemas que ustedes identificaron en la actividad 14-29. Hagan lo siguiente:

1. Intercambien la información que encontraron sobre los problemas que eligieron. Expliquen cuál es el más serio y por qué.

2. Luego, háganse preguntas relacionadas con ese problema. Utilicen en sus respuestas las expresiones indicadas en *En directo* y tomen nota de las respuestas del grupo.

MODELO la falta de seguridad en las escuelas

E1: *¿Creen que haya solución al problema de la falta de seguridad en las escuelas?*

E2: *Sí, la solución es tener/establecer más comunicación con la administración de las escuelas, para que controlen mejor la seguridad de los alumnos.*

E3: *A mí me parece que la solución es instalar máquinas en las entradas de las escuelas que registren a todas las personas que quieran entrar en la escuela.*

En directo

To present a group's conclusion:

Después de hablar sobre el tema, hemos llegado a la siguiente conclusión. Nuestro grupo cree/piensa que...

A nuestro grupo le parece que...

Para nosotros, el problema más serio es...

To support a group's view or position:

No tenemos duda de que es el problema más serio porque...

Si miramos/observamos... nos damos cuenta de que...

Las estadísticas/La opinión de los expertos apoya(n) nuestra conclusión.

Listen to a conversation with these expressions.

Comprueba

I was able to ...

____ **inform myself well about the problem, and identify possible solutions.**

____ **organize my ideas in a logical sequence: identification of a problem and possible solutions to share with my classmate.**

14-31 

Un paso más. Preséntenle a la clase la información y conclusión a la que llegaron en la actividad 14-30. Prepárense para defender su posición.

LEE

Preparación. Responde a las siguientes preguntas. Compara tus respuestas con las de tu compañero/a.

1. ¿Qué fábulas conoces o recuerdas de tu niñez?
2. ¿Cuáles son los elementos de las fábulas?
3. ¿Cuál es el propósito de una fábula?
4. ¿Qué diferencias hay entre una mosca y un águila? ¿Qué tienen en común?
5. Imagínate que no eres un ser humano, sino un animal. ¿Preferirías ser una mosca o un águila? ¿Por qué?

ESTRATEGIA

Identify the tone of a text

Identifying the tone of a text is important when reading literature. A writer may use subtle irony or sarcasm to convey social criticism. Sometimes the writer adopts a traditional genre (e.g., fairy tale, fable) to present a message about contemporary life.

Augusto Monterroso (1921–2003) nació en Honduras de un padre guatemalteco y una madre hondureña, pero se crio en Guatemala y siempre se consideró guatemalteco. Por sus actividades políticas, estuvo encarcelado brevemente en 1944 pero escapó y vivió exiliado en Chile y luego en México, donde vivió hasta su muerte. Monterroso, conocido por sus relatos breves que tratan sobre temas complejos del comportamiento humano, es uno de los maestros de la minificción. Su microcuento "El dinosaurio" es considerado uno de los más breves de la literatura universal (*Cuando despertó, el dinosaurio todavía estaba allí.*), aunque el escritor mexicano Luis Felipe Lomelí ha escrito uno más corto de solo cuatro palabras.

14-33 

Lee. Desde la perspectiva de la Mosca del cuento, indica cuáles son las ventajas (**V**) y las desventajas (**D**) de ser un águila.

1. _____ volar por los Alpes
2. _____ tener alas grandes
3. _____ tener un cuerpo pesado
4. _____ tener un pico duro
5. _____ tener garras fuertes
6. _____ remontar montañas

Comprueba

I was able to …

_____ **understand the story literally.**

_____ **understand the fly's internal conflict.**

_____ **apply the message of the story to human behavior.**

LA MOSCA QUE SOÑABA QUE ERA UN ÁGUILA

Había una vez una Mosca que todas las noches soñaba que era un Águila y que se encontraba volando por los Alpes y por los Andes.

En los primeros momentos esto la volvía loca de felicidad; pero pasado un tiempo le causaba una sensación de angustia, pues hallaba las alas[1] demasiado grandes, el cuerpo demasiado pesado, el pico[2] demasiado duro y las garras[3] demasiado fuertes; bueno, que todo ese gran aparato le impedía posarse a gusto sobre los ricos pasteles o sobre las inmundicias[4] humanas, así como sufrir a conciencia dándose topes contra los vidrios de su cuarto.

En realidad no quería andar en las grandes alturas o en los espacios libres, ni mucho menos.

Pero cuando volvía en sí lamentaba con toda el alma no ser un Águila para remontar montañas, y se sentía tristísima de ser una Mosca, y por eso volaba tanto, y estaba tan inquieta, y daba tantas vueltas, hasta que lentamente, por la noche, volvía a poner las sienes en la almohada.

Monterroso, Augusto. *La oveja negra y demás fábulas.* Alfaguara. México: 2a edición. 1998.

[1] *wings* [2] *beak* [3] *claws* [4] *filth*

14-34 

Un paso más. En grupos, escriban su interpretación del minicuento y preséntenla a la clase. Enfóquense en cómo se puede aplicar el conflicto de la Mosca al comportamiento humano.

ESCRIBE

14-35

Preparación. Lee el siguiente poema que alude a las emociones de una persona que se siente atrapada en una relación. Luego, indica si estás de acuerdo (**A**) o en desacuerdo (**D**) con las afirmaciones sobre el poema.

Hombre pequeñito
de Alfonsina Storni

Hombre pequeñito, hombre pequeñito,
Suelta a tu canario, que quiere volar…
Yo soy el canario, hombre pequeñito,
Déjame saltar.
Estuve en tu jaula, hombre pequeñito,
Hombre pequeñito que jaula me das,
Digo pequeñito porque no me entiendes,
Ni me entenderás.
Tampoco te entiendo, pero mientras tanto
Ábreme la jaula que quiero escapar;
Hombre pequeñito, te amé media hora.
No me pidas más.

1. ____________ El poema tiene un tono alegre.
2. ____________ La persona que habla en este poema es un hombre.
3. ____________ La voz del poema expresa un sentimiento de disgusto por la opresión en la que ha vivido.
4. ____________ La persona expresa la esperanza de que su pareja la comprenda en el futuro.
5. ____________ Al usar la palabra *pequeñito* la voz del poema expresa irónicamente su desprecio por su pareja.
6. ____________ La voz del poema quiere continuar viviendo con su compañero/a.

ESTRATEGIA

Use language to express emotions

Poetry is well suited to the expression of emotions. Poets paint with words experiences or feelings of heroism, beauty, love, sadness, loss, or injustice. To compose an effective poem, it is important to think carefully about the feelings we want to convey. Because poetry is a reflection of human experience, it is available to everyone both as readers and writers.

14-36

Escribe. **PREPARACIÓN.** Vas a escribir tu propio poema de cinco líneas. Primero, escoge el tema principal (una persona, un animal, un objeto) y piensa en el tono y las emociones que quieres expresar. Luego, sigue las instrucciones para escribir tu poema.

Tema: ______________

Tono, emociones: ______________________

Comprueba

I was able to …

____ **decide on a topic, tone, and message for my poem.**

____ **follow the instructions to create an original 5-line poem.**

Mi poema de cinco líneas:

Título (el tema en una palabra) ______________________________

Dos adjetivos que describan el tema ______________, ______________

Tres gerundios (*-ando/-iendo*) relacionados con el tema ______________, ______________, ______________

Una frase de cuatro palabras relacionada con el tema ______________________________

Una palabra que exprese lo mismo que el título ______________________________.

14-37 

Un paso más. Lean sus poemas y decidan si evocan las emociones que cada uno de ustedes quería expresar. Luego, háganles preguntas específicas a los miembros de su grupo sobre el uso de las palabras que han escogido.

¿Por qué dices en el poema que…?

En este capítulo...

Comprueba lo que sabes

Go to ***MySpanishLab*** to review what you have learned in this chapter. Practice with the following:

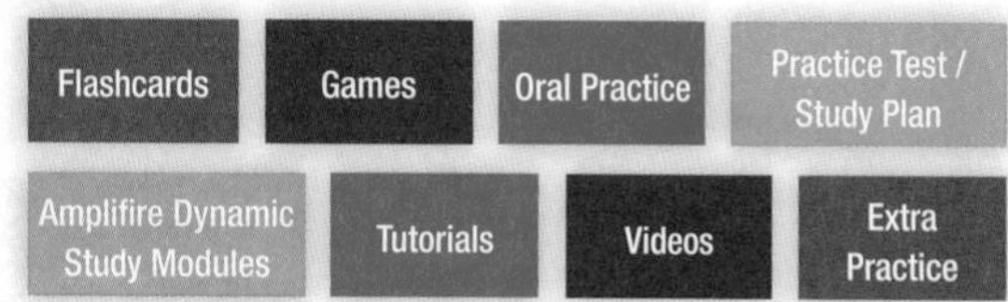

Vocabulario

LA SOCIEDAD
Society

la adaptación *adjustment, adaptation*
el alfabetismo *literacy*
el analfabetismo *illiteracy*
el cambio *change*
la confianza *trust*
la democracia *democracy*
el derecho *right*
el desempleo *unemployment*
el desplazamiento *movement, displacement*
la dictadura *dictatorship*
la diversificación *diversification*
la eficiencia *efficiency*
la elección *election*
la emigración *emigration*
la esperanza de vida *life expectancy*
la exportación *export*
la honestidad *honesty*
la igualdad *equality*
la inmigración *immigration*
la lucha *fight*
la migración *migration*
la mortalidad *mortality*
la pobreza *poverty*
la proximidad *proximity*
el régimen *regime*
el tráfico de drogas *drug trafficking*

LAS ENCUESTAS
Surveys/Polls

los datos *data, information*
la mayoría *majority*
la minoría *minority*
el porcentaje *percentage*
el promedio *average*
la tasa *rate*

LAS PERSONAS
People

el/la emigrante *emigrant*
el/la habitante *inhabitant*
el/la inmigrante *immigrant*
la población *population*
el/la presidente/a *president*

LAS DESCRIPCIONES
Descriptions

amplio/a *ample*
analfabeto/a *illiterate*
dictatorial *dictatorial*
económico/a *economic*
enérgico/a *energetic*
infantil *children's*
políglota *polyglot, multilingual*

VERBOS
Verbs

destacarse *to stand out*
defender (ie) *to defend*
elegir (i, i) *to choose, elect*
emigrar *to emigrate*
gobernar (ie) *to govern*
luchar *fight*
mejorar *to improve*
preceder *to precede*
realizar (c) *to carry out*

PALABRAS Y EXPRESIONES ÚTILES
Useful words and expressions

en vez de *instead of*
el nivel *level*
la sucursal *branch (business)*

See pages 488 and 491 for a list of adverbial conjunctions.

¿Qué nos trae el futuro?

ENFOQUE CULTURAL
Puerto Rico

VOCABULARIO EN CONTEXTO
La ciencia y la tecnología en el mundo de hoy
La conservación del medio ambiente
Otros retos del futuro

MOSAICO CULTURAL
La investigación tecnológica en Latinoamérica

FUNCIONES Y FORMAS
The imperfect subjunctive
If-clauses
Se for unplanned occurrences

EN ACCIÓN
¡Cuidemos el medio ambiente!

MOSAICOS
ESCUCHA Identify the speaker's intention through the main idea and specific information
HABLA Use drama and humor in telling a personal anecdote
LEE Identify the narrator's perspective
ESCRIBE Use imagination and humor in writing a narrative

EN ESTE CAPÍTULO...
Comprueba lo que sabes
Vocabulario

LEARNING **OUTCOMES**

You will be able to:

- talk about advances in science and technology
- express wishes and recommendations in the past
- hypothesize and share information about the present and the future
- express unexpected occurrences
- talk about Puerto Rico in terms of its advances in science and technology

ENFOQUE *cultural* PUERTO RICO

Enfoque cultural

To learn more about Puerto Rico, go to MySpanishLab to view the *Vistas culturales* videos.

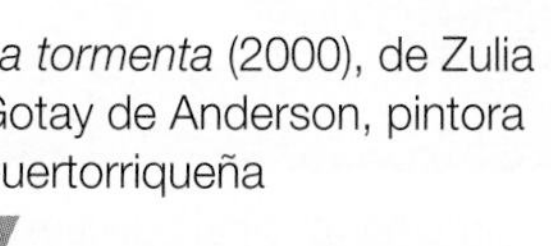

La tormenta (2000), de Zulia Gotay de Anderson, pintora puertorriqueña

¿QUÉ TE PARECE?

- En Puerto Rico se mide la temperatura ambiental en grados Farenheit mientras que la temperatura corporal se mide en grados centígrados.
- En Puerto Rico se usa el sistema monetario de Estados Unidos, pero se han mantenido los nombres de las antiguas monedas españolas. Un dólar se conoce como un peso y la moneda de 25 centavos es una peseta.
- En Puerto Rico hay cientos de especies de bananas. La palabra genérica para esta fruta es guineo porque en la época colonial las importaban del país africano Guinea. En vez de naranja, se usa la palabra china porque esta fruta se trajo de China.
- Puerto Rico participa como país independiente en los Juegos Olímpicos. Ha ganado siete medallas: cinco en boxeo, una en lucha libre y otra en atletismo. Javier Culson es el atleta olímpico más conocido.

ENFOQUE cultural

◀ La Parguera, en Lajas, es una bahía llena de casas flotantes y una de las tres bahías de Puerto Rico donde en las noches sin luna se puede observar el fenómeno de la bioluminiscencia. Las bahías sorprenden por la intensidad de la luz emitida por los organismos microscópicos al agitarse. Es como un espectáculo de luces bajo el mar.

◀ El Observatorio de Arecibo, en el norte de la isla, tiene el radiotelescopio más grande del mundo. Allí se filmaron las películas *Contact* y *Goldeneye* del famoso Agente 007. Además ha aparecido en episodios de *X Files* y más recientemente en *Covert Affairs.* Desde 1999 el Instituto SETI ha analizado los datos recolectados por este radiotelescopio en búsqueda de evidencia de la existencia de inteligencia extraterrestre y, por eso, en el mundo del cine muchas veces se asocia con los temas de ciencia ficción.

▲ La expresión musical en Puerto Rico es el resultado de una gran mezcla de culturas. El *reguetón,* una expresión de música urbana, es una fusión del reggae en español que proviene de Panamá, del hip hop y de otros ritmos caribeños. En sus comienzos fue prohibido por sus temas sociales muy controvertidos, pero hoy, gracias a la persistencia de cantantes famosos como Tego Calderón, el reguetón es popular en todas partes del mundo.

Las Fiestas de la Calle San Sebastián, que se celebran cada año en el Viejo San Juan a finales de enero, duran cuatro días. Hay desfiles, música, artesanía y exhibiciones de arte. Con ellas se pone fin a la temporada navideña puertorriqueña. En la Comparsa de los Cabezudos, los cabezudos (muñecos con cabezas enormes) representan a las figuras más destacadas de la historia, la cultura y la política, al igual que a otras figuras populares del momento. ▶

¿CUÁNTO SABES?

Completa estas oraciones con la información correcta.

1. El coquí es una ____________ que vive exclusivamente en Puerto Rico.
2. El reguetón es una mezcla de ritmos de hip hop, ____________ en español y otros ritmos caribeños.
3. Una china en Puerto Rico es una ____________.
4. En Puerto Rico un peso equivale a ____________ pesetas.
5. El Observatorio de Arecibo es famoso por tener el ____________ más grande del mundo y por las investigaciones sobre la vida ____________ que se realizan allí.

Vocabulario en contexto

Talking about science, technology, and the environment

La ciencia y la tecnología en el mundo de hoy

MySpanishLab
Learn more using Amplifire Dynamic Study Modules, Pronunciation, and Vocabulary Tutorials.

▲ Antes de salir para la universidad, Ángel, un joven puertorriqueño, **se conecta** con sus amigos por Internet. Entra en Twitter y le manda un *tweet* sobre la nueva película de **ciencia ficción** a Carmen. Luego, baja el último *podcast* para su clase *online* y le envía a su profesor de ciencias naturales un **mensaje** con un **documento adjunto.**

▲ Entonces, Lorena, la hermana de Ángel, le pide que la ayude a bajar una canción de Internet para tenerla en su **tableta.** Por último, entra en el *blog* de su amigo Juanjo para leer las últimas novedades sobre sus **videojuegos** preferidos. Allí encuentra un **enlace** que le interesa.

▲ Actualmente, la ciencia y la tecnología **contribuyen** a un mejor **conocimiento** y comprensión de las diferencias culturales que existen entre los pueblos. Los jóvenes de Europa e Hispanoamérica tienen muchas cosas en común con los de Asia, África o Estados Unidos. El **acceso** a Internet a través de las tabletas, computadoras y **móviles** hacen más fluida la comunicación y facilitan la **diseminación** y el **intercambio** de información.

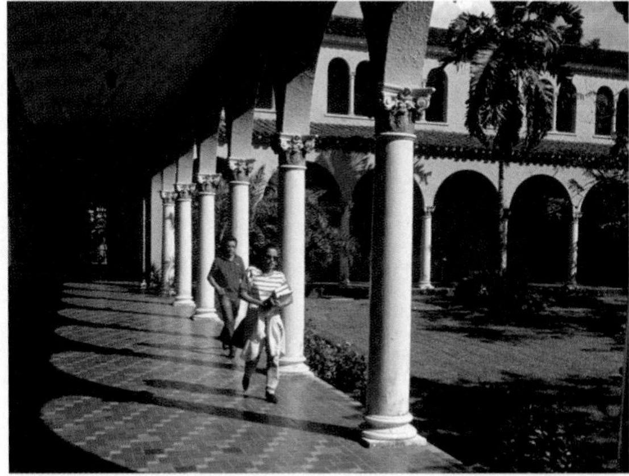

▲ Hace unos años, se estableció el Instituto de Ciencias y Tecnología (ICT) de la Universidad de Puerto Rico con el fin de **promover** el estudio de las ciencias entre los jóvenes. La Escuela Graduada de Ciencias y Tecnología de la Información (EGCTI), de la misma universidad, tiene una **biblioteca digital** que sirve como una importante **fuente de recursos** para los interesados en el campo de las ciencias de la información.

PRÁCTICA

15-1  

Escucha y confirma. Escucha el anuncio radiofónico y decide si las afirmaciones son ciertas (**C**) o falsas (**F**). Corrige las falsas, dando la información correcta.

1. _____ Es el anuncio de una tienda digital.
2. _____ Según el anuncio se puede obtener un título de maestría *online*.
3. _____ Se ofrecen clases de humanidades solamente.
4. _____ Los expertos en recursos digitales son los profesores.
5. _____ La calidad de la enseñanza es más importante que la interacción.
6. _____ Los estudiantes no necesitan acceso a Internet.

15-2 

¿Para qué lo usamos? En las siguientes afirmaciones relacionadas con diversos usos de tecnología, indica el uso que *no* corresponde.

1. Internet sirve para...
   - **a.** acceder a información sobre muchas disciplinas.
   - **b.** ver películas.
   - **c.** enviar felicitaciones.
   - **d.** examinar a un paciente.
2. El correo electrónico se usa para...
   - **a.** comunicarse con los amigos.
   - **b.** hacer fotografías.
   - **c.** enviar un documento adjunto.
   - **d.** recibir mensajes.
3. La biblioteca digital se utiliza para...
   - **a.** comunicarse con los profesores de la universidad.
   - **b.** encontrar enlaces.
   - **c.** bajar artículos.
   - **d.** identificar documentación.
4. Los videojuegos sirven para...
   - **a.** divertirse con los amigos.
   - **b.** practicar deportes al aire libre.
   - **c.** diseminar ciertos conocimientos.
   - **d.** intercambiar información.

Cultura

Universidad de Río Piedras

La Universidad de Puerto Rico está formada por once campus que se encuentran por toda la isla. El campus de Río Piedras es el más importante de todos y el que cuenta con mayor número de estudiantes, más de 17.000. Está situado en el centro de la zona comercial y cultural de Río Piedras, a las afueras de San Juan. El campus es fácilmente identificable desde diferentes puntos de la ciudad por su llamativa torre.

Comparaciones. ¿Cuál es el campus más importante de la universidad pública de tu estado? ¿Cuántos alumnos tiene? ¿Qué programas, actividades o edificios de esa universidad son los más conocidos?

15-3

Usa la tecnología.

PREPARACIÓN. Usa la tecnología para preparar una presentación sobre Puerto Rico que incluya lo siguiente.

1. ubicación de un lugar en un mapa
2. descripción y tres datos que se refieran a las características físicas del lugar, la gente del lugar y una costumbre del lugar
3. fotos

 **INTERCAMBIOS.** Comparte la información con tu grupo, incluyendo una descripción de los recursos tecnológicos que utilizaste.

15-4

Una noticia. PREPARACIÓN. Busca una noticia que te interese en un periódico virtual de Puerto Rico. Léela y toma apuntes sobre lo esencial de la noticia.

INTERCAMBIOS. Mándales a tres personas de la clase un mensaje electrónico incluyendo un resumen de la noticia y tu opinión sobre ella.

La conservación del medio ambiente

La contribución de América Latina a la ciencia **se ha enfocado** principalmente en la biología, **debido a** la riqueza de la flora y la fauna, la **conservación** de la **naturaleza,** la agricultura y la medicina. Aunque a veces las **infraestructuras** y los recursos son insuficientes, algunos científicos de esta región han hecho **descubrimientos** importantes. Esta es una foto de El Yunque en Puerto Rico, una de las muchas **reservas naturales** de Hispanoamérica.

La reserva de la biosfera del Alto Golfo de California y del delta del río Colorado puede ser la salvación de nuestra cultura pesquera. Juntos vamos a desarrollar un plan que nos permita manejar la reproducción y recuperación de los recursos naturales y de esta manera, asegurar nuestro bienestar y el de nuestros hijos.

¡El éxito depende de nuestra participación!

La **cuenca** del río Amazonas cubre un área de más de siete millones de kilómetros cuadrados, región comparable en extensión a dos terceras partes del territorio continental de Estados Unidos. Debido a su densa vegetación selvática, esta zona es conocida como el pulmón del **planeta.** Hoy en día, miles de campesinos llegan a la selva **en busca de tierra** para cultivar. La **deforestación** de nuestros **bosques** se considera una **pérdida** irreparable para el **medio ambiente.**

PRÁCTICA

15-5 

Para confirmar. PREPARACIÓN. Indica cuáles de los siguientes problemas se asocian **a)** con la industria pesquera, **b)** con los bosques tropicales o **c)** con los dos.

1. _____ la construcción de carreteras
2. _____ la desertización
3. _____ la erosión
4. _____ la exterminación de especies animales
5. _____ la tala (*felling*) de árboles
6. _____ la contaminación provocada por aguas residuales (*sewage*) y substancias químicas
7. _____ la disminución de la capa de ozono
8. _____ la pesca ilimitada

 INTERCAMBIOS. Intercambien ideas y recomendaciones para resolver cada problema.

15-6

Los adelantos (*Advances*) científicos.
PREPARACIÓN. Haz una lista de tres adelantos científicos y tres cambios sociales que esperas que se realicen en las próximas décadas.

ADELANTOS CIENTÍFICOS	CAMBIOS SOCIALES
_____	_____
_____	_____
_____	_____

INTERCAMBIOS. Comparen sus listas y justifiquen la razón de los cambios que indicaron en *Preparación*. ¿Por qué ocurrirán? ¿Son cambios necesarios?

Cultura

El coquí

El coquí es el nombre general para designar de manera popular un conjunto de ranas específico de Puerto Rico. El nombre es una onomatopeya del sonido emitido por las ranas. Debido a los cambios medioambientales su población ha disminuido considerablemente en los últimos años. Muchas organizaciones ecologistas siguen luchando por la protección del hábitat del coquí, que se ha convertido en símbolo nacional de Puerto Rico, y hoy día el coquí llanero está protegido bajo la Ley Federal de Especies en Peligro de Extinción.

Conexiones. Busca información sobre las causas de la destrucción del hábitat del coquí llanero. ¿Qué animales están en peligro de extinción en tu estado o región? ¿Qué hacen los grupos ecologistas y el gobierno para protegerlos?

15-7

Organizaciones ecologistas.
Busca información en Internet sobre organizaciones como Greenpeace o el Club Sierra, cuyo propósito es proteger el medio ambiente. Escoge una de esas organizaciones y prepara un breve informe oral con la siguiente información.

1. ¿Qué objetivos tiene la organización?
2. ¿Cómo se financia?
3. ¿Quiénes trabajan o hacen voluntariado en ella?
4. ¿Cuál fue una de sus campañas recientes?
5. ¿Qué objetivos tenía la campaña?
6. ¿Cómo la realizaron?
7. ¿Cuál fue el resultado de la campaña?
8. ¿En qué capacidad crees que podrías ayudar tú?

Otros retos del futuro

LAS CIUDADES

- Se **construirán** ciudades verticales con edificios **climatizados** por medio de **energía solar** o **energía de fusión.**
- El 90% de la población vivirá en las ciudades.
- Todas las basuras urbanas serán **recicladas.**

EL MAR

- El nivel del mar subirá por los **deshielos** debido al **calentamiento** de la atmósfera y causará **inundaciones** y **la desaparición** de algunas costas.
- La contaminación de los mares provocará la **extinción** de los **bancos de peces.**

LA ATMÓSFERA

- El **agujero** de la **capa de ozono** hará aumentar el número de enfermos de cáncer de piel.
- Se cultivarán plantas que mejoren la calidad del aire.

LAS VIVIENDAS

- Todos los hogares estarán conectados a Internet. Las compras se harán siempre **virtualmente.**
- Las puertas y los aparatos electrónicos serán activados por la voz o con sensores que reconocerán a cada individuo.
- Habrá **robots** que se ocuparán de hacer la limpieza.

EL TRANSPORTE

- Los trenes de alta velocidad conectarán las grandes ciudades y circularán por **rieles** suspendidos a la altura de los edificios.
- Los coches combinarán la energía eléctrica y la energía solar. Serán pequeñas **cápsulas voladoras** que podrán **despegar** y **aterrizar** verticalmente como los helicópteros.
- El tráfico aéreo será controlado por **satélite**.

LA CIENCIA Y LA TECNOLOGÍA

- Habrá **clonaciones** de animales **extinguidos.**
- Los embriones humanos se seleccionarán **genéticamente.**
- Los **chips electrónicos** se implantarán en el cerebro mediante **microcirugía**.
- Se explorarán energías alternativas.
- Se **repoblarán** los bosques con técnicas avanzadas para eliminar la desertización.

PRÁCTICA

15-8

Para confirmar. PREPARACIÓN. Tomando como base las fotos y textos anteriores, haz una lista de tus propias predicciones para el futuro en dos de las siguientes áreas: el transporte, la tecnología, las formas de vida, la vivienda o la planificación de las ciudades.

 INTERCAMBIOS. Compartan sus predicciones sobre el mundo del futuro.

- Hablen de dos problemas específicos que existen en el mundo contemporáneo.
- Sugieran posibles soluciones para cada uno de los problemas.
- Presenten sus ideas ante la clase.

El tráfico en las ciudades es un problema muy grande. Proponemos construir aparcamientos en las afueras de las ciudades y tener más zonas peatonales.

15-9 

El reto más serio de hoy. Preparen un informe oral sobre el reto más serio que enfrentan el mundo y el ser humano hoy, según su opinión. Describan detalladamente el problema y ofrezcan algunas soluciones.

15-10 

¡El futuro es hoy! Primero, individualmente hagan una lista de cinco cosas (aparatos, sistemas de comunicación, transporte, etc.) que existen hoy y que no existían cuando sus padres tenían su edad. Luego, comparen sus listas y expliquen el impacto y las consecuencias de estas nuevas cosas en sus vidas.

15-11 

Los OVNIS (Objetos Voladores No Identificados). PREPARACIÓN. Observen la imagen y contesten las preguntas.

1. ¿Qué va a pasar cuando lleguen las cápsulas voladoras a la Tierra?
2. ¿Qué van a encontrar los extraterrestres?
3. ¿Cómo van a reaccionar los habitantes de la Tierra?

INTERCAMBIOS. Imaginen que visitaron un planeta desconocido. Hablen entre ustedes sobre los siguientes asuntos. Luego, escriban un párrafo sobre sus observaciones para compartir con la clase. Incluyan la siguiente información.

1. nombre y descripción del planeta
2. descripción de sus habitantes
3. descripción de sus ciudades, viviendas y medios de transporte

15-12 

Un viaje a Marte. Planeen un viaje a Marte y expliquen con quiénes irán, qué llevarán, cuánto tiempo tardarán en llegar, qué verán allí y cómo se sentirán física y emocionalmente en este nuevo ambiente. Compartan su plan con otros dos astronautas (sus compañeros/as) para formular el mejor plan posible.

Cultura

Agricultura ecológica

Debido a la riqueza medioambiental y a la biodiversidad de la isla, Puerto Rico es un lugar apropiado para la explotación agrícola que respeta la naturaleza y el medio ambiente. En los últimos años, se ha incrementado la práctica de agricultura ecológica que cumple unas normas éticas y de sostenibilidad con el fin de proteger los recursos naturales para las futuras generaciones.

Comparaciones. ¿En qué lugares de tu comunidad puedes comprar productos agrícolas ecológicos? ¿Qué ventajas tienen estos productos?

15-13  

El problema de la alimentación. You will listen to a short talk about the problem of feeding the world's population. Before you listen, list two problems you think the speaker may mention and two solutions you think she may provide.

First, read the following incomplete ideas. Then, as you listen, pay attention to the general idea of what is said and mark (✓) the appropriate ending to each statement.

1. Los gobiernos tienen que solucionar el problema de…
   - a. ______ la agricultura tradicional.
   - b. ______ la falta de alimentos para la población.
   - c. ______ las pocas variedades de productos.
2. La tecnología y los científicos…
   - a. ______ pueden ayudar a solucionar este problema.
   - b. ______ trabajan en las islas Filipinas.
   - c. ______ desarrollan computadoras de mucha utilidad.
3. Si se aumenta la producción del arroz, los gobiernos pueden…
   - a. ______ exportarlo y ganar más dinero.
   - b. ______ alimentar a más personas.
   - c. ______ obtener variedades más nutritivas.
4. Hay que aprovechar los avances de la tecnología, pero también es necesario…
   - a. ______ aumentar la productividad en un 70%.
   - b. ______ conseguir alimentos básicos.
   - c. ______ preservar el medio ambiente.

MOSAICO cultural

La investigación tecnológica en Latinoamérica

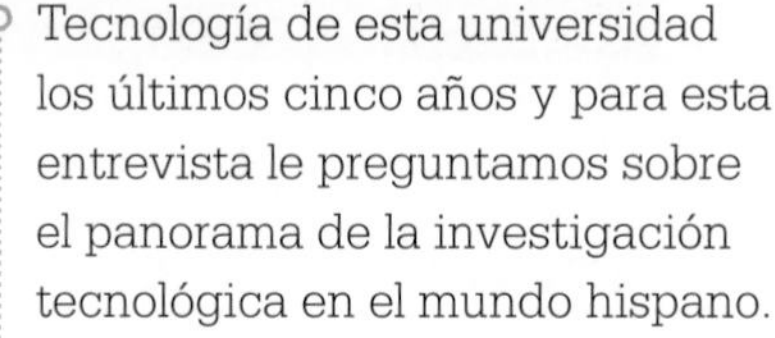

En los últimos años, América Latina ha firmado importantes tratados (*treaties*) de comercio con Estados Unidos, Europa, Rusia y China. "Estamos ante un cambio de mentalidad importante", afirma el investigador cubano Pablo Oliveros de la Universidad de Estocolmo. El profesor Oliveros ha dirigido el Departamento de Investigación, Ciencia y Tecnología de esta universidad los últimos cinco años y para esta entrevista le preguntamos sobre el panorama de la investigación tecnológica en el mundo hispano.

"La academia hispana históricamente ha tenido poca participación en avances tecnológicos en el mundo. Aproximadamente el 3% de los ingenieros realizan tareas de investigación y desarrollo en el planeta y solo el 1% de los recursos se invierte con este fin. Por esta razón, muchos científicos preferimos salir de nuestros países hacia Europa o Estados Unidos". A pesar de (*despite*) esto, muchos inventos importantes de hispanos han impactado el mundo: la píldora anticonceptiva (*birth control pill*) del químico mexicano Luis Miramontes, o el test de paternidad, del venezolano Baruj Benacerraf, son dos ejemplos.

▲ **Juan Manuel Santos, el presidente de Colombia, y Barack Obama, el presidente de EE.UU., reunidos para discutir el Tratado de Libre Comercio.**

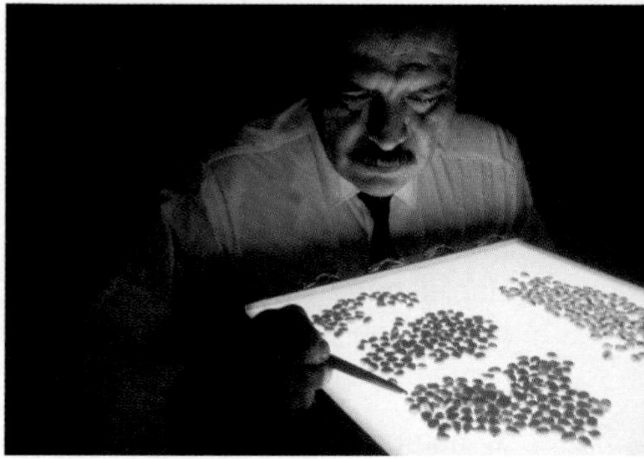

▲ **Un científico hispano trabaja en su laboratorio.**

"Estos científicos tuvieron que hacer grandes esfuerzos para producir avances tan importantes. Los tratados de comercio son buenas oportunidades para la ciencia y la tecnología hispanas. Si hacemos bien las cosas, en el futuro tendremos muchos más investigadores y científicos importantes sin tantos inconvenientes", dice Oliveros. "La verdad es que la inversión extranjera, los grandes avances en educación y estos tratados de comercio comienzan a mostrar a una Latinoamérica menos dependiente; nos veo como una potencia mundial en el futuro." Comenta Oliveros: "El futuro de la ciencia hispana es brillante: gracias a estos proyectos habrá mejores oportunidades, habrá menos desequilibrios sociales y la educación será una base sólida para la comunidad". También es necesario recordar que los cambios demográficos harán que para el 2020 el español sea una de las tres lenguas más importantes, junto con el inglés y el mandarín.

Compara

1. ¿Qué otras invenciones de hispanos conoces? ¿Cuáles son las principales contribuciones tecnológicas de científicos de tu comunidad para el mundo?
2. ¿Qué beneficios sociales trae la investigación científica? ¿Cuáles serán las principales contribuciones de la tecnología hispana? Elabora tu respuesta.
3. ¿Crees que el rol de la comunidad hispana cambiará para el año 2040? ¿Cómo afectará a tu comunidad el incremento de la población hispana? Explica y justifica tu respuesta.
4. ¿Crees que en el futuro será importante hablar español? ¿Cuáles serán las principales lenguas en 2040? Explica tu respuesta.

Funciones y formas

1 Expressing wishes and recommendations in the past

PADRE: ¿Qué quieres que **hagamos** ahora?

NIÑA: Papá, quiero que me **cuentes** un cuento.

PADRE: Muy bien, hija. Cuando mi abuelo era niño, los seres humanos querían que los robots **hicieran** todo su trabajo. Mis abuelos limpiaban la casa, preparaban las comidas, hacían las tareas de los niños…

NIÑA: ¡Qué terrible, papá! Pero luego, ¿qué pasó?

PADRE: Los políticos recomendaron que los científicos **produjeran** robots más complejos. Querían que los robots **tuvieran** computadoras muy potentes (*powerful*). Los científicos temían que los robots **fueran** más inteligentes que ellos, pero los políticos insistieron en que los científicos los **construyeran** con más capacidad intelectual. Entonces…

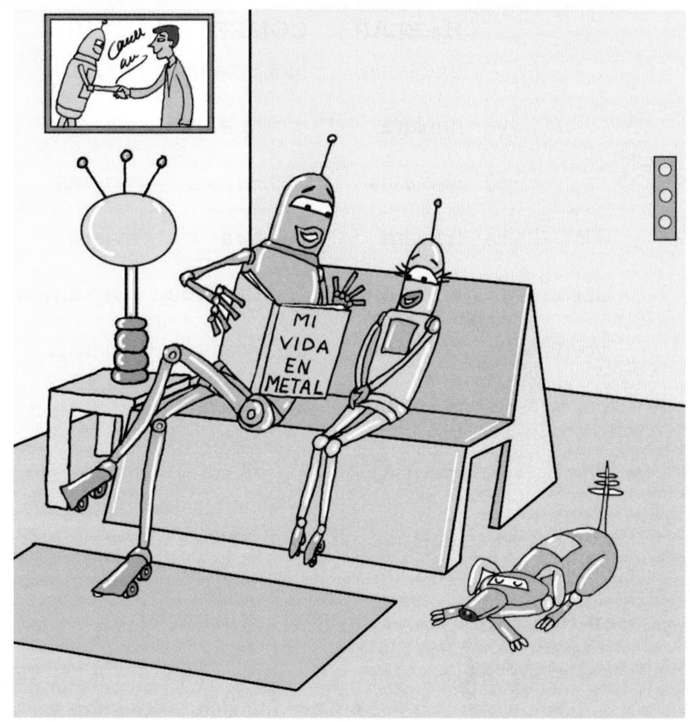

Piénsalo. Indica (✓) si las siguientes oraciones se refieren al presente/al futuro o al pasado.

	PRESENTE/FUTURO	PASADO
1. ¿Qué quieres que **hagamos** ahora?	_____	_____
2. Quiero que me **cuentes** un cuento.	_____	_____
3. Los seres humanos querían que los robots **hicieran** todo su trabajo.	_____	_____
4. Los políticos recomendaron que los científicos **produjeran** robots más complejos.	_____	_____
5. Querían que los robots **tuvieran** computadoras muy potentes.	_____	_____
6. Los científicos temían que los robots **fueran** más inteligentes que ellos.	_____	_____
7. Los políticos insistieron en que los **construyeran** con más capacidad intelectual.	_____	_____

The imperfect subjunctive

- In previous chapters, you studied the forms and uses of the present subjunctive. Now you will study the past subjunctive, also called the imperfect subjunctive. All regular and irregular past subjunctive verb forms are based on the **ustedes/ellos/ellas** form of the preterit. Drop the **-on** preterit ending and substitute the past subjunctive endings. Note the written accent on the **nosotros/as** forms.

PAST OR IMPERFECT SUBJUNCTIVE

	HABLAR (hablar~~on~~)	**COMER** (comier~~on~~)	**VIVIR** (vivier~~on~~)	**ESTAR** (estuvier~~on~~)
yo	hablar**a**	comier**a**	vivier**a**	estuvier**a**
tú	hablar**as**	comier**as**	vivier**as**	estuvier**as**
Ud., él, ella	hablar**a**	comier**a**	vivier**a**	estuvier**a**
nosotros/as	hablár**amos**	comiér**amos**	viviér**amos**	estuviér**amos**
vosotros/as	hablar**ais**	comier**ais**	vivier**ais**	estuvier**ais**
Uds., ellos/as	hablar**an**	comier**an**	vivier**an**	estuvier**an**

- The present subjunctive is oriented to the present or future, whereas the past subjunctive generally focuses on the past. In general, the same rules that determine the use of the present subjunctive also apply to the past subjunctive.

HOY O MAÑANA → PRESENT SUBJUNCTIVE

Sandra quiere comprar una computadora portátil que **sea** ligera.
Sandra wants to buy a laptop that does not weigh a lot.

Hablará con sus amigos para que le **den** unas recomendaciones.
She will talk to her friends so that they can give her some recommendations.

AYER → PAST SUBJUNCTIVE

Sandra quería una computadora portátil que **fuera** ligera.
Sandra wanted a laptop that did not weigh a lot.

Habló con sus amigos para que le **dieran** unas recomendaciones.
She talked to her friends so that they could give her some recommendations.

- Always use the past subjunctive after **como si** (*as if, as though*).

Gastan dinero en aparatos electrónicos **como si fueran** millonarios.
They spend money on electronic gadgets as though they were millionaires.

Hablaba con la científica **como si entendiera** el problema.
He talked with the scientist as if he understood the problem.

e **¿COMPRENDES?**

Completa las oraciones con la forma apropiada del subjuntivo (presente o pasado) de los verbos entre paréntesis.

1. Juan me recomendó que ________ (ir) a ver una película de ciencia ficción.
2. Mi profesora quiere que nosotros ________ (usar) tecnología en nuestras presentaciones.
3. El gobierno les pidió a los científicos que ________ (explorar) energías alternativas.
4. Los viajeros prefieren que los trenes ________ (ser) rápidos y puntuales.
5. Es necesario que los edificios climatizados ________ (conservar) mejor la energía.
6. Era inevitable que la contaminación de los mares ________ (afectar) a los peces.

MySpanishLab

Learn more using Amplifire Dynamic Study Modules, Grammar Tutorials, and Extra Practice activities.

PRÁCTICA

15-14 

Cuando era niño/a. **PREPARACIÓN.** Marca (✓) lo que tus padres querían o no querían que hicieras cuando eras niño/a. Después, compara tus respuestas con las de tu compañero/a.

1. _____ Querían que yo comiera muchos vegetales y frutas.
2. _____ Querían que yo estudiara ciencias.
3. _____ No querían que yo viera programas violentos en la televisión.
4. _____ Querían que yo cuidara el medio ambiente.
5. _____ Querían que yo leyera sobre el programa espacial y los astronautas.
6. _____ No querían que yo estuviera sin hacer nada.

INTERCAMBIOS. Marca con un círculo lo que tú querías que tus padres hicieran cuando eras niño/a. Luego, compara tus respuestas con las de tu compañero/a. Añade otra opción si es necesario.

1. Para divertirme con la tecnología...
   - **a.** yo quería que mis padres me llevaran a ver una nave espacial.
   - **b.** deseaba que mis padres me permitieran jugar a videojuegos muchas horas.
2. Para estar con mis amigos...
   - **a.** yo quería que mis padres me llevaran al parque los fines de semana.
   - **b.** les pedía a mis padres que me permitieran jugar en las casas de ellos.
3. Para pasarlo bien los fines de semana...
   - **a.** yo quería que mis padres me dieran más dinero.
   - **b.** insistía en que mis padres me permitieran hacer fiestas en casa.
4. Para mi cumpleaños...
   - **a.** siempre quería que mis padres me regalaran juguetes electrónicos.
   - **b.** prefería que mis padres me compraran ropa.

15-15 

En el laboratorio. Miguel es un estudiante inteligente, pero muy distraído. Hoy hizo unos experimentos con su profesor de química en el laboratorio. ¿Qué le dijo el profesor en estas situaciones? Túrnense para dar respuestas lógicas.

Miguel no se puso los guantes para hacer el experimento.

El profesor le dijo que se pusiera los guantes.

1. Llegó tarde al laboratorio.
2. Escuchaba música mientras hacía un experimento.
3. Dejó una botella de alcohol cerca de una estufa.
4. No esterilizó unos instrumentos.
5. Recibió una llamada en su celular.
6. La mesa donde Miguel trabajaba estaba muy desordenada.
7. No comparó sus resultados con los del ayudante del profesor.
8. Salió del laboratorio durante un experimento para conversar con su novia.

EN OTRAS PALABRAS

Cell phones are **teléfonos móviles** or **teléfonos celulares.** The name of these devices is usually shortened to **móvil, celular** o **cel.**

15-16 

Alguien que no nos cae bien. PREPARACIÓN. Imagínense que ustedes conocen a una persona arrogante que cree que es mejor que todos. Digan cómo se comporta esta persona en los siguientes aspectos de su vida. Pueden usar los verbos que aparecen más abajo u otros.

cuando va de un lugar a otro a pie
Camina como si fuera la única persona en la calle.

cambiar	manejar
caminar	usar
discutir	vestirse
gastar	vivir

1. cuando quiere comprar algo
2. cuando se prepara para salir con un grupo de amigos
3. cuando habla con otras personas
4. cuando se sube a (*gets into*) su automóvil

INTERCAMBIOS. Ahora háganse las siguientes preguntas e informen a la clase.

1. ¿Conoces a alguna persona que sea arrogante?
2. ¿Qué hábito o comportamiento de esa persona te molesta? ¿Por qué?
3. ¿Te gustaría que esta persona cambiara? Si es así, ¿cómo te gustaría que cambiara?

Situación

PREPARACIÓN. Lean esta situación. Luego, compartan ejemplos de vocabulario, gramática y otra información que necesitan para desarrollar la conversación.

Role A. You are unhappy with your new digital device (cell phone, tablet, laptop, etc.). You go back to the electronics store and tell the manager:

a. your friend had recommended that you buy this device;
b. you hoped the device would be of better quality; and
c. you want to return it and expect them to give you back your money.

Role B. You are the manager of the computer department at an electronics store. A customer is unhappy with a recent purchase of a digital device and tells you why. Explain:

a. the store does not give refunds (**devolver el dinero**); but
b. you would be glad to exchange the device for a different one; and
c. you hope that the customer will like the new device.

	ROLE A	ROLE B
Vocabulario	Digital technology	Digital technology
Funciones y formas	Expressing wishes Present and past subjunctive	Expressing wishes Present and past subjunctive

INTERCAMBIOS. Practica la conversación con tu compañero/a incorporando el vocabulario y las funciones de *Preparación*. Luego, represéntenla ante la clase.

2 Hypothesizing about the present and the future

MATEO: Oye, Lucía. ¿Has visto la calidad de las nuevas cámaras digitales? ¡Es increíble! **Si** la tecnología **continúa** avanzando así, pronto **producirán** minicámaras para controlar a toda la población, incluso en sus casas.

LUCÍA: **Si** lo **hicieran, pondrían** en peligro las libertades individuales. Pero **si** la ciencia **avanza** tan rápidamente, ¿por qué no **podemos** trabajar por la paz? Yo no quiero que se perfeccione la tecnología para vigilar a la gente y controlarla, sino para protegerla.

MATEO: Tienes razón, Lucía. **Si** los jóvenes no **hacemos** nada para dar un buen uso a la tecnología, **tendremos** problemas en el futuro.

Piénsalo. Indica si las siguientes afirmaciones hechas por Mateo y Lucía indican una condición relacionada con el presente (**P**), con el futuro (**F**) o si indican una condición que es improbable (**I**) que se cumpla (*come to pass*).

1. _____ **Si** la tecnología **continúa** avanzando así, pronto **producirán** minicámaras para controlar a toda la población, incluso en sus casas.
2. _____ **Si** lo **hicieran, pondrían** en peligro las libertades individuales.
3. _____ Pero **si** la ciencia **avanza** tan rápidamente, ¿por qué no **podemos** trabajar por la paz?
4. _____ **Si** los jóvenes no **hacemos** nada para dar un buen uso a la tecnología, **tendremos** problemas en el futuro.

If-clauses

- To express what happens or will happen *if* certain conditions are met, use the present or future indicative in the main clause and the present indicative in the *if*-clause.

  Si **continuamos** cortando árboles, los bosques **van a** desaparecer.
  If we continue cutting down trees, the forests will disappear.

  Si **creamos** tecnología para cuidar los recursos naturales, las generaciones futuras **tendrán** una vida mejor.
  If we create technology to protect the natural resources, future generations will have a better life.

  Puedes obtener información sobre las últimas novedades tecnológicas si la **buscas** en Internet.
  You can get information on the latest technology if you look for it on the Internet.

- To express a condition that is unlikely or contrary to fact, use the imperfect subjunctive in the *if*-clause. Use the conditional in the main clause.

  Si **invirtieran** más dinero en el aeropuerto, el tráfico aéreo **podría** mejorar.
  If they invested more money in the airport, air traffic could improve.

  Si **usáramos** la energía solar en las casas, **ahorraríamos** mucho petróleo.
  If we used solar energy in our homes, we would save a lot of oil.

¿COMPRENDES?

Completa las oraciones con el presente de indicativo o el imperfecto de subjuntivo del verbo entre paréntesis según su grado de probabilidad.

1. Si los habitantes ________ (mantener) limpias las ciudades, será más agradable pasear por ellas.
2. Si los perros ________ (hablar), dirían que los humanos estamos locos.
3. Si el gobierno ________ (proteger) más el medio ambiente, habría menos contaminación.
4. Si los ingenieros ________ (hacer) un cohete espacial más barato, irían turistas al espacio.
5. Si tú ________ (tener) más imaginación, inventarías una máquina para viajar en el tiempo.
6. Si los estudiantes ________ (practicar) mucho el español, aprenderán más rápidamente.

MySpanishLab

Learn more using Amplifire Dynamic Study Modules, Grammar Tutorials, and Extra Practice activities.

PRÁCTICA

Cultura

Problemas ecológicos de Puerto Rico

Puerto Rico es una de las islas con mayor densidad de población del mundo. Esto ha causado graves problemas medioambientales que han deteriorado el patrimonio natural. Entre los problemas ecológicos más importantes se puede mencionar la deforestación, la contaminación del aire —a menudo por la congestión del tráfico— la mala calidad del agua y el tratamiento y reciclaje de basura.

Comparaciones. ¿Crees que los problemas ecológicos de Puerto Rico son similares a los que existen en tu comunidad? ¿Cuáles son algunas soluciones posibles a estos problemas?

15-17

El mundo que todos queremos. Completa cada idea de la izquierda con una de las conclusiones de la derecha. En algunos casos, puede haber más de una respuesta lógica. Luego, compara tus respuestas con las de tu compañero/a.

1. _____ Si las escuelas tuvieran más dinero…	**a.** no contaminaríamos tanto el medio ambiente.
2. _____ Si hubiera menos armas de fuego en manos de la gente…	**b.** todos los alumnos tendrían acceso a los laboratorios para hacer investigación.
3. _____ Si cuidáramos más nuestro planeta…	**c.** si todos nos respetáramos y dialogáramos en vez de pelear.
4. _____ Tendríamos un mundo mejor…	**d.** las personas manejarían menos en las carreteras.
5. _____ Si hubiera trenes de alta velocidad…	**e.** habría menos homicidios en la sociedad.
6. _____ Gastaríamos menos gasolina…	**f.** si usáramos el transporte público.

15-18 

¿Qué pasa si...? Túrnense para decir qué resultados se pueden obtener si se hacen ciertas cosas.

 leer los periódicos

Si todos leen los periódicos regularmente, sabrán qué está pasando en el mundo.

1. usar solamente tecnología para aprender otra lengua
2. inventar aparatos electrónicos desechables (*disposable*)
3. proteger los recursos naturales
4. legalizar las drogas
5. comunicarse solamente por correo electrónico
6. construir más estaciones espaciales

15-19 

¿Cómo sería el mundo? Expliquen cómo sería el mundo si se dieran las siguientes circunstancias. Después, compartan sus ideas con otros/as estudiantes.

1. si no hubiera televisión
2. si los seres humanos viviéramos más de 150 años
3. si la clonación fuera legal
4. si no existieran fronteras entre los países
5. si pudiéramos viajar en autos supersónicos a todas partes
6. si toda la educación se hiciera por Internet

15-20

Cambios. PREPARACIÓN. Identifica un problema serio en tu comunidad, en tu país o en el mundo, en cada una de las siguientes áreas en la vida de tu comunidad, de tu país o del mundo. Explica por qué lo consideras un problema serio.

1. la seguridad personal y/o colectiva
2. el consumo excesivo de alcohol entre los jóvenes
3. el transporte público
4. el costo de las necesidades básicas, como la comida y la gasolina

INTERCAMBIOS. Ahora digan cuál creen ustedes que es el problema más serio en cada área. Explíquenles a sus compañeros por qué lo consideran serio. Si pudieran, ¿qué harían para eliminar cada problema?

MODELO **ÁREA:** el medio ambiente

PROBLEMA SERIO: *la contaminación del aire y el agua*

RAZÓN: *El mal uso y el descuido* (neglect) *de los recursos naturales como el petróleo han causado el calentamiento del planeta. Todos usamos carros que contaminan el aire. Además, las industrias ponen sus desperdicios* (waste) *en los ríos. Contaminan el agua que todos bebemos.*

PLAN HIPOTÉTICO: *Crearíamos incentivos para usar el transporte público y pondríamos multas* (fines) *muy altas a las compañías que tiran desperdicios en los ríos.*

En directo

To ask that people request the floor before speaking:

Por favor, no interrumpa(n) sin pedir la palabra.
Please don't interrupt without requesting the floor.

Pida(n) la palabra. *Request the floor.*

To request the floor:

Yo quisiera decir/añadir/explicar algo.
I would like to say/add/explain something.

¿Podría añadir/agregar algo?
Could I add something?

To give the floor to someone:

X tiene la palabra. *X has the floor.*

Dinos lo que tú piensas. *Tell us what you think.*

Listen to a conversation with these expressions.

Situación

PREPARACIÓN. Lean esta situación. Luego, compartan ejemplos de vocabulario, gramática y otra información que necesitan para desarrollar la conversación.

Role A. You are a billionaire who believes that education should be radically different. You would give your local college 20 million dollars if they did the following:

a. there would be no required courses; students could choose all their own courses;
b. there would be no exams, only projects and papers; and
c. students would tell the faculty what courses should be taught.

Respond to the reaction of the college president.

Role B. You are a college president. A billionaire (your classmate) would donate 20 million dollars to the college if you agreed to make radical changes. Listen to the potential donor's proposal and respond with your hypotheses of what would happen if:

a. there were no required courses; students could choose all their own courses;
b. there were no exams, only projects and papers; and
c. students told the faculty what courses should be taught.

	ROLE A	ROLE B
Vocabulario	Numbers Academic policies	Numbers Academic policies
Funciones y formas	Talking about hypothetical situations	Talking about hypothetical situations

INTERCAMBIOS. Practica la conversación con tu compañero/a incorporando el vocabulario y las funciones de *Preparación*. Luego, represéntenla ante la clase.

3 Expressing the unexpected

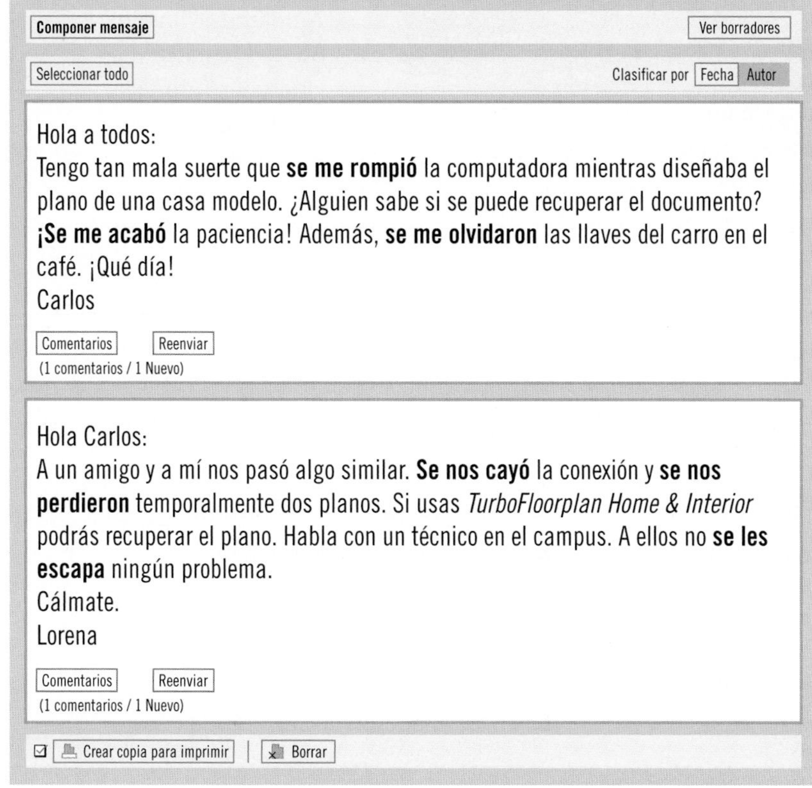

Componer mensaje | Ver borradores

Seleccionar todo | Clasificar por Fecha Autor

Hola a todos:
Tengo tan mala suerte que **se me rompió** la computadora mientras diseñaba el plano de una casa modelo. ¿Alguien sabe si se puede recuperar el documento? ¡**Se me acabó** la paciencia! Además, **se me olvidaron** las llaves del carro en el café. ¡Qué día!
Carlos

Comentarios | Reenviar
(1 comentarios / 1 Nuevo)

Hola Carlos:
A un amigo y a mí nos pasó algo similar. **Se nos cayó** la conexión y **se nos perdieron** temporalmente dos planos. Si usas *TurboFloorplan Home & Interior* podrás recuperar el plano. Habla con un técnico en el campus. A ellos no **se les escapa** ningún problema.
Cálmate.
Lorena

Comentarios | Reenviar
(1 comentarios / 1 Nuevo)

Crear copia para imprimir | Borrar

Piénsalo. Indica si en las siguientes afirmaciones se pone énfasis en el evento (**E**) o en la persona responsable del evento (**PR**).

1. _____ **Se me rompió** la computadora.
2. _____ **Rompí** la computadora.
3. _____ **Olvidé** las llaves del carro en el café.
4. _____ **Se me olvidaron** las llaves del carro en el café.
5. _____ **Se nos perdieron** temporalmente dos planos.
6. _____ **Perdimos** temporalmente dos planos.

Se for unplanned occurrences

- Use **se** + *indirect object* + *verb* to express unplanned or accidental events. This construction puts the focus on the unexpected nature of the event rather than on personal responsibility for its occurrence. Some verbs often used with this construction include **olvidar** (*to forget*), **apagar** (*to turn off*), **acabar** (*to run out of something*), **romper** (*to break, to tear*), and **quedar** (*to leave something behind*).

Se les apagaron las luces del carro.	*The headlights of their car went out.*
A él **se le acabó** el dinero.	*He ran out of money.*
Se nos olvidó el código.	*We forgot the code.*
Se te rompió la chaqueta.	*Your jacket got torn.*

- Use an indirect object pronoun (**me**, **te**, **le**, **nos**, **os**, **les**) to indicate whom the unplanned event affects. Place the pronoun between **se** and the verb. If what is lost, forgotten, and so on, is plural, the verb also must be plural.

Se me quedó el DVD en la computadora.	*I left the DVD in the computer.*
Se me quedaron los cables en casa.	*I left the cables at home.*

¿COMPRENDES?

Completa las oraciones con el pronombre de objeto indirecto apropiado.

1. A Miguel se _____ estropeó la computadora.
2. A mí se _____ perdió el pasaporte.
3. A Juan y Elisa se _____ olvidó comprar la comida.
4. A ti se _____ acabó la tinta (*ink*) de la impresora.
5. A Elena se _____ apagaron las luces cuando trabajaba.
6. A ustedes se _____ rompieron los platos.

MySpanishLab
Learn more using Amplifire Dynamic Study Modules, Grammar Tutorials, and Extra Practice activities.

PRÁCTICA

15-21

¿Qué les pasó? Termina lógicamente las ideas de la columna de la izquierda, usando las ideas de la columna de la derecha.

1. _____ Hablaron con el plomero porque…	**a.** se me quedó el dinero en casa.
2. _____ Tuve que usar la tarjeta de crédito porque…	**b.** se nos rompió la computadora.
3. _____ No pude llamarte por el celular porque…	**c.** se me olvidó tu nuevo número de teléfono.
4. _____ Tuvieron que llamar al electricista porque…	**d.** se me perdió la llave del coche.
5. _____ Tuvimos que llamar al técnico porque…	**e.** se les inundó el baño.
6. _____ Llegué tarde a casa de mi novia porque…	**f.** se les apagaron las luces en la casa.

15-22

Problemas. Tú trabajas en un laboratorio de ingeniería genética. Ayer hubo muchos problemas técnicos. Explica qué pasó usando las opciones de la lista u otras.

El investigador no pudo completar el experimento.
Se le olvidó la fórmula.

perder las llaves	acabarse la gasolina
enfermarse un hijo	romper el microscopio
romper la computadora	escapar el perro en el parque
perder unos datos importantes	quedar documentos confidenciales en un café

1. Los científicos no pudieron hacer el experimento con las bacterias.
2. El director nunca falta al trabajo, pero ayer no fue a trabajar.
3. Los ayudantes llegaron tarde de un viaje a un laboratorio en otra ciudad.
4. La doctora Milán no pudo entrar en el laboratorio durante el fin de semana.
5. El subdirector no recibió un correo electrónico importante.
6. El presidente de la compañía estaba histérico cuando llegó a la oficina y se dio cuenta de lo que le había ocurrido.

Momentos difíciles. Miren los dibujos y túrnense para contestar las preguntas que siguen.

1. ¿Qué les pasó a las personas en los dos dibujos? Inventen una historia para cada situación: ¿Cuándo y dónde pasó, cómo se sintieron las personas y qué hicieron después?
2. ¿Les ha pasado a ustedes una situación semejante? Cuéntense la historia de su problema y cómo lo resolvió cada uno de ustedes.
3. Si vivieras una experiencia semejante otra vez, ¿harías algo diferente esta vez? ¿Tu respuesta es similar o diferente a la de tu compañero/a?

a

b

Situación

PREPARACIÓN. Lean esta situación. Luego, compartan ejemplos de vocabulario, gramática y otra información que necesitan para desarrollar la conversación.

Role A. You have had a bad day and you call your friend to vent. Say that:

a. you forgot to set your alarm clock so you got up late and missed your first class;
b. you ran out of gas on the highway;
c. you left your homework for your Spanish class at home; and
d. in the cafeteria you accidentally dropped your soup and salad on your friend's backpack.

Role B. Your friend calls to complain about his/her day. Commiserate with him/her and describe what happened to you last night:

a. there was a big storm in your city and the lights went out so you could not watch your favorite TV show;
b. you decided to drive to your parents' house, but when were leaving your apartment, both of your cats accidentally escaped; and
c. when you were walking in the dark (**oscuridad**), you accidentally dropped your wallet and could not find it.

	ROLE A	ROLE B
Vocabulario	Time Problems at school Food	Weather Pets Personal belongings
Funciones y formas	Past tense *Se* for unplanned occurrences	Past tense *Se* for unplanned occurrences

INTERCAMBIOS. Practica la conversación con tu compañero/a incorporando el vocabulario y las funciones de *Preparación*. Luego, represéntenla ante la clase.

EN ACCIÓN

¡Cuidemos el medio ambiente!

15-24 Antes de ver

Un futuro mejor. Marca (✓) las situaciones que contribuirían a mejorar el medio ambiente.

Mejoraríamos el medio ambiente si...

1. _____ usáramos más autos eléctricos.
2. _____ plantáramos más árboles.
3. _____ elimináramos el transporte público.
4. _____ no compráramos agua en botellas de plástico.
5. _____ lleváramos bolsas de tela al supermercado.
6. _____ aumentáramos el uso de la energía solar.
7. _____ continuáramos la deforestación de nuestros bosques.

15-25 Mientras ves

La tecnología al servicio del medio ambiente. En este segmento de video, Yolanda y Federico comparten sus proyectos con los otros chicos. Indica si las siguientes afirmaciones son ciertas (**C**) o falsas (**F**). Corrige las afirmaciones falsas.

Techos verdes:

1. _____ Es un programa del gobierno de Estados Unidos para mejorar el problema de la contaminación en México.
2. _____ El principal beneficiario de este programa es la Ciudad de México.
3. _____ En la Ciudad de México hay muy pocos espacios verdes.
4. _____ En los techos y paredes de edificios se planta vegetación nativa.

Coches eléctricos y taxis solares:

5. _____ El gobierno de California está en la vanguardia de la tecnología de autos eléctricos.
6. _____ El plan ZEV es un programa del gobierno mexicano que promueve la creación de autos con cero emisiones.
7. _____ Telsa Motors ofrece autos de energía solar.
8. _____ En la Ciudad de México hay algunos taxis ecológicos.

15-26 Después de ver 

¡Bienvenida sea la tecnología! **PREPARACIÓN.** Empareja las oraciones de la columna de la izquierda con las de la columna de la derecha.

1. _____ Si más ciudades implementaran programas como Techos verdes...
2. _____ Si no quisiéramos usar nuestros coches de gasolina...
3. _____ Si otros gobernadores siguieran el ejemplo del gobernador de California...

a. no habría tantas emisiones de monóxido de carbono en la atmósfera.
b. habría más oxígeno en el medio ambiente.
c. podríamos usar autobuses o taxis solares.

INTERCAMBIOS. Comparen sus respuestas de *Preparación* y háganse las siguientes preguntas.

1. ¿Qué otros planes o proyectos conocen ustedes para mejorar los problemas del medio ambiente?
2. ¿Quiénes son los responsables de enfrentar los problemas del medio ambiente? ¿Los individuos? ¿Los gobiernos? ¿Las organizaciones internacionales? Hablen de los beneficios y desafíos de cada una de estas opciones.

La beca. **PREPARACIÓN.** Los estudiantes llevan todo el verano trabajando en sus proyectos cinematográficos. Ahora, te toca a ti decidir quién va a ganar la beca. Vuelve a ver los proyectos finales y decide a quién le darías la beca.

___ Esteban ___ Fede ___ Héctor
___ Vanesa ___ Yolanda

INTERCAMBIOS. Hablen con los otros miembros de su grupo para justificar su selección. ¿Están de acuerdo ustedes en quién va a ganar la beca? Expliquen las razones por las que seleccionaron al ganador/a la ganadora y compartan sus ideas con la clase.

Mosaicos

ESCUCHA

15-27

Preparación. Vas a escuchar una breve presentación sobre el futuro de la tecnología en la medicina. Antes de escuchar, escribe dos avances tecnológicos o médicos que, en tu opinión, ayudarán a los pacientes del futuro. Comparte tus ideas con la clase.

ESTRATEGIA

Identify the speaker's intention through the main idea and specific information

To understand what a speaker says, it is necessary to use a number of strategies. To identify the main idea, you should anticipate key concepts that may be associated with the topic and focus on phrases that signal the presentation of the main idea. Keep track of the speaker's message by organizing the information mentally as you listen. Pay attention to the speaker's verbal and nonverbal cues, such as word choice, tone, and gestures.

15-28  

Escucha. Read the statements below and then listen to the presentation. As you listen, indicate the statements that reflect the main idea and the supporting details. Then, explain what the speaker's intention is for sharing this information.

	IDEA PRINCIPAL	DETALLES
1. _____ El marcapasos…	**a.** se usa para ayudar a los corredores. **b.** les ha salvado la vida a muchas personas. **c.** es un tipo de tecnología obsoleta.	**a.** regula los latidos del corazón. **b.** se inventó hace diez años. **c.** es una microcomputadora.
2. _____ Con el implante en el oído…	**a.** los sonidos suenan como una lengua extranjera. **b.** los sordos pueden oír muy pocos sonidos. **c.** los sordos no sufren de dolor de oídos.	**a.** el aparato se pone en la parte externa del oído. **b.** el aparato aumenta el volumen. **c.** el aparato se coloca en el oído interno.

3. _____ What is the speaker's intention in sharing this information?

a. aliviar a los pacientes

b. informar al público

c. entretener a la familia de los pacientes

Comprueba

I was able to …

__ identify the main idea of each section.

__ understand the details in each section.

__ understand the speaker's intention.

15-29 

Un paso más. Trabajen juntos para responder a las siguientes preguntas. Presenten sus repuestas a la clase.

1. Según ustedes, ¿de qué otra forma la tecnología puede ayudar a la medicina?
2. ¿En qué otras áreas, puede ayudar la tecnología? Expliquen.

HABLA

15-30

Preparación. Lee las anécdotas que les ocurrieron a dos celebridades y luego sigue las instrucciones para analizar las estrategias de las narradoras.

"Hace dos años, una amiga mía vino a San Francisco para visitarme. Como era su cumpleaños, el sábado por la noche fuimos a un restaurante francés muy elegante y caro para celebrarlo. Después de comer muy bien y beber el mejor champán que tenían, me trajeron la cuenta. La cantidad era enorme, pero no había problema, porque mis películas siempre tenían mucho éxito y me pagaban bien. Llevé la mano al bolsillo de mi chaqueta y me di cuenta de que la billetera estaba en casa, no en mi chaqueta. Llamé al camarero y le expliqué la situación. Incluso le dije quién era. Con una mirada irónica y un tono más frío que la Antártida en invierno, el camarero me dijo: Si usted es…, yo soy Brad Pitt. Por favor, no me cuente historias."

"Una tarde de verano decidí ir de incógnito a Manhattan. Iba a pasar unas horas comprando, y luego iba a ver una película. Después de viajar como veinte minutos por la carretera, se me descompuso el Jag. ¡Qué feo! Había mucho tráfico y hacía un calor insoportable. Me bajé del carro, levanté el capó y revisé lo que había allí dentro. Como aparentemente no había ningún problema mecánico, volví al carro. De repente, me acordé de que el marcador de gasolina no funcionaba, y que ¡se me había olvidado llenar el tanque! En ese momento llegaron dos policías y me preguntaron cuál era el problema. Les conté la historia, pero no me creyeron y me pusieron una multa altísima. ¡Claro, estaba en Nueva York, donde todo es carísimo!"

1. En la primera anécdota:
   - **a.** Subraya (*Underline*) los adjetivos que describen el restaurante y la comida.
   - **b.** ¿Qué palabras y frases indican que la narradora se cree rica y famosa? Subráyalas.
   - **c.** Subraya la frase que indica la perspectiva del camarero.
2. En la segunda anécdota:
   - **a.** Subraya las palabras que indican que la narradora se cree famosa.
   - **b.** ¿Qué palabras y frases indican las emociones de la narradora? subráyalas.
   - **c.** Subraya la frase que indica la perspectiva de los policías.

ESTRATEGIA

Use drama and humor in telling a personal anecdote

You learned in *Capítulo 13* to keep your listeners interested in your story by inserting remarks to draw their attention to moments that are particularly funny, frightening, or surprising. You can use these remarks, called *evaluations,* to make your story humorous or to heighten the drama. You can also increase the drama by strategically using descriptive details to slow down the pace and thus create suspense.

LENGUA

Spanish has several expressions with **se** that speakers use daily. Read the following and think of possible situations in which they may be used.

Se me puso la piel de gallina.
I got goosebumps.

Se me fue el alma a los pies.
My heart sank.

Se me fue la lengua.
I gave myself away.

Se me congeló la pantalla.
The screen froze up on me.

Habla. Prepara una anécdota (real o ficticia) de una experiencia y cuéntasela a tu grupo. Usa las expresiones de *En directo* para que tu anécdota tenga humor y un tono dramático. Cada miembro del grupo debe hacerte preguntas y consultar el segundo recuadro de *En directo* para expresar sus reacciones efectivamente.

Comprueba

I was able to ...

___ organize the events of my story in a logical sequence.

___ insert descriptive elements to flesh out the events.

___ use exclamations or direct quotes to make my story humorous or dramatic.

En directo

To make your story dramatic:

¿Y qué crees/creen que pasó después? *And what do you think happened then?*

¡No vas/van a creerlo! *You're not going to believe it!*

Espera/Esperen, que todavía no has/han escuchado la mejor parte. *Wait, you still haven't heard the best part.*

To incorporate humor:

Hacía más frío/calor que... *It was colder/warmer than ...*

Me/Nos miró con cara de... *You/He/She looked at me/us with an expression of ...*

Me/Nos respondió como si... *You/He/She answered me/us as if ...*

 Listen to a conversation with these expressions.

En directo

To express sympathy:

¡Qué lástima!/¡Cuánto lo siento! *I am (so) sorry.*

¡Qué triste/horrible! *How sad/horrible!*

To express happiness:

¡Qué bueno/bien! *Great!*

¡Cuánto me alegro! *I am really happy!*

To express relief after a tense situation:

¡Qué alivio! *What a relief!*

¡Por fin! *Finally!*

¡Gracias a Dios! *Thank goodness!*

 Listen to a conversation with these expressions.

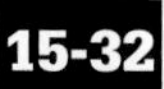 

Un paso más. Seleccionen la anécdota más dramática o graciosa de su grupo. Conviertan la anécdota en una pequeña obra de teatro y represéntenla frente a la clase.

LEE

15-33 

Preparación. Comenten entre ustedes cuáles de las máquinas, aparatos o servicios de la lista se encontrarían en una sociedad donde se usa una tecnología avanzada. Expliquen su selección.

1. automóviles voladores
2. electricidad generada por la energía eólica (energía del viento)
3. servicio postal automatizado
4. computadoras nanomecánicas
5. impresoras que escanean, faxean y fotocopian
6. aviones de pasajeros sin pilotos

ESTRATEGIA

Identify the narrator's perspective

A narrative can be told from one of several perspectives. Two important points of view are the perspective of the protagonist (someone who tells his/her own experiences: I, we) and that of a witness (someone who tells what he/she sees or witnesses: he, she, they). Therefore, to identify the perspective of the narrator, the following questions will help you: Who witnesses the event? Who is speaking? Who is responding?

Marco Denevi (1922–1998), escritor argentino, fue autor de novelas, obras de teatro y cuentos cortos (entre ellos, cuentos muy cortos o *microcuentos*). También fue abogado y periodista. Tanto en su ficción como en sus escritos periodísticos expresó su preocupación por los problemas políticos y sociales de su tiempo.

15-34 

Lee. Lee el siguiente microcuento escrito por Marco Denevi, un conocido escritor argentino, y luego sigue las instrucciones.

APOCALIPSIS

La extinción de la raza de los hombres se sitúa aproximadamente a fines del siglo XXXI. La cosa sucedió así: las máquinas habían alcanzado tal perfección que los hombres no necesitaban comer, ni dormir, ni leer, ni escribir, ni siquiera pensar. Les bastaba apretar botones y las máquinas lo hacían todo por ellos.

Gradualmente fueron desapareciendo las mesas, los teléfonos, los Leonardo da Vinci, las rosas de té, las tiendas de antigüedades, los discos con las nueve sinfonías de Beethoven, el vino de Burdeos[1], las golondrinas, los cuadros de Salvador Dalí[2], los relojes, los sellos postales, los alfileres[3], el Museo del Prado, la sopa de cebolla, los transatlánticos, las pirámides de Egipto, las Obras Completas de don Benito Pérez Galdós.[4] Sólo había máquinas.

Después los hombres empezaron a notar que ellos mismos iban desapareciendo paulatinamente[5] y que en cambio las máquinas se multiplicaban. Bastó poco tiempo para que el número de los hombres quedase reducido a la mitad y el de las máquinas aumentase al doble y luego al décuplo.[6] Las máquinas terminaron por ocupar todo el espacio disponible. Nadie podía dar un paso, hacer un simple ademán[7] sin tropezarse[8] con una de ellas. Finalmente los hombres se extinguieron.

Como el último se olvidó de desconectar las máquinas, desde entonces seguimos funcionando.

[1]región de Francia famosa por sus vinos [2]famoso pintor y diseñador español conocido por su estilo surrealista y su excentricidad [3]*pins* [4]famoso novelista español (1843–1920) [5]gradualmente [6]*tenfold* [7]*gesture* [8]*stumble*

Marca (✓) la información relacionada con la perspectiva del narrador.

1. ______ El narrador habla de una experiencia que le contaron.

2. ______ El narrador habla de una experiencia que ha vivido.

Marca (✓) la información relacionada con el narrador.

3. ______ Al final del cuento descubrimos quién es el narrador.

4. ______ El narrador habla desde la perspectiva del tiempo futuro.

5. ______ El narrador es una máquina.

Marca (✓) la información relacionada con la trama de esta historia.

6. ______ El ser humano, según el narrador, se dio cuenta de que las máquinas lo estaban controlando, y las destruyó.

7. ______ Al final del cuento, ya no había seres humanos, sino solamente máquinas.

Comprueba

I was able to …

___ **identify the narrator.**

___ **understand the ending.**

___ **understand the meaning of the title *Apocalipsis*.**

15-35 

Un paso más. Respondan a las preguntas y apunten las ideas que salgan en su discusión. Presenten sus respuestas y justificaciones a la clase.

1. ¿Cuál es el significado del título de este cuento? Explíquenlo.

2. ¿Hace un comentario social este cuento? ¿Cuál es el mensaje?

3. ¿Están ustedes de acuerdo con el mensaje? Expliquen sus ideas.

ESCRIBE

Preparación. Imagínense que ustedes son las máquinas que quedaron funcionando después de la desaparición de los seres humanos.

1. Intercambien algunas ideas que describan la existencia de las máquinas después de la desaparición del ser humano: ¿Es su existencia semejante o diferente a la del pasado? ¿Es más o menos divertida? ¿Qué hacían ustedes antes que ya no hacen hoy o viceversa?
2. Mencionen tres errores cometidos por el ser humano que, según ustedes, tuvieron relación directa con su desaparición y expliquen por qué.

ESTRATEGIA

Use imagination and humor in writing a narrative

In creative writing you can use your imagination to invent events and characters that would be impossible in real life. You can use fantasy and humor to exaggerate events and characters' behaviors to entertain your readers. To write an imaginative and humorous story, consider the following tips:

- Create situations or behaviors that differ from people's expectations.
- Use contradictions within a character to create humor. The humor will be apparent when you poke fun at the contradictions.
- Base your humor on situations and characterizations that will be familiar to your audience.

15-37

Escribe. Ahora, en el papel de una de las máquinas que sobrevivió la desaparición del ser humano, escribe una narración. Usa la información que preparaste en la actividad 15-36.

1. Describe tu existencia antes y después de la desaparición de los seres humanos. Usa humor para captar la atención del lector.
2. Indica con humor algunos aspectos de tu interacción y trabajo cotidianos con los humanos que extrañas con nostalgia.
3. Especula sobre algunos errores que, en tu opinión, provocaron la extinción de la raza humana.

Comprueba

I was able to ...

___ **use fantasy to make my story interesting.**

___ **create a humorous situation by using contradictions or exaggerations.**

15-38

Un paso más. Lee la narración de tu compañero/a y escoge una situación o un personaje que te guste de su narración. Haz lo mismo con la de otros compañeros/otras compañeras y revisa tu propia narración incorporando estas nuevas ideas.

En este capítulo...

Comprueba lo que sabes

Go to ***MySpanishLab*** to review what you have learned in this chapter. Practice with the following:

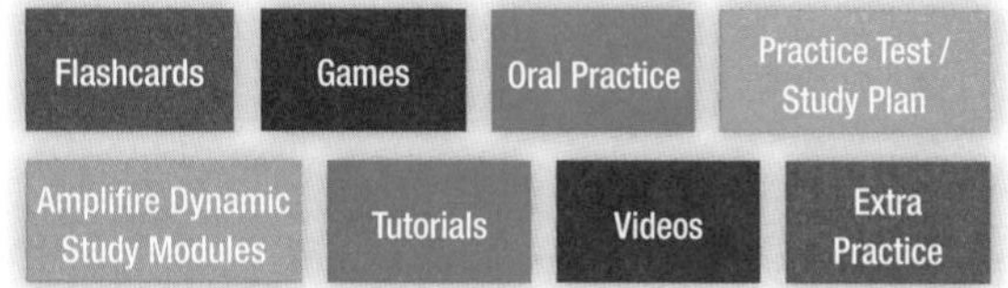

Vocabulario

LA CIENCIA Y LA TECNOLOGÍA
Science and technology

el acceso *access*
el agujero *hole*
la biblioteca digital *digital library*
la cápsula *capsule*
el chip electrónico *integrated circuit*
la ciencia ficción *science fiction*
la clonación *cloning*
el conocimiento *knowledge*
el descubrimiento *discovery*
la diseminación *dispersal, dissemination*
el documento adjunto *attachment, attached document*
la energía solar/de fusión *solar/fusion energy*
el enlace *link*
la fuente *source*
la infraestructura *infrastructure*
el intercambio *exchange*
el mensaje *message*
la microcirugía *microsurgery*
el móvil *cell phone*
el reto *challenge*
el riel *rail*
el robot *robot*
la tableta *tablet (computer)*
el videojuego *video game*

EL MEDIO AMBIENTE
Environment

el banco de peces *shoal; school of fish*
el bosque *forest*
el calentamiento *warming*
la capa de ozono *ozone layer*
la conservación *preservation*
la cuenca *(river) basin*
la deforestación *deforestation*
la desaparición *disappearance*
el deshielo *thaw, thawing*
la extinción *extinction*
la inundación *flood*
la naturaleza *nature*
la pérdida *loss*
el planeta *planet*
los recursos *resources*
la reserva natural *nature preserve*
el satélite *satellite*
la tierra *land, soil*

LAS DESCRIPCIONES
Descriptions

climatizado/a *air-conditioned*
extinguido/a *extinguished*
ligero/a *light*
reciclado/a *recycled*
volador/a *flying*

VERBOS
Verbs

aterrizar (c) *to land*
avanzar *to progress, to advance*
bajar *to download*
conectarse *to connect*
construir (y) *to build*
contribuir (y) *to contribute*
despegar (u) *to take off (airplane)*
encender (ie) *to turn on*
enfocarse (qu) *to focus*
meter *to insert*
promover (ue) *to promote*
repoblar *to reforest*
unificar (qu) *to unify*

PALABRAS Y EXPRESIONES ÚTILES
Useful words and expressions

debido a *due to*
en busca de *in search of*
genéticamente *genetically*

Appendix 1

Stress and Written Accents in Spanish

Rules for Written Accents

The following rules are based on pronunciation.

1. If a word ends in *n*, *s*, or a vowel, the penultimate (second-to-last) syllable is usually stressed.

   Examples: ca**mi**nan
   muchos
   silla

2. If a word ends in a consonant other than *n* or *s*, the last syllable is stressed.

   Example: fa**tal**

3. Words that are exceptions to the preceding rules have an accent mark on the stressed vowel.

   Examples: sar**tén**
   lápices
   ma**má**
   fácil

4. **Separation of diphthongs.** When *i* or *u* is combined with another vowel, the two vowels are pronounced as one sound (a diphthong). When each vowel sound is pronounced separately, a written accent mark is placed over the stressed vowel (either the *i* or the *u*).

   Example: gracias día

Because the written accents in the following examples are not determined by pronunciation, the accent mark must be memorized as part of the spelling of the words as they are learned.

5. **Homonyms.** When two words are spelled the same, but have different meanings, a written accent is used to distinguish and differentiate meaning.

Examples:				
	de	*of*	**dé**	*give* (formal command)
	el	*the*	**él**	*he*
	mas	*but*	**más**	*more*
	mi	my	**mí**	me
	se	*him/herself, (to) him/her/them*	**sé**	*I know, be* (formal command)
	si	*if*	**sí**	*yes*
	te	*(to) you*	**té**	*tea*
	tu	*your*	**tú**	*you*

6. **Interrogatives and exclamations.** In questions (direct and indirect) and exclamations, a written accent is placed over the following words: **dónde, cómo, cuándo, cuál(es), quién(es), cuánto(s)/cuánta(s),** and **qué.**

Word Formation in Spanish

Recognizing certain patterns in Spanish word formation can be a big help in deciphering meaning. Use the following information about word formation to help you as you read.

- **Prefixes.** Spanish and English share a number of prefixes that shade the meaning of the word to which they are attached: **inter-** (between, among); **intro/a-** (within); **ex-** (former, toward the outside); **en-/em-** (the state of becoming); **in-/a-** (not, without), among others.

inter-	interdisciplinario, interacción
intro/a-	introvertido, introspección
ex-	exponer (*expose*)
en-/em-	enrojecer (*to turn red*), empobrecer (*to become poor*)
in-/a-	inmoral, incompleto, amoral, asexual

- **Suffixes.** Suffixes and, in general, word endings will help you identify various aspects of words such as part of speech, gender, meaning, degree, etc. Common Spanish suffixes are **-ría, -za, -miento, -dad/tad, -ura, -oso/a, -izo/a, -(c)ito/a,** and **-mente.**

-ría	place where something is made and/or bought: **panadería**, **zapatería** (*shoe store*), **librería**
-za	feminine, abstract noun: **pobreza** (*poverty*), **riqueza** (*wealth, richness*)
-miento	masculine, abstract noun: **empobrecimiento** (*impoverishment*), **entrenamiento** (*training*)
-dad/tad	feminine noun: **ciudad** (*city*), **libertad** (*liberty, freedom*)
-ura	feminine noun: **verdura, locura** (*craziness*)
-oso/a	adjective meaning having the characteristics of the noun to which it's attached: **montañoso, lluvioso** (*rainy*)
-izo/a	adjective meaning having the characteristics of the noun to which it's attached: **rojizo** (*reddish*), **enfermizo** (*sickly*)
-(c)ito/a	diminutive form of noun or adjective: **Juanito, mesita** (*little table*), **Carmencita**
-mente	attached to the feminine form of adjective to form an adverb: **rápidamente, felizmente** (*happily*)

- **Compounds.** Compounds are made up of two words (e.g., *mailman*), each of which has meaning in and of itself: **altavoz** (*loudspeaker*) from **alto/a** and **voz; sacacorchos** (*corkscrew*) from **sacar** and **corcho.** Your knowledge of the root words will help you recognize the compound; and likewise, learning compounds can help you to learn the root words. What do you think **sacar** means?

- **Spanish–English associations.** Learning to associate aspects of word formation in Spanish with aspects of word formation in English can be very helpful. Look at the associations below.

SPANISH	ENGLISH
es/ex + consonant	*s* + consonant
esclerosis, extraño	*sclerosis, strange*
gu-	*w-*
guerra, Guillermo	*war, William*
-tad/dad	*-ty*
libertad, calidad	*liberty, quality*
-sión/-ción	*-sion/-tion*
tensión, emoción	*tension, emotion*

Appendix 2

Verb Charts

Regular Verbs: Simple Tenses

Infinitive Present Participle Past Participle	Indicative					Subjunctive		Imperative
	Present	Imperfect	Preterit	Future	Conditional	Present	Imperfect	Commands
hablar hablando hablado	hablo hablas habla hablamos habláis hablan	hablaba hablabas hablaba hablábamos hablabais hablaban	hablé hablaste habló hablamos hablasteis hablaron	hablaré hablarás hablará hablaremos hablaréis hablarán	hablaría hablarías hablaría hablaríamos hablaríais hablarían	hable hables hable hablemos habléis hablen	hablara hablaras hablara habláramos hablarais hablaran	habla (tú), no hables hable (usted) hablemos hablad (vosotros), no habléis hablen (Uds.)
comer comiendo comido	como comes come comemos coméis comen	comía comías comía comíamos comíais comían	comí comiste comió comimos comisteis comieron	comeré comerás comerá comeremos comeréis comerán	comería comerías comería comeríamos comeríais comerían	coma comas coma comamos comáis coman	comiera comieras comiera comiéramos comierais comieran	come (tú), no comas coma (usted) comamos comed (vosotros), no comáis coman (Uds.)
vivir viviendo vivido	vivo vives vive vivimos vivís viven	vivía vivías vivía vivíamos vivíais vivían	viví viviste vivió vivimos vivisteis vivieron	viviré vivirás vivirá viviremos viviréis vivirán	viviría vivirías viviría viviríamos viviríais vivirían	viva vivas viva vivamos viváis vivan	viviera vivieras viviera viviéramos vivierais vivieran	vive (tú), no vivas viva (usted) vivamos vivid (vosotros), no viváis vivan (Uds.)

Regular Verbs: Perfect Tenses

Indicative										Subjunctive			
Present Perfect		Past Perfect		Preterit Perfect		Future Perfect		Conditional Perfect		Present Perfect		Past Perfect	
he has ha hemos habéis han	hablado comido vivido	había habías había habíamos habíais habían	hablado comido vivido	hube hubiste hubo hubimos hubisteis hubieron	hablado comido vivido	habré habrás habrá habremos habréis habrán	hablado comido vivido	habría habrías habría habríamos habríais habrían	hablado comido vivido	haya hayas haya hayamos hayáis hayan	hablado comido vivido	hubiera hubieras hubiera hubiéramos hubierais hubieran	hablado comido vivido

Irregular Verbs

Infinitive Present Participle Past Participle	**Indicative**					**Subjunctive**		**Imperative**
	Present	**Imperfect**	**Preterit**	**Future**	**Conditional**	**Present**	**Imperfect**	**Commands**
andar andando andado	ando andas anda andamos andáis andan	andaba andabas andaba andábamos andabais andaban	anduve anduviste anduvo anduvimos anduvisteis anduvieron	andaré andarás andará andaremos andaréis andarán	andaría andarías andaría andaríamos andaríais andarían	ande andes ande andemos andéis anden	anduviera anduvieras anduviera anduviéramos anduvierais anduvieran	anda (tú), no andes ande (usted) andemos andad (vosotros), no andéis anden (Uds.)
caer cayendo caído	caigo caes cae caemos caéis caen	caía caías caía caíamos caíais caían	caí caíste cayó caímos caísteis cayeron	caeré caerás caerá caeremos caeréis caerán	caería caerías caería caeríamos caeríais caerían	caiga caigas caiga caigamos caigáis caigan	cayera cayeras cayera cayéramos cayerais cayeran	cae (tú), no caigas caiga (usted) caigamos caed (vosotros), no caigáis caigan (Uds.)
dar dando dado	doy das da damos dais dan	daba dabas daba dábamos dabais daban	di diste dio dimos disteis dieron	daré darás dará daremos daréis darán	daría darías daría daríamos daríais darían	dé des dé demos deis den	diera dieras diera diéramos dierais dieran	da (tú), no des dé (usted) demos dad (vosotros), no deis den (Uds.)
decir diciendo dicho	digo dices dice decimos decís dicen	decía decías decía decíamos decíais decían	dije dijiste dijo dijimos dijisteis dijeron	diré dirás dirá diremos diréis dirán	diría dirías diría diríamos diríais dirían	diga digas diga digamos digáis digan	dijera dijeras dijera dijéramos dijerais dijeran	di (tú), no digas diga (usted) digamos decid (vosotros), no digáis digan (Uds.)
estar estando estado	estoy estás está estamos estáis están	estaba estabas estaba estábamos estabais estaban	estuve estuviste estuvo estuvimos estuvisteis estuvieron	estaré estarás estará estaremos estaréis estarán	estaría estarías estaría estaríamos estaríais estarían	esté estés esté estemos estéis estén	estuviera estuvieras estuviera estuviéramos estuvierais estuvieran	está (tú), no estés esté (usted) estemos estad (vosotros), no estéis estén (Uds.)
haber habiendo habido	he has ha hemos habéis han	había habías había habíamos habíais habían	hube hubiste hubo hubimos hubisteis hubieron	habré habrás habrá habremos habréis habrán	habría habrías habría habríamos habríais habrían	haya hayas haya hayamos hayáis hayan	hubiera hubieras hubiera hubiéramos hubierais hubieran	
hacer haciendo hecho	hago haces hace hacemos hacéis hacen	hacía hacías hacía hacíamos hacíais hacían	hice hiciste hizo hicimos hicisteis hicieron	haré harás hará haremos haréis harán	haría harías haría haríamos haríais harían	haga hagas haga hagamos hagáis hagan	hiciera hicieras hiciera hiciéramos hicierais hicieran	haz (tú), no hagas haga (usted) hagamos haced (vosotros), no hagáis hagan (Uds.)

Irregular Verbs *(continued)*

Infinitive Present Participle Past Participle	Indicative					Subjunctive		Imperative
	Present	**Imperfect**	**Preterit**	**Future**	**Conditional**	**Present**	**Imperfect**	**Commands**
ir yendo ido	voy vas va vamos vais van	iba ibas iba íbamos ibais iban	fui fuiste fue fuimos fuisteis fueron	iré irás irá iremos iréis irán	iría irías iría iríamos iríais irían	vaya vayas vaya vayamos vayáis vayan	fuera fueras fuera fuéramos fuerais fueran	ve (tú), no vayas vaya (usted) vamos, no vayamos id (vosotros), no vayáis vayan (Uds.)
oír oyendo oído	oigo oyes oye oímos oís oyen	oía oías oía oíamos oíais oían	oí oíste oyó oímos oísteis oyeron	oiré oirás oirá oiremos oiréis oirán	oiría oirías oiría oiríamos oiríais oirían	oiga oigas oiga oigamos oigáis oigan	oyera oyeras oyera oyéramos oyerais oyeran	oye (tú), no oigas oiga (usted) oigamos oíd (vosotros), no oigáis oigan (Uds.)
poder pudiendo podido	puedo puedes puede podemos podéis pueden	podía podías podía podíamos podíais podían	pude pudiste pudo pudimos pudisteis pudieron	podré podrás podrá podremos podréis podrán	podría podrías podría podríamos podríais podrían	pueda puedas pueda podamos podáis puedan	pudiera pudieras pudiera pudiéramos pudierais pudieran	
poner poniendo puesto	pongo pones pone ponemos ponéis ponen	ponía ponías ponía poníamos poníais ponían	puse pusiste puso pusimos pusisteis pusieron	pondré pondrás pondrá pondremos pondréis pondrán	pondría pondrías pondría pondríamos pondríais pondrían	ponga pongas ponga pongamos pongáis pongan	pusiera pusieras pusiera pusiéramos pusierais pusieran	pon (tú), no pongas ponga (usted) pongamos poned (vosotros), no pongáis pongan (Uds.)
querer queriendo querido	quiero quieres quiere queremos queréis quieren	quería querías quería queríamos queríais querían	quise quisiste quiso quisimos quisisteis quisieron	querré querrás querrá querremos querréis querrán	querría querrías querría querríamos querríais querrían	quiera quieras quiera queramos queráis quieran	quisiera quisieras quisiera quisiéramos quisierais quisieran	quiere (tú), no quieras quiera (usted) queramos quered (vosotros), no queráis quieran (Uds.)
saber sabiendo sabido	sé sabes sabe sabemos sabéis saben	sabía sabías sabía sabíamos sabíais sabían	supe supiste supo supimos supisteis supieron	sabré sabrás sabrá sabremos sabréis sabrán	sabría sabrías sabría sabríamos sabríais sabrían	sepa sepas sepa sepamos sepáis sepan	supiera supieras supiera supiéramos supierais supieran	sabe (tú), no sepas sepa (usted) sepamos sabed (vosotros), no sepáis sepan (Uds.)

Irregular Verbs *(continued)*

Infinitive Present Participle Past Participle	Indicative					Subjunctive		Imperative
	Present	Imperfect	Preterit	Future	Conditional	Present	Imperfect	Commands
salir saliendo salido	salgo sales sale salimos salís salen	salía salías salía salíamos salíais salían	salí saliste salió salimos salisteis salieron	saldré saldrás saldrá saldremos saldréis saldrán	saldría saldrías saldría saldríamos saldríais saldrían	salga salgas salga salgamos salgáis salgan	saliera salieras saliera saliéramos salierais salieran	sal (tú), no salgas salga (usted) salgamos salid (vosotros), no salgáis salgan (Uds.)
ser siendo sido	soy eres es somos sois son	era eras era éramos erais eran	fui fuiste fue fuimos fuisteis fueron	seré serás será seremos seréis serán	sería serías sería seríamos seríais serían	sea seas sea seamos seáis sean	fuera fueras fuera fuéramos fuerais fueran	sé (tú), no seas sea (usted) seamos sed (vosotros), no seáis sean (Uds.)
tener teniendo tenido	tengo tienes tiene tenemos tenéis tienen	tenía tenías tenía teníamos teníais tenían	tuve tuviste tuvo tuvimos tuvisteis tuvieron	tendré tendrás tendrá tendremos tendréis tendrán	tendría tendrías tendría tendríamos tendríais tendrían	tenga tengas tenga tengamos tengáis tengan	tuviera tuvieras tuviera tuviéramos tuvierais tuvieran	ten (tú), no tengas tenga (usted) tengamos tened (vosotros), no tengáis tengan (Uds.)
traer trayendo traído	traigo traes trae traemos traéis traen	traía traías traía traíamos traíais traían	traje trajiste trajo trajimos trajisteis trajeron	traeré traerás traerá traeremos traeréis traerán	traería traerías traería traeríamos traeríais traerían	traiga traigas traiga traigamos traigáis traigan	trajera trajeras trajera trajéramos trajerais trajeran	trae (tú), no traigas traiga (usted) traigamos traed (vosotros), no traigáis traigan (Uds.)
venir viniendo venido	vengo vienes viene venimos venís vienen	venía venías venía veníamos veníais venían	vine viniste vino vinimos vinisteis vinieron	vendré vendrás vendrá vendremos vendréis vendrán	vendría vendrías vendría vendríamos vendríais vendrían	venga vengas venga vengamos vengáis vengan	viniera vinieras viniera viniéramos vinierais vinieran	ven (tú), no vengas venga (usted) vengamos venid (vosotros), no vengáis vengan (Uds.)
ver viendo visto	veo ves ve vemos veis ven	veía veías veía veíamos veíais veían	vi viste vio vimos visteis vieron	veré verás verá veremos veréis verán	vería verías vería veríamos veríais verían	vea veas vea veamos veáis vean	viera vieras viera viéramos vierais vieran	ve (tú), no veas vea (usted) veamos ved (vosotros), no veáis vean (Uds.)

Stem-Changing and Orthographic-Changing Verbs

Infinitive Present Participle Past Participle	Indicative					Subjunctive		Imperative
	Present	Imperfect	Preterit	Future	Conditional	Present	Imperfect	Commands
almorzar (ue) (c) almorzando almorzado	almuerzo almuerzas almuerza almorzamos almorzáis almuerzan	almorzaba almorzabas almorzaba almorzábamos almorzabais almorzaban	almorcé almorzaste almorzó almorzamos almorzasteis almorzaron	almorzaré almorzarás almorzará almorzaremos almorzaréis almorzarán	almorzaría almorzarías almorzaría almorzaríamos almorzaríais almorzarían	almuerce almuerces almuerce almorcemos almorcéis almuercen	almorzara almorzaras almorzara almorzáramos almorzarais almorzaran	almuerza (tú), no almuerces almuerce (usted) almorcemos almorzad (vosotros), no almorcéis almuercen (Uds.)
buscar (qu) buscando buscado	busco buscas busca buscamos buscáis buscan	buscaba buscabas buscaba buscábamos buscabais buscaban	busqué buscaste buscó buscamos buscasteis buscaron	buscaré buscarás buscará buscaremos buscaréis buscarán	buscaría buscarías buscaría buscaríamos buscaríais buscarían	busque busques busque busquemos busquéis busquen	buscara buscaras buscara buscáramos buscarais buscaran	busca (tú), no busques busque (usted) busquemos buscad (vosotros), no busquéis busquen (Uds.)
corregir (i, i) (j) corrigiendo corregido	corrijo corriges corrige corregimos corregís corrigen	corregía corregías corregía corregíamos corregíais corregían	corregí corregiste corrigió corregimos corregisteis corrigieron	corregiré corregirás corregirá corregiremos corregiréis corregirán	corregiría corregirías corregiría corregiríamos corregiríais corregirían	corrija corrijas corrija corrijamos corrijáis corrijan	corrigiera corrigieras corrigiera corrigiéramos corrigierais corrigieran	corrige (tú), no corrijas corrija (usted) corrijamos corregid (vosotros), no corrijáis corrijan (Uds.)
dormir (ue, u) durmiendo dormido	duermo duermes duerme dormimos dormís duermen	dormía dormías dormía dormíamos dormíais dormían	dormí dormiste durmió dormimos dormisteis durmieron	dormiré dormirás dormirá dormiremos dormiréis dormirán	dormiría dormirías dormiría dormiríamos dormiríais dormirían	duerma duermas duerma durmamos durmáis duerman	durmiera durmieras durmiera durmiéramos durmierais durmieran	duerme (tú), no duermas duerma (usted) durmamos dormid (vosotros), no durmáis duerman (Uds.)
incluir (y) incluyendo incluido	incluyo incluyes incluye incluimos incluís incluyen	incluía incluías incluía incluíamos incluíais incluían	incluí incluiste incluyó incluimos incluisteis incluyeron	incluiré incluirás incluirá incluiremos incluiréis incluirán	incluiría incluirías incluiría incluiríamos incluiríais incluirían	incluya incluyas incluya incluyamos incluyáis incluyan	incluyera incluyeras incluyera incluyéramos incluyerais incluyeran	incluye (tú), no incluyas incluya (usted) incluyamos incluid (vosotros), no incluyáis incluyan (Uds.)

Infinitive Present Participle Past Participle	Indicative					Subjunctive		Imperative
	Present	**Imperfect**	**Preterit**	**Future**	**Conditional**	**Present**	**Imperfect**	**Commands**
llegar (gu) llegando llegado	llego llegas llega llegamos llegáis llegan	llegaba llegabas llegaba llegábamos llegabais llegaban	llegué llegaste llegó llegamos llegasteis llegaron	llegaré llegarás llegará llegaremos llegaréis llegarán	llegaría llegarías llegaría llegaríamos llegaríais llegarían	llegue llegues llegue lleguemos lleguéis lleguen	llegara llegaras llegara llegáramos llegarais llegaran	llega (tú), no llegues llegue (usted) lleguemos llegad (vosotros), no lleguéis lleguen (Uds.)
pedir (i, i) pidiendo pedido	pido pides pide pedimos pedís piden	pedía pedías pedía pedíamos pedíais pedían	pedí pediste pidió pedimos pedisteis pidieron	pediré pedirás pedirá pediremos pediréis pedirán	pediría pedirías pediría pediríamos pediríais pedirían	pida pidas pida pidamos pidáis pidan	pidiera pidieras pidiera pidiéramos pidierais pidieran	pide (tú), no pidas pida (usted) pidamos pedid (vosotros), no pidáis pidan (Uds.)
pensar (ie) pensando pensado	pienso piensas piensa pensamos pensáis piensan	pensaba pensabas pensaba pensábamos pensabais pensaban	pensé pensaste pensó pensamos pensasteis pensaron	pensaré pensarás pensará pensaremos pensaréis pensarán	pensaría pensarías pensaría pensaríamos pensaríais pensarían	piense pienses piense pensemos penséis piensen	pensara pensaras pensara pensáramos pensarais pensaran	piensa (tú), no pienses piense (usted) pensemos pensad (vosotros), no penséis piensen (Uds.)
producir (zc) (j) produciendo producido	produzco produces produce producimos producís producen	producía producías producía producíamos producíais producían	produje produjiste produjo produjimos produjisteis produjeron	produciré producirás producirá produciremos produciréis producirán	produciría producirías produciría produciríamos produciríais producirían	produzca produzcas produzca produzcamos produzcáis produzcan	produjera produjeras produjera produjéramos produjerais produjeran	produce (tú), no produzcas produzca (usted) produzcamos producid (vosotros), no produzcáis produzcan (Uds.)
reír (i, i) riendo reído	río ríes ríe reímos reís ríen	reía reías reía reíamos reíais reían	reí reíste rió/rio reímos reísteis rieron	reiré reirás reirá reiremos reiréis reirán	reiría reirías reiría reiríamos reiríais reirían	ría rías ría riamos riáis/riais rían	riera rieras riera riéramos rierais rieran	ríe (tú), no rías ría (usted) riamos reíd (vosotros), no riáis/riais rían (Uds.)
seguir (i, i) (ga) siguiendo seguido	sigo sigues sigue seguimos seguís siguen	seguía seguías seguía seguíamos seguíais seguían	seguí seguiste siguió seguimos seguisteis siguieron	seguiré seguirás seguirá seguiremos seguiréis seguirán	seguiría seguirías seguiría seguiríamos seguiríais seguirían	siga sigas siga sigamos sigáis sigan	siguiera siguieras siguiera siguiéramos siguierais siguieran	sigue (tú), no sigas siga (usted) sigamos seguid (vosotros), no sigáis sigan (Uds.)

Stem-Changing and Orthographic-Changing Verbs *(continued)*

Infinitive Present Participle Past Participle	Indicative					Subjunctive		Imperative
	Present	Imperfect	Preterit	Future	Conditional	Present	Imperfect	Commands
sentir (ie, i) sintiendo sentido	siento sientes siente sentimos sentís sienten	sentía sentías sentía sentíamos sentíais sentían	sentí sentiste sintió sentimos sentisteis sintieron	sentiré sentirás sentirá sentiremos sentiréis sentirán	sentiría sentirías sentiría sentiríamos sentiríais sentirían	sienta sientas sienta sintamos sintáis sientan	sintiera sintieras sintiera sintiéramos sintierais sintieran	siente (tú), no sientas sienta (usted) sintamos sentid (vosotros), no sintáis sientan (Uds.)
volver (ue) volviendo vuelto	vuelvo vuelves vuelve volvemos volvéis vuelven	volvía volvías volvía volvíamos volvíais volvían	volví volviste volvió volvimos volvisteis volvieron	volveré volverás volverá volveremos volveréis volverán	volvería volverías volvería volveríamos volveríais volverían	vuelva vuelvas vuelva volvamos volváis vuelvan	volviera volvieras volviera volviéramos volvierais volvieran	vuelve (tú), no vuelvas vuelva (usted) volvamos volved (vosotros), no volváis vuelvan (Uds.)

Appendix 3

Spanish-English Glossary

This vocabulary includes all words and expressions presented in the text, except for proper nouns spelled the same in English and Spanish, diminutives with a literal meaning, typical expressions of the Hispanic countries presented in the *Enfoque cultural*, and cardinal numbers (found on page 23). Cognates and words easily recognized because of the context are not included either.

The number following each entry in bold corresponds to the **capítulo** in which the the word is introduced for active mastery. Non-bold numbers correspond to introduction of words for receptive use.

A

a *at, to* **P**
a menos que *unless* 14
a pesar de *despite* 15
¿A qué hora es? *At what time is [it]?* P
a sí misma/o(s) *himself/herself/themselves* 4
a través de *through* **13**
a veces *sometimes* **1;** 3 *at times* 12
abandonar *to abandon* 14
el/la abogado/a *lawyer* **9**
abrazar(se) (c) *to embrace* **13**
el abrazo *hug* 4
el abrigo *coat* **6**
abril *April* **P**
abrir *to open* 10
la abuela *grandmother* **4**
el abuelo *grandfather* **4**
abundar *to abound* **13**
aburrido/a *boring* **1**, 4, 6; *bored* 6
aburrirse *to get bored* 7, **8**
a caballo *horseback* **8**
acabar(se) *to run out of* 9, 15
el acceso *access* **15**
el accesorio *accessory* **6**
el aceite *oil* **10**
la aceituna *olive* **3**
acompañar *to accompany* **8**
aconsejar *to advise* 5
el acontecimiento *event* 13
acostar(se) (ue) *to put to bed; to go to bed* **4**, 7 ; *to lie down* 4
el actor/la actriz *actor/actress* **9**
actual *present, current* **14**
actualmente *at the present time* **9**
la adaptación *adjustment, adaptation* **14**
Adelante. *Come in.* 5
el adelanto *advance* 15
el ademán *gesture* 15
además *in addition* 3, *besides, furthermore* 11
el aderezo *salad dressing* **10**
adiós *good-bye* **P**
adivinanza *guess* 2
adivinar *to guess* 5
¿adónde? *where (to)?* **3**
adornado/a *decorated* **8**
la aduana *customs* **12**
la aerolínea/línea aérea *airline* **12**
el/la aeromozo/a *flight attendant* 12
afeitar(se) *to shave; to shave (oneself)* **4**
las afueras *outskirts* **5**
la agencia de viajes *travel agency* **12**
el/la agente de viajes *travel agent* **12**
agosto *Augost* **P**
agradable *nice* **2**
agregar *to add* **10**, 15
agrícola *agricultural* **9**
el/la agricultor/a *farmer* **9**
la agricultura *farming* **9**
agrio/a *sour* **10**
el agua *water* **3**
el aguacate *avocado* 6, **10**
las aguas residuales *sewage* 15
el agujero *hole* **15**
ahora *now* **1**
ahorrar to save 14, 15
el aire acondicionado *air conditioning* **5**
el ají *pepper (hot, spicy)* 10
el ajo *garlic* **10**
al (*contraction of* **a** + **el**) *to the* **3**
al aire libre *outdoors* 3
al fondo *at the back, in the rear* **13**
al lado (de) *next to* **P**
el ala wing 14
alegrarse (de) *to be glad (about)* **11**
alegre *happy, glad* **2**
la alegría *joy* **8**
alemán/alemana *German* **2**
la alergia *allergy* **11**
el alfabetismo *literacy* **14**
el alfiler *pin* 15
la alfombra *carpet, rug* 5
algo *something* **1,** *anything* 12
alguien *someone, anyone* 12
algún, alguno (-os, -as) *some, any, several* 12
alguna vez *sometime, ever* 12
algunas veces *sometimes* 12
el alivio *relief* 15
el almacén *department store; warehouse* **6**
la almeja *clam* 10
la almohada *pillow* **5**
almorzar (ue) *to have lunch* **4**
el almuerzo *lunch* **3**
¿Aló? *Hello? (on the telephone)* 3
el alojamiento *lodging* **12**
alquilar *to rent* 1, **3**
el alquiler *rent* **5**
alto/a *tall* **2**
el/la alumno/a *student* **1**
el ama/o de casa *housewife, homemaker* **9**
la amabilidad *kindless* 9
amarillo/a *yellow* **2**
el ambiente setting 8
el amigo/la amiga *friend* **P,** 2
la amistad *friendship* 6, **13,** 13
el amor *love* **13**
amplio/a *ample* **14**
el analfabetismo *illiteracy* **14**
analfabeto/a *illiterate* **14**
el análisis *test* 11
anaranjado/a *orange* **2**
ancho/a *wide* **6**
el anillo *ring* **6**
animado/a *lively* **8**
el ánimo *mood* 5
anoche *last night* **6**
la ansiedad *anxiety* 12
ante(a)noche *the night before last* **6**
anteayer *the day before yesterday* **6**
el antepasado *ancestor* **8**

antes *before* **8**
antes de eso *before that* 6
antes (de) que *before* 14
el antibiótico *antibiotic* **11**
antiguo/a *old* **1**
antipático/a *unpleasant* **2**
la antropología *anthropology* **1**
el anuncio *ad, advertisement* 5, 9
añadir *to add* **10**, 4, 15
el año *year* **P**
el año/mes pasado *last year/month* ***6***
el Año Nuevo *New Year's Day* **8**
apagar *to extinguish, turn off* **9**, 15
el apagón *power outage* 9
el apartamento *apartment* **5**
apoyar *to support* 7, 14
aprender *to learn* Pr, **1**
aquel/aquella/aquello *that (over there)* 5
aquellos/aquellas *those (over there)* 5
el árbitro *umpire, referee* **7**
el árbol *tree* **7**
el arete *earring* **6**
argentino/a *Argentinian* **2**
el armario *closet, armoire* **5**
el aro *earring* 6
el arpa *harp* 13
el/la arquitecto/a *architect* **9**
la arquitectura *architecture* **1**
arrepentirse (ie) *to regret* 7
el arroz *rice* **3**
la artesanía *handicrafts* **6**
el/la artesano/a *craftsman/woman, craftsperson* **13**
el artículo de belleza *beauty item* **11**
asado/a *roasted* **10**
el ascensor *elevator* 4
el aserrín *sawdust* 8
el asiento *seat* **12**
el asiento de pasillo/ventanilla *aisle/ window seat* **12**
la asignatura *subject* **1**
asistir *to attend* **1**
el asma *asthma* **11**
asomarse *to look inside* 13
la aspiradora *vacuum cleaner* **5**
atender (ie) *to help* (a customer) 9
atentamente *kindly* 4
aterrizar (c) *to land* **15**
el atletismo *track and field* **7**
atreverse *to dare* 7
aunque *although, even though, even if* 12, 14
el auto *car* **2**
el autobús/bus *bus* **12**
la autopista *freeway* **12**
el autorretrato *self-portrait* **13**
el/la auxiliar de vuelo *flight attendant* **12**
avanzar (c) *to advance* **15**
la avenida *avenue* Pr
averiguar *to find out* 5
las aves *poultry, fowl* **10**
el avión *plane* **12**
ayer *yesterday* **6**
ayudar *to help* 1, **4,** 5
el/la azafato/a flight attendant 12
el azúcar *sugar* **10**
azul *blue* **2**

B

bailar *to dance* **1,** 6
el bailarín/la bailarina *dancer* **13**
la bajada *slope* 7
bajar *to download* 1, **3, 15**
bajar de peso *lose weight* 3, 10
bajo *under* 5
bajo/a *short (in stature)* **2,** 2
la ballena jorobada *humpback whale* 11
el balón/la pelota/bola *ball* **7,** *7*
el baloncesto/el básquetbol *basketball* **7**
el banano *banana, plantain* 10
el banco de peces *shoal; school of fish* **15**
la bandeja *tray 9,* **10**
la bandera *flag* 2
la bañadera *bathtab* 5
bañar(se) *to bathe; to take a bath* **4**
la bañera *bathtub* **5,** 5
el baño *bathroom* **5**
barato/a *inexpensive, cheap* **6**; *moderate* 12
la barbacoa *barbecue pit; barbecue (event)* **5**
el barco *ship/boat* **12**
barrer *to sweep* **5**
el barrio *neighborhood* **5**
bastante *rather* **P**
la basura *garbage, trash* **5**
la bata *robe* **6**
el bate *bat* **7**
el batido *shake* 3; *smothie* 10
batir *to beat* **10**
el bautizo *baptism, christening* **4**
beber *to drink* ***1***; *beber(se) 10*
la bebida *drink* **3**
la beca *scholarship* 1
el béisbol *baseball* **7**
besar(se) *to kiss* **13**
el beso *kiss 4*
la biblioteca *library* **1; digital** *digital library* **15**
el/la bibliotecario/a *librarian* **9**
bien *well* **P,** 2
bien/mal aparcado *well/badly parked* **12**
bilingüe *bilingual* **2**
el billete ticket 12
la billetera *wallet* **6**
el bistec *steak* **3**
blanco/a *white* **2**
blando/a *soft* **13**
la blusa *blouse* **6**
la boca *mouth* 10, **11**
el boleto/el pasaje *ticket* **12**
el bolígrafo *ballpoint pen* **P**
boliviano/a *Bolivian* **2**
la bolsa/el bolso *purse* **6**
el/la bombero/a *firefighter* **9**
bonito/a *pretty* **2,** 2
el borrador *eraser* **P**
el bosque *forest* **9, 15**
las botas *boots* **6**
la botella *bottle* **10**
el brazo *arm* 6, **11**
¡Buena suerte! *Good luck!* **1**
buenas noches *good night* **P**
buenas tardes *good afternoon/good evening* **P**
¡Bueno! *Hello? (on the telephone)* 3
bueno/a *good* **1;** *well* (health); *physically attractive* 6
buenos días *good morning* **P**
la bufanda *scarf* **6**
el burgués/la burguesa *middle class person* 13
el buscador *search engine* 15
buscar *to look for* **1,** 11, 15
la butaca *armchair* **5**

C

el cabello *hair* **11**
la cabeza *head* 6, **11**
cada *each* 4
cada día each 3
cada... horas *every … hours* **11**
la cadera *hip* **11**
caer bien (y) *to like* 6
caer mal (y) *to dislike* 6
caer simpático *to be liked* **15**
caer(se) (y) *to fall* **11**
café (color) *brown* 2
el café *cafe, coffee shop* **1;** *coffee* **3**
la cafetería *cafetería* **1**
la caja fuerte *safe* **12**
el cajero automático *ATM* **12**
el/la cajero/a *cashier* **9**
los calcetines *socks* **6**
la calculadora *calculator* P
la calefacción *heating* **5**

el calentamiento *warm-up* 7; *warming* **15**
la calidad *quality* 6, **13**
caliente *hot* **3**
callado/a *quiet* **2**
la calle *street* Pr, **15**
el calzado *footwear* **6**
calzar (c) *to wear a shoe size* **6**
los calzoncillos *boxer shorts* **6**
la cama *bed* **5**
la Cámara de Representantes *Congress* 3
el/la camarero/a *server, waiter/ waitress* **3,** 9
el camarón/la gamba *shrimp* **10**
cambiar *to change, to exchange* 3, **6,** 8
el cambio *change* **14**
el cambur *plantain* 10
caminar *to walk* **1**
el camión *bus* 12
la camisa *shirt* **6; de manga corta** *short sleeve shirt* **15**
la camiseta *T-shirt* **6**
el camisón *nightgown* **6**
la campanada *bell chime* 8
el campeón/la campeona *champion* **7**
el campeonato *championship* **7,** *tournament* 7
el/la campesino/a *peasant* **10**
el campo *field* **7**; *countryside* **9**
el campo de fútbol *soccer field* **7**
canadiense *Canadian* **2**
cancelar *to cancel* 12
la cancha *court, golf course* **7**
la canción *song* **3**
la canela *cinnamon* 10
cansado/a *tired* **2**
cantar *to sing* **3,** *6*
la capa de ozono *ozone layer* **15**
el capó *hood* **12**
la cápsula *capsule* **15**
la cara *face* 4, **11**
el cargador *charger* 5
carmelita *brown* 2
el carnaval *carnaval* **8**
la carne *meat*; **de res** *beef/steak*; **molida** *ground meat* **10**
caro/a *expensive* **6**
el/la carpintero/a *carpenter* **9**
la carrera *race* **7**
la carrera *major* 1
la carreta *cart, wagon* **8**
la carretera *highway* **12**
el carro *car* **2**
la carroza *float (in a parade)* **8**
la casa *house, home* **1**
casado/a *married* **2, 4**
casar(se) *to get married* **4,** *5, 8*
el casco *helmet* 7
casi almost 1
castaño/a *brown* 2
el catarro *cold* 11
la cebolla *onion* **10**
la ceja *eyebrow* **11**
el cel/celular *cell phone* 15
la celebración *celebration* 3, **8**
celebrar *to celebrate* **3**
la célula troncal *stem cell* 14
el cementerio *cemetery* **8**
la cena *dinner, supper* **3**
cenar *to have dinner* **3,** 7
Cenicienta Cinderella 3
el centro *downtown, center* **5**
el centro comercial *shopping center* **6**
el centro turístico privado *resort* 11
cerca (de) *near, close (to)* **3, 5**
el cerdo *pork* **10**
el cereal *cereal* **3**
el cerebro *brain* **11**
la cereza *cherry* **10**
cerrar (ie) *to close* **4**
el certamen *contest* 9
la cerveza *beer* **3**
el césped *lawn* **5**, *grass* 5
el cesto *wastebasket* **P**
el cesto/la cesta *basket, hoop* **7**
el ceviche *dish of marinated raw fish* **3**
chao (chau) *good-bye* **P**
la chaqueta *jacket* **6**
el/la chef *chef* **9**
el chico/la chica *boy/girl* **P**
el chile *pepper (hot, spicy)* 10
chileno/a *Chilean* **2**
la chimenea *fireplace* **5**
chino/a *Chinese* **2**
el chip electrónico *integrated circuit* **15**
la chiva *bus* 12
el choclo *corn* 10
el/la chofer, chófer *driver* **9**
la chuleta *chop* **10**
los churros *fried dough* **10**
el ciclismo *cycling* **7**
el/la ciclista *cyclist* 7
el cielo *sky* 7
cien/ciento *hundred* 3
la ciencia ficción *science fiction* **15**
las ciencias *sciences* **1**
las ciencias políticas *political science* **1**
el/la científico/a *scientist* **9**
cierto *true* **Pr**
el cine *movies* 2, **3**
el/la cineasta *filmmaker* 13
la cintura *waist* **11**
el cinturón *belt* **6**
ciudad *city* **3**
¡claro! *of course!* **3**
la clase turista *tourist class* **12**
la clave *key* 13
el/la cliente/a *client* **9**
climatizado/a *air-conditioned* **15**
la clínica/el centro de salud/el sanatorio *clinic* **11**
la clonación *cloning* **15**
el clóset *closet* 5
la cobija *blanket* 5
el coche *car* **2**
la cocina *kitchen* **5;** *stove* 5
cocinar *to cook* **5**
codiciado/a *sought after* 13
el codo *elbow* **11**
coger (j) *to hold* 13
el colectivo *bus* 12
el collar *necklace* **6**
colombiano/a *Colombian* **2**
el color *color* **2**
el comedor *dining room* **5**
comenzar (ie) *to start 1, to begin 6,* **8**
comer *to eat* **1,** 3, 6
comer(se) *to eat* 10
la cometa *kite 8*
la comida *food; meal; dinner, supper* **3**
la comida basura *junk food* 10
el comienzo *origen* 7; *beginning* **8**
el comino *cumin* 10
¿cómo? *how?/what?* **1**
¿Cómo es? *What is he/she/it like?* **P**
¿Cómo está? *How are you? (formal)* **P**
¿Cómo estás? *How are you? (familiar)* **P,** 2
¡Cómo no! *Of course!* **9**
¿Cómo se dice... en español? *How do you say ... in Spanish?* **P**
¿Cómo se llama usted? *What's your name? (formal)* **P**
como si *as if, as though* 15
¿Cómo te llamas? *What's your name? (familiar)* **P**
¿Cómo te va? *How is it going?* **1**
cómoda *dresser* **5**
cómodo/a *comfortable* 9
el/la compañero/a *partner, classmate* **1,** 2; **de cuarto** *roommate* 2
la compañía (de danza, de teatro) *(dance, theater) company* **13**
la compañía/la empresa *company* **9**
la comparsa *group dressed in similar costumes* **8**
compartir *to share* 4
el comportamiento *behavior* 9
comprar *to buy* **1,** *6*
las compras *shopping* 6
¿Comprenden?/¿Comprendes? *Do you understand?* **P**
comprender *to understand* **1,** *10*
el compromiso *engagement* 8
el/la computador/a *computer* 1

la computadora portátil *laptop* **P**
la comunicación *communication* **3**
comunicarse con *to reach out to* 14
con *with* **1**
con cariño *affectionately* 4
con ellos/ellas *with them* 7
con mucho cariño *with much love* 4
Con mucho gusto. *With pleasure./ Gladly.* 1
con permiso *pardon me, excuse me* **P**
con qué frecuencia *how often* 1
con quien *with whom* 12
con tal (de) que *provided that* 14
el concejo municipal *city council* 14
la concha *shell* 8
concordar (ue) *to agree* 14
el concurso *contest* 5
el condimento *seasoning* **10**
conectarse *to connect* **15**
conectarse a *to connect to* **4**
confiable *trustworthy* 13
la confianza *trust* **14**
congelar(se) *to freeze* **7**
conmigo *with me* **7,** 7
conocer (zc) *to know* 3, 13
conocer(se) (zc) *to meet; to know (each other)* 13
el conocimiento *knowledge* **15**
el/la consejero/a *adviser* **1**
el consejo *advice* 5
el consenso *consensus* 12
la conservación *preservation* **15**
la consola de videojuegos *games console* 5
construir (y) *to develop* **7,** *to build* **15**
el consultorio *office (of doctor, dentist, etc.)* **9**
consumir *consume* **10**
el/la contador/a, el/la contable *accountant* **9,** 9
contar (ue) *to count* 3, 6; *to tell* 15
contento/a *happy, glad* **2**
contestar *to answer* 4
Contesten, por favor./Contesta, por favor. *Please answer.* P
contigo *with you (familiar)* **7,** 7
continuar *to continue* 15
contraer *to contract* 11
contrario/a *opposing* **7**
el/la contratista *contractor* **9**
contribuir (y) *to contribute* **15**
controlar *to control* 7, **8**
conversador/a *talkative* **2**
conversar *to talk, to converse* **1**
la copa *(stemmed) glass* **10**
el corazón *heart* **11**
la corbata *tie* **6**
el cordero *lamb* **10**
correr *to run* **1**
la correspondencia *mail* 9
la corrida (de toros) *bullfight* 8, 2
la corriente *current* 12
cortar *to cut; to mow (lawn)* 5
la cortesía *courtesy* P
la cortina *curtain* **5**
corto/a *short (in length)* **2,** 2
la cosa *thing* **6**
cosechar *to harvest* **9**
costar (ue) *to cost* **4,** 13
costarricense *Costa Rican* **2**
la costilla *rib* **10**
la costumbre *custom* **8**
la costurera *seamstress* 13
cotidiano/a everyday 13
crear *to create* 15
crecer *to grow* 5
creer (y) *to believe* **5,** 7
la crema *cream* **10**
el crucero *cruise* **12**
el cuaderno *notebook* **P**
cuadra *city block* **12**
el cuadro *picture, painting* **5**
¿Cuál es la fecha? *What is the date today?* **P**
¿cuál(es)? *which?* **1**
cuando *when* 14
¿cuándo? *when?* **1**
¿Cuántas clases tienes? *How many classes do you have?* **1**
¿cuánto/a? *how much?* **1**
¿Cuánto cuesta? *How much is it?* **1**
¿Cuánto tiempo hace que...? *How long has it been since...?* 4
¿cuántos/as? *how many?* **1**
Cuaresma *Lent* 4
cuarto/a *fourth* **5**
el cuarto *room; bedroom* 2, **5**
cubano/a *Cuban* **2**
cubierto *overcast (sky)* **7**
cubista *cubist* **13**
cubrir *to cover* 10
la cuchara *spoon* **10**
la cucharada *spoonful* 10
la cucharita *teaspoon* **10**
el cuchillo *knife* **10**
el cuello *neck* 6, **11**
la cuenca *(river) basin* **15**
la cuenta *bead* 8
el cuento *story* **13**
el cuero *leather* **6**
el cuerpo *body* 6
cuidar(se) (de) *to take care of* **11**
cultivar *to grow, cultivate* **9**
el cumpleaños *birthday* **3**
cumplir *to fulfill* 7
cumplir (requisitos) *meet (requirements)* 9
curar *to cure* **11**
el currículum *résumé* **9**
el cuy *guinea pig* 10

D

dañino/a *harmful* 10
dar *to give, to hand* **6,** *6, 10*
dar de comer *to feed* 9
dar órdenes *to order around* 5
dar una vuelta *to take a walk* **8**
darse cuenta *to realize* 14
los datos *data* 14
de *of, from* **2**
de acuerdo con *according to* 4
de color entero *solid* **6**
de cuadros *plaid* **6**
de estatura mediana *average, medium height* **2**
de ida y vuelta *round trip* **12**
de la mañana *A.M. (from midnight to noon)* **P**
de la noche *P.M. (from nightfall to midnight)* **P**
de la tarde *P.M. (from noon to nightfall)* **P**
de lunares *dots* **6**
de moda *stylish* 6
de nada *you're welcome* **P**
de ninguna manera *absolutely not* 2
¿de quién? *whose?* **2**
de rayas *stripes* **6**
debajo (de) *under* **P**
deber *should* **1**
debido a *due to* **15**
débil *weak* **2**
décimo/a *tenth* **5**
decir (g, i) *to say, to tell* **4,** 6, 7, 10, 11, 15
el décuplo *tenfold* 15
dedicar *to dedicate* **4**
el dedo *finger* **11**
defender (ie) *to defend* 14
la deforestación *deforestation* **15**
dejar *to leave* **9**
del *of the (contraction of de* + el) 1, **2**
delgado/a *thin* **2**
la democracia *democracy* **14**
denunciar *to denounce* **13**
el departamento *apartment* 5
el dependiente/la dependienta *salesperson* **1**
el deporte *sport* 1, 4
el/la deportista *sportsman, sportswoman* 7
la derecha *right* 4
derecho *law* **1**
el derecho *right* **14**

derretido/a *melted* 10
el desafío *challenge* 13, 14
la desaparición *disappearance* **15**
desarmar *to disassemble* 9
desarrollar *to develop* 8
el desarrollo *development* **13**
desayunar *to have breakfast* **4**
el desayuno *breakfast* **3**
descansar *to rest* **3**
descomponerse *to break down* **12**; *to break* 9
describir *to describe* 6
la descripción *description* **1**
el descubrimiento *discovery* **15**
el descuido *neglect* 15
desde *since* **13**
desear *to want to, to wish* **1, 2,** 3, 5
desechable *disposable* 15
el desempleo *unemployment* 5, **14**
el desfile *parade* **8**
deshacer (g) *to dissolve* 13
el deshielo *thaw, thawing* **15**
el desorden *mess* 3
la despedida *leavetaking* **P**
despedir (i) *to fire* 9
despedir(se) (i) *to say goodbye* 7
despegar (u) *to take off (airplane)* **15**
desperdicios *waste* 15
despertar(se) (ie) *to wake (someone up); to wake up* **4**
el desplazamiento *movement, displacement* **14**
después *after, later* **3**
después (de eso) after (that) 3, 6
después (de) que *after* 14
destacado/a *outstanding* **13**
destacarse *to stand out* **14**
destapar *uncover* 10
la desventaja *disadvantage* **5**
detrás (de) *behind* **P**
devolver (ue) *to return an item* 6
el día *day* **P**
el Día de Acción de Gracias *Thanksgiving Day* **8**
el Día de la Independencia de México *Mexican Independence Day* **8**
el Día de la Madre *Mother's Day* ***8***
el Día de las Brujas *Halloween* **8**
el Día de los Enamorados/del Amor y la Amistad *Valentine's Day* **8**
el Día del Padre *Father's Day* **8**
el día feriado *legal holiday* **8**
el día festivo *holiday* **8**
el dibujo *drawing* 5
el diccionario *dictionary* **1**
diciembre *December* **P**
dictadura *dictatorship* **14**
dictatorial *dictatorial* **14**
el diente *tooth* **11**
el diente de ajo *clove of garlic* 10
difícil *difficult* **1**
difundir *to spread, disseminate* 15
difunto/a *dead* **8**
¿Diga?, ¿Dígame? *Hello? (on the telephone)* 3
Dile a tu compañero/a... *Tell your partner ...* **P**
el dinero *money* 4; **en efectivo** *money in cash* **6**
dirigir (j) *to direct* **13**
la discoteca *dance club* **1**
disculparse *to apologize* 7
el discurso *speech* 8
discutir *to argue* **7**
la diseminación *dispersal, dissemination* **15**
el diseño *design* **6**
disfrazarse (c) *to wear a costume* **8**
disfrutar *to enjoy* 5
distinguir *to distinguish* **13**
la distribución *layout* 5
la diversificación *diversification* **14**
la diversión *entertainment* **3**
divertido/a *funny, amusing* **2;** *fun* 4, 10
divertirse (ie, i) *to have fun, to enjoy* 7
divorciado/a *divorced* **4**
doblar *to fold* **5;** *to turn* **12**
el documento adjunto *attachment, attached document* **15**
doler (ue) *to hurt, ache* 2, **11**
el dolor *pain* **11**
domingo *Sunday* **P**
dominicano/a *Dominican* **2**
donde *where, wherever* 14
¿dónde? *where?* **1**
¿Dónde está...? *Where is...?* **P**
dormir (ue) la siesta *to take a nap* **4,** 4
dormir(se) (ue) *to sleep; to fall asleep* **4,** 7, 10. 11
dos veces *twice* 3
la ducha *shower* **5**
duchar(se) *to give a shower to; to take a shower* **4,** 7
la duda *doubt* 14
el dulce *candy/sweets* **10; de higos** *candied figs* 10
duplicar *to duplicate* 10
durante *during* **3**
durar *to last* **7**
el durazno *peach* 10
el DVD *DVD; DVD player* **P**

E

economía *economics* **1**
económico/a *economic* **14**
ecuatoriano/a *Ecuadorian* **2**
el edificio *building* **5**
la eficiencia *efficiency* **14**
el/la ejecutivo/a *executive* **9**
él *he* **P**
el/la *the* **1**
elaborar *to produce* 9
la elección *election* **14**
el/la electricista *electrician* **9**
los electrodomésticos *appliances* **5**
elegir (ie, i) *to choose, elect* 5, 13, **14**
elenco *cast* 4
ella *she* **P**
ellos/ellas *they* **1**
el elote *corn* 10
la emergencia *emergency* *9*
la emigración *emigration* **14**, 14
el/la emigrante *emigrant* **14**
emigrar *to emigrate* **14**
empezar (ie) *to begin, to start* **4,** 6, 13
el/la empleado/a *employee* **9**
en *in* **P**
en busca de *in search of* **15**
En cambio... *On the other hand ...* 4
En contraste... *In contrast ...* 4
en cuanto *as soon as* 14
en la actualidad *at the present time* **13**
en punto *on the dot, sharp (time)* **P**
¿En qué página? *On what page?* **P**
¿En qué puedo servirle(s)? *How may I help you?* **6**
en realidad/realmente *in fact, really* ***9;*** *actually 9*
en vez de *instead of* **14**
Encantado/a. *Pleased/Nice to meet you.* **P**
encantar *to delight, to love* **6,** 6, 11
encender (ie) *to turn on* 15
encontrar (ue) *to find* **4, 6**
encontrarse *to run into* 13
el encuentro *encounter* Pr
la energía solar *solar energy* **15**
enérgico/a *energetic* **14**
enero *January* **P**
enfadarse *to get angry 7, 7*
la enfermedad *illness* 2, **11**
el/la enfermero/a *nurse* **9**
el/la enfermo/a *ill/sick person* 3, **11**
enfocarse (qu) *to focus* **15**
enfrente (de) *in front of* **P**
el enlace *link* **15**
enojado/a *angry* **2**
la ensalada *salad* **3**
enseguida *immediately* **6**
entender (ie) *to understand* **4**
enterar(se) *to find out* 7
enterrar *to burry* 8
entonces *then* **8**
entrar (en) *to go in, to enter* **6**

entre *between, among* **P,** 7
entregar *to turn in* 9
el/la entrenador/a *coach* **7**
la entrevista *interview* 1, **9**
entrevistar(se) *to interview (each other)* 4
enviar *to send* 3, **9**
en vivo *live* **8**
el equipaje *luggage* 11, **12**
el equipo *team; equipment* **7**
eres *you are (familiar)* **P**
es *you are (formal), he/she is* **P**
la escala *stopover* **12**
la escalera *stair* **5**
el escaparate *store window* **6**
la escena *scene* **13**
escoger *to choose* 4
Escribe. *Write.* **P**
escribir *to write* **1,** 6, 10
escribirse *to write to each other* 4
el/la escritor/a *writer* **13**
el escritorio *desk* **P**
escuchar *to listen (to)* **1**
el/la escultor/a *sculptor* **13**
ese/a *that* (*adjective*) P
ese/esa/eso *that* 5
esos/esas *those* 5
los espaguetis *spaghetti* **3**
la espalda *back* **11**
el español *Spanish* **1**
español/a *Spanish* **2**
la especialidad *specialty 9*
las especias *spices* **10**
el espejo *mirror* **5; retrovisor** *rearview mirror* **12**
la esperanza de vida *life expectancy* **14**
esperar *to wait for* **9**; *to wish 11*
las espinacas *spinach* **10**
la esposa *wife* **2, 4**
el esposo *husband* **2, 4**
el esquí *skiing, ski* **7**
esquiar *to ski* **7**
la esquina *corner* **12**
está *he/she is, you are (formal)* **P**
está despejado *it's clear* 7
esta noche *tonight* 3
está nublado *it's cloudy 7*
la estación *season* **6**
el estadio *stadium* 7
la estadística *statistics* **1**
el estado libre asociado *commonwealth* 2
estadounidense *U.S. citizen* 2
estar *to be,* **P, 1**, 1, 2, 5, 6, 7, 8, 12
estar aburrido/a *to be bored* 2
estar cansado/a *to be tired* 2
estar contento/a *to be happy* 2, 11
estar de acuerdo *to agree* 11
estar de moda *to be fashionable* **6**
estar en forma *to keep in shape* 7
estar enojado/a *to be angry* 2
estar listo/a *to be ready* 2
estar malo/a *to be ill* 2
estar verde *to be unripe* 2
estás *you are (familiar)* **P**
este/a *this* **1,** 1
este/esta/esto *this* 5
el estilo *style* **5**
estimado/a *dear 4*
el estómago *stomach* 2, **11**
estornudar *to sneeze* **11**
estos/estas *these* 5
estrecho/a *narrow, tight* **6**
la estrella *star* 13
estremecerse *to tremble* 13
el/la estudiante *student* **P**
estudiar *to study* **1**
estudioso/a *studious* **1**
la estufa *stove* 5
¡estupendo! *fabulous!* **3**
la etnia *ethnicity* 14
evitar *avoid* 2, 10
el examen *test* **1**
examinar *to examine* **11**
excelente *excellent* **1**
la excursión *outing, trip* **12**
exigir *to demand* 14
el éxito *success* **13**
la experiencia *experience* **9**
explicar *to explain* 4, 15
explicarse *to explain to each other* 6
explotar *to exploit* **9**
exponer (g) *to exhibit* **13**
la exportación *export* **9, 14**
la expresión *expression* P
la extinción *extinction* **15**
extinguido/a *extinguished* **15**
extrañar *to miss* 10
extrovertido/a *extrovert, outgoing* 4

F

fabuloso/a *fabulous, great* **3**
fácil *easy* **1**
facturar *to check in (luggage)* **12**
la facultad *school, department* **1**
la falda *skirt* **6**
falso/a *false* Pr
la familia *family* **4**
el fantasma *ghost* 8
el/la farmacéutico/a *pharmacist* **11**
la farmacia *pharmacy* **11**
fascinar *to fascinate, to be pleasing to* **6,** 6
favorito/a *favorite* **1**
febrero *February* **P**
felicidades *congratulations* **3**
felicitar *to congratulate* 11
feo/a *ugly* **2**
el festival *festival 8; event or celebration (public)* 8
la festividad, la fiesta *festivity; holiday; celebration* **8;** (*public*) *festivity* **8**
la ficha *note card* 7
la fiebre *fever* **11**
fielmente *faithfully* 7
la fiesta *party 3; holiday, celebration* 8
fijar(se) *to focus 4; to take note* 14
el fin de semana *weekend* **1**
finalmente *finally 5, 6*
la finca *ranch, farm* **9**
la flor *flower* 2
el/la fontanero/a *plumber* 9
la forma *shape, form* **13**
fortalecer (zc) *to strenghten* 10
la foto(grafía) *photo(graph)* **4**
el fracaso *failure* **13**
fracturar(se) *to fracture, to break* **11**
francés/francesa *French* **2**
la frazada *blanket* 5
la frecuencia *frequency* **1**
frecuentemente *frequently, often* **4,** 5, **8**
el fregadero *kitchen sink* **5**
freír (i) *to fry* **10**
la frente *forehead* **11**
la fresa *strawberry* **10**
frijoles *beans* **3**
frío/a *cold* **3**
frito/a *fried* **3, 10**
la fruta *fruit* **3, 10; de la pasión** *passion fruit* 10
los fuegos artificiales *fireworks* **8**
la fuente bowl 10; *source* 8, **15**
la fuente de ingresos *source of income* **9**
fuerte *strong* **2**
la fuerza laboral *workforce* **9**
fumar *to smoke* **11**
funcionar *to work* 4
la fundación *founding* (*noun*) **13**
el fútbol (americano) *soccer (football)* 3, **7**

G

las gafas de sol *sunglasses* **6**
la galleta *cookie* **10**
las gambas *shrimp* 10
el ganado cattle 10
ganar *to win* 3, **7,** 12, 14; *to earn (money)* 14
la ganga *bargain* 6

el garaje *garaje* **5**
los garbanzos *garbanzo beans* **10**
la garganta *throat* **11**
la garra *claw* 14
gastar *to spend* **6,** 13
gemelo/a *twin* **4**
generalmente *generally* **8**
genéticamente *genetically* **15**
la gente *people* **8**
la geografía *geography* **1**
el/la gerente (de ventas) *(sales) manager* **9**
el gimnasio *gymnasium* **1**
el gitano *gypsy* 13
gobernante *ruler* 8
gobernar (ie) *to govern* **14**
el gobierno *government* **11**
el gol *goal* **7**
el golf *golf* **7**
gordo/a *fat* **2**
la gorra *cap* **6**
grabar *to record* 13
gracias *thanks* **P**
¡Gracias a Dios! *Thank goodness!* 15
graduarse *to graduate* 14
grande *big* **1**
grave *serious* **11**; *seriously ill* 6
la gripe *flu* **11**
gris *gray* **2**
la guagua *bus* 12
el guajolote *turkey* 10
el guante *glove* **6**
la guantera *glove compartment* **12**
guapo/a *good-looking, handsome* **2**
guardar silencio *to keep silent* 14
guatemalteco/a *Guatemalan* **2**
la guía *guide* 6
la guitarra *guitar* **3**
el/la guitarrista *guitar player* **13**
gustar *to like* **2;** *to be pleasing to, to like* **6,** 11

H

haber consenso *to agree* 12
la habitación *bedroom* **5**
la habitación doble/sencilla *double/single room* **12**
el/la habitante *inhabitant* **14**
hablar *to speak* **1,** 9, 10
Hablen (sobre...) *Talk (about . . .)* **P**
hace *ago* 7
Hace (+ expresión de tiempo) que... *It's been (time expression) since...* 4
Hace buen/mal tiempo. *The weather is good.* **P,** 7
hace fresco *it's cool* **7**
Hace sol. *It's sunny.* **P**
hace un día/mes/año (que) *it has been a day/month/year since* **6**
hace viento *it's windy* **7**
hacer (g) *to do* 1, **3,** 7, 9, 10, 15
hacer cola *to stand in line* **12**
hacer la cama *to make the bed* **3**
hacer malabarismo *to juggle* 9
hacer parapente *to go paragliding* **7**
hacer surf *to surf* **7**
hacerse *to become* 14
hacerse daño *to hurt oneself* 8
la hamburguesa *hamburger* **3**
la harina *flour* **10**
hasta *even* 7; *including* **13**
hasta luego *see you later* **P**
hasta mañana *see you tomorrow* **P**
hasta pronto *see you soon* **P**
hasta que *until* 14
hay *there is, there are* **P**
el hecho *fact* 6
la heladera *refrigerator* 5
el helado *ice cream* **3**
la herida *wound* 11
la hermana *sister* **4,** 1
el hermano *brother* **4**
hervir (ie, i) *to boil* **10**
el hielo *ice* **7**
las hierbas *herbs* **10**
el hierro *iron* **9**
la hija *daughter* **4**
el hijo *son* **4**
el hijo único/la hija única *only child* 4
el/la hincha *fan* **7**
hinchado/a *swollen* 11
la hinchazón *swelling* 11
hispano/a *Hispanic* **2**
la historia *history* **1**
el hockey sobre hierba *field hockey* **7**
hoja *leaf* **5**
hola *hi, hello* P
el hombre *man* **3**
el hombre/la mujer de negocios *businessman/woman* **9**
el hombro *shoulder* **11**
el homenaje homage 8
hondureño/a *Honduran* **2**
la honestidad *honesty* **14**
el hospital *hospital* **11**
hoy *today* **P**
hoy en día *nowadays* **8**
Hoy es (día de la semana). *Today is (day of the week.)* **P**
el hueso *bone* 8, **11**
el huevo *egg* **3**
las humanidades *humanities* **1**

I

la iglesia *church* 8
la igualdad *equality* **14**
Igualmente. *Likewise.* **P**
el impermeable *raincoat* **6**
la impresora *printer* 5
el incendio *fire* **9**
independizarse *to become independent* 5
la industria textil *textile industry* **9**
la infancia *childhood* 7
infantil *children's* **14**
la infección *infection* **11**
influir (y) *to influence* 3, 13
la información de fondo *background information* 8
la informática/la computación *computer science* **1**, 1
el informe *report* 9
la infraestructura *infrastructure* **15**
el/la ingeniero/a *engineer* **9**
la inmigración *immigration* **14,** 14
el/la inmigrante *immigrant* **14**
la inmundicia filth 14
el inodoro *toilet* **5**
inolvidable *unforgettable* **13**
el/la inspector/a de aduana *customs agent* **12**
el intercambio *exchange* **15**
interesante *interesting* **1**
interesar *to interest* **6,** *6*
el/la intérprete *interpreter* **9**; *performer, artist* **13**
interrumpir *to interrupt* 15
la inundación *flood* **15**
invertir (ie) *to invest* 15
el invierno *Winter* **6, 7**
la invitación *invitation* 8
invitar *to invite* 8
la inyección *injection* **11**
ir *to go* **3,** 6, 11
ir bien con... *to go well with* 6
ir de bowling *to bowl* 7
ir de compras *to shop* 3, *to go shopping* **6**
ir de tapas *to go out for tapas* 1
ir(se) *to go away, to leave* **7,** 7, 11
irse la luz *to be a blackout* 8
la izquierda *left* 4

J

el jabón *soap* **5**
jamás *never, (not ever)* 12
el jamón *ham* **3**
japonés/japonesa *Japanese* **2**
el jardín *garden* **5**
el/la jefe/a *boss* **9**

joven *young* **2**
el/la joven *young man/woman 3*
la joya jewel 4; *piece of jewelry* **6**
jubilarse *to retire*14
el juego/el partido *game* **7**
jueves *Thursday* **P**
el/la juez *judge* **9**
el/la jugador/a *player* **7**
jugar (ue) *to play (a game, sport)* **4**
jugar (ue) a los bolos/(al) boliche *to bowl* 4, **7,** 7
el jugo *juice* **3**
el juguete *toy* **6**
julio *July* P
junio *June* P
juntos/as *together 4*

L

el labio *lip* **11**
lácteo/a *dairy (product)* **10**
el/la ladrón/a *thief* 8
el lago *lake* **7**
lamentar *to be sorry* 11
la lámpara *lamp* **5**
la langosta *lobster* **10**
lanzar *to throw* 7
el lápiz *pencil* **P**
largo/a *long* **2**
la lástima *shame 11*
el lavabo *bathroom sink* **5**
la lavadora *washer* 5
la lavandería *laundry room* **5**
el lavaplatos *dishwasher* 4, **5**
lavar(se) *to wash (oneself)* ***4***
le gusta(n) *you (formal) like* **2**
la leche *milk* **3**
la leche de coco *coconut milk* **10**
la lechuga *lettuce* **3**
Lee. *Read.* **P**
leer *to read* **1, 7,** 10
las legumbres *legumes* 10
lejos (de) *far (from)* 4, **5**
las lentejas *lentils* **10**
lentes de contacto *contact lenses* **2**
Levanta la mano. *Raise your hand.* **P**
levantar pesas *to lift weights* **7**
levantar(se) *to raise; to get up* **4,** 7
levantarse con el pie izquierdo *to get up on the wrong side of the bed* 7
la libertad *freedom* 14; **de expresión** *freedom of expression* 14
la librería *bookstore* ***1***
el libro *book* **P**
la licencia de conducir *driver's license* **12**
el limón *lemon* **10**
el limpiaparabrisas *windshield wiper* **12**
limpiar *to clean* **5,** 11; **en seco** *to dry clean* 14
limpio/a *clean* **5**
listo/a *smart; ready* **2;** *clever* 6
la literatura *literature* ***1***
el litio *lithium* 13
llamarse *to be called* **4,** 8
la llanta *tire* **12**
la llave *key* **12**
la llegada *arrival* **12**
llegar *to arrive* 1, 6
llenar *to fill (out)* **9**
lleno/a *full* **12**
llevar *to take* 4; *to wear, to take* **6**
llorar *to cry* 8
llover (ue) *to rain* **7**
Llueve./Está lloviendo. *It's raining.* P
la lluvia *rain* **7**
lo importante *the important thing* **9**
lo mismo *the same* 5
lo siento *I'm sorry (to hear that)* **P**
el/la locutor/a *radio announcer* **9**
lograr *to accomplish* 7; *to achieve* 12
los/las *the (plural)* **1**
las luces intermitentes *flashers/ hazard lights* **12**
la lucha *fight* **14**
luchar *to fight* **14**
luego *after, later* **3**
luego *then* 4, 5, 6
el lugar *place* **1**
el lujo *luxury* 12
luna de miel *honeymoon 4*
lunes *Monday* **P**
la luz (las luces) *light(s)* **12**

M

machacar *to crush* 10
la madera *wood* **9**
la madrastra *stepmother* **4**
la madre *mother* **4**
la madrina *godmother* 4
magnífico/a *great* **6**
el maíz *corn* **10**
mal *bad* **P**
la maleta *suitcase* 6, **12**
el maletero/el baúl *trunk* **12**
el maletín *briefcase* **12**
malo/a *bad* **1;** *ill* 6
la malva *mallow* 11
la mamá *mom* **4**
la mami/mamita *mommy* 4
mandar *to send* ***9***
mandar saludos *to say hello* 5
manejar *to drive* **12**
la mano *hand* 6, **11**
la manta *blanket* **5**
la manteca/la mantequilla *butter* **10**
el mantel *tablecloth* **10**
mantener (g, ie) *to maintain* **8**
mantenerse *to stay* 14
mantenerse en contacto *to stay in touch* 13
mantenerse en forma *to keep in shape* 11
la manzana *apple* **10**
manzanilla *chamomile* 11
mañana (adv.) *tomorrow* **P;** 3
la mañana *morning* **P**
el mapa *map* **1**
maquillar(se) *to put makeup on (someone); to put makeup on (oneself)* **4**
el mar *sea* **3**
el maracuyá *passion fruit* **10**
maravilloso/a *marvelous* **8**
la marca *brandname* 6; *brand* 7
el marcador *scoreboard* 5
el marcador/el rotulador *marker* **P;** *highlighter* 10
la margarina *margarine* **10**
el marido *husband* 4
los mariscos *shellfish* 3, **10**
marrón *brown* **2**
marroquí *Moroccan* **2**
martes *Tuesday* **P**
marzo *March* **P**
más (+ adj.) *most (+ adj.) 1*
Más alto, por favor. *Louder, please.* **P**
más de *more than* 8
Más despacio/lento, por favor. *More slowly, please.* **P**
más o menos *about, more or less* **P**
más tarde *later* 3, 4, 5, 6
el/la más... *the most...*8
más... que *more...than* 8
matar *to kill* 8
la materia *subject* **1**
el material *material* 6
el matrimonio *marriage* **4**
mayo *May* **P**
la mayonesa *mayonnaise* **10**
mayor *old* **2**
mayor que *older than* 8
el/la mayor *the oldest* **4**
la mayoría *majority* **14**
me gusta(n) *I like* **2**
Me gustaría... *I would like . . .* 3, **6**
Me llamo... *My name is...* **P**
el médano *sand dune* 7
la media hermana *half-sister* **4**
las medias *stockings, socks* **6, 6**
la medicina *medicine* **1, 11**
el/la médico/a *medical doctor* **9**
el/la médico/a de cabecera/de familia *doctor (primary care)* 11
el medio ambiente *environment* 11
el medio hermano *half-brother* **4**

la mejilla *cheek* **11**
el/la mejor *the best* 8
mejor que *better than* 4, 8
mejorar *to improve* **14**
el melocotón *peach 10*
la melodía *melody* **8**
el melón *melon* **10**
el/la menor *the youngest* **4**
menos... que *less...than* 8
el mensaje *message* **15**
el mercado *market 6*
la merienda *snack* 12
el mes *month* **P**
la mesa *table* **P**
meter *to insert* 15
meter un gol *to score a goal* **7**
el metro *subway* **12**
el metro cuadrado *square meter* 4
mexicano/a *Mexican* **2**
mi amor *(term of endearment)* 3
mi vida *(term of endearment)* 3
mi(s) *mine* 2
mi(s) *my* P
el micro *bus* 12
la microcirugía *microsurgery* **15**
el (horno de) microondas *microwave (oven)* **5**
mientras *while* **3, 8,** 14
miércoles *Wednesday* **P**
la migración *migration* **14**
mil *thousand* 3
millón *million* 3
la minoría *minority* **14**
el minuto *minute* P
mirar *to look (at)* **1**
mismo/a *same* 2
mitad *half* 2
el móvil *mobile* **15**
la mochila *backpack* **P**
mojado/a *wet* 7
módico/a *moderate* 12
moler (ue) *to grind* 10
molestar(le) *to bother, be bothered by* **11**
montar (en bicicleta) *to ride (a bicycle)* **1**
morado/a *purple* **2**
moreno/a *brunette; of African ancestry; of dark skin or hair color* **2**
morir (ue) *to die* 6, 7, 10, 13
la mortalidad *mortality* **14**
la mostaza *mustard* **10**
el mostrador *counter* **12**
mostrar (ue) *to show* ***6***
el motor *motor* **12**
mover(se) *to move* 7
el móvil *cell phone* 15
muchas veces *many times* **1**
mucho *(adv.) much, a lot* **2**
mucho/a *(adj.) many* **2**
Mucho gusto. *Nice to meet you.* **P**
mudar(se) *to move* 5
los muebles *furniture* **5**
muerto/a *dead* **8,** *deceased* 6
la mujer *woman* ***3;*** *wife* 4
la multa *fine* **12,** 15
la muñeca *wrist* **11**
el mural *mural* **13**
el/la muralista *muralist* **13**
el músculo *muscle* **11**
la música *music* **3**
muy *very* **P,** 2

N

nacer *to be born* 8
la nacionalidad *nationality* **2**
nada *nothing* 12
nadar *to swim* **3, 7**
nadie *no one, nobody* 12
la [la naranja] **naranja** *orange* **3;** (color) *orange* 2
la nariz *nose* 6, **11**
la natación *swimming* ***7***
natal *native* 10
la naturaleza *nature* ***7*, 15**
la Navidad *Christmas* ***8***
necesario/a *necessary* 11
necesitar *to need* **1,** 13
negro/a *black* **2;** *of African ancestry; of dark skin or hair color* 2
el nervio *nerve* **11**
nervioso/a *nervous* **2**
nevar (ie) *to snow* **7**
la nevera *refrigerator* 5
ni... ni *neither . . . nor* 12
nicaragüense *Nicaraguan* **2**
la nieta *granddaughter* **4**
el nieto *grandson* **4**
la nieve *snow* **7**
nigeriano/a *Nigerian* **2**
ningún, ninguno/a *no, not any, none* 12
el niño/la niña *child* **4**
nivel *level* **14**
¿no? *isn't it?* 1
No comprendo. *I don't understand.* **P**
no obstante *however* 11
No sé. *I don't know.* **P**
la Nochebuena *Christmas Eve* **8**
la Nochevieja *New Year's Eve* **8**
nominar *to nominate* **13**
norteamericano/a *North American* **1**
nosotros/as *we* **1**
la noticia *news* 4
las noticias *news* 2
la novela *novel* **13**
el/la novelista *novelist* **13**
noveno/a *ninth* **5**
la novia *fiancée; girlfriend* **4,** 2
noviembre *November* **P**
el novio *fiancé; boyfriend* 2, **4**
nuestro(s), nuestra(s) our **2**
nuevo/a *new* **2**
el número *size (shoes)* **6**
nunca *never* **1** *(not ever)* 12

O

o... o either ... or 12
la obra *work* **13**
el/la obrero/a *worker* **9**
octavo/a *eighth* **5**
octubre *October* **P**
ocupado/a *busy* **4**
ocurrir *to occur* 10
odiar *to hate* ***8***
la odontología *dentistry* 11
la oficina *office* **1**
ofrecer (zc) *to offer* ***9***
el oído *(inner) ear* **11**
Oiga, por favor. *Listen, please.* 1
¡Oigo! *Hello? (on the telephone)* 3
oír *to listen to* 3, **7**
ojalá que... *I/we hope that . . .* 11
el ojo *eye* **2**
la ola *wave* 7
olvidar to forget 10, 15
el ómnibus *bus* 12
ordenado/a *tidy* **5**
el ordenador *computer* 1
ordenar *to tidy up* **5**
la oreja *(outer) ear* 6, **11**
el oro *gold* **6**
la orquesta *orchestra* **8**
oscuro/a *dark 2*
el otoño *fall* **6, 7**
Otra vez. *Again.* P
otro/a *other, another* **3**
la oveja *sheep* **10**
el OVNI *UFO* 15
¡Oye! *Hey!* 1

P

el/la paciente *patient* **11**
el padrastro *stepfather* **4**
el padre *father* **4**
los padres *parents 2,* **4**
el padrino *godfather* 4
pagar *to pay (for)* **6**
el país *country, nation* 1, **3**
el paisaje *landscape* 13
la paiteña *a type of onion* 10
la palabra *word* **P**
las palomitas de maíz *popcorn 10*
los palos *golf clubs* **7**
la palta avocado 10
el pan dulce *bun, small cake* **10**
el pan tostado/la tostada *toast* **3**

panameño/a *Panamanian* **2**
la pantalla *earring* 6; *screen* **P**
los pantalones *pants;* **cortos** *shorts* **6**
las pantimedias *pantyhose* **6**
el pañuelo *handkerchief* **6**
el papá *dad* **4**
la papa *potato* **3**
las papas fritas *French fries* **3**
la papaya *papaya* **10**
el papi/papito daddy 4
para *in order (to)*; *towards* 3; *for, to* 3, **1**
para mí *for me* 7
para que *so that* 14
¿para qué? *why?/what for?* **1**
para ti *for you (familiar)* 7
el parabrisas *windshield* **12**
el paraguas *umbrella* **6**
paraguayo/a *Paraguayan* **2**
la parchita *passion fruit* 10
pardo/a *brown* 2
parecer (zc) *to seem* **6;** to think 14
parecido *similar* 1
la pareja *couple* 4
el parentesco *kinship* 4
el pariente *relative* **4**
el parque de atracciones *amusement park* 3
participar *to participate* **1**
pasado mañana *the day after tomorrow* 3
el/la pasajero/a *passenger* **12**
el pasaporte *passport* **12**
pasar *to spend (time)* **4;** *to happen* 13
pasar (muy) bien/pasarlo bien *to have a good time* 3, **8**
pasar la aspiradora *to vacuum* **5**
la Pascua *Easter* **8**
Pase(n). *Come in.* 5
pasear *to take a walk, to stroll* **4**
el pasillo *corridor, hall* **5**
el paso *step* 5
la pasta de dientes *toothpaste* 10
el pastel *cake* 5; *pastry* **10**
la pastilla *pill* **11;** *medication* 11
la pata *foot, leg (in animals and furniture)* 2
patinar *to skate* **7**
patriótico/a *patriotic* 8
patrocinar *to sponsor* 12
el pavo *turkey* **10**
el pecho *chest* **11**
la pechuga de pollo *chicken breast* 10
pedir (i) *to ask for; to order* **4,** 7; *to request* 15
pedir la palabra *to request the floor* 15
peinar(se) *to comb (someone's hair); to comb (one's hair)* **4**
pelar to *peel* 10
pelear *to argue* 4
la película *movie, film* 2, **3**
el peligro *danger* 8
pelirrojo/a *redhead* **2**
el pelo *hair* **2**
la peluquería *beauty salon, barbershop* 9
el/la peluquero/a *hairdresser* **9**
el penalti *penalty (in sports)* **7**
el pendiente *earring* 6
pensar (en) (ie) *to think (about)* 3, **4,** *6, 11*
pensar (ie) + *infinitive to plan to* + verb **4**
el pepino *cucumber* **10**
pequeño/a *small* **1**
la pera *pear* **10**
percibido/a *noticed* 13
perder (ie) *to lose 7, 15*
perderse *to miss out on* 8; *to get lost* **12**
la pérdida *loss* **15**
perdón *pardon me, excuse me* **P**
¿Perdón? *What?* 1
el/la peregrino/a *pilgrim, traveller* **8**
el perejil *parsley* 10
el perezoso (Zool.) sloth 12
perezoso/a *lazy* **2,** 4
perfecto/a *perfect* 10
el periódico *newspaper* **3,** 1
el/la periodista *journalist* **9**
permitir *to allow* 5, 11
pero *but* **1**
el/la perro/a *dog* 5
la persona *person* **P**
el personaje principal *main character* **13**
las personas *people* **P**
las pertenencias *things you own* 2
peruano/a *Peruvian* **2**
la pesa *weight* 10
la pesadilla nightmare 12
el pescado *fish* **3, 10**
la pestaña *eyelash* **11**
el petróleo *petroleum* **9**
picado/a *chopped* 10
picante *spicy* 8
picar *to chop* 10
el pico *peak* 14
el pie *foot* 2, 6, **11**
la piel *skin* 11
la pierna *leg* 6, **11,** 12
el pijama *pajamas* 6
la píldora anticonceptiva *birth control pill* 15
la pileta *pool* 7
la pimienta *pepper* 10; *ground pepper* 10; **roja** *cayenne* 10
el pimiento *pepper (vegetable);* **rojo** *red bell pepper* 10 ; **verde** *green pepper* **10**
pintar *to paint* 13
el/la pintor/a *painter* **13**
la pintura *painting* **13**
la piña *pineapple* **10**
piscina *swimming pool* **5, 7**
el piso *floor* ***4, 5;*** *apartment* **5**
la pista *slope; court; track* **7**
pitar *to whistle* **7**
el/la piyama *pajamas* **6**
la pizarra *chalkboard* **P**
la placa *license plate* **12**
planchar *to iron* **5**
el planeta *planet* **15**
la planta baja *first floor, ground floor* **5**; *lobby* 4
la plata *silver* **6**
el plátano/la banana *banana, plantain* **10**
el plato *plate* **5,** *dish* **5, 10**
la playa *beach 1*
la plaza *plaza, square 1*
el/la plomero/a *plumber* **9**
la población *population* **14**
pobre *poor* **2**
la pobreza *poverty* **14**
poco después *shortly after* 4
poder (ue) *to be able to, can* **4,** 7, 9, 10, 15
el poema *poem* **13**
la poesía *poetry* **13**
el/la poeta *poet* **13**
polaco/a *Polish* **2**
polémico/a *controversial* 7
el/la policía *policeman/woman* **9**
políglota *polyglot, multilingual* **14**
la pollera *skirt* 6
el pollo *chicken* **3**
poner (g) *to put* 4, 10, 15
poner (la tele) (g) *to turn on (the TV)* ***3***
poner la mesa (g) *to set the table* **3**
poner una película *to show a movie* **3**
ponerse (g) la ropa *to put one's clothes on* **4**
popularizar (c) *to popularize* 13
por *along* 3; *for* 2, 3; *per* 1; *through* 3
por ciento *percent* **3**
por cierto *by the way* **9**
por ejemplo *for example* **3**
por eso *for this reason* **3**
por favor *please* **P**
por fin *at last* **3;** *finally* 15
por lo menos *at least* **3,** *5*
Por otro lado... *On the other hand . . .* 4, 11
por primera vez *for the first time* 3
por qué *why* 3
¿por qué? *why?* **1**
por supuesto *of course* 1, **3**

por último *finally* 4
Por un lado... *On the one hand . . .* 4, 11
el porcentaje *percentage* **14**
porque *because* **1, 3**
portugués/portuguesa *Portuguese* **2**
la posición *position* **P**
practicar *to practice* **1**
preceder *to precede* **14**
el precio *price* **6**
precioso/a *beautiful* **6**
preferir (ie) *to prefer* **4,** 7, 11
el premio *award, prize* **13**
prendas de vestir *articles of clothing* 6
preocupar(se) *to be worried* 11
preparar *to train* **7;** *to prepare* **8,** 11
el preparativo *preparation* **8**
la presentación *introduction* P
Presente. *Here (present).* P
el/la presidente/a *president* **14**
prestar *to lend* **6,** 13
el presupuesto *budget* 10
la primavera *spring* **6, 7**
el primer piso *second floor* 4
la primera clase *first class* **12**
la primera planta *second floor* 4
primer/primero/a *first* 4, **5,** 6
el primo/la prima *cousin* **4**
probar (ue) *to try, to taste* **10**
probarse (ue) *to try on* **6**
la procesión *procession* **8**
producir *produce* 15
el/la profesor/a *professor, teacher* **P,** 2, 4
el promedio *average* 8, **14**
prometedor/a *promising* **13**
promover *to promote* **15**
el pronóstico del tiempo *weather forecast* 7
propio/a *own* **9**
proponer (g) to propose 14
el propósito *purpose* **4**
protestar *to protest* 14
la próxima semana *next week* 3
la proximidad *proximity 14*
próximo/a *next* 5
el próximo mes/año *next month/year* 3
la psicología *psychology* **1**
el/la (p)sicólogo/a *psychologist* **9**
el pueblo *village* 5
el puerco *pork* 10
la puerta *door* **P; de salida** *departure gate* **12**
puertorriqueño/a *Puerto Rican* **2**
el puesto *position* **9**
el pulmón *lung* **11**
la pulsera *bracelet* **6**
el punto de vista *point of view* 11

Q

¿qué? *what?* Pr, **1**
¡Qué aburrido! *How boring!* 1, 3
¡Qué bien! *How nice!* 3
¡Qué casualidad! *What a coincidence!* 1
¿Qué día es hoy? *What day is today?* **P**
¡Qué divertido! *How funny!* 1, 3
¿Qué fecha es hoy? *What date is today?* **P**
¿Qué hay? *Hello? (on the telephone)* 3
¿Qué hora es? *What time is it?* **P**
¡Qué increíble! *That's unbelievable!* 1
¡Qué interesante! *That's so interesting!* 1, 3, 8
¡Qué lástima! *What a pity!* **1**
¡Qué lata! *What a nuisance!* 3
¡Qué maravilla! *How wonderful!* 3
¡Qué suerte! *How lucky!* 3
¿Qué tal? *What's up? What's new? (familiar)* **P,** 2
¿qué te parece? *what do you think?* **3**
¿Qué te/le(s) pasa? *What's wrong (with you/them)?* **11**
¿Qué tiempo hace? *What's the weather like?* **P**
quedar *to be left over; to fit;* **6;** *to leave something behind* 15;
quedar(se) *to stay* 11, 14
quejarse to complain 5, 7
querer (ie) *to want* 3, **4,** 7, 9, 11; to wish 3, 11; to love 8
querido/a *dear* 3
el queso *cheese* **3; crema** *cream cheese* **10**
¿Quién es...? *Who is . . . ?* **P**
¿quién(es)? *who?* **1**
la quinceañera *celebration for a girl's 15th birthday* 4
quinto/a *fifth* **5**
Quisiera... *I would like . . .* 3, 6
quitar(se) *to take away; to take off* **4**

R

el radiador *radiator* **12**
el/la radio *radio* **5**
rápido/a *fast* 3
la raqueta *racquet* **7**
el rasgo *trait* 14
la razón *reason* 4
realizar (c) *to carry out* **14**
realmente *actually* 9
la rebaja *sale* **6**
rebajado/a *marked down* **6**
la rebanada *slice* 10
la recepción *front desk* **12**
la receta *recipe* **10;** *prescription* **11**
recetar *to prescribe* **11**
reciclado/a *recycled* **15**
reclamar *to demand* 14
recoger (j) *to pick up* 3, **5**
recomendar (ie) *to recommend* **10,** 11
el reconocimiento *recognition* 7
recopilar *to compile* 14
recordar (ue) *to remember* 2, 4, **8**
recorrer *to travel, to cover (distance)* **7, 12**
el recuerdo *memory* **13**
los recuerdos *souvenirs* 6
los recursos *resources* **15**
la red *net* **7**
las redes sociales *social networks* 3
reducir *to reduce* 11
reflejar *to reflect* 5, **13**
el refrán *proverb* 12
el refresco *soda, soft drink* **3**
el refrigerador *refrigerator* **5**
regalar *to give (a present)* **6**
el regalo *gift* 3, *present* **6**
regar (ie) *to water* 5
regatear *to haggle* **6**
el régimen *regime* **14**
regular *fair* **P**
reír (i) *to laugh* 7
rellenar *fill out* **1**
relleno/a *filled* 10
el reloj *clock* **P**
el remedio *remedy, medicine* **11**
remunerado/a *paid* 9
el renacimiento *rebirth* 8
el rendimiento *performance* 9
reparar *to fix* 5
repetir (i) *to repeat* **4,** *7*
Repite./Repitan. *Repeat.* **P**
repoblar *to reforest* **15**
el repollo *cabbage* 6
la reserva natural *nature preserve* **15**
reservar *to make a reservation* 12
respetar(se) *to respect (each other)* 13
respirar *to breathe* **11**
responder *to respond* **1,** 9
el reto *challenge* **15**
retratar *to portray* **13**
la reunión *meeting, gathering* **3**
la revista *magazine* **3**
la revista del corazón *gossip magazine* **13**
rico/a *rich, wealthy* **2;** *delicious (food)* 6
el riel *rail* **15**
el robot *robot* **15**
rociar *to spray, to sprinkle* 8
rodear *to surround* **13**

la rodilla *knee* **11**
rojo/a *red* **2**
romper *to break* 10; *to tear* 15
la ropa clothes **6**
la ropa interior *underwear* **6**
rosado/a, rosa *pink* **2**
rubio/a *blond* **2**
la rueda *wheel* **12**
el ruido *noise* 8
las ruinas *ruins* 5

S

sábado *Saturday* P
la sábana *sheet* **5**
saber *to know* 3, 9
el sacacorchos *corkscrew* **10**
sacar buenas/malas notas *to get good/bad grades* **1**
sacar *to take out* 5, 6
el saco *blazer, jacket* ***6***
la sal *salt* **10**
la sala *living room* **5; de espera** *waiting room* **12**
la salida *departure* **12**
la salida de emergencia *emergency exit* **12**
salir *to go out* **3;** *to leave* **12**
el salón de clase *classroom* **P**
la salsa con queso *nacho cheese sauce* 10
la salsa de tomate *tomato sauce* **10**
saludable *healthful* 2, 10
saludar *to greet* **13**
el saludo *greeting* **P**
salvadoreño/a *Salvadoran* **2**
el sanatorio *hospital* 11
las sandalias *sandals* **6**
el sándwich *sandwich* **3**
la sangre *blood* **11**
el satélite *satellite* **15**
el saúco *elder* 11
Se me congeló la pantalla. *The screen froze up on me.* 15
Se me fue el alma a los pies. *My heart sank.* 15
Se me fue la lengua. *I gave myself away.* 15
Se me puso la piel de gallina. *I got goosebumps.* 15
la secadora *dryer* 5
secar(se) *to dry (oneself)* **4, 5**
seco/a *dry* **5**
seguir (i) *to follow, to go on* ***4,*** *7, 11*
seguir (i) derecho *to go straight* **12**
según *according to 4, 5; as* 14
segundo/a *second* **5**
la seguridad *security* 8
la semana *week* **P**
la semana pasada *last week* **6**
la semilla *seed* **8**
sentarse (ie) *to sit down 4*
el sentimiento *feeling* 3
sentir (ie, i) *to feel* **11;** *to be sorry* 11
sentir(se) (ie) *to feel* **4,** *7*
la señal *signal* **9**
el señor (Sr.) *Mr.* **P**
la señora (Sra.) *Ms., Mrs.* **P**
la señorita (Srta.) *Ms, Miss* **P**
septiembre *September* **P**
séptimo/a *seventh* **5**
ser *to be* **P, 2,** 6, 8, 10, 11, 12, 13, 15
ser aburrido/a *to be boring* 2
ser listo/a *to be clever, smart* 2
ser malo/a *to be bad/evil* 2
ser verde *to be green* 2
serio/a *serious* **11**
la servilleta *napkin* **10**
servir (i) *to serve* **4,** 7
sexto/a *sixth* **5**
si *if* **3**
sí *yes* **P**
siempre *always* **1, 8,** 12
Siga(n). *Come in.* 5
siguiente *following* 12
la silla *chair* **P, 5**
silvestre *wild* 10
el símbolo *symbol* **13**
simpático/a *nice, charming* **2**
sin embargo *nevertheless 1,* **9,** 6, 11
sin fines de lucro *non-profit 7*
sin nosotros/as *without us* 7
sin que *without* 14
sino que *but rather 1*
el síntoma *symptom* **11**
sobre *on, above* **P**
el sobrenombre *nickname* 5
sobrevivir *to survive* 9
la sobrina *niece* **4**
el sobrino *nephew* **4**
la sociología *sociology* **1**
el sofá *sofa* **5**
solicitar *to apply (for)* 9
la solicitud *application* **9**
solo *only* **1,** 2
soltero/a *single* **2;** *unmarried* 5
el sombrero *hat* **6**
la sopa *soup* **3**
la sorpresa *surprise* 4
el sostén *bra* **6**
el sótano *basement* 5
soy *I am* **P**
su(s) *your (formal), his, her, its, their* **2**
suave *soft* 8
subir *upload* 9
subir a *to get into* 15
subir de peso *to gain weight* 3
subrayar *to underline* 15
sucio/a *dirty* **5**
la sucursal *branch (business)* **14**
la sudadera *sweatshirt; jogging suit* **6**
el sueldo *salary, wage* **9**
el suéter *sweater* **6**
sugerir (ie) *to suggest* 11
el supermercado *supermarket* **6**
surgir (j) *to emerge* **13**
surrealista *surrealist* **13**
sustentar *to support* 12

T

la tableta *tablet* **P, 15**
la tala *felling* 15
la talla *size (clothes)* **6**
los tallarines *spaghetti* **3**
el taller *workshop* 9
los tamales *tamales* **3**
el tamaño *size* 6
también *also* **1**; *also, too 12*
tampoco *neither, not* 12
tan bien como *as well as* 8
tan bueno/a como *as good as* 8
tan pronto (como) *as soon as* 14
tan... como *as . . . as* 8
tanto/a... como *as much . . . as* 8
tapar *to cover* **10**
tarde *late* **4**
la tarea *homework 1*
La tarea, por favor. *Homework please.* **P**
la tarjeta de crédito *credit card* **6; de embarque** *boarding pass*; **magnética** *key card* **12**
la tarta de manzana *apple pie* 10
la tasa *rate* **14**
la taza *cup* **10**
te gusta(n) *you (familiar) like* **2**
el té *tea* **3**
el teatro *theater* 8
el/la técnico/a *technician* **9**
la tela *fabric* **6**
el teléfono *telephone* **3; celular/ móvil** *cell pone* 15
el televisor *television set* **P**
el tema *topic* 4; *theme* **13**
temer *to fear* **11**
temprano *early* **4**
tender (ie) *to hang (clothes)* **5**
el tenedor *fork* **10**
tener (g, ie) *to have* **4,** *7, 10, 11, 12, 13, 14, 15*
tener calor *to be hot* **5**
tener cuidado *to be careful* **5**
tener dolor de... *to have a(n) ... ache* **11**
tener éxito *to be successful* 10, **13**
tener frío *to be cold* **5**
tener hambre *to be hungry* **5**

tener la palabra *to have the floor* 15
tener mala cara *to look terrible* **11**
tener miedo *to be afraid* **5**
tener prisa *to be in a hurry* **5**
tener que *to have to* **4**
tener razón *to be right* **5**
tener sed *to be thirsty* **5**
tener sueño *to be sleepy* **5**
tener suerte *to be lucky* **5**
tener tiempo *to have time* 3
tener... años *to be . . . years old* 5
tengo/tienes *I have/you have* **1**
Tengo... años. *I am ... years old.* **2**
el tenis *tennis* **7**
el/la tenista *tennis player* **7**
la tensión/la presión (arterial) *(blood) pressure* **11**
tercer/tercero/a *third* **5**
terminar *to finish* **4,** 6, 10, 14
el termómetro *thermometer* **11**
la terraza *deck, balcony* **5**
el terreno *land* **9**
la tía *aunt* **4**
el tiburón *shark* 5
el tiempo *weather* **7**
el tiempo libre *free time* ***3***
la tienda *store* **6**; *tent* 12
la tienda de 24 horas *convenience store* 10
la tienda de conveniencia *convenience store* 10
la tienda de gasolinera *convenience store* 10
la tienda de la esquina o del barrio *convenience store* 10
tiene *he/she has; you (formal) have* **2**
¿Tienen preguntas?/¿Tienes preguntas? *Do you have any questions?* **P**
la tierra *land, soil* **15**
tímido/a *shy* 4
la tina *bathtab* 5
la tintorería *dry cleaner* 14
el tío *uncle* **4**
típico/a *typical* 3
titular(se) *to be called* **13**
el título *degree* 14
la toalla *towel* **5**
el tobillo *ankle* **11**
el toca DVD *DVD player* **P**
tocar (un instrumento) *to play (an instrument)* **3**
todas las semanas *every week* **1**
todavía *still, yet* **10**
todo *everything* 12
todos los días *every day* **1**
todos los meses *every month* **1**
todos/as *everybody* **2;** *all* 12
tomar *to drink* 3, 11; *to take, to drink* **1,** 10
tomar apuntes/notas *to take notes* **1**
tomar asiento *to have/take a seat 9*
tomar el sol *to sunbathe* **3**
el tomate *tomato* **3**
tonto/a *silly, foolish* **2**
torcer(se) (ue) *to twist* **11**
el torero *bullfighter* 2
el torneo *tournament* 7
el toro *bull* **8**
la toronja/el pomelo *grapefruit* **10**
la tos *cough* **11**
toser *to cough* **11**
trabajador/a *hardworking* **2**
trabajar *to work* **1,** *10, 14*
trabajo *job 1*
el trabajo *work* **5**
la tradición *tradition* **8**
traducir (zc) *to translate* 7, 7
traer (j) *to bring* **3,** 7, 11, 13
el tráfico de drogas *drug trafficking* **14**
el traje *suit* **6; de baño** *bathing suit* **6**
el tramo *stretch* 12
el tratado *treaty* 15
tratar *to treat, be about* **11, 13;** to try 5, 10
trazado/a *drawn* 3
el tren *train* **12**
trigo *wheat* 2
trigueño/a *of lightbrown skin color* 2
triste *sad* **2,** 11, 15
tropezarse *to stumble* 15
tú *you (familiar)* **P,** Pr
tú *you (familiar)* **P**
tu(s) *your (familiar)* **P**
tu(s) *your (familiar)* 2
turnarse *to take turns* 4
Túrnense. *Take turns* **P**

U

la ubicación *location* 4, 5
último/a *last* **8**
un/una *a, an* **P,** 1
Un cordial saludo. *Yours; Sincerely* 4
un poco *a little* **4**
una semana atrás *a week ago* **6**
una vez *once* 3, **12**
unificar (qu) *to unify* 15
la universidad *university* **1**
unos/as *some* **1**
unos/unas *some (plural)* 1
urgente *urgent* 11
uruguayo/a *Uruguayan* **2**
usar *to use* **2,** 15
usted *you (formal)* **P**
ustedes *you (plural)* **1**
útil *useful* **P**
la uva *grape* **10**

V

las vacaciones *vacation* **3**
la vacante *opening* **9**
vacío/a *empty* **12**
la vainilla *vanilla* **10**
valer (g) *to be worth* **6**
los vaqueros/los jeans *jeans* **6**
el vaso *glass* 3, **10**
Vayan a la pizarra./Ve a la pizarra. *Go to the board.* P
el/la vecino/a *neighbor* 5
el vegetal/la verdura *vegetable* **3, 10**
la velocidad *speed* **12**
¡Ven/Anda, anímate! *Come on, cheer up!* 3
la vena *vein* **11**
el/la vendedor/a *salesman, saleswoman* **9**
vender *to sell* **6,** 13
venerar *to worship* 8
venezolano/a *Venezuelan* 2
venir (g, ie) *to come* **4,** 7, 8
la ventaja *advantage* **5**
la ventana *window* **P**
las ventas *sales* ***9***
ver *to see* **1,** 10, 13
ver(se) *to look* 6
el verano *summer* **6, 7**
el verbo *verb* **P**
¿verdad? *don't you?, right?* **1**
verde *green* 2; *unripe* 6
el verso *line (poem)* **13**
el vestido *dress* **6**
vestir(se) (i) *to dress; to get dressed* 4, 7
vestuario *lockerroom* 7
el/la veterinario/a *vet* 9
viajar *to travel* **12,** 13
viaje *trip* 3
la vida *life* 2
el videojuego *video game* **15**
viejo/a *old* **2,** 8
el viento *wind* 6
viernes *Friday* **P**
el vinagre *vinegar* **10**
el vino *wine* **3**
la viruela *smallpox* 11
virtualmente *virtually* **15**
visitar *to visit* ***4***
la vista *view* **5**
viudo/a *widower; widow* 4
la vivienda *housing* **5**
vivir *to live* **1,** 8, 5, 10
vivo/a *lively (personality); alive* 6
volador/a *flying* **15**

el volante *steering wheel* **12**
volar (ue) *to fly* 6
el vóleibol/volibol *volleyball* **7**
volver (ue) *to return* **4,** 6, 10,
vosotros/as *you (familiar, plural)* **1**
votar *to vote* 14
la voz *voice* **13**
el vuelo *flight* **12**
vuestro(s), vuestra(s) *your (familiar plural)* 2

Y

y *and* **P**
yuca frita *fried yuca* **3**
Y tú, ¿cómo te llamas? *And what is your name?* **P**
ya *already* **10**
ya que since 5
yo *I* **P**
el yogur *yogurt* **10**

Z

la zanahoria *carrot* **10**
las zapatillas *slippers* **6; de deporte** *tennis shoes* **6**
los zapatos *shoes*; **de tacón** *highheeled shoes* **6**
el zarcillo *earring* 6
la zona *area* **5**
la zona peatonal *pedestrian area* 10

Appendix 4

English-Spanish Glossary

A

a little un poco
a lot (adv.) mucho
a week ago una semana atrás
a week ago una semana atrás
a, an un/una
A.M. (from midnight to noon) de la mañana
to abandon abandonar
to abound abundar
about más o menos
above sobre
absolutely not de ninguna manera
access el acceso
accessory el accesorio
to accompany acompañar
to accomplish lograr
according to según, de acuerdo con
accountant el/la contador/a , el/la contable *(Spain)*
to ache doler
actor/actress el actor/la actriz
actually en realidad
actually realmente
ad el anuncio
adaptation la adaptación
to add agregar/añadir
adjustment la adaptación
to advance avanzar
advance el adelanto
advantage la ventaja
advertisement el anuncio
advice el consejo
to advise aconsejar
adviser el/la consejero/a
affectionately con cariño
after después (de) que
after después, luego
again otra vez
ago hace
to agree concordar; estar de acuerdo; haber consenso
agricultural agrícola
air conditioning el aire acondicionado
air-conditioned climatizado/a
airline la aerolínea, la línea aérea
aisle seat el asiento de pasillo
alive vivo/a
all todos/as
allergy la alergia
to allow permitir
almost casi
alone solo/a
along por
already ya
also también
although aunque
always siempre
among entre
ample amplio/a
amusement park el parque de atracciones
amusing divertido/a
ancestor el antepasado
And what is your name? Y tú, ¿cómo te llamas?
and y
angry enojado/a
ankle el tobillo
another otro/a
to answer contestar
anthropology la antropología
antibiotic el antibiótico
anxiety la ansiedad
any algún, alguno (-os, -as)
anyone alguien
anything algo
apartment el apartamento, el departamento, el piso *(Spain)*
to apologize disculparse
apple la manzana
apple pie la tarta de manzana
appliances los electrodomésticos
application la solicitud
to apply (for) solicitar
April abril
architect el/la arquitecto/a
architecture la arquitectura
area la zona
Argentinian argentino/a
to argue discutir, pelear
arm el brazo
armchair la butaca
armoire el armario, el clóset
arrival la llegada
to arrive llegar
articles of clothing prendas de vestir
as . . . as tan... como
as good as tan bueno/a como
as if como si
as much . . . as tanto/a... como
as según
as soon as en cuanto
as soon as tan pronto (como)
as though como si
as well as tan bien como
to ask for pedir
asthma el asma
at a
at last por fin
at least por lo menos
at the back al fondo
at the present time actualmente, en la actualidad
at times a veces
At what time is it? A qué hora es?
ATM el cajero automático
attachment, attached document el documento adjunto
to attend asistir
August agosto
aunt la tía
avenue la avenida
average el promedio
average height de estatura mediana
avocado el aguacate, la palta
avoid evitar
award el premio

B

back la espalda
background information la información de fondo
backpack la mochila
bad malo/a
badly parked mal aparcado
balcony la terraza
ball el balón, la pelota/bola
ballpoint pen el bolígrafo
banana el banano *(Colom.)*, la banana *(Urug.)*, el plátano *(Spain)*, el cambur *(Venez.)*
bank el banco
baptism el bautizo

barbecue pit; barbecue (event) la barbacoa
barbershop la peluquería
bargain la ganga
baseball el béisbol
basement el sótano
basin (river) la cuenca
basket el cesto/la cesta
basketball el baloncesto/básquetbol
bat el bate
to bathe bañar
bathing suit el traje de baño
bathroom el baño
bathroom sink el lavabo
bathtub la bañera, la bañadera, la tina
to be ser; estar
to be . . . years old tener... años
to be a blackout irse la luz
to be able to, can poder
to be about tratar
to be afraid tener miedo
to be angry estar enojado/a
to be bad/evil ser malo/a
to be bored estar aburrido/a
to be boring ser aburrido/a
to be born nacer
to be called lamarse
to be called titularse
to be clever ser listo/a
to be careful tener cuidado
to be cold tener frío
to be fashionable estar de moda
to be glad (about) alegrarse (de)
to be green ser verde
to be happy estar contento/a
to be hot tener calor
to be hungry tener hambre
to be ill estar malo/a
to be in a hurry tener prisa
to be left over quedar
to be liked caer simpático
to be lucky tener suerte
to be not ripe estar verde
to be pleasing fascinar
to be pleasing to gustar
to be ready estar listo/a
to be right tener razón
to be sleepy tener sueño
to be smart ser listo/a
to be sorry sentir, lamentar
to be successful tener éxito
to be thirsty tener sed
to be tired estar cansado/a
to be worried preocuparse
to be worth valer
beach la playa
bead la cuenta
beans los frijoles
to beat batir
beautiful precioso/a
beauty item el artículo de belleza
beauty salon la peluquería
because porque
to become hacerse
to become independent independizarse
bed la cama
bedroom el cuarto
beef la carne de res
beer la cerveza
before antes, antes (de) que
to begin comenzar, empezar
beginning el comienzo
behavior el comportamiento
behind detrás (de)
to believe creer
bell chime la campanada
belt el cinturón
besides además
better than mejor que
between entre
bicycle la bicicleta
big grande
bilingual bilingüe
birth control pill la píldora anticonceptiva
birthday el cumpleaños
black negro/a
blanket la manta, la cobija, la frazada
blazer el saco
blond rubio/a
blood la sangre
blouse la blusa
blue azul
boarding pass la tarjeta de embarque
body el cuerpo
to boil hervir
Bolivian boliviano/a
bone el hueso
book el libro
bookstore la librería
boots las botas
boring aburrido/a
boss el/la jefe/a
to bother, be bothered by molestar
bottle la botella
to bowl jugar a los bolos, jugar (al) boliche, ir de bowling
bowl la fuente
boxer shorts los calzoncillos
boy el chico
boyfriend el novio
bra el sostén
bracelet la pulsera
brain el cerebro
branch (business) la sucursal
brand, brandname la marca
bread el pan
to break fracturarse; romper; descomponerse
to break down descomponerse
breakfast el desayuno
to breathe respirar
briefcase el maletín
to bring traer
brother el hermano
brown marrón, café, carmelita, castaño/a, pardo/a
brunette moreno/a
budget el presupuesto
to build construir
building el edificio
bull el toro
bullfight la corrida de toros
bullfighter el torero
bun, small cake el pan dulce
to bury enterrar
bus el autobús/bus, el camión *(Mex.)*, el colectivo *(Arg.)*, el micro *(Chile)*, el bus/la guagua *(P.R., Cuba)*, la chiva *(Colom.)*, el ómnibus *(Peru)*
businessman el hombre de negocios
businesswoman la mujer de negocios
busy ocupado/a
but pero
but rather sino que
butter la manteca/mantequilla
to buy comprar
by the way por cierto

C

cabbage el repollo
cafe el café
cafeteria la cafetería
cake el pastel
calculator la calculadora
Canadian canadiense
to cancel cancelar
candied figs el dulce de higos
candy/sweets el dulce
cap la gorra
capsule la cápsula
car el auto/carro/coche
careful cuidado
carnival el carnaval
carpenter el/la carpintero/a
carpet la alfombra
carrot la zanahoria
to carry out realizar
cart la carreta
cashier el/la cajero/a
cast elenco
cattle el ganado
cayenne la pimienta roja

to celebrate celebrar
celebration (public) el festival
celebration for a girl's 15th birthday la quinceañera
celebration la celebración/fiesta
celebration la festividad, la fiesta
cell phone el teléfono móvil/celular, el móvil/celular/cel
cemetery el cementerio
center el centro
cereal el cereal
chair la silla
chalkboard la pizarra
challenge el reto, el desafío
chamomile la manzanilla
champion el campeón/la campeona
championship el campeonato
to change cambiar
change el cambio
charger el cargador
charming simpático/a
cheap barato/a
to check in (luggage) facturar
cheek la mejilla
cheese el queso
chef el/la chef
cherry la cereza
chest el pecho
chicken el pollo
chicken breast la pechuga de pollo
to achieve lograr
child el niño/la niña
childhood la infancia
children's infantil
Chilean chileno/a
Chinese chino/a
to choose elegir, escoger
to chop picar
chop la chuleta
chopped picado/a
christening el bautizo
Christmas Eve la Nochebuena
Christmas la Navidad
church la iglesia
Cinderella Cenicienta
cinnamon la canela
city block la cuadra
city council el concejo municipal
city la ciudad
clam la almeja
classmate el/la compañero/a
classroom el salón de clase
claw la garra
to clean limpiar
clean limpio/a
clever listo/a
client el/la cliente/a
clinic la clínica, el centro de salud, el sanatorio
clock el reloj
clock el reloj
cloning la clonación
close (to) cerca (de)
to close cerrar
closet el clóset, el armario
clothes la ropa
clove of garlic el diente de ajo
coach el/la entrenador/a
coat el abrigo
coconut milk la leche de coco
coffee el café
coffee shop el café
cold el catarro
cold el frío; **(adj.)** frío/a
Colombian colombiano/a
color el color
to comb (one's hair) peinar(se)
Come in. Pase(n). Adelante. Siga(n). *(Colomb.)*
Come on, cheer up! ¡Ven/Anda, anímate!
to come venir
comfortable cómodo/a
commonwealth el estado libre asociado
communication la comunicación
company (dance, theater) la compañía (de danza, de teatro)
company la compañía, la empresa
to compile recopilar
to complain quejarse
computer la computadora, el computador, el ordenador *(Spain)*
computer science la computación, la informática *(Spain)*
conclusion la conclusión
to congratulate felicitar
congratulations las felicidades
Congress la Cámara de Representantes
to connect conectarse
to connect to conectarse a
consensus el consenso
to consume consumir
contact lenses los lentes de contacto
contest el certamen, el concurso
to continue continuar
to contract contraer
contractor el/la contratista
to contribute contribuir
to control controlar
controversial polémico/a
convenience store la tienda de conveniencia *(Mex.),* de gasolinera *(C.R.),* de la esquina/del barrio, de 24 horas *(Spain)*
to converse conversar
to cook cocinar
cookie la galleta
corkscrew el sacacorchos
corn el maíz, el elote *(Mex./Central America),* choclo *(South America)*
corner la esquina
corridor el pasillo
to cost costar
Costa Rican costarricense
cough la tos
to cough toser
to count contar
counter el mostrador
country el país
countryside el campo
couple la pareja
court la pista
court (golf) la cancha
courtesy la cortesía
cousin el/la primo/a
to cover cubrir; tapar; **(distance)** recorrer
craftsman/woman, craftsperson el/la artesano/a
cream cheese el queso crema
cream la crema
to create crear
credit card la tarjeta de crédito
cruise el crucero
to crush machacar
to cry llorar
Cuban cubano/a
cubist cubista
cucumber el pepino
to cultivate cultivar
cumin el comino
cup la taza
to cure curar
current actual
current la corriente
curtain la cortina
custom la costumbre
customs la aduana; **agent** el/la inspector/a de aduana
to cut cortar
cycling el ciclismo
cyclist el/la ciclista

D

dad el papá
daddy el papi/papito
dairy (product) lácteo/a
to dance bailar
dance club la discoteca
dancer el bailarín/la bailarina
danger el peligro
to dare atreverse
dark oscuro/a

darse cuenta to realize
data los datos
daughter la hija
day before yesterday anteayer
day el día
dead difunto/a, muerto/a
dear estimado/a; querido/a; mi amor/ vida/corazón *(terms of endearment)*
deceased muerto/a
December diciembre
deck la terraza
decorated adornado/a
to dedicate dedicar
to defend defender
deforestation la deforestación
degree el título
delicious rico/a
description la descripción
to delight encantar
to demand exigir; reclamar
democracy la democracia
to denounce denunciar
dentistry la odontología
department store el almacén
departure la salida
depressed deprimido/a
to describe describir
design el diseño
desk el escritorio
despite a pesar de
to develop desarrollar; contruir
development el desarrollo
dictatorial dictatorial
dictatorship dictadura
dictionary el diccionario
to die morir
difficult difícil
dining room el comedor
dinner la cena
dinner la comida
to direct dirigir
dirty sucio/a
disadvantage la desventaja
disappearance la desaparición
to disassemble desarmar
discovery el descubrimiento
dish el plato
dish of marinated raw fish el ceviche
dishwasher el lavaplatos
to dislike caer mal
dispersal la diseminación
displacement el desplazamiento
disposable desechable
to disseminate difundir
dissemination la diseminación
to dissolve deshacer
to distinguish distinguir
diversification la diversificación
divorced divorciado/a
to do hacer
Do you have any questions? ¿Tienen preguntas?/¿Tienes preguntas?
Do you understand? ¿Comprenden?/¿Comprendes?
doctor (primary care) el/la médico/a de familia/de cabecera; el/la doctor/a
dog el/la perro/a
Dominican dominicano/a
don't you? ¿verdad?
door la puerta
dots de lunares
double room la habitación doble
doubt la duda
to download bajar
downtown el centro
drawing el dibujo
drawn trazado/a
dress el vestido
to dress; to get dressed vestir(se)
dresser la cómoda
to drink beber, tomar
drink la bebida
to drive manejar
driver el/la chofer
driver's license la licencia de conducir
drug trafficking el tráfico de drogas
to dry (oneself) secar(se)
to dry clean limpiar en seco
dry cleaner la tintorería
dry seco/a
dryer la secadora
due to debido a
to duplicate duplicar
during durante
DVD el DVD
DVD player el toca DVD

E

each cada
each day cada día
ear (inner) el oído
ear (outer) la oreja
ear la oreja
early temprano
to earn ganar
earring el arete, el aro, el pendiente, el zarcillo, la pantalla
Easter la Pascua
easy fácil
to eat comer
economic económico/a
economics economía
Ecuadorian ecuatoriano/a
efficiency la eficiencia
egg el huevo
eighth octavo
either ... or o... o
elbow el codo
elder (herb) el saúco
to elect elegir
election la elección
electrician el/la electricista
elevator el ascensor
to embrace abrazar(se)
to emerge surgir
emergency exit la salida de emergencia
emergency la emergencia
emigrant el/la emigrante
to emigrate emigrar
emigration la emigración
employee el/la empleado/a
empty vacío/a
encounter el encuentro
energetic enérgico/a
engagement el compromiso
engineer el/la ingeniero/a
to enjoy disfrutar, divertirse
to enter entrar en
entertainment la diversión
environment el medio ambiente
equality la igualdad
equipment el equipo
eraser el borrador
ethnicity la etnia
even hasta
even if, even though aunque
event el acontecimiento
event el festival
ever alguna vez
every ... hours cada... horas
every day todos los días
every month todos los meses
every week todas las semanas
everybody todos/as
everyday cotidiano/a
everything todo
to examine examinar
excellent excelente
to exchange cambiar
exchange el intercambio
excuse me perdón; con permiso
executive el/la ejecutivo/a
expensive caro/a
experience la experiencia
to explain explicar
to exploit explotar
export la exportación
expression la expresión
extinction la extinción
to extinguish apagar, extinguir
extinguished extinguido/a
extroverted extrovertido/a
eye el ojo
eyebrow la ceja
eyelash la pestaña

F

fabric la tela
fabulous estupendo, fabuloso/a
face la cara
fact el hecho
failure el fracaso
fair regular
faithfully fielmente
to fall asleep dormirse
to fall caer(se)
fall el otoño
false falso/a
family la familia
fan (admirer) el/la hincha
fan el ventilador
far (from) lejos (de)
farm la finca
farmer el/la agricultor/a
farming la agricultura
to fascinate fascinar
fast rápido/a
fat gordo/a
father el padre
Father's Day el Día del Padre
favorite favorito/a
to fear temer
February febrero
to feed dar de comer
to feel sentir(se)
feeling el sentimiento
felling la tala
festival el festival
festivity (public) la festividad, la fiesta
fever la fiebre
fiancé/fiancée el novio/la novia
field el campo
field hockey el hockey sobre hierba
fifth quinto/a
fight la lucha
to fight luchar
to fill (out) llenar, rellenar
filled relleno/a
film la película
filmmaker el/la cineasta
filth la inmundicia
finally finalmente; por fin; por último
to find encontrar
to find out enterarse, averiguar
fine la multa
finger el dedo
to finish terminar
to fire despedir
fire el incendio
firefighter el/la bombero/a
fireplace la chimenea
fireworks los fuegos artificiales
first class la primera clase
first floor la planta baja
first primer/o/a, primer
fish el pescado
to fit quedar
to fix reparar
flag la bandera
flashers las luces intermitentes
flight attendant el/la auxiliar de vuelo, el/la azafato/a *(Spain),* el/la aeromozo/a *(Latin Am.)*
flight el vuelo
float (in a parade) la carroza
flood la inundación
floor el piso
flour la harina
flower la flor
flu la gripe
to fly volar
flying volador/a
to focus enfocarse, fijarse
to fold doblar
to follow seguir
following siguiente
food la comida
foolish tonto/a
foot (in animals) la pata
foot el pie
football el fútbol (americano)
footwear el calzado
for por, para
for example por ejemplo
for me para mí
for the first time por primera vez
for this reason por eso
for you (familiar) para ti
forehead la frente
forest el bosque
to forget olvidar
fork el tenedor
founding (noun) la fundación
fourth cuarto
fowl las aves
to fracture fracturarse
free time el tiempo libre
freedom la libertad
freedom of expression la libertad de expresión
freeway la autopista
to freeze congelar(se)
French francés/francesa
French fries las papas fritas
frequency la frecuencia
frequently frecuentemente
Friday viernes
fried frito/a
fried dough los churros
fried yuca yuca frita
friend el/la amigo/a
friendship la amistad
from de
front desk la recepción
fruit la fruta
to fry freír
to fulfill cumplir
full lleno/a
fun, funny divertido/a
furniture los muebles
furthermore además

G

to gain weight subir de peso
game el juego/el partido
games console la consola de videojuegos
garage el garaje
garbage la basura
garbanzo beans los garbanzos
garden el jardín
garlic el ajo
gate (departure) la puerta (de salida)
gathering la reunión
generally generalmente
genetically genéticamente
geography la geografía
German alemán/alemana
gesture el ademán
to get angry enfadarse
to get bored aburrirse
to get good/bad grades sacar buenas/malas notas
to get into subir a
to get lost perderse
to get married casarse
to get up levantarse
to get up on the wrong side of the bed levantarse con el pie izquierdo
ghost el fantasma
gift el regalo
girl la chica
to give (a present) dar, regalar
to give a shower to duchar
to give dar
glad contento/a, alegre
glass (stemmed) la copa
glass el vaso
glove compartment la guantera
glove el guante
Go to the board. Vayan a la pizarra. *(plural);* Ve a la pizarra. *(sing./fam.)*
to go ir
to go away irse
to go in entrar en
to go on seguir
to go out for tapas ir de tapas
to go out salir
to go paragliding hacer parapente
to go shopping ir de compras
to go straight seguir derecho

to go to bed acostarse
to go well with... ir bien con...
goal el gol
godchild el/la ahijado/a
godfather el padrino
godmother la madrina
gold el oro
golf clubs los palos
golf course la cancha de golf
golf el golf
good bueno/a
Good afternoon. Buenas tardes.
Good evening. Buenas tardes.
Good luck! ¡Buena suerte!
Good morning. Buenos días.
Good night. Buenas noches.
good-bye adiós, chao (chau)
good-looking guapo/a
gossip magazine la revista del corazón
to govern gobernar
government el gobierno
to graduate graduarse
granddaughter la nieta
grandfather el abuelo
grandmother la abuela
grandson el nieto
grape la uva
grapefruit la toronja, el pomelo
grass el césped
gray gris
great magnífico/a
green verde
green pepper el pimiento verde
to greet saludar
greeting el saludo
to grind moler
ground floor la planta baja
ground meat la carne molida
ground pepper la pimienta
group dressed in similar costumes la comparsa
to grow crecer
to grow cultivar
Guatemalan guatemalteco/a
guess la adivinanza
to guess adivinar
guide la guía
guinea pig el cuy
guitar la guitarra
guitar player el/la guitarrista
gymnasium el gimnasio
gypsy el gitano

H

to haggle regatear
hair el cabello, el pelo
hairdresser el/la peluquero/a
half la mitad
half-brother el medio hermano
half-sister la media hermana
hall el pasillo
Halloween el Día de las Brujas
ham el jamón
hamburger la hamburguesa
to hand dar
hand la mano
handicrafts la artesanía
handkerchief el pañuelo
handsome guapo, bien parecido, buen mozo
to hang (clothes) tender
to happen pasar
happy, alegre, contento/a
hard-working trabajador/a
harmful dañino/a
harp el arpa
to harvest cosechar
hat el sombrero
to hate odiar
to have tener
to have a good time pasar (muy) bien
to have a(n) ... ache tener dolor de...
to have a seat tomar asiento
to have breakfast desayunar
to have dinner cenar
to have fun divertirse
to have lunch almorzar
to have the floor tener la palabra
to have time tener tiempo
to have to tener que
hazard lights las luces intermitentes
he él
he/she has; you (formal) have tiene
head la cabeza
healthful saludable
healthy saludable
heart el corazón
heating la calefacción
hello hola
Hello? (on the telephone) ¿Diga?/¿Dígame? *(Spain),* ¡Bueno! *(Mex.),* ¿Aló? *(Arg., Peru, Chile),* ¡Oigo!/¿Qué hay? *(Cuba)*
helmet el casco
to help (a customer) atender
to help ayudar
her su(s)
herbs las hierbas
Here (present). Presente.
herself a sí mismo/a(s)
Hey! ¡Oye!
hi hola
highheeled shoes los zapatos de tacón
highlighter el marcador, el rotulador
highway la carretera
himself a sí mismo/a(s)
hip la cadera
his su(s)
Hispanic hispano/a
history la historia
to hold coger
hole el agujero
holiday (legal) el día feriado
holiday el día festivo, la festividad, la fiesta
homage el homenaje
home la casa
homework la tarea
Homework please. La tarea, por favor.
Honduran hondureño/a
honesty la honestidad
honeymoon la luna de miel
hood el capó
hoop el cesto/la cesta
horseback a caballo
hospital el hospital, el sanatorio, la clínica
hot caliente
house la casa
housewife, homemaker el ama/o de casa
housing la vivienda
How are you? (formal) ¿Cómo está?
How are you? (informal) ¿Cómo estás?
How boring! ¡Qué aburrido!
How do you say. . . in Spanish? ¿Cómo se dice... en español?
How fun!/How funny! ¡Qué divertido!
How interesting! ¡Qué interesante!
How is it going? ¿Cómo te va?
How long has it been since. . .? ¿Cuánto tiempo hace que...?
How lucky! ¡Qué suerte!
how many? ¿cuántos/as?
How many classes do you have? ¿Cuántas clases tienes?
How may I help you? ¿En qué puedo servirle(s)?
How much is it? ¿Cuánto cuesta?
how much? ¿cuánto/a?
How nice! ¡Qué bien!
how often con qué frecuencia
How wonderful! ¡Qué maravilla!
how? ¿cómo?
however no obstante, sin embargo
hug el abrazo
humanities las humanidades
humpback whale la ballena jorobada
hundred cien/ciento
to hurt doler
to hurt oneself hacerse daño
husband el esposo, el marido

I

I yo
I am soy
I am ... years old. Tengo... años.

I don't know. No sé.
I don't understand. No comprendo.
I gave myself away. Se me fue la lengua.
I got goosebumps. Se me puso la piel de gallina.
I have tengo
I hope that . . . Ojalá que...
I like me gusta(n)
I would like ... Quisiera/ Me gustaría...
I'm sorry (to hear that) lo siento
ice cream el helado
ice el hielo
if si
ill person el/la enfermo/a
illiteracy el analfabetismo
illiterate analfabeto/a
illness la enfermedad
immediately enseguida
immigrant el/la inmigrante
immigration la inmigración
to improve mejorar
in addition además
in contrast . . . en contraste...
in en
in fact en realidad, realmente
in front of enfrente (de)
in order (to) para
in search of en busca de
in the rear al fondo
inappropriate inapropiado/a
including hasta
inexpensive barato/a
infection la infección
to influence influir
infrastructure la infraestructura
inhabitant el/la habitante
injection la inyección
to insert meter
to inspect revisar
instead of en vez de
integrated circuit el chip electrónico
to interest interesar
interesting interesante
interpreter el/la intérprete
to interrupt interrumpir
to interview (each other) entrevistar(se)
interview la entrevista
introduction la presentación
to invest invertir
invitation la invitación
to invite invitar
iron el hierro
to iron planchar
isn't it? ¿no?
it has been a day/month/year since hace un día/mes/año (que)
It is (time of the day). Es la/Son las (hora del día).
it's clear está despejado
it's cloudy está nublado
it's cool hace fresco
it's raining llueve, está lloviendo
it's sunny hace sol
it's windy hace viento
It's been (time expression) since... Hace (+ expresión de tiempo) que... **4**
its su(s)

J

jacket el saco, la chaqueta
January enero
Japanese japonés/japonesa
jeans los vaqueros/jeans
jewel la joya
jeweller el/la joyero/a
job el trabajo
jogging suit la sudadera
journalist el/la periodista
joy la alegría
judge el/la juez
to juggle hacer malabarismo
juice el jugo
July julio
June junio
junk food la comida basura

K

to keep in shape estar en forma, mantenerse en forma
to keep silent guardar silencio
key card la tarjeta magnética
key la llave; la clave
to kill matar
kindless la amabilidad
kindly atentamente
kinship el parentesco
to kiss besar(se)
kiss el beso
kitchen la cocina
kitchen sink el fregadero
kite la cometa
knee la rodilla
knife el cuchillo
to know (each other) conocer(se)
to know conocer; saber
knowledge el conocimiento

L

lake el lago
lamb el cordero
lamp la lámpara
to land aterrizar
land el terreno (terrain); la tierra (ground, soil)
landscape el paisaje
laptop la computadora portátil
last último/a
to last durar
last night anoche
last week la semana pasada
last year/month el año/mes pasado
last último/a; por último
late tarde
later después, luego, más tarde
to laugh reír
laundry room la lavandería
law derecho
lawn el césped
lawyer el/la abogado/a
layout la distribución
lazy perezoso/a
leaf la hoja
to learn aprender
leather el cuero
to leave dejar; irse
to leave something behind quedar
leavetaking la despedida
left la izquierda
leg la pierna
legumes las legumbres
lemon el limón
to lend prestar
Lent la Cuaresma
lentils las lentejas
less . . . than menos... que
lettuce la lechuga
level el nivel
librarian el/la bibliotecario/a
library la biblioteca
license plate la placa
to lie down acostarse
life expectancy la esperanza de vida
life la vida
to lift weights levantar pesas
light(s) la luz (las luces)
to like gustar; caer bien
Likewise. Igualmente.
line (in a poem) el verso
link el enlace
lip el labio
to listen (to) escuchar; oír
Listen, please. Oiga, por favor.
literacy el alfabetismo
literature la literatura
lithium el litio
live en vivo
to live vivir
lively animado/a, vivo/a
living room la sala
lobby la planta baja
lobster la langosta

location la ubicación
to lock up encerrar
locker room el vestuario
lodging el alojamiento
long largo/a
to look at mirar
to look for buscar
to look inside asomarse
to look terrible tener mala cara
to look ver(se)
to lose perder
to lose weight bajar de peso
loss la pérdida
Louder, please. Más alto, por favor.
love el amor
to love querer; encantar
luggage el equipaje
lunch el almuerzo
lung el pulmón
luxury el lujo

M

magazine la revista
mail la correspondencia
main character el personaje principal
to maintain mantener
major la carrera
majority la mayoría
to make a reservation reservar
to make the bed hacer la cama
mallow la malva
man el hombre
manager, (sales) manager el/la gerente (de ventas)
many (adj.) mucho/a
many times muchas veces
map el mapa
March marzo
margarine la margarina
marked down rebajado/a
marker el marcador/el rotulador
market el mercado
marriage el matrimonio
married casado/a
marvelous maravilloso/a
marvelously estupendamente
material el material
May mayo
mayonnaise la mayonesa
meal la comida
meat la carne
medical doctor el/la médico/a
medication la pastilla
medicine el remedio; la medicina
medium height de estatura mediana
to meet conocer; **(each other)** conocer(se)
to meet (requirements) cumplir (requisites)
meeting la reunión
melody la melodía
melon el melón
melted derretido/a
memory el recuerdo
mess el desorden
message el mensaje
Mexican Independence Day el Día de la Independencia de México
Mexican mexicano/a
microsurgery le microcirugía
microwave (oven) el (horno de) microondas
middle class person el burgués/la burguesa
migration la migración
milk la leche
million millón
mine mi(s)
minority la minoría
minute el minuto
mirror el espejo
to miss extrañar
to miss out on perderse
mobile el móvil barato/a
mom la mamá
mommy la mami/mamita
Monday lunes
money el dinero
money (in cash) el dinero (en efectivo)
month el mes
mood el ánimo
more . . . than más... que
more or less más o menos
More slowly, please. Más despacio/ lento, por favor.
more than más de
morning la mañana
Moroccan marroquí
mortality la mortalidad
most (+ adj.) más (+ adj.)
mother la madre
Mother's Day el Día de la Madre
motor el motor
mouth la boca
to move mover(se); mudarse
movement el desplazamiento
movie la película
movies el cine
to mow (lawn) cortar
Mr. el señor (Sr.)
Ms, Miss la señorita (Srta.)
Ms., Mrs. la señora (Sra.)
much mucho/a
multilingual políglota
mural el mural
muralist el/la muralista
muscle el músculo
music la música
mustard la mostaza
my mi(s)
My heart sank. Se me fue el alma a los pies.
My name is... Me llamo...

N

nacho cheese sauce la salsa con queso
napkin la servilleta
narrow estrecho/a
nation el país
nationality la nacionalidad
native natal
nature la naturaleza
nature preserve la reserva natural
near cerca de
necessary necesario/a
neck el cuello
necklace el collar
to need necesitar
neglect el descuido
neighbor el/la vecino/a
neighborhood el barrio
neither . . . nor ni... ni
neither, not tampoco
nephew el sobrino
nerve el nervio
nervous nervioso/a
net la red
never (not ever) jamás, nunca
nevertheless sin embargo
new nuevo/a
New Year's Day el Año Nuevo
New Year's Eve la Nochevieja
news la noticia
newspaper el periódico
next month/year el próximo mes/año
next próximo/a
next to al lado (de)
next week la próxima semana
Nicaraguan nicaragüense
nice agradable, simpático/a
Nice to meet you. Mucho gusto.
nickname el sobrenombre
niece la sobrina
Nigerian nigeriano/a
nightgown el camisón
nightmare la pesadilla
ninth noveno
no one nadie
no, not any, none ningún, ninguno/a
nobody nadie
noise el ruido
to nominate nominar
non-profit sin fines de lucro
North American norteamericano/a

nose la nariz
note card la ficha
notebook el cuaderno
nothing nada
novel la novela
novelist el/la novelista
November noviembre
now ahora
nowadays hoy en día
nurse el/la enfermero/a

O

to occur ocurrir
October octubre
of de
of African ancestry moreno/a, negro/a
of course por supuesto
Of course! ¡Cómo no!/¡Claro!
of dark skin moreno/a, negro/a
of lightbrown skin color trigueño/a
of the (contraction of de + el**)** del
to offer ofrecer
office (of doctor, dentist, etc.) el consultorio
office la oficina
often frecuentemente
oil el aceite
old antiguo/a
old mayor; viejo/a
older than mayor que
olive la aceituna
on sobre
on the dot (time) en punto
On the one hand . . . Por un lado...
On the other hand . . . En cambio/Por otro lado...
On what page? ¿En qué página?
once una vez
onion la cebolla
only child el hijo único/la hija única
only solo
to open abrir
opening la vacante
opposing contrario/a
orange (adj.) anaranjado/a, naranja; **(noun)** la naranja
orchestra la orquesta
to order around dar órdenes
to order pedir
origen el comienzo
other otro/a
our nuestro(s), nuestra(s)
outdoors al aire libre
outgoing extrovertido/a
outing la excursión
outskirts las afueras
outstanding destacado/a
overcast (sky) cubierto
own propio/a
ozone layer la capa de ozono

P

P.M. (from nightfall to midnight) de la noche
P.M. (from noon to nightfall) de la tarde
paid remunerado/a
pain el dolor
to paint pintar
painter el/la pintor/a
painting el cuadro
painting la pintura
pajamas el/la piyama, el pijama *(Spain)*
Panamanian panameño/a
pants los pantalones
pantsuit el traje pantalón
pantyhose las pantimedias
papaya la papaya
parade el desfile
Paraguayan paraguayo/a
pardon me perdón; con permiso
parents los padres
parsley el perejil
to participate participar
partner el/la compañero/a
party la fiesta
passenger el/la pasajero/a
passion fruit el maracuyá *(Colom.)*, la fruta de la pasión *(Spain)*, la parchita *(Venez., Mex.)*
passport el pasaporte
pastry el pastel
patient el/la paciente
patrotic patriótico/a
to pay (for) pagar
peach el melocotón *(Spain)*, el durazno *(Latin America)*
peak el pico
pear la pera
peasant el/la campesino/a
pedestrian area la zona peatonal
to peel pelar
penalty (in sports) el penalti
pencil el lápiz
people la gente, las personas
pepper la pimienta; **(hot, spicy)** el chile/ají **(vegetable)** el pimiento
per por
percent por ciento
percentage el porcentaje
percibido/a noticed
perfect perfecto/a
performance el rendimiento
performer, artist el/la intérprete
person la persona
Peruvian peruano/a
petroleum el petróleo
pharmacist el/la farmacéutico/a
pharmacy la farmacia
photo(graph) la foto(grafía)
to pick up recoger
picture el cuadro
piece of jewelry la joya
pilgrim el/la peregrino/a
pill la pastilla
pillow la almohada
pin el alfiler
pineapple la piña
pink rosado/a, rosa
place el lugar
plaid de cuadros
to plan to + verb pensar + *infinitive*
plane el avión
planet el planeta
plantain el plátano/la banana
plate el plato
to play (a game, sport) jugar
to play (an instrument) tocar (un instrumento)
player el/la jugador/a
Please answer. Contesten, por favor./ Contesta, por favor.
please por favor
Pleased/Nice to meet you. Encantado/a.
plumber el/la plomero/a, el/la fontanero/a *(Spain)*
poem el poema
poet el/la poeta
poetry la poesía
point of view el punto de vista
policeman/woman el/la policía
Polish polaco/a
political science las ciencias políticas
polyglot el/la políglota
pool la piscina, la pileta
poor pobre
popcorn las palomitas de maíz
to popularize popularizar
population la población
pork el cerdo, el puerco
to portray retratar
Portuguese portugués/portuguesa
position el puesto; la posición
potato la papa
poultry las aves
poverty la pobreza
power outage el apagón
to practice practicar
to precede preceder
to prefer preferir
preparation el preparativo
to prepare preparar
to prescribe recetar
prescription la receta

present actual
present el regalo
preservation la conservación
president el/la presidente/a
pressure (blood) la tensión/la presión (arterial)
pretty bonito/a, linda, guapa
price el precio
printer la impresora
prize el premio
procession la procesión
to produce producir
professor el/la profesor/a
promising prometedor/a
to promote promover
to propose proponer
to protest protestar
proverb el refrán
provided that con tal (de) que
proximity la proximidad
psychologist el/la sicólogo/a
psychology la psicología
Puerto Rican puertorriqueño/a
purple morado/a
purpose el propósito
purse la bolsa/el bolso
to put poner
to put makeup on (someone); to put makeup on (oneself) maquillar(se)
to put one's clothes on ponerse la ropa
to put to bed acostar

Q

quality la calidad
quiet callado/a

R

race la carrera
racquet la raqueta
radiator el radiador
radio announcer el/la locutor/a
radio el/la radio
rail el riel
rain forest el bosque tropical
rain la lluvia
to rain llover
raincoat el impermeable
to raise levantar
Raise your hand. Levanta la mano.
ranch la finca
rate la tasa
rather bastante
to reach out to comunicarse con
to read leer
Read. Lee.
ready listo/a
to realize darse cuenta
really en realidad, realmente
rearview mirror el espejo retrovisor
reason la razón
rebirth el renacimiento
recipe la receta
recognition el reconocimiento
to recommend recomendar
to record grabar
recycled reciclado/a
red bell pepper el pimiento rojo
red rojo/a
redhead pelirrojo/a
to reduce reducir
referee el árbitro
to reflect reflejar
to reforest repoblar
refrigerator el refrigerador
refrigerator el refrigerador/la nevera/ heladera
regime el régimen
to regret arrepentirse
relative el/la pariente
relief el alivio
remedy el remedio
to remember recordar
to rent alquilar
rent el alquiler
Repeat. Repite./Repitan.
to repeat repetir
report el informe
to request pedir
to request the floor pedir la palabra
resort el centro turístico privado
resources los recursos
to respond responder
to rest descansar
résumé el currículum
to retire jubilarse
to return an item devolver
to return volver
rib la costilla
rice el arroz
rich rico/a
to ride (a bicycle) montar (en bicicleta)
right el derecho; la derecha
to be right tener razón
right? ¿verdad?
ring el anillo
roasted asado/a
robe la bata
robot el robot
room el cuarto
roommate el/la compañero/a de cuarto
round trip de ida y vuelta
rug la alfombra
ruins las ruinas
ruler el/la gobernante
to run correr
to run into encontrarse
to run out of acabarse

S

sad triste
safe la caja fuerte
salad dressing el aderezo
salad la ensalada
salary el sueldo
sale la rebaja
sales las ventas
salesman, saleswoman el/la vendedor/a
salesperson el dependiente/la dependienta
salt la sal
Salvadoran salvadoreño/a
same mismo/a
sand dune el médano
sandals las sandalias
sandwich el sándwich
satellite el satélite
Saturday sábado
to save ahorrar
sawdust el aserrín
to say decir
to say goodbye despedirse
to say hello mandar saludos
scarf la bufanda
scene la escena
scholarship la beca
school of fish el banco de peces
school, department la facultad
science fiction la ciencia ficción
sciences las ciencias
scientist el/la científico/a
to score a goal meter un gol
scoreboard el marcador
screen la pantalla
sculptor el/la escultor/a
sea el mar
seafood los mariscos
seamstress la costurera
search engine el buscador
season la estación
seasoning el condimento
seat el asiento
second floor el primer piso; la primera planta
second segundo
security la seguridad
to see ver
see you later hasta luego
see you soon hasta pronto
see you tomorrow hasta mañana
seed la semilla
to seem parecer
self-portrait el autorretrato

to sell vender
to send enviar, mandar
September septiembre
serious (situation) grave; serio/a
seriously ill grave
to serve servir
server el/la camarero/a
to set the table poner la mesa
setting el ambiente
seventh séptimo/a
several algún, alguno (-os, -as)
sewage las aguas residuales
shake el batido
shame la lástima
shape la forma
to share compartir
shark el tiburón
sharp (time) en punto
to shave; to shave (oneself) afeitar(se)
she ella
sheep la oveja
sheet la sábana
shell la concha
shellfish los mariscos
ship/boat el barco
shirt la camisa
shoal el banco de peces
shoes los zapatos
to shop ir de compras
shopping center el centro comercial
shopping las compras
short (in length) corto/a
short (in stature) bajo/a
short sleeve shirt camisa de manga corta
shortly after poco después
shorts los pantalones cortos
should deber
shoulder el hombro
to show mostrar
to show a movie poner una película
shower la ducha
shrimp el camarón, la gamba *(Spain)*
to shut in encerrar
shy tímido/a
sick enfermo/a
signal la señal
silly tonto/a
silver la plata
similar parecido/a
since desde; ya que
to sing cantar
single room la habitación sencilla
single soltero/a
sister la hermana
to sit down sentarse
sixth sexto/a
size el tamaño **(clothes)** la talla; **(shoes)** el número
to skate patinar
to ski esquiar
skiing, ski el esquí
skin la piel
skirt la falda, pollera *(Arg., Urug.)*
sky el cielo
to sleep dormir
slice la rebanada
slippers las zapatillas
slope la bajada; la pista
sloth el perezoso (Zool.)
small pequeño/a
smallpox la viruela
smart listo/a
to smoke fumar
smothie el batido
snack la merienda
to sneeze estornudar
snow la nieve
to snow nevar
so that para que
soap el jabón
soccer el fútbol
soccer field el campo de fútbol
social networks las redes sociales
sociology la sociología
socks los calcetines, las medias
soda el refresco
sofa el sofá
soft blando/a; suave
soft drink el refresco
soil la tierra
solar energy la energía solar
solid de color entero
some algún, alguno (-os, -as)
some unos/as
someone alguien
something algo
sometime alguna vez
sometimes a veces, algunas veces
son el hijo
song la canción
sought after codiciado/a
soup la sopa
sour agrio/a
source la fuente
source of income la fuente de ingresos
souvenirs los recuerdos
spaghetti los espaguetis, tallarines
Spanish español/a; el español
to speak hablar
specialty la especialidad
speech el discurso
speed la velocidad
to spend gastar; **(time)** pasar
spices las especias
spicy picante
spinach las espinacas
to sponsor patrocinar
spoon la cuchara
spoonful la cucharada
sport el deporte
sportsman, sportswoman el/la deportista
to spray rociar
to spread difundir
spring la primavera
to sprinkle rociar
square la plaza
square meter el metro cuadrado
stadium el estadio
stairs la escalera
to stand in line hacer cola
to stand out destacarse
star la estrella
to start comenzar, empezar
statistics la estadística
to stay quedarse
to stay in touch mantenerse en contacto
steak el bistec, la carne de res
steering wheel el volante
stem cell la célula troncal
step el paso
stepbrother el hermanastro
stepfather el padrastro
stepmother la madrastra
stepsister la hermanastra
still todavía
stockings las medias
stomach el estómago
stopover la escala
store la tienda
store window el escaparate
story el cuento
stove la estufa, la cocina
strawberry la fresa
street la calle
to strenghten fortalecer
stretch el tramo
stripes de rayas
stroke la campanada
to stroll pasear
strong fuerte
student el/la estudiante, alumno/a
studious estudioso/a
to study estudiar
to stumble tropezarse
style el estilo
stylish de moda
subject la materia, la asignatura
subway el metro
success el éxito
sugar el azúcar
to suggest sugerir
suit el traje

suit el traje de chaqueta
suitcase la maleta
summer el verano
to sunbathe tomar el sol
Sunday domingo
sunglasses las gafas de sol
supermarket el supermercado
supper la cena, la comida
to support apoyar; sustentar
to surf hacer surf
surprise la sorpresa
surrealist surrealista
to surround rodear
to survive sobrevivir
sweater el suéter
sweatshirt la sudadera
to sweep barrer
swelling la hinchazón
to swim nadar
swimming la natación
swimming pool la piscina
swollen hinchado/a
symbol el símbolo
symptom el síntoma

T

table la mesa
tablecloth el mantel
tablet la tableta
to take a bath bañarse
to take a nap dormir la siesta
to take a seat tomar asiento
to take a shower ducharse
to take a walk dar una vuelta; pasear
to take advantage aprovechar
to take away quitar
to take care of cuidar(se) (de)
to take llevar
to take note fijar(se)
to take notes tomar apuntes/notas
to take off (airplane) despegar
to take off quitarse
to take out sacar
to take tomar
to take turns turnarse
Take turns Túrnense.
Talk (about ...) Hablen (sobre...)
to talk conversar
talkative conversador/a
tall alto/a
to taste probar
tea el té
teacher el/la profesor/a
team el equipo
to tear romper
teaspoon la cucharita
technician el/la técnico/a
telephone el teléfono
television set el televisor
to tell decir; contar
Tell your partner ... Dile a tu compañero/a...
tenfold el décuplo
tennis el tenis
tennis player el/la tenista
tennis shoes las zapatillas de deporte
tent la tienda
tenth décimo/a
test el análisis; el examen
to exhibit exponer
textile industry industria textil
Thank goodness! ¡Gracias a Dios!
thanks gracias
Thanksgiving Day el Día de Acción de Gracias
that (adjective) ese/a
that (over there) aquel/aquella/aquello
that ese/esa/eso
That's so interesting! ¡Qué interesante!
That's unbelievable! ¡Qué increíble!
thaw, thawing el deshielo
the (singular) el/la; **(plural)** los/las
the best el/la mejor
the day after tomorrow pasado mañana
the day before yesterday anteayer
the important thing lo importante
the most el/la... más
the night before last ante(a)noche
the oldest el/la mayor
the same lo mismo
The screen froze up on me. Se me congeló la pantalla.
The weather is good/bad. Hace buen/mal tiempo.
the youngest el/la menor
theater el teatro
their su(s)
theme el tema
themselves a sí mismo/a(s)
then entonces, luego
there is, there are hay
thermometer el termómetro
these estos/estas
they ellos/ellas
thief el/la ladrón/a
thin delgado/a
thing la cosa
things you own las pertenencias
to think parecer; **(about)** pensar (en)
third tercero/la, tercer
this este/esta/esto
those esos/esas
those (over there) aquellos/aquellas
thousand mil
throat la garganta
through a través de; por
to throw lanzar
Thursday jueves
ticket el boleto, el pasaje, el billete *(Spain)*
tidy ordenado/a
to tidy up ordenar
tie la corbata
tight estrecho/a
tire la llanta
tired cansado/a
to a; para
to the al (*contraction of* **a** + **el**)
toast el pan tostado, la tostada
today hoy
Today is (day of the week.) Hoy es (día de la semana).
together juntos/as
toilet el inodoro
tomato el tomate
tomato sauce la salsa de tomate
tomorrow mañana
tonight esta noche
too también
tooth el diente
toothpaste la pasta de dientes
topic el tema
tourist class la clase turista
tournament el campeonato, el torneo
towards para
towel la toalla
toy el juguete
to turn doblar
track and field el atletismo
track la pista
tradition la tradición
train el tren
to train prepararse
trait el rasgo
to translate traducir
trash la basura
travel agency la agencia de viajes
travel agent el/la agente de viajes
to travel viajar; recorrer
traveller el/la viajero/a
tray la bandeja
to treat tratar
treaty el tratado
tree el árbol
to tremble estremecerse
trip la excursión
trip el viaje
true cierto/a
trunk el maletero, el baúl
trust la confianza
trustworthy confiable

to try on probarse
to try tratar; probar
T-shirt la camiseta
Tuesday martes
turkey el pavo, el guajolote *(Mex.)*
to turn in entregar
to turn off apagar
to turn on encender; (the TV) poner
twice dos veces
twin gemelo/a
to twist torcer(se)
typical típico/a

U

U.S. citizen estadounidense
UFO el OVNI
ugly feo/a
umbrella el paraguas
umpire el árbitro
uncle el tío
to uncover destapar
under bajo; debajo (de)
to underline subrayar
to understand comprender, entender
underwear la ropa interior
unemployment el desempleo
unforgettable inolvidable
to unify unificar
university la universidad
unless a menos que
unmarried soltero/a
unpleasant antipático/a
unripe verde
until hasta(que)
to upload subir
urgent urgente
Uruguayan uruguayo/a
to use usar
useful útil

V

vacation las vacaciones
vacuum cleaner la aspiradora
to vacuum pasar la aspiradora
Valentine's Day el Día de los Enamorados/del Amor y la Amistad
vanilla la vainilla
vegetable el vegetal, la verdura
vein la vena
Venezuelan venezolano/a
verb el verbo
very muy
vet el/la veterinario/a
video game el videojuego
view la vista
village el pueblo
vinegar el vinagre
virtual library la biblioteca virtual
virtually virtualmente
to visit visitar
voice la voz
volleyball el vóleibol/volibol
to vote votar

W

wage el sueldo
wagon la carreta
waist la cintura
to wait for esperar
waiter/waitress el/la camarero/a
waiting room la sala de espera
to wake up despertarse
to wake someone up despertar
to walk caminar
wallet la billetera
to want querer, desear
warehouse el almacén
warming el calentamiento
warm-up el calentamiento
to wash (oneself) lavar(se)
washer la lavadora
waste los desperdicios
wastebasket el cesto
water el agua
to water regar
wave la ola
We hope that . . . Ojalá que...
we nosotros/as
weak débil
wealthy rico/a
to wear a costume disfrazarse
to wear a shoe size calzar
to wear llevar
weather el tiempo
weather forecast el pronóstico del tiempo
wedding la boda
Wednesday miércoles
week la semana
weekend el fin de semana
weight la pesa
well bien
well parked bien aparcado
wet mojado/a
What a coincidence! ¡Qué casualidad!
What a nuisance! ¡Qué lata!
What a pity! ¡Qué lástima!
What day is today? ¿Qué día es hoy?
What do you think? ¿qué te parece?
What for? ¿para qué?
What is he/she/it like? ¿Cómo es?
What is the date today? ¿Qué fecha es hoy?/¿Cuál es la fecha?
What time is it? ¿Qué hora es?
What? ¿Qué?; ¿Cómo?; ¿Perdón?
What's the weather like? ¿Qué tiempo hace?
What's up? What's new? (informal) ¿Qué tal?
What's your name? (familiar) ¿Cómo te llamas?
What's your name? (formal) ¿Cómo se llama usted?
What's wrong (with you/them)? ¿Qué te/le(s) pasa?
wheat el trigo
wheel la rueda
when cuando
When? ¿Cuándo?
Where (to)? ¿Adónde?
Where is ... ? ¿Dónde está...?
where, wherever donde
Where? ¿Dónde?
Which? ¿Cuál(es)?
while mientras
to whistle pitar
white blanco/a
Who is . . .? ¿Quién es...?
Who? Quién(es)?
whose? ¿De ¿quién?
why por qué
Why? ¿Para qué?; ¿Por qué?
wide ancho/a
widower viudo/a
wife la esposa, la mujer *(Spain)*
wild silvestre
to win ganar
wind el viento
window la ventana
window seat el asiento de ventanilla
windshield el parabrisas
windshield wiper el limpiaparabrisas
wine el vino
wing el ala
winter el invierno
to wish desear; esperar; querer
with con
with me conmigo
with much love con mucho cariño
With pleasure./Gladly. Con mucho gusto.
with them con ellos/ellas
with whom con quien
with you (familiar) contigo
without sin(que)
without us sin nosotros/as
woman la mujer
wood la madera
word la palabra

work el trabajo; la obra
to work trabajar; funcionar
worker el/la obrero/a; el/la trabajador/a
workforce la fuerza laboral
workshop el taller
to worship venerar
wound la herida
wrist la muñeca
to write escribir
to write to each other escribirse
Write. Escribe.
writer el/la escritor/a

Y

year el año
yellow amarillo/a
yes sí
yesterday ayer
yet todavía
yogurt el yogur
you (familiar) like te gusta(n)
you (familiar) tú; **(plural)** vosotros/as *(Spain)*
you (formal) like le gusta(n)
you (formal) usted; **(plural)** ustedes
you are (familiar) eres; estás
you are (formal) es; está
you have (familiar) tienes
you're welcome de nada
young joven
young man/woman el/la joven
your (familiar plural) vuestro(s), vuestra(s)
your (familiar) tu(s)
your (formal) su(s)
Yours, sincerely. Un cordial saludo.

Text & Photo Credits

Text Credits

Capítulo 13

p. 453: Gabriela Mistral, "Dame la mano." La Orden Franciscana de Chile autoriza el uso de la obra de Gabriela Mistral. Lo equivalente a los derechos de autoría es entregado a la Orden Franciscana de Chile, para los niños de Montegrande y de Chile, de conformidad a la voluntad testamentaria de Gabriela Mistral; **p. 475:** Gloria Fuertes, "Las Cosas" by Gloria Fuertes from OBRAS INCOMPLETAS, Cátedra, 2006. Used by permission of Fundación Gloria Fuertes

Capítulo 14

p. 506: "La mosca que soñaba que era un aguila" by Augusto Monterroso from EL PARAÍSO IMPERFECTO: ANTOLOGÍA TÍMIDA. Debolsillo, 2013. Used by permission of International Editors Company, S. L.

Photo Credits

Front Matter

p. ix: adimas/fotolia; **p. x:** LUIS ACOSTA/AFP/ Getty Images; **p. xi:** Monkey Business Images/ Shutterstock/Dorling Kindersley, Ltd.; **p. xiii(t):** Marcos Brindicci/Reuters/Corbis; **p. xiii(b):** Eduardo Rivero/Shutterstock; **p. xiv(r):** Christian Kieffer/Shutterstock ; **p. xiv(l):** Skylines/ Shutterstock; **p. xv:** Andresr/Shutterstock; **p. xvi:** Nik Niklz/Shutterstock; **p. xvii:** Jose Luis Stephens/Alamy; **p. xiii:** Fotolia; **p. xxiii(l):** Fotolia; **p. xxiii:** Fotolia; **p. xviii:** Imagery-Majestic/Shutterstock; **p. xxxvi(b):** Elizabeth E. Guzman; **p. xxxvi:** Judith Liskin-Gasparro

Capítulo Preliminar

p. 2: Contrastwerkstatt / Fotolia; **p. 3:** Jeff Greenberg / Alamy; **p. 4(tl):** Mikesch112 / Fotolia; **p. 4(tr):** Atm2003 / Fotolia; **p. 4(c):** Joan Albert Lluch / Fotolia; **p. 4(bl):** BlueOrange Studio / Fotolia; **p. 5:** Zurijeta / Shutterstock; **p. 6(t):** Michael Jung / Fotolia; **p. 7(tl):** Ian O'Leary /Getty Images; **p. 7(tc):** Dorling Kindersley, Ltd; **p. 7(bl):** Shutterstock; **p. 8(tr):** Mike Good / Dorling Kindersley, Ltd; **p. 9(bl):** Bonga1965 / Fotolia; **p. 10-11(tl):** Priganica / Fotolia; **p. 11(br):** Brenda Carson / Fotolia; **p. 13(tc):** Alexmillos / Fotolia; **p. 14(bl):** Vannphoto / Fotolia; **p. 14(b):** Vmelinda/fotolia; **p. 16(b):** Diego Cervo / Fotolia; **p. 18(tl):** Pedrosala / Fotolia; **p. 18(cr):** Alex Havret / DK Images; **p. 18(bc):** StockLite / Shutterstock; **p. 20:** Runzelkorn / Fotolia; **p. 22(b):** Chokniti / Fotolia; **p. 23(tr):** Scanrail / Fotolia; **p. 23(b):** Petr Vaclavek / Fotolia; **p. 24(cl):** Adimas / Fotolia; **p. 24(bl):** Brad Pict / Fotolia; **p. 25(tl):** Faraways / Fotolia; **p. 25(tr):** Paul Bricknell / Dorling Kindersley, Ltd; **p. 25(c):** Barone Rosso / Fotolia; **p. 25(bl):** Andy Crawford / Dorling Kindersley, Ltd; **p. 25(br):** Tim Ridley / Dorling Kindersley, Ltd; **p. 26(b):** Silkstock / Fotolia; **p. 27(cr):** Igor Mojzes / Fotolia;

Capítulo 1

p. 30(cr): Yuraliaits Albert / Shutterstock; **p. 31(c):** Matt Trommer / Shutterstock; **p. 31(cr):** Pilar Echevarria / Shutterstock; **p. 31(tc):** Dorota Jarymowicz and Mariusz Ja / DK Images; **p. 31(c):** Rafael Ramirez Lee / Shutterstock; **p. 31(tl):** Carlos Nieto / Age Fotostock / Robert Harding; **p. 31(bl):** Album / Prisma / Newscom; **p. 32(tl):** Akulamatiau / Fotolia; **p. 32(bl):** Aleksandar Todorovic / Fotolia; **p. 32(cr):** Travelwitness / Fotolia; **p. 32(cl):** Mrks V / Fotolia; **p. 33(cr):** Andresr / Shutterstock; **p. 33(bl):** Pkchai / Shutterstock; **p. 34(br):** Andres Rodriguez; **p. 35(tr):** Jenkedco /Shutterstock; **p. 36:** Roman Sigaev / Fotolia; **p. 38(br):** Hemeroskopion / Fotolia; **p. 39:** Santiago Pais / Fotolia; **p. 40(b):** Tim Draper / Dorling Kindersley,Ltd; **p. 41(tr):** Pearson Education Ltd; **p. 41(br):** Yakor / Fotolia; **p. 41(cl):** Fxegs / Fotolia; **p. 47(cl):** Aaron Amat / Fotolia; **p. 47(br):** Hill Street Studios / Blend Images/Alamy; **p. 48(tr):** JHershPhoto / Shutterstock; **p. 49(tr):** Mimohe / Fotolia; **p. 55(tc):** Spencer Grant / PhotoEdit; **p. 56:** Auremar / Fotolia; **p. 57(tr):** Gabriel Blaj / Fotolia LLC; **p. 62:** Dmitriy Shironosov / Shutterstock;

Capítulo 2

p. 64(cr): Andres Rodriguez / Fotolia; **p. 65(l):** Everett Collection Inc / Alamy; **p. 65(l):** Everett Collection Inc / Alamy; **p. 65(tc):** April Turner / Shutterstock; **p. 65(bc):** Robin Holden Sr / Shutterstock; **p. 65(cr):** Hola Images / Alamy; **p. 65(tr):** EPA / Alamy; **p. 65(c):** Gvictoria / Shutterstock; **p. 65(br):** Images / Alamy; **p. 66(tc):** Alessandra Santarell i/ Jeoff Davis / Dorling Kindersley,Ltd; **p. 66(cr):** Everett Collection Inc / Alamy; **p. 66(bl):** Henryk Sadura / Fotolia; **p. 66(br):** ZUMA Press, Inc. / Alamy; **p. 67(tl):** Andres Rodriguez / Fotolia; **p. 67(tc):** Samuel Borges / Fotolia; **p. 67(tr):** Mel Lindstrom / Mira; **p. 67(l):** Mangostock / Fotolia; **p. 67(br):** Andresr / Shutterstock; **p. 68(br):** Avava / Fotolia; **p. 71(cl):** Wallenrock / Shutterstock; **p. 71(cl):** Dallas Events Inc / Shutterstock; **p. 71(c):** Michaeljung / Fotolia; **p. 71(cr):** Shutterstock; **p. 71(b):** Wong Sze Fei / Fotolia; **p. 72(tl):** EPA / Alamy; **p. 72(tr):** EPA / Alamy; **p. 73(bl):** Greg Roden / Dorling Kindersley,Ltd; **p. 74(tr):** Berc / Fotolia; **p. 75(br):** Max / Fotolia; **p. 75(tl):** Igorigorevich / Fotolia; **p. 75(tr):** Dgmata / Fotolia; **p. 77(br):** Shutterstock; **p. 78(tr):** WavebreakMediaMicro / Fotolia; **p. 78(bl):** Michael Germana / Landov; **p. 78(bc):** Front Row Photos; **p. 78(b):** Taylor Jones / The Palm Beach Post / Zumapress / Alamy; **p. 78(br):** Ramon Espinosa / AP Images; **p. 78(cl):** Max Alexander / DK Images; **p. 80(tr):** AP Images; **p. 81** Tyler Olson / Shutterstock; **p. 86(tr):** Dwphotos / Shutterstock; **p. 87(tr):** Andresr / Shutterstock; **p. 89(tl):** Andres Rodriguez / Fotolia; **p. 89(cl):** ArchMen / Fotolia; **p. 90(tl):** Andres Rodriguez / Fotolia LLC; **p. 91(br):** Andres Rodriguez / Fotolia LLC; **p. 92(tr):** Skylines / Shutterstock; **p. 94(br):** Shutterstock; **p. 95(tc):** Alliance Images / Alamy; **p. 96(br):** Scanrail / Fotolia; **p. 97** Andresr / Shutterstock; **p. 98** Leonidovich / Shutterstock;

Capítulo 3

p. 100(cr): Auremar / Fotolia; **p. 101(tl):** Suzanne Porter / Dorling Kindersley, Ltd; **p. 101(cl):** Mike Von Bergen / Shutterstock; **p. 101(cr):** Shutterstock; **p. 101(bl):** Mireille Vautier / Alamy; **p. 102(tl):** Ocphoto / Shutterstock; **p. 102(cl):** Bob Krist / Corbis; **p. 102(bl):** Richard Smith / Corbis; **p. 102(cr):** Silvia Izquierdo/Reuters/Corbis; **p. 103(tl):** Creatas / Thinkstock; **p. 103(tl):** Tim Draper / Rough Guides / DK Images; **p. 103(tc):** iStockphoto / Thinkstock; **p. 103(tr):** Mangostock / Fotolia; **p. 104** Travel Pictures / Alamy; **p. 105(cr):** Luis Santos /shutterstock; **p. 105(tr):** Giuseppe_R / Shutterstock; **p. 105(br):** Goodluz / Fotolia; **p. 106** Grant Hindsley / AP images; **p. 107(br):** Subbotina Anna / Shutterstock; **p. 107(tl):** Jennifer Boggs / Amy Paliwoda / Alamy; **p. 107(bl):** Cameron Whitman / Shutterstock; **p. 107(tr):** Dinner, Allison / the food passionates /Corbis; **p. 108** Jeff Greenberg / Alamy; **p. 109(bc):** John Van Hasselt / Sygma / Corbis; **p. 110(tr):** karelnoppe / Fotolia; **p. 110(cl):** Segismundo Trivero / Fotolia; **p. 110(br):** Jeff Greenberg / Alamy; **p. 113(br):** James Thew / Fotolia; **p. 115(br):** Kitch Bain / Shutterstock; **p. 116(bl):** Fotolia; **p. 116(bc):** Aaron Oberlander / Getty Images; **p. 116(br):** Oscar Pinto Sanchez; **p. 116(br):** Jeff Greenberg / Alamy; **p. 117(br):** Elenathewise / Fotolia; **p. 122** Germanskydive110 / Fotolia; **p. 124** Zuma Press, Inc / Alamy; **p. 125(t):** Robert Lerich / Fotolia; **p. 125(b):** Neale Cousland / Shutterstock; **p. 134** iPics / Fotolia;

Capítulo 4

p. 136(cr): Andres Rodriguez / Fotolia; **p. 137(tc):** Amra Pasic / Shutterstock; **p. 137(cr):** Pies Specifics / Alamy; **p. 137(cl):** Archivo el Tiempo / El Tiempo de Colombia / Newscom; **p. 137(cr):** Richard Gunion / Thinkstock / Getty Images; **p. 137(bl):** Galyna Andrushko / Shutterstock; **p. 137(br):** Marlborough Gallery; **p. 138(tl):** Luis Acosta / AFP / Getty Images; **p. 138(bl):** Fotolia; **p. 138(tr):** Rodrigo Arangua / AFP / Getty Images / Newscom; **p. 138(br):** Jenny Leonard / Shutterstock; **p. 139(tl):** Paloma Lapuerta; **p. 139(tr):** bst2012 / Fotolia; **p. 139(br):** Blend Images / Shutterstock; **p. 139(bl):** Ton Koene / Horizons WWP / Alamy; **p. 141(b):** JackF / Fotolia; **p. 142(tr):** Montserrat Diez / EPA / Newscom; **p. 142(br):** Fotoluminate LLC / Fotolia; **p. 143(cr):** Lucky Dragon USA / Fotolia; **p. 145(bl):** Dennis jacobsen / Fotolia; **p. 145(br):** Monkey Business Images / Shutterstock; **p. 146(br):** Jose R. Aguirre / Cover / Getty Images; **p. 146(t):** Jupiterimages / Brand X Pictures / Thinkstock; **p. 147(tr):** Scott Griessel / Fotolia; **p. 147(br):** Africa Studio /

Fotolia; **p. 148(tr):** Samuel Borges / Fotolia; **p. 149(bl):** Monkey Business Images / Shutterstock / Dorling Kindersley, Ltd.; **p. 149:** Vision images / Fotolia; **p. 150(t):** Doruk Sikman / Fotolia; **p. 150(b):** Noam / Fotolia; **p. 151(bl):** Monkey Business / Fotolia; **p. 151(tr):** Nick White / Getty Images; **p. 152(tr):** Blend Images / Thinkstock; **p. 154(tl):** Stefanolunardi / Fotolia; **p. 155(br):** Giuseppe R / Fotolia; **p. 155(tr):** Gabriel Blaj / Fotolia; **p. 156(tr):** Blaz Kure / Shutterstock; **p. 157(br):** Daria Filiminova / Fotolia; **p. 158(bl):** Helen Kattai / Shutterstock; **p. 159(tr):** GalinaSt / Fotolia; **p. 161:** AVAVA / Shutterstock; **p. 163(tc):** Omkara.V / Fotolia; **p. 164(tc):** Orange Line Media / Fotolia; **p. 166(tl):** Shutterstock; **p. 166(br):** Bill Aron / PhotoEdit; **p. 167(br):** Andres Rodriguez / Fotolia; **p. 168(br):** Ra2studio / Shutterstock;

Capítulo 5

p. 170(cr): Rtimages / Fotolia; **p. 171(tc):** Oscar Espinosa / Shutterstock; **p. 171(cl):** Tatiana Popova / Shutterstock; **p. 171(cr):** Getty Images; **p. 171(bc):** Getty Images; **p. 171(br):** Eli Coory/Fotolia; **p. 171(l):** Shutterstock.com; **p. 171(bl):** Cindy Miller Hopkins / Danita Delimont / Alamy; **p. 172(cr):** Christian Heeb / JAI / Corbis; **p. 172(bl):** Tazzymon / Fotolia; **p. 172(tc):** Ariane Citron / Fotolia; **p. 173(cr):** Nik Wheeler / Alamy; **p. 175(br):** Kochneva Tetyana / Shutterstock; **p. 176(br):** Oswaldo Rivas / Reuters / Corbis; **p. 180(br):** Ruth Jenkinson / DK Images; **p. 181(bc):** Andres Rodriguez / Alamy; **p. 181(br):** Robert Harrison / Alamy; **p. 184(tl):** Randy Green / Alamy; **p. 184(c):** Bruce Ayres / Getty Images; **p. 184(cr):** Jan Sochor / Alamy; **p. 188(tl):** Tony Freeman / PhotoEdit; **p. 188(tr):** Fotolia; **p. 188(cr):** Erwinova / Fotolia; **p. 192(tr):** Enigmatico / Fotolia; **p. 199(bl):** Diego Cervo / Shutterstock; **p. 200(tc):** Kablonk Micro / Fotolia; **p. 201(br):** Giovanni Cancemi / Fotolia;

Capítulo 6

p. 204(cr): Conrado/Shutterstock; **p. 205(tl):** E Mike / Fotolia; **p. 205(tc):** Enrique Molina / Age Fotostock; **p. 205(cl):** Gastromedia / Alamy; **p. 205(cr):** Mark Cosslett / National Geographic Image Collection / Getty Images; **p. 205(bl):** Simon Bolivar (1783-1830) (chromolitho), . / Private Collection / Archives Charmet / The Bridgeman Art Library; **p. 205(bc):** Malcolm Schuyl / Alamy; **p. 206** Volff / Fotolia; **p. 206(tl):** Malcolm Schuyl / Alamy; **p. 206(cl):** Volff / Fotolia; **p. 206(tr):** Vladimir Melnik / Fotolia; **p. 206(cr):** Hemeroskopion / Fotolia; **p. 207(tr):** Dan Herrick / Alamy; **p. 207(tl):** Rob Crandall/Stock Connection / Glow Images; **p. 207(tc):** Jeff Greenberg / PhotoEdit, Inc.; **p. 208(cr):** Adam Gregor / Fotolia; **p. 209(cl):** Brand X Pictures / Thinkstock; **p. 212(tr):** lunamarina / Fotolia; **p. 214(c):** Glamour / Shutterstock; **p. 215(bl):** Dorothy Alexander / Alamy; **p. 215(tr):** Scott Dalton / Bloomberg / Getty Images; **p. 220(tr):** Patrick Keen / Getty Images; **p. 220(tl):** JKaczka Digital Imaging / Fotolia; **p. 220(bl):** Yann Arthus-Bertrand / Documentary / Corbis; **p. 220(br):** Juan Silva / The Image Bank / Getty Images; **p. 224(cr):** Carlos / Fotolia; **p. 228(bc):** Gelpi JM / Shutterstock; **p. 228(br):** Jason Maehl / Shutterstock; **p. 228(bl):** East / Shutterstock; **p. 228(bc):** Iko / Shutterstock; **p. 228(cr):** Paco Ayala / Fotolia; **p. 229(bc):** Sauletas / Fotolia; **p. 232(br):** Monkey Business Images /Shutterstock; **p. 232(tr):** Antonio Guillem / Shutterstock; **p. 232(bl):** Kurhan / Shutterstock; **p. 232(cr):** Konradbak / Fotolia; **p. 233(tl):** Goodluz / Shutterstock; **p. 233(tc):** Artem Furman / Shutterstock; **p. 233(tr):** Viacheslav Nikolaenko / Shutterstock; **p. 235(cr):** Julia Pivovarova / Shutterstock; **p. 237(cl):** WoGi / Fotolia;

Capítulo 7

p. 240(cr): Jiang Dao Hua / Shutterstock; **p. 241** Zurbaran Galeria / SuperStock; **p. 241(tc):** Elxeneize / Fotolia; **p. 241(bc):** Christopher Pillitz/Alamy; **p. 241(cr):** Eye Ubiquitous / Robert Harding; **p. 241(tl):** Galina Barskaya / Shutterstock; **p. 242(tl):** Demetrio Carrasco / DK Images; **p. 242(bl):** Nicoletaraftu / Fotolia; **p. 242(br):** Kseniya Ragozina / Fotolia; **p. 242(cl):** Fernando Giani / Fotolia; **p. 242(cr):** Toniflap / Fotolia; **p. 243(tl):** Marcos Brindicci / Reuters / Corbis; **p. 243(bl):** Bikeriderlondon / Shutterstock; **p. 243(cr):** Daily Mail / Rex / Alamy; **p. 244(cr):** Gal Schweizer / Getty Images; **p. 245(br):** Corbis Sports/Corbis; **p. 245(bl):** Tim Farrell / Corbis Sports / Corbis; **p. 245(bc):** Fred Thornhill / Reuters / Corbis; **p. 249(cl):** Photocreo / Fotolia; **p. 250(cl):** Maxi Failla / LatinContent / Getty Images; **p. 250(tr):** Alfredo Herms / LatinContent / Getty Images; **p. 250(br):** Richard Rad / LatinContent / Getty Images; **p. 253(bc):** Fotokostic / Shutterstock; **p. 254(cr):** Cusp / SuperStock; **p. 254(tc):** Carlos / Fotolia; **p. 254(br):** Bikeriderlondon / Shutterstock; **p. 261(tr):** Tobias Titz / Getty Images; **p. 264(bl):** Fotolia; **p. 270(br):** Morten Andersen/Corbis; **p. 272(br):** Nicolas Celaya / Xinhua /Landov; **p. 273(cl):** Fotokostic / Shutterstock; **p. 273(tr):** Fotoember / Fotolia;

Capítulo 8

p. 276(cr): Monkey Business /Fotolia; **p. 277(tc):** Chris Ronneseth / Getty Images; **p. 277(tr):** Steven Allan / Getty Images; **p. 277(bc):** Nathalie Speliers Ufermann / Shutterstock; **p. 277(tl):** Ken Welsh / Age Fotostock; **p. 277(cr):** Kinetic Imagery / Shutterstock; **p. 277(bl):** Frida Kahlo / Museo Nacional de Arte Moderno,2001 Banco de Mexico Diego Rivera & Frida Kahlo Museums Trust/Artists Rights Society (ARS), NY. Av./D.F. Reproduction authorized by the Instituto Nacional de Bellas Artes y Literatura / Christie's Images / Corbis; **p. 278(tl):** Ulga / Fotolia; **p. 278(br):** DK Images; **p. 278(bl):** Danny Lehman / Corbis; **p. 278(tr):** Horticulture / Fotolia; **p. 279(tl):** German_click / Fotolia; **p. 279(tc):** Kim Karpeles / Alamy; **p. 279(tr):** Eduardo Rivero /Shutterstock; **p. 279(bl):** Phil Clarke-Hill / Robert Harding World Imagery / Alamy; **p. 279(bc):** Fabienne Fossez / Alamy; **p. 279(br):** Jan Sochor / Alamy; **p. 280(c):** Orlando Sierra / AFP / Getty Images; **p. 281(r):** Danita Delimont / Alamy; **p. 282(bc):** Nito / Fotolia; **p. 283(tr):** Phase4Photography / Fotolia; **p. 284(cl):** Guillermo Gonzalez / Notimex / Newscom; **p. 285(cl):** Jan Sochor / Demotix / Corbis; **p. 285(tr):** Jan Sochor / Demotix / Corbis; **p. 285(br):** Jmstock / Getty Images; **p. 291(bl):** DmitriMaruta / Shutterstock; **p. 291(bc):** Juriah Mosin / Shutterstock; **p. 291(br):** Anetlanda / Shutterstock; **p. 294(bc):** Dan Bannister / DK Images; **p. 294(br):** Hector Vivas / Jam Media / LatinContent / Getty Images; **p. 295(bc):** John Mitchell / Alamy; **p. 295(br):** Sandra van der Steen / Fotlia; **p. 296(tl):** EPA / Alamy; **p. 296(tr):** Peter Kneffel / EPA / Newscom; **p. 298(tr):** Memofoto / Fotolia; **p. 307(tr):** Mireille Vautier / Alamy; **p. 307(cl):** Holbox / Shutterstock; **p. 308(br):** Michaeljung / Fotolia;

Capítulo 9

p. 310(cr): Goodluz / Shutterstock; **p. 311(tc):** Kschrei / Shutterstock; **p. 311(tr):** Linda Whitwam / DK Images; **p. 311(cr):** Robert Lerich / Fotolia; **p. 311(bl):** Kim Seidl / Shutterstock; **p. 311(bc):** Stefano Paterna / Alamy; **p. 311(bl):** Arte Maya; **p. 312(cr):** Simon Dannhauer / Fotolia; **p. 312(cl):** hotshotsworldwide / Fotolia; **p. 312(bl):** Johan Ordonez / AFP / Getty Images; **p. 312(tl):** Tim Draper / DK Images; **p. 313(br):** EPA / Corbis; **p. 313(bl):** Karl Kummels / SuperStock; **p. 313(bc):** Fernando Morales / AFP / Newscom; **p. 313(tc):** Arte Maya; **p. 313(tr):** Arte Maya; **p. 313(tl):** Arte Maya; **p. 315(tl):** Science Photo Library / Alamy; **p. 315(tc):** Shutterstock; **p. 315(tr):** Kokotewan /Fotolia; **p. 315(bl):** Fotolia; **p. 315(bc):** Tsian / Shutterstock; **p. 315(br):** Wavebreakmedia / Shutterstock; **p. 316(bl):** Gabriela Trojanowska / Shutterstock; **p. 317(cr):** Andres Rodriguez / Fotolia; **p. 318(bl):** Dave Rock / Shutterstock; **p. 318(tl):** Shutterstock; **p. 320(bl):** Monkey Business / Fotolia; **p. 320(br):** Snowwhiteimages / Fotolia; **p. 321(tr):** Blickwinkel / LO / Alamy; **p. 321(cr):** Christian Kieffer / Shutterstock; **p. 321(bl):** Homer Sykes / Photonica World / Getty Images; **p. 324(tl):** Lev Kropotov / Shutterstock; **p. 325(tr):** Yuri Arcurs / Shutterstock; **p. 328(br):** Wavebreakmedia /Shutterstock; **p. 329(tr):** Corepics VOF / Shutterstock; **p. 336(cr):** Scott T. Baxter / Photodisc /Getty Images; **p. 341(bc):** Paul Kennedy / Alamy; **p. 342(br):** Daboost / Fotolia; **p. 342(bl):** Daboost / Fotolia; **p. 342(bc):** Daboost / Fotolia; **p. 343(br):** Mark Harmel / Alamy; **p. 343(tc):** A. Ramey / PhotoEdit;

Capítulo 10

p. 346(cr): Lucky Business / Shutterstock; **p. 347(bc):** Jennifer Elizabeth / Fotolia; **p. 347(tc):** iStockphoto / Getty Images; **p. 347(tr):** Steve100 / Fotolia; **p. 347(tl):** Kletr / Shutterstock; **p. 347(cr):** Andrew Linscott / Alamy; **p. 347(br):** Yumbo Indian from the neighbourhood of Quito, Ecuador, with various fruits and trees (oil on canvas), American School, (18th century) / Museo de America, Madrid, Spain / Index / The Bridgeman Art Library; **p. 348(tl):** Rechitan Sorin / Shutterstock; **p. 348(tr):** PB Pictures / Fotolia; **p. 348(bl):** Alexander / Fotolia; **p. 348(br):** Tommypic / Fotolia; **p. 349(tl):** Owen Franken / Corbis; **p. 349(tr):** Greg Roden / Rough Guides / DK Images; **p. 349(bl):** Arco Images G / Newscom; **p. 349(bc):** Imagebroker / Alamy; **p. 349(tc):** Janice Hazeldine / Alamy; **p. 353(cr):** Redav / Shutterstock; **p. 355(cr):** Santiago Cornejo / Shutterstock; **p. 356(cl):** Sven Schermer / Shutterstock; **p. 356(tc):** Margie Politzer / Lonely Planet Images / Getty Images; **p. 356(br):** Pablo Aneli / AP Images; **p. 359(tl):** Lily / Fotolia; **p. 359(tc):** Paul Brighton / Fotolia; **p. 363(tr):** Sergey Peterman / Fotolia; **p. 366(bc):** John Mitchell / Alamy; **p. 367(cr):** Skylines / Shutterstock; **p. 370(cr):** Greg Roden / Dorling Kindersely,Ltd; **p. 370(cl):** Robert Lerich / Fotolia; **p. 371(tr):** Danita Delimont / Alamy; **p. 377(tr):** Julenochek / Fotolia; **p. 377(tc):** Christian Vinces / Shutterstock; **p. 378(bl):** Pressmaster / Fotolia;

Capítulo 11

p. 380(tr): Mangostock / Fotolia; **p. 381(tl):** Alex James Bramwell / Shutterstock; **p. 381(cl):** Osov / Shutterstock; **p. 381(c):** Elias H. Debbas II / Shutterstock; **p. 381(cr):** Rob Huntley / Shutterstock; **p. 381(bl):** Mireille Vautier / Alamy; **p. 382(tl):** Fotolia; **p. 382(cr):** Brelsbil / Fotolia; **p. 382(cl):** Salazar / Fotolia; **p. 382(tr):** Cstyle / Fotolia; **p. 383(tl):** Andresr / Shutterstock; **p. 383(tr):** Adam Eastland / Alamy; **p. 383(bl):** Dorothy Alexander / Alamy; **p. 383(br):** Nigel Hicks / Dorling Kindersely, Ltd; **p. 384(c):** Simone Voigt / Shutterstock; **p. 390(tc):** Paul Almasy / Corbis; **p. 390(tr):** Greg Roden / DK Images; **p. 390(br):** Jorge Adorno / Reuters / Corbis; **p. 391(tr):** Rob Bayer / Shutterstock; **p. 397(tr):** Donya Nedomam / Shutterstock; **p. 398(cr):** Graham Harrison / Alamy; **p. 401(tl):** Linda Whitwam / Dorling Kindersley,Ltd; **p. 401(cl):** Galina Barskaya / Fotolia; **p. 409(br):** Angellodeco / Fotolia; **p. 410(tr):** BrazilPhotos / Alamy; **p. 411(c):** Pablocalvog / Fotolia; **p. 412(b):** Rangizzz / Fotolia;

Capítulo 12

p. 414(c): vilainecrevette / Fotolia; **p. 415(cr):** Marcus / Fotolia; **p. 415(tr):** Jim Lipschutz / Shutterstock; **p. 415(c):** RJ Lerich / Shutterstock; **p. 415(tl):** Brandon / Shutterstock; **p. 415(cl):** Jon Spaull / Dorling Kindersley, Ltd.; **p. 415(bl):** Kevin Schafer / Alamy; **p. 416(t):** Vilant / Fotolia; **p. 416(cr):** AustralianDream / Fotolia; **p. 416(cl):** Searagen / Fotolia; **p. 416(b):** Fotolia; **p. 417(tl):** Jose Luis Stephens / Alamy; **p. 417(tr):** Prisma Archivo / Alamy; **p. 417(bl):** Aleksey Stemmer / Shutterstock; **p. 419(tr):** Michaeljung / Fotolia; **p. 420(bl):** Ethan Daniels / Shutterstock; **p. 421(tr):** Getty Images; **p. 422(bl):** Alfredo Maiquez / Alamy; **p. 425(cl):** Nik Niklz / Shutterstock; **p. 425(tc):** Ariane Citron / Fotolia; **p. 425(cr):** Greg Roden / Dorling Kindersley, Ltd.; **p. 425(c):** Isaac Koval / The Agency Collection /Getty Images; **p. 425(bc):** Ty Milford / Radius Images / Getty Images; **p. 425(br):** Jordan Siemens / Digital Vision / Getty Images; **p. 425(cr):** Todd Warnock / Stockbyte / Getty Images; **p. 426(tr):** Jarno Gonzalez Zarraonandia / Shutterstock; **p. 428(cr):** Blaine Harrington III / Corbis; **p. 429(cl):** Jarno Gonzalez Zarraonandia / Shutterstock; **p. 439(br):** Stuart Pearce / Age Fotostock; **p. 440(tr):** Tony Northrup / Shutterstock; **p. 442(br):** Maisant Ludovic / Hemis / Alamy; **p. 445(br):** Csaba Peterdi / Fotolia; **p. 446(bl):** Fuste Rag a/ Age Fotostock / Getty Images;

Capítulo 13

p. 448(cr): Bikeriderlondon / Shutterstock; **p. 449(tl):** Shutterstock; **p. 449(cl):** Katarzyna Citko / Shutterstock; **p. 449(cr):** Ildar Turumtaev / Fotolia; **p. 449(br):** Leeman / Thinkstock / Getty Images; **p. 449(tc):** Travelscape Images / Alamy; **p. 449(c):** Vario Images GmbH & Co.KG / Alamy; **p. 449(bl):** Gianni Dagli Orti / The Art Archive at Art Resource, NY; **p. 450(tl):** Julio Etchart / Alamy; **p. 450(cl):** Juan Karita / AP Images; **p. 450(tr):** Aukasz Kurbiel / Fotolia; **p. 450(c):** AdStock RF / Shutterstock; **p. 451(tr):** Ulf Andersen / Hulton Archive / Getty Images; **p. 451(tl):** Piero Pomponi / Liaison / Getty Images; **p. 451(c):** Bettmann / Corbis; **p. 451(br):** Carlos Alvarez / Getty Images Entertainment / Getty Images; **p. 452(bl):** Ppicture-Alliance / Geisler-Fotopres / Clemens Niehaus/AP Images; **p. 453(cr):** Victor Potasyev / Shutterstock; **p. 454(tl):** Francis G. Mayer / Corbis; **p. 454(cr):** The Museum of Modern Art /Licensed by SCALA / Art Resource, NY; **p. 454(bl):** Museum Associates / LACMA/ Licensed by Art Resource, NY; **p. 455(bc):** Ray Roberts / Alamy; **p. 455(t):** Mondadori / Getty Images; **p. 456 (tl):** Enrique Arnal; **p. 456(bl):** Francis G. Mayer / Corbis; **p. 456(bl):** Bridgeman-Giraudon / Art Resource, NY; **p. 456(cl):** Adam Lee / Alamy; **p. 457(tr):** Dale Mitchell / Fotolia; **p. 457(c):** Marcos Brindicci / Reuters / Corbis; **p. 457(cr):** Riccardo Cesari / Splash News / Corbis; **p. 457(br):** Sue Cunningham Photographic / Alamy; **p. 458(cr):** Salah Malkawi / Getty Images; **p. 459(cr):** Robert Harding World Imagery / Alamy; **p. 460(tl):** Brent Winebrenner / Lonely Planet Images / Getty Images; **p. 460(bl):** Benoit Paill / Flickr / Getty Images; **p. 460(tr):** Krzysztof Dydynski / Lonely Planet Images / Getty Images; **p. 462(br):** Fotomicar / Shutterstock; **p. 464(tr):** Thinkstock; **p. 466(b):** RoxyFer / Shutterstock.com; **p. 467(tr):** MJ Photography / Alamy; **p. 474(br):** Paco Torrente / AFP / Newscom;

Capítulo 14

p. 478(cr): Gianni Muratore / Alamy; **p. 479(tl):** Jeremy Horner / Corbis; **p. 479(cl):** Art Wolfe / The Image Bank / Getty Images; **p. 479(tc):** Marc C. Johnson / Shutterstock; **p. 479(c):** Ene / Shutterstock; **p. 479(bc):** Travel Bug / Shutterstock; **p. 479(bl):** Stephanie Jackson / Photographsofaustralia / Alamy; **p. 480(tl):** Nataliya Hora /Shutterstock; **p. 480(c):** Michele Pautasso / Fotolia; **p. 480(tc):** Pablo Rogat /Shutterstock; **p. 480(cl):** Tero Hakala /Shutterstock; **p. 480(tr):** Tifonimages / Shutterstock; **p. 480(bc):** Travel Bug / Shutterstock; **p. 481(tl):** Rodrigo Arangua / AFP / Getty Images; **p. 481(tr):** Jorge Villegas / Age Fotostock / Alamy; **p. 481(br):** Martin Alipaz / epa / Corbis; **p. 483(tr):** Bill Bachmann / Alamy; **p. 485(tl):** Monkey Business / Fotolia; **p. 485(cr):** Db2stock/Blend Images / Corbis; **p. 487(cl):** Philippe Lissac / Godong / Corbis; **p. 487(tr):** Hans Neleman / Corbis; **p. 488(tr):** Jack Kurtz / The Image Works; **p. 493(tr):** Jorge Villegas / Xinhua / Newscom; **p. 496(tr):** Corbis; **p. 499(tr):** Carlos Carrion / Sygma / Corbis; **p. 500(tr):** Prisma Archivo / Alamy; **p. 503(br):** Diego Cervo / Fotolia; **p. 505(cr):** Moises Castillo / AP Images; **p. 506(b):** Africa Studio / Fotolia; **p. 508(b):** PhotoSG / Fotolia;

Capítulo 15

p. 510(cr): Alexander Raths / Fotolia; **p. 511(tl):** David Parker / Science Source; **p. 511(tc):** Lori Froeb / Shutterstock; **p. 511(tr):** Eddtoro / Shutterstock; **p. 511(c):** Joseph / Shutterstock; **p. 511(c):** Richard Ellis / Alamy; **p. 511(bl):** Zulia Gotay de Anderson; **p. 512(tl):** Hemis / Alamy; **p. 512(cl):** Tim Draper / Dorling Kindersley,Ltd; **p. 512(bc):** Thais Llorca / EPA / Newscom; **p. 512(cr):** Torkil Adsersen / EPA / Newscom; **p. 513(tl):** Liv Friis-Larsen / Shutterstock; **p. 513(tr):** Sadeugra / E+ / Getty Images; **p. 513(bl):** Ilolab / Shutterstock; **p. 513(br):** David R. Frazier Photolibrary, Inc. / Alamy; **p. 514(cr):** Interfoto / Alamy; **p. 515(tr):** Jennifer Stone / Shutterstock; **p. 515(bl):** Xico Putini / Fotolia; **p. 516(bl):** Joseph / Shutterstock; **p. 517(tl):** Andrea Crisante / Alamy; **p. 517(tr):** Jack Jackson / Robert Harding; **p. 517(bl):** Ziqiu / Fotolia; **p. 517(br):** Vadym Andrushchenko / Shutterstock; **p. 518(tl):** Antonis Papantoniou / Shutterstock; **p. 518(tr):** Jim West / Alamy; **p. 519 (tr):** iLexx/Getty Images; **p. 519(bl):** Lunatic67 / Shutterstock; **p. 520(cl):** Cesar Carrion / Notimex / Newscom; **p. 520(tr):** Ted Spiegel / Nomad / Corbis; **p. 523(br):** Kirill Kedrinski / Fotolia; **p. 526(cr):** Alberto Paredes / Alamy; **p. 527(b):** WavebreakMediaMicro / Fotolia; **p. 536(c):** Ra2 Studio / Fotolia

Communicative Functions and Learning Strategies Index

Index

W

Y